Philip's
COMPACT
WORLD
ATLAS

Philip's
COMPACT
WORLD
ATLAS

CHANCELLOR
PRESS

CONTENTS

Cartography by Philip's

Text
Keith Lye

Picture Acknowledgements
© **Corbis** /Stephen Frink, cover top right, / Hans
Georg Roth, cover bottom right
Courtesy of NPA Group, Edenbridge, UK 1
Image Bank /Lionel Brown 10
Images Colour Library /cover bottom left
Rex Features /Sipa 6, 24
Still Pictures 26, /Anne Piantanida 8, /Chris
Caldicott 16, /Mark Edwards 18, 20, /Hartmut
Schwarzbach 14, 22, /Luke White 4, /Francois Pierrel
cover top left
Tony Stone Images /Kevin Kelley 2, /Art Wolfe 12

Material in this book has also appeared in
Philip's Desk Reference Atlas (George Philip Ltd.,
1996)
Essential World Atlas (George Philip Ltd., 1998)

This 2002 edition published by Cancellor Press,
an imprint of Bounty Books, a division of
Octopus Publishing Group Limited,
2–4 Heron Quays, London E14 4JP

© 2001 George Philip Limited

A CIP catalogue record for this book is available
from the British Library.

ISBN 0 7537 0594 X

Printed in China

WORLD STATISTICS

vi–ix	*Countries*
x–xi	*Cities*
xii–xv	*Physical*
xvi	*Climate*

THE EARTH IN FOCUS

2–3	*The Universe and Solar System*
4–5	*The Changing Earth*
6–7	*Earthquakes and Volcanoes*
8–9	*Water and Ice*
10–11	*Weather and Climate*
12–13	*Landforms and Vegetation*
14–15	*Population*
16–17	*Languages and Religions*
18–19	*Agriculture and Industry*
20–21	*Trade and Commerce*
22–23	*Transport and Travel*
24–27	*International Organizations*
28–29	*Regions in the News*
30–32	*World Flags*

WORLD MAPS

1	General Reference	54–55	North-west Africa
2–3	Northern Hemisphere	56–57	Central Africa
4–5	Southern Hemisphere	58–59	Southern Africa
6–7	Europe	60–61	Australia
8–9	Scandinavia	62–63	South-east Australia
10–11	British Isles	64–65	New Zealand, Central
12–13	France		and South-west Pacific
14–15	Germany and Benelux	66–67	North America
16–17	Central Europe	68–69	Eastern Canada
18–19	Spain and Portugal	70–71	Western Canada
20–21	Italy and the Adriatic	72–73	North-east USA
22–23	Greece and the Balkans	74–75	South-east USA
24–25	Eastern Europe	76–77	North-central USA
26–27	Asia	78–79	Southern USA
28–29	Western Russia and	80–81	North-west USA
	Central Asia	82–83	South-west USA
30–31	Eastern Siberia	84–85	Mexico
32–33	Japan	86–87	Caribbean and Central
34–35	China		America
36–37	South-east Asia	88–89	South America
38–39	Philippines and Eastern	90–91	South America –
	Indonesia		North-west
40–41	Eastern India, Bangladesh and	92–93	South America –
	Burma		North-east
42–43	Western India and Pakistan	94–95	South America –
44–45	Iran, the Gulf and Afghanistan		South
46–47	The Middle East and Turkey	96	Antarctica
48–49	Arabia and the Horn of Africa		
50–51	Africa		
52–53	North-east Africa	97–160	**Index to World Maps**

WORLD STATISTICS – COUNTRIES

Listed below are the principal countries of the world; the more important territories are also included. If a territory is not completely independent, then the country it is associated with is named. The area figures give the total area of land, inland water and ice. Annual income is the GNP per capita. The figures are the latest available: usually 1998.

Country / Territory	Area (1,000 sq km)	Area (1,000 sq mls)	Population (1,000s)	Capital City	Annual Income US$
Afghanistan	652	252	26,511	Kabul	800
Albania	28.8	11.1	3,795	Tirana	810
Algeria	2,382	920	32,904	Algiers	1,550
Andorra	0.45	0.17	49	Andorra La Vella	18,000
Angola	1,247	481	13,295	Luanda	340
Argentina	2,767	1,068	36,238	Buenos Aires	8,970
Armenia	29.8	11.5	3,968	Yerevan	480
Australia	7,687	2,968	18,855	Canberra	20,300
Austria	83.9	32.4	7,613	Vienna	26,850
Azerbaijan	86.6	33.4	8,324	Baku	490
Azores (Portugal)	2.2	0.87	238	Ponta Delgada	–
Bahamas	13.9	5.4	295	Nassau	20,100
Bahrain	0.68	0.26	683	Manama	7,660
Bangladesh	144	56	150,589	Dhaka	350
Barbados	0.43	0.17	265	Bridgetown	7,890
Belarus	207.6	80.1	10,697	Minsk	2,200
Belgium	30.5	11.8	9,832	Brussels	25,380
Belize	23	8.9	230	Belmopan	2,700
Benin	113	43	6,369	Porto-Novo	380
Bhutan	47	18.1	1,906	Thimphu	1,000
Bolivia	1,099	424	9,724	La Paz/Sucre	1,000
Bosnia-Herzegovina	51	20	4,601	Sarajevo	1,720
Botswana	582	225	1,822	Gaborone	3,600
Brazil	8,512	3,286	179,487	Brasília	4,570
Brunei	5.8	2.2	333	Bandar Seri Begawan	24,000
Bulgaria	111	43	9,071	Sofia	1,230
Burkina Faso	274	106	12,092	Ouagadougou	240
Burma (= Myanmar)	677	261	51,129	Rangoon	1,200
Burundi	27.8	10.7	7,358	Bujumbura	140
Cambodia	181	70	10,046	Phnom Penh	280
Cameroon	475	184	16,701	Yaoundé	610
Canada	9,976	3,852	28,488	Ottawa	20,020
Canary Is. (Spain)	7.3	2.8	1,494	Las Palmas/Santa Cruz	–
Cape Verde Is.	4	1.6	515	Praia	1,060
Central African Republic	623	241	4,074	Bangui	300
Chad	1,284	496	7,337	Ndjaména	230
Chile	757	292	15,272	Santiago	4,810
China	9,597	3,705	1,299,180	Beijing	750
Colombia	1,139	440	39,397	Bogotá	2,600
Comoros	2.2	0.86	670	Moroni	370
Congo	342	132	3,167	Brazzaville	690
Congo (Dem. Rep. of the)	2,345	905	49,190	Kinshasa	110
Costa Rica	51.1	19.7	3,711	San José	2,780
Croatia	56.5	21.8	4,960	Zagreb	4,520
Cuba	111	43	11,504	Havana	1,560

Country / Territory	Area (1,000 sq km)	Area (1,000 sq mls)	Population (1,000s)	Capital City	Annual Income US$
Cyprus	9.3	3.6	762	Nicosia	13,000
Czech Republic	78.9	30.4	10,500	Prague	5,040
Denmark	43.1	16.6	5,153	Copenhagen	33,260
Djibouti	23.2	9	552	Djibouti	1,200
Dominica	0.75	0.29	87	Roseau	3,010
Dominican Republic	48.7	18.8	8,621	Santo Domingo	1,770
Ecuador	284	109	13,319	Quito	1,530
Egypt	1,001	387	64,210	Cairo	1,290
El Salvador	21	8.1	6,739	San Salvador	1,850
Equatorial Guinea	28.1	10.8	455	Malabo	1,500
Eritrea	94	36	4,523	Asmara	200
Estonia	44.7	17.3	1,647	Tallinn	3,390
Ethiopia	1,128	436	61,841	Addis Ababa	100
Fiji	18.3	7.1	883	Suva	2,110
Finland	338	131	5,077	Helsinki	24,110
France	552	213	58,145	Paris	24,940
French Guiana (France)	90	34.7	130	Cayenne	6,000
French Polynesia (France)	4	1.5	268	Papeete	10,800
Gabon	268	103	1,612	Libreville	3,950
Gambia, The	11.3	4.4	1,119	Banjul	340
Georgia	69.7	26.9	5,777	Tbilisi	930
Germany	357	138	76,962	Berlin/Bonn	25,850
Ghana	239	92	20,564	Accra	390
Greece	132	51	10,193	Athens	11,650
Grenada	0.34	0.13	83	St George's	3,170
Guadeloupe (France)	1.7	0.66	365	Basse-Terre	9,200
Guatemala	109	42	12,222	Guatemala City	1,640
Guinea	246	95	7,830	Conakry	540
Guinea-Bissau	36.1	13.9	1,197	Bissau	160
Guyana	215	83	891	Georgetown	770
Haiti	27.8	10.7	8,003	Port-au-Prince	410
Honduras	112	43	6,846	Tegucigalpa	730
Hong Kong (China)	1.1	0.40	6,336	–	23,670
Hungary	93	35.9	10,531	Budapest	4,510
Iceland	103	40	274	Reykjavik	28,010
India	3,288	1,269	1,041,543	New Delhi	430
Indonesia	1,905	735	218,661	Jakarta	680
Iran	1,648	636	68,759	Tehran	1,770
Iraq	438	169	26,339	Baghdad	2,400
Ireland	70.3	27.1	4,086	Dublin	18,340
Israel	27	10.3	5,321	Jerusalem	15,940
Italy	301	116	57,195	Rome	20,250
Ivory Coast (Côte d'Ivoire)	322	125	17,600	Yamoussoukro	700
Jamaica	11	4.2	2,735	Kingston	1,680
Japan	378	146	128,470	Tokyo	32,380
Jordan	89.2	34.4	5,558	Amman	1,520
Kazakstan	2,717	1,049	19,006	Astana	1,310
Kenya	580	224	35,060	Nairobi	330
Korea, North	121	47	26,117	Pyŏngyang	1,000
Korea, South	99	38.2	46,403	Seoul	7,970

Country / Territory	Area (1,000 sq km)	Area (1,000 sq mls)	Population (1,000s)	Capital City	Annual Income US$
Kuwait	17.8	6.9	2,639	Kuwait City	22,700
Kyrgyzstan	198.5	76.6	5,403	Bishkek	350
Laos	237	91	5,463	Vientiane	330
Latvia	65	25	2,768	Riga	2,430
Lebanon	10.4	4	3,327	Beirut	3,560
Lesotho	30.4	11.7	2,370	Maseru	570
Liberia	111	43	3,575	Monrovia	1,000
Libya	1,760	679	6,500	Tripoli	6,700
Lithuania	65.2	25.2	3,935	Vilnius	2,440
Luxembourg	2.6	1	377	Luxembourg	43,570
Macau (China)	0.02	0.006	656	Macau	16,000
Macedonia (F.Y.R.O.M.)	25.7	9.9	2,157	Skopje	1,290
Madagascar	587	227	16,627	Antananarivo	260
Madeira (Portugal)	0.81	0.31	253	Funchal	–
Malawi	118	46	12,458	Lilongwe	200
Malaysia	330	127	21,983	Kuala Lumpur	3,600
Maldives	0.30	0.12	283	Malé	1,230
Mali	1,240	479	12,685	Bamako	250
Malta	0.32	0.12	366	Valletta	9,440
Martinique (France)	1.1	0.42	362	Fort-de-France	10,700
Mauritania	1,030	412	2,702	Nouakchott	410
Mauritius	2.0	0.72	1,201	Port Louis	3,700
Mexico	1,958	756	107,233	Mexico City	3,970
Micronesia, Fed. States of	0.70	0.27	110	Palikir	1,800
Moldova	33.7	13	4,707	Chişinău	410
Mongolia	1,567	605	2,847	Ulan Bator	400
Morocco	447	172	31,559	Rabat	1,250
Mozambique	802	309	20,493	Maputo	210
Namibia	825	318	2,437	Windhoek	1,940
Nepal	141	54	24,084	Katmandu	210
Netherlands	41.5	16	15,829	Amsterdam/The Hague	24,760
Netherlands Antilles (Neths)	0.99	0.38	203	Willemstad	11,500
New Caledonia (France)	18.6	7.2	195	Nouméa	11,400
New Zealand	269	104	3,662	Wellington	14,700
Nicaragua	130	50	5,261	Managua	390
Niger	1,267	489	10,752	Niamey	190
Nigeria	924	357	105,000	Abuja	300
Norway	324	125	4,331	Oslo	34,330
Oman	212	82	2,176	Muscat	7,900
Pakistan	796	307	162,409	Islamabad	480
Panama	77.1	29.8	2,893	Panama City	3,080
Papua New Guinea	463	179	4,845	Port Moresby	890
Paraguay	407	157	5,538	Asunción	1,760
Peru	1,285	496	26,276	Lima	2,460
Philippines	300	116	77,473	Manila	1,050
Poland	313	121	40,366	Warsaw	3,900
Portugal	92.4	35.7	10,587	Lisbon	10,690
Puerto Rico (US)	9	3.5	3,836	San Juan	9,000
Qatar	11	4.2	499	Doha	17,100
Réunion (France)	2.5	0.97	692	Saint-Denis	4,800

Country / Territory	Area (1,000 sq km)	Area (1,000 sq mls)	Population (1,000s)	Capital City	Annual Income US$
Romania	238	92	24,000	Bucharest	1,390
Russia	17,075	6,592	155,096	Moscow	2,300
Rwanda	26.3	10.2	10,200	Kigali	230
St Lucia	0.62	0.24	177	Castries	3,410
St Vincent & Grenadines	0.39	0.15	128	Kingstown	2,420
Samoa	2.8	1.1	171	Apia	1,020
São Tomé & Príncipe	0.96	0.37	151	São Tomé	280
Saudi Arabia	2,150	830	20,697	Riyadh	9,000
Senegal	197	76	8,716	Dakar	530
Sierra Leone	71.7	27.7	5,437	Freetown	140
Singapore	0.62	0.24	3,000	Singapore	30,060
Slovak Republic	49	18.9	5,500	Bratislava	3,700
Slovenia	20.3	7.8	2,055	Ljubljana	9,760
Solomon Is.	28.9	11.2	429	Honiara	750
Somalia	638	246	9,736	Mogadishu	600
South Africa	1,220	471	43,666	C. Town/Pretoria/ Bloemfontein	2,880
Spain	505	195	40,667	Madrid	14,080
Sri Lanka	65.6	25.3	19,416	Colombo	810
Sudan	2,506	967	33,625	Khartoum	290
Surinam	163	63	497	Paramaribo	1,660
Swaziland	17.4	6.7	1,121	Mbabane	1,400
Sweden	450	174	8,560	Stockholm	25,620
Switzerland	41.3	15.9	6,762	Bern	40,080
Syria	185	71	17,826	Damascus	1,020
Taiwan	36	13.9	22,000	Taipei	12,400
Tajikistan	143.1	55.2	7,041	Dushanbe	350
Tanzania	945	365	39,639	Dodoma	210
Thailand	513	198	63,670	Bangkok	2,200
Togo	56.8	21.9	4,861	Lomé	330
Trinidad & Tobago	5.1	2	1,484	Port of Spain	4,430
Tunisia	164	63	9,924	Tunis	2,050
Turkey	779	301	66,789	Ankara	3,160
Turkmenistan	488.1	188.5	4,585	Ashkhabad	1,630
Uganda	236	91	26,958	Kampala	320
Ukraine	603.7	233.1	52,558	Kiev	850
United Arab Emirates	83.6	32.3	1,951	Abu Dhabi	18,220
United Kingdom	243.3	94	58,393	London	21,400
United States of America	9,373	3,619	266,096	Washington, DC	29,340
Uruguay	177	68	3,274	Montevideo	6,180
Uzbekistan	447.4	172.7	26,044	Tashkent	870
Vanuatu	12.2	4.7	206	Port-Vila	1,270
Venezuela	912	352	24,715	Caracas	350
Vietnam	332	127	82,427	Hanoi	330
Virgin Is. (US)	0.34	0.13	135	Charlotte Amalie	12,500
Western Sahara	266	103	228	El Aaiún	300
Yemen	528	204	13,219	Sana	300
Yugoslavia	102.3	39.5	10,761	Belgrade	2,300
Zambia	753	291	12,267	Lusaka	330
Zimbabwe	391	151	13,123	Harare	610

WORLD STATISTICS – CITIES

Listed below are all the cities with more than 600,000 inhabitants (only cities with more than 1 million inhabitants are included for Brazil, China and India). The figures are taken from the most recent censuses and surveys, and are in thousands. As far as possible the figures are for the metropolitan area, e.g. greater New York or Mexico City.

	Population (1,000s)		Population (1,000s)		Population (1,000s)		Population (1,000s)

Afghanistan
Kabul 1,565
Algeria
Algiers 2,168
Oran 916
Angola
Luanda 2,418
Argentina
Buenos Aires 11,256
Córdoba. 1,208
Rosario. 1,118
Mendoza 773
La Plata 642
San Miguel de
Tucumán 622
Armenia
Yerevan. 1,248
Australia
Sydney 3,770
Melbourne 3,217
Brisbane 1,489
Perth. 1,262
Adelaide 1,080
Austria
Vienna. 1,595
Azerbaijan
Baku 1,720
Bangladesh
Dhaka. 6,105
Chittagong 2,041
Khulna 877
Belarus
Minsk 1,700
Belgium
Brussels 948
Bolivia
La Paz 1,126
Santa Cruz. 767
Brazil
São Paulo 16,417
Rio de Janeiro 9,888
Salvador 2,211
Belo Horizonte 2,091
Fortaleza. 1,965
Brasília 1,821
Curitiba 1,476
Recife 1,346
Pôrto Alegre 1,288
Manaus 1,157
Belém 1,144
Goiânia. 1,004
Bulgaria
Sofia 1,116
Burkina Faso
Ouagadougou 690
Burma (Myanmar)
Rangoon 2,513
Cambodia
Phnom Penh 920
Cameroon
Douala 1,200
Yaoundé. 800
Canada
Toronto 4,344
Montréal. 3,337
Vancouver 1,831

Ottawa–Hull 1,022
Edmonton 885
Calgary 831
Québec 693
Winnipeg. 677
Hamilton 643
Chile
Santiago 5,067
China
Shanghai 15,082
Beijing. 12,362
Tianjin. 10,687
Hong Kong (SAR)* . . 6,502
Chongqing 3,870
Shenyang. 3,860
Wuhan 3,520
Guangzhou 3,114
Harbin. 2,505
Nanjing 2,211
Xi'an 2,115
Chengdu 1,933
Dalian 1,855
Changchun 1,810
Jinan 1,660
Taiyuan 1,642
Qingdao 1,584
Fuzhou, Fujian 1,380
Zibo 1,346
Zhengzhou 1,324
Lanzhou 1,296
Anshan 1,252
Fushun 1,246
Kunming 1,242
Changsha 1,198
Hangzhou 1,185
Nanchang 1,169
Shijiazhuang 1,159
Guiyang. 1,131
Ürümqi 1,130
Jilin 1,118
Tangshan. 1,110
Qiqihar 1,104
Baotou 1,033
Hefei 1,000
Colombia
Bogotá 6,004
Cali 1,985
Medellín 1,970
Barranquilla 1,157
Cartagena 812
Congo
Brazzaville 937
Congo (Dem. Rep. of the)
Kinshasa 1,655
Lubumbashi. 851
Mbuji-Mayi. 806
Costa Rica
San José 1,220
Croatia
Zagreb 931
Cuba
Havana 2,241
Czech Republic
Prague 1,209
Denmark
Copenhagen. 1,362

Dominican Republic
Santo Domingo 2,135
Santiago 691
Ecuador
Guayaquil 1,973
Quito 1,487
Egypt
Cairo. 9,900
Alexandria 3,431
El Gîza 2,144
Shubra el Kheima 834
El Salvador
San Salvador. 1,522
Ethiopia
Addis Ababa. 2,112
France
Paris 9,319
Lyon 1,262
Marseille. 1,087
Lille 959
Bordeaux. 696
Toulouse 650
Georgia
Tbilisi 1,300
Germany
Berlin 3,470
Hamburg 1,706
Munich 1,240
Cologne. 964
Frankfurt. 651
Essen 616
Dortmund. 600
Ghana
Accra. 949
Greece
Athens 3,097
Guatemala
Guatemala 1,167
Guinea
Conakry 1,508
Haiti
Port-au-Prince 1,255
Honduras
Tegucigalpa 813
Hungary
Budapest. 1,885
India
Mumbai (Bombay) . . . 12,572
Kolkata 10,916
Delhi. 7,207
Chennai (Madras) 5,361
Hyderabad 4,280
Bangalore 4,087
Ahmadabad 3,298
Pune 2,485
Kanpur 2,111
Nagpur 1,661
Lucknow. 1,642
Surat. 1,517
Jaipur 1,514
Coimbatore 1,136
Vadodara 1,115
Indore. 1,104
Patna. 1,099
Madurai 1,094
Bhopal. 1,064

Vishakhapatnam 1,052
Varanasi 1,026
Ludhiana. 1,012
Indonesia
Jakarta 11,500
Surabaya 2,701
Bandung 2,368
Medan. 1,910
Semarang 1,366
Palembang 1,352
Tangerang. 1,198
Ujung Pandang 1,092
Bandar Lampung. 832
Malang 763
Padang 721
Iran
Tehran. 6,750
Mashhad 1,964
Esfahan 1,221
Tabriz 1,166
Shiraz 1,043
Ahvaz. 828
Qom 780
Bakhtaran 666
Iraq
Baghdad 3,841
Diyala. 961
As Sulaymaniyah 952
Arbil. 770
Al Mawsil. 664
Ireland
Dublin 952
Israel
Tel Aviv-Yafo. 1,502
Italy
Rome 2,775
Milan. 1,369
Naples 1,067
Turin 962
Palermo. 698
Genoa 678
**Ivory Coast
(Côte d'Ivoire)**
Abidjan 2,500
Jamaica
Kingston 644
Japan
Tokyo–
Yokohama. 26,836
Osaka 10,601
Nagoya 2,152
Sapporo 1,757
Kyoto 1,464
Kobe. 1,424
Fukuoka 1,285
Kawasaki. 1,203
Hiroshima. 1,109
Kitakyushu 1,020
Sendai 971
Chiba 857
Sakai. 803
Kumamoto 650
Okayama 616
Jordan
Amman. 1,300
Az-Zarqā 609

	Population (1,000s)		Population (1,000s)		Population (1,000s)		Population (1,000s)

Kazakstan
Almaty 1,150
Kenya
Nairobi 2,000
Mombasa 600
Korea, North
Pyŏngyang 2,639
Hamhung 775
Chŏngjin 754
Chinnampo 691
Korea, South
Seoul 11,641
Pusan 3,814
Taegu 2,449
Inchon 2,308
Taejŏn 1,272
Kwangju 1,258
Ulsan 967
Sŏngnam 869
Puch'on 779
Suwŏn 756
Latvia
Riga 846
Lebanon
Beirut 1,900
Libya
Tripoli 1,083
Madagascar
Antananarivo 1,053
Malaysia
Kuala Lumpur 1,145
Mali
Bamako 800
Mauritania
Nouakchott 735
Mexico
Mexico City 15,048
Guadalajara 2,847
Monterrey 2,522
Puebla 1,055
León 872
Ciudad Juárez 798
Tijuana 743
Culiacán Rosales 602
Mexicali 602
Moldova
Chişinău 700
Mongolia
Ulan Bator 627
Morocco
Casablanca 3,079
Rabat-Salé 1,344
Fès 735
Marrakesh 621
Mozambique
Maputo 2,000
Netherlands
Amsterdam 1,101
Rotterdam 1,076
The Hague 694
New Zealand
Auckland 997
Nicaragua
Managua 864
Nigeria
Lagos 10,287
Ibadan 1,365
Ogbomosho 712
Kano 657
Norway
Oslo 714

Pakistan
Karachi 9,863
Lahore 5,085
Faisalabad 1,875
Peshawar 1,676
Gujranwala 1,663
Rawalpindi 1,290
Multan 1,257
Hyderabad 1,107
Paraguay
Asunción 945
Peru
Lima–Callao 6,601
Callao 638
Arequipa 620
Philippines
Manila 9,280
Quezon City 1,989
Davao 1,191
Caloocan 1,023
Cebu 662
Poland
Warsaw 1,638
Lódz 825
Kraków 745
Wroclaw 642
Portugal
Lisbon 2,561
Oporto 1,174
Romania
Bucharest 2,060
Russia
Moscow 9,233
St Petersburg 4,883
Nizhniy Novgorod 1,425
Novosibirsk 1,400
Yekaterinburg 1,300
Samara 1,200
Omsk 1,200
Chelyabinsk 1,100
Kazan 1,100
Ufa 1,100
Volgograd 1,003
Perm 1,000
Rostov 1,000
Voronezh 908
Saratov 895
Krasnoyarsk 869
Togliatti 689
Simbirsk 678
Izhevsk 654
Krasnodar 645
Vladivostok 632
Yaroslavl 629
Khabarovsk 618
Saudi Arabia
Riyadh 1,800
Jedda 1,500
Mecca 630
Senegal
Dakar 1,571
Singapore
Singapore 3,104
Somalia
Mogadishu 1,000
South Africa
Cape Town 2,350
East Rand 1,379
Johannesburg 1,196
Durban 1,137
Pretoria 1,080

West Rand 870
Port Elizabeth 853
Vanderbijlpark–
Vereeniging 774
Spain
Madrid 3,029
Barcelona 1,614
Valencia 763
Sevilla 719
Zaragoza 607
Sri Lanka
Colombo 1,863
Sudan
Omdurman 1,267
Khartoum 925
Khartoum North 879
Sweden
Stockholm 1,744
Göteborg 775
Switzerland
Zürich 1,175
Bern 942
Syria
Aleppo 1,591
Damascus 1,549
Homs 644
Taiwan
Taipei 2,653
Kaohsiung 1,405
Taichung 817
Tainan 700
Tanzania
Dar-es-Salaam 1,361
Thailand
Bangkok 5,572
Togo
Lomé 590
Tunisia
Tunis 1,827
Turkey
Istanbul 7,490
Ankara 3,028
Izmir 2,333
Adana 1,472
Bursa 1,317
Konya 1,040
Gaziantep 930
Icel 908
Antalya 734
Diyarbakir 677
Kocaeli 661
Urfa 649
Kayseri 648
Manisa 641
Uganda
Kampala 773
Ukraine
Kiev 2,630
Kharkiv 1,555
Dnipropetrovsk 1,147
Donetsk 1,088
Odesa 1,046
Zaporizhzhya 887
Lviv 802
Kryvyy Rih 720
United Kingdom
London 8,089
Birmingham 2,373
Manchester 2,353
Liverpool 852
Glasgow 832

Sheffield 661
Nottingham 649
Newcastle 617
United States
New York 16,329
Los Angeles 12,410
Chicago 7,668
Philadelphia 4,949
Washington, DC 4,466
Detroit 4,307
Houston 3,653
Atlanta 3,331
Boston 3,240
Dallas 2,898
Minneapolis–St Paul . . . 2,688
San Diego 2,632
St Louis 2,536
Phoenix 2,473
Baltimore 2,458
Pittsburgh 2,402
Cleveland 2,222
San Francisco 2,182
Seattle 2,180
Tampa 2,157
Miami 2,025
Newark 1,934
Denver 1,796
Portland (Or.) 1,676
Kansas City (Mo.) 1,647
Cincinnati 1,581
San Jose 1,557
Norfolk 1,529
Indianapolis 1,462
Milwaukee 1,456
Sacramento 1,441
San Antonio 1,437
Columbus (Oh.) 1,423
New Orleans 1,309
Charlotte 1,260
Buffalo 1,189
Salt Lake City 1,178
Hartford 1,151
Oklahoma 1,007
Jacksonville (Fl.) 665
Omaha 663
Memphis 614
Uruguay
Montevideo 1,378
Uzbekistan
Tashkent 2,107
Venezuela
Caracas 2,784
Maracaibo 1,364
Valencia 1,032
Maracay 800
Barquisimeto 745
Vietnam
Ho Chi Minh City 4,322
Hanoi 3,056
Haiphong 783
Yemen
Sana 972
Yugoslavia
Belgrade 1,137
Zambia
Lusaka 982
Zimbabwe
Harare 1,189
Bulawayo 622

* SAR = Special Administrative Region
of China

WORLD STATISTICS – PHYSICAL

Under each subject heading, the statistics are listed by continent. The figures are in size order beginning with the largest, longest or deepest, and are rounded as appropriate. Both metric and imperial measurements are given. The lists are complete down to the > mark; below this mark they are selective.

Land and Water

	km²	miles²	%
The World	509,450,000	196,672,000	–
Land	149,450,000	57,688,000	29.3
Water	360,000,000	138,984,000	70.7
Asia	44,500,000	17,177,000	29.8
Africa	30,302,000	11,697,000	20.3
North America	24,241,000	9,357,000	16.2
South America	17,793,000	6,868,000	11.9
Antarctica	14,100,000	5,443,000	9.4
Europe	9,957,000	3,843,000	6.7
Australia & Oceania	8,557,000	3,303,000	5.7
Pacific Ocean	179,679,000	69,356,000	49.9
Atlantic Ocean	92,373,000	35,657,000	25.7
Indian Ocean	73,917,000	28,532,000	20.5
Arctic Ocean	14,090,000	5,439,000	3.9

Seas

Pacific Ocean	km²	miles²
South China Sea	2,974,600	1,148,500
Bering Sea	2,268,000	875,000
Sea of Okhotsk	1,528,000	590,000
East China & Yellow	1,249,000	482,000
Sea of Japan	1,008,000	389,000
Gulf of California	162,000	62,500
Bass Strait	75,000	29,000

Atlantic Ocean	km²	miles²
Caribbean Sea	2,766,000	1,068,000
Mediterranean Sea	2,516,000	971,000
Gulf of Mexico	1,543,000	596,000
Hudson Bay	1,232,000	476,000
North Sea	575,000	223,000
Black Sea	462,000	178,000
Baltic Sea	422,170	163,000
Gulf of St Lawrence	238,000	92,000

Indian Ocean	km²	miles²
Red Sea	438,000	169,000
The Gulf	239,000	92,000

Mountains

Europe		m	ft
Elbrus	Russia	5,642	18,510
Mont Blanc	France/Italy	4,807	15,771
Monte Rosa	Italy/Switzerland	4,634	15,203
Dom	Switzerland	4,545	14,911
Liskamm	Switzerland	4,527	14,852
Weisshorn	Switzerland	4,505	14,780
Taschorn	Switzerland	4,490	14,730
Matterhorn/Cervino	Italy/Switzerland	4,478	14,691
Mont Maudit	France/Italy	4,465	14,649
Dent Blanche	Switzerland	4,356	14,291
> Nadelhorn	Switzerland	4,327	14,196
Grandes Jorasses	France/Italy	4,208	13,806
Jungfrau	Switzerland	4,158	13,642
Barre des Ecrins	France	4,103	13,461
Gran Paradiso	Italy	4,061	13,323
Piz Bernina	Italy/Switzerland	4,049	13,284

Europe (cont.)		m	ft
Eiger	Switzerland	3,970	13,025
Monte Viso	Italy	3,841	12,602
Grossglockner	Austria	3,797	12,457
Wildspitze	Austria	3,772	12,382
Monte Disgrazia	Italy	3,678	12,066
Mulhacén	Spain	3,478	11,411
Pico de Aneto	Spain	3,404	11,168
Marmolada	Italy	3,342	10,964
Etna	Italy	3,340	10,958
Zugspitze	Germany	2,962	9,718
Musala	Bulgaria	2,925	9,596
Olympus	Greece	2,917	9,570
Triglav	Slovenia	2,863	9,393
Monte Cinto	France (Corsica)	2,710	8,891
Gerlachovka	Slovak Republic	2,655	8,711
Torre de Cerredo	Spain	2,648	8,688
Galdhöpiggen	Norway	2,468	8,100
Hvannadalshnúkur	Iceland	2,119	6,952
Kebnekaise	Sweden	2,117	6,946
Ben Nevis	UK	1,343	4,406

Asia		m	ft
Everest	China/Nepal	8,850	29,035
K2 (Godwin Austen)	China/Kashmir	8,611	28,251
Kanchenjunga	India/Nepal	8,598	28,208
Lhotse	China/Nepal	8,516	27,939
Makalu	China/Nepal	8,481	27,824
Cho Oyu	China/Nepal	8,201	26,906
Dhaulagiri	Nepal	8,172	26,811
Manaslu	Nepal	8,156	26,758
Nanga Parbat	Kashmir	8,126	26,660
Annapurna	Nepal	8,078	26,502
Gasherbrum	China/Kashmir	8,068	26,469
Broad Peak	China/Kashmir	8,051	26,414
Xixabangma	China	8,012	26,286
Kangbachen	India/Nepal	7,902	25,925
Jannu	India/Nepal	7,902	25,925
Gayachung Kang	Nepal	7,897	25,909
Himalchuli	Nepal	7,893	25,896
Disteghil Sar	Kashmir	7,885	25,869
Nuptse	Nepal	7,879	25,849
Khunyang Chhish	Kashmir	7,852	25,761
Masherbrum	Kashmir	7,821	25,659
Nanda Devi	India	7,817	25,646
Rakaposhi	Kashmir	7,788	25,551
Batura	Kashmir	7,785	25,541
Namche Barwa	China	7,756	25,446
Kamet	India	7,756	25,446
Soltoro Kangri	Kashmir	7,742	25,400
Gurla Mandhata	China	7,728	25,354
> Trivor	Pakistan	7,720	25,328
Kongur Shan	China	7,719	25,324
Tirich Mir	Pakistan	7,690	25,229
K'ula Shan	Bhutan/China	7,543	24,747
Pik Kommunizma	Tajikistan	7,495	24,590
Demavend	Iran	5,604	18,386
Ararat	Turkey	5,165	16,945
Gunong Kinabalu	Malaysia (Borneo)	4,101	13,455
Yu Shan	Taiwan	3,997	13,113
Fuji-San	Japan	3,776	12,388

Africa		m	ft
Kilimanjaro	Tanzania	5,895	19,340
Mt Kenya	Kenya	5,199	17,057
Ruwenzori	Uganda/Congo (D. Rep.)	5,109	16,762
Ras Dashan	Ethiopia	4,620	15,157

Africa (cont.)		m	ft
Meru	Tanzania	4,565	14,977
Karisimbi	Rwanda/Congo (D. Rep.)	4,507	14,787
Mt Elgon	Kenya/Uganda	4,321	14,176
Batu	Ethiopia	4,307	14,130
Guna	Ethiopia	4,231	13,882
Toubkal	Morocco	4,165	13,665
Irhil Mgoun	Morocco	4,071	13,356
Mt Cameroon	Cameroon	4,070	13,353
Amba Ferit	Ethiopia	3,875	13,042
Pico del Teide	Spain (Tenerife)	3,718	12,198
Thabana Ntlenyana	Lesotho	3,482	11,424
Emi Koussi	Chad	3,415	11,204
>Mt aux Sources	Lesotho/South Africa	3,282	10,768
Mt Piton	Réunion	3,069	10,069

Oceania		m	ft
Puncak Jaya	Indonesia	5,029	16,499
Puncak Trikora	Indonesia	4,750	15,584
Puncak Mandala	Indonesia	4,702	15,427
>Mt Wilhelm	Papua New Guinea	4,508	14,790
Mauna Kea	USA (Hawaii)	4,205	13,796
Mauna Loa	USA (Hawaii)	4,169	13,681
Mt Cook (Aoraki)	New Zealand	3,753	12,313
Mt Balbi	Solomon Is.	2,439	8,002
Orohena	Tahiti	2,241	7,352
Mt Kosciuszko	Australia	2,237	7,339

North America		m	ft
Mt McKinley (Denali)	USA (Alaska)	6,194	20,321
Pierre Elliott Trudeau	Canada	5,959	19,551
Citlaltepetl	Mexico	5,700	18,701
Mt St Elias	USA/Canada	5,489	18,008
Popocatepetl	Mexico	5,452	17,887
Mt Foraker	USA (Alaska)	5,304	17,401
Ixtaccihuatl	Mexico	5,286	17,342
Lucania	Canada	5,227	17,149
Mt Steele	Canada	5,073	16,644
Mt Bona	USA (Alaska)	5,005	16,420
Mt Blackburn	USA (Alaska)	4,996	16,391
Mt Sanford	USA (Alaska)	4,940	16,207
Mt Wood	Canada	4,848	15,905
Nevado de Toluca	Mexico	4,670	15,321
Mt Fairweather	USA (Alaska)	4,663	15,298
Mt Hunter	USA (Alaska)	4,442	14,573
Mt Whitney	USA	4,418	14,495
Mt Elbert	USA	4,399	14,432
Mt Harvard	USA	4,395	14,419
Mt Rainier	USA	4,392	14,409
Blanca Peak	USA	4,372	14,344
>Longs Peak	USA	4,345	14,255
Tajumulco	Guatemala	4,220	13,845
Grand Teton	USA	4,197	13,770
Mt Waddington	Canada	3,994	13,104
Mt Robson	Canada	3,954	12,972
Chirripó Grande	Costa Rica	3,837	12,589
Mt Assiniboine	Canada	3,619	11,873
Pico Duarte	Dominican Rep.	3,175	10,417

South America		m	ft
Aconcagua	Argentina	6,960	22,834
Bonete	Argentina	6,872	22,546
Ojos del Salado	Argentina/Chile	6,863	22,516
Pissis	Argentina	6,779	22,241
Mercedario	Argentina/Chile	6,770	22,211
Huascaran	Peru	6,768	22,204
Llullaillaco	Argentina/Chile	6,723	22,057
Nudo de Cachi	Argentina	6,720	22,047
Yerupaja	Peru	6,632	21,758
N. de Tres Cruces	Argentina/Chile	6,620	21,719
Incahuasi	Argentina/Chile	6,601	21,654
Cerro Galan	Argentina	6,600	21,654
Tupungato	Argentina/Chile	6,570	21,555

South America (cont.)		m	ft
>Sajama	Bolivia	6,542	21,463
Illimani	Bolivia	6,485	21,276
Coropuna	Peru	6,425	21,079
Ausangate	Peru	6,384	20,945
Cerro del Toro	Argentina	6,380	20,932
Siula Grande	Peru	6,356	20,853
Chimborazo	Ecuador	6,267	20,561
Cotapaxi	Ecuador	5,896	19,344
Pico Colon	Colombia	5,800	19,029
Pico Bolivar	Venezuela	5,007	16,427

Antarctica	m	ft
Vinson Massif	4,897	16,066
Mt Kirkpatrick	4,528	14,855
Mt Markham	4,349	14,268

Ocean Depths

Atlantic Ocean	m	ft
Puerto Rico (Milwaukee) Deep	9,220	30,249
Cayman Trench	7,680	25,197
Gulf of Mexico	5,203	17,070
Mediterranean Sea	5,121	16,801
Black Sea	2,211	7,254
North Sea	660	2,165
Baltic Sea	463	1,519

Indian Ocean	m	ft
Java Trench	7,450	24,442
Red Sea	2,635	8,454
Persian Gulf	73	239

Pacific Ocean	m	ft
Mariana Trench	11,022	36,161
Tonga Trench	10,882	35,702
Japan Trench	10,554	34,626
Kuril Trench	10,542	34,587
Mindanao Trench	10,497	34,439
Kermadec Trench	10,047	32,962
New Guinea Trench	9,140	29,987
Peru–Chile Trench	8,050	26,410

Arctic Ocean	m	ft
Molloy Deep	5,608	18,399

Land Lows

		m	ft
Dead Sea	Asia	−411	−1,348
Lake Assal	Africa	−156	−512
Death Valley	North America	−86	−282
Valdés Peninsula	South America	−40	−131
Caspian Sea	Europe	−28	−92
Lake Eyre North	Oceania	−16	−52

Rivers

Europe		km	miles
Volga	Caspian Sea	3,700	2,300
Danube	Black Sea	2,850	1,770
Ural	Caspian Sea	2,535	1,575
Dnepr (Dnipro)	Black Sea	2,285	1,420
Kama	Volga	2,030	1,260
Don	Black Sea	1,990	1,240
Petchora	Arctic Ocean	1,790	1,110
Oka	Volga	1,480	920
Belaya	Kama	1,420	880

xiii

Europe (cont.)		km	miles
Dnister (Dniester)	Black Sea	1,400	870
Vyatka	Kama	1,370	850
Rhine	North Sea	1,320	820
North Dvina	Arctic Ocean	1,290	800
Desna	Dnepr (Dnipro)	1,190	740
Elbe	North Sea	1,145	710
Wisla	Baltic Sea	1,090	675
Loire	Atlantic Ocean	1,020	635
West Dvina	Baltic Sea	1,019	633

Asia		km	miles
Yangtze	Pacific Ocean	6,380	3,960
Yenisey–Angara	Arctic Ocean	5,550	3,445
Huang He	Pacific Ocean	5,464	3,395
Ob–Irtysh	Arctic Ocean	5,410	3,360
Mekong	Pacific Ocean	4,500	2,795
Amur	Pacific Ocean	4,400	2,730
Lena	Arctic Ocean	4,400	2,730
Irtysh	Ob	4,250	2,640
Yenisey	Arctic Ocean	4,090	2,540
Ob	Arctic Ocean	3,680	2,285
Indus	Indian Ocean	3,100	1,925
Brahmaputra	Indian Ocean	2,900	1,800
Syrdarya	Aral Sea	2,860	1,775
Salween	Indian Ocean	2,800	1,740
Euphrates	Indian Ocean	2,700	1,675
Vilyuy	Lena	2,650	1,645
Kolyma	Arctic Ocean	2,600	1,615
Amudarya	Aral Sea	2,540	1,575
Ural	Caspian Sea	2,535	1,575
Ganges	Indian Ocean	2,510	1,560
Si Kiang	Pacific Ocean	2,100	1,305
Irrawaddy	Indian Ocean	2,010	1,250
Tarim–Yarkand	Lop Nor	2,000	1,240
Tigris	Indian Ocean	1,900	1,180
Angara	Yenisey	1,830	1,135
Godavari	Indian Ocean	1,470	915
Sutlej	Indian Ocean	1,450	900
Yamuna	Indian Ocean	1,400	870

Africa		km	miles
Nile	Mediterranean	6,670	4,140
Congo	Atlantic Ocean	4,670	2,900
Niger	Atlantic Ocean	4,180	2,595
Zambezi	Indian Ocean	3,540	2,200
Oubangi/Uele	Congo (Dem. Rep.)	2,250	1,400
Kasai	Congo (Dem. Rep.)	1,950	1,210
Shaballe	Indian Ocean	1,930	1,200
Orange	Atlantic Ocean	1,860	1,155
Cubango	Okavango Swamps	1,800	1,120
Limpopo	Indian Ocean	1,600	995
Senegal	Atlantic Ocean	1,600	995
Volta	Atlantic Ocean	1,500	930
Benue	Niger	1,350	840

Australia		km	miles
Murray–Darling	Indian Ocean	3,750	2,330
Darling	Murray	3,070	1,905
Murray	Indian Ocean	2,575	1,600
Murrumbidgee	Murray	1,690	1,050

North America		km	miles
Mississippi–Missouri	Gulf of Mexico	6,020	3,740
Mackenzie	Arctic Ocean	4,240	2,630
Mississippi	Gulf of Mexico	3,780	2,350
Missouri	Mississippi	3,780	2,350
Yukon	Pacific Ocean	3,185	1,980
Rio Grande	Gulf of Mexico	3,030	1,880
Arkansas	Mississippi	2,340	1,450
Colorado	Pacific Ocean	2,330	1,445
Red	Mississippi	2,040	1,270

North America (cont.)		km	miles
Saskatchewan	Lake Winnipeg	1,940	1,205
Snake	Columbia	1,670	1,040
Churchill	Hudson Bay	1,600	990
Ohio	Mississippi	1,580	980
Brazos	Gulf of Mexico	1,400	870
St Lawrence	Atlantic Ocean	1,170	730

South America		km	miles
Amazon	Atlantic Ocean	6,450	4,010
Paraná–Plate	Atlantic Ocean	4,500	2,800
Purus	Amazon	3,350	2,080
Madeira	Amazon	3,200	1,990
São Francisco	Atlantic Ocean	2,900	1,800
Paraná	Plate	2,800	1,740
Tocantins	Atlantic Ocean	2,750	1,710
Paraguay	Paraná	2,550	1,580
Orinoco	Atlantic Ocean	2,500	1,550
Pilcomayo	Paraná	2,500	1,550
Araguaia	Tocantins	2,250	1,400
Juruá	Amazon	2,000	1,240
Xingu	Amazon	1,980	1,230
Ucayali	Amazon	1,900	1,180
Maranón	Amazon	1,600	990
Uruguay	Plate	1,600	990
Magdalena	Caribbean Sea	1,540	960

Lakes

Europe		km²	miles²
Lake Ladoga	Russia	17,700	6,800
Lake Onega	Russia	9,700	3,700
Saimaa system	Finland	8,000	3,100
Vänern	Sweden	5,500	2,100
Rybinskoye Reservoir	Russia	4,700	1,800

Asia		km²	miles²
Caspian Sea	Asia	371,800	143,550
Lake Baykal	Russia	30,500	11,780
Aral Sea	Kazak./Uzbek.	28,687	11,086
Tonlé Sap	Cambodia	20,000	7,700
Lake Balqash	Kazakstan	18,500	7,100
Lake Dongting	China	12,000	4,600
Lake Ysyk	Kyrgyzstan	6,200	2,400
Lake Orumiyeh	Iran	5,900	2,300
Lake Koko	China	5,700	2,200
Lake Poyang	China	5,000	1,900
Lake Khanka	China/Russia	4,400	1,700
Lake Van	Turkey	3,500	1,400
Lake Ubsa	China	3,400	1,300

Africa		km²	miles²
Lake Victoria	East Africa	68,000	26,000
Lake Tanganyika	Central Africa	33,000	13,000
Lake Malawi/Nyasa	East Africa	29,600	11,430
Lake Chad	Central Africa	25,000	9,700
Lake Turkana	Ethiopia/Kenya	8,500	3,300
Lake Volta	Ghana	8,500	3,300
Lake Bangweulu	Zambia	8,000	3,100
Lake Rukwa	Tanzania	7,000	2,700
Lake Mai-Ndombe	Congo (D. Rep.)	6,500	2,500
Lake Kariba	Zambia/Zimbabwe	5,300	2,000
Lake Mobutu	Uganda/Congo (D. Rep.)	5,300	2,000
Lake Nasser	Egypt/Sudan	5,200	2,000
Lake Mweru	Zambia/Congo (D. Rep.)	4,900	1,900
Lake Cabora Bassa	Mozambique	4,500	1,700
Lake Kyoga	Uganda	4,400	1,700
Lake Tana	Ethiopia	3,630	1,400
Lake Kivu	Rwanda/Congo (D. Rep.)	2,650	1,000
Lake Edward	Uganda/Congo (D. Rep.)	2,200	850

Australia		km²	miles²
Lake Eyre	Australia	8,900	3,400
Lake Torrens	Australia	5,800	2,200
Lake Gairdner	Australia	4,800	1,900

North America		km²	miles²
Lake Superior	Canada/USA	82,350	31,800
Lake Huron	Canada/USA	59,600	23,010
Lake Michigan	USA	58,000	22,400
Great Bear Lake	Canada	31,800	12,280
Great Slave Lake	Canada	28,500	11,000
Lake Erie	Canada/USA	25,700	9,900
Lake Winnipeg	Canada	24,400	9,400
Lake Ontario	Canada/USA	19,500	7,500
Lake Nicaragua	Nicaragua	8,200	3,200
Lake Athabasca	Canada	8,100	3,100
Smallwood Reservoir	Canada	6,530	2,520
Reindeer Lake	Canada	6,400	2,500
Nettilling Lake	Canada	5,500	2,100
Lake Winnipegosis	Canada	5,400	2,100
Lake Nipigon	Canada	4,850	1,900
Lake Manitoba	Canada	4,700	1,800

South America		km²	miles²
Lake Titicaca	Bolivia/Peru	8,300	3,200
Lake Poopo	Peru	2,800	1,100

Islands

Europe		km²	miles²
Great Britain	UK	229,880	88,700
Iceland	Atlantic Ocean	103,000	39,800
Ireland	Ireland/UK	84,400	32,600
Novaya Zemlya (North)	Russia	48,200	18,600
West Spitzbergen	Norway	39,000	15,100
Novaya Zemlya (South)	Russia	33,200	12,800
Sicily	Italy	25,500	9,800
Sardinia	Italy	24,000	9,300
North-east Spitzbergen	Norway	15,000	5,600
Corsica	France	8,700	3,400
Crete	Greece	8,350	3,200
Zealand	Denmark	6,850	2,600

Asia		km²	miles²
Borneo	South-east Asia	744,360	287,400
Sumatra	Indonesia	473,600	182,860
Honshu	Japan	230,500	88,980
Sulawesi (Celebes)	Indonesia	189,000	73,000
Java	Indonesia	126,700	48,900
Luzon	Philippines	104,700	40,400
Mindanao	Philippines	101,500	39,200
Hokkaido	Japan	78,400	30,300
Sakhalin	Russia	74,060	28,600
Sri Lanka	Indian Ocean	65,600	25,300
Taiwan	Pacific Ocean	36,000	13,900
Kyushu	Japan	35,700	13,800
Hainan	China	34,000	13,100
Timor	Indonesia	33,600	13,000
Shikoku	Japan	18,800	7,300
Halmahera	Indonesia	18,000	6,900
Ceram	Indonesia	17,150	6,600
Sumbawa	Indonesia	15,450	6,000
Flores	Indonesia	15,200	5,900
Samar	Philippines	13,100	5,100
Negros	Philippines	12,700	4,900
Bangka	Indonesia	12,000	4,600
Palawan	Philippines	12,000	4,600
Panay	Philippines	11,500	4,400
Sumba	Indonesia	11,100	4,300
Mindoro	Philippines	9,750	3,800

Asia (cont.)		km²	miles²
Buru	Indonesia	9,500	3,700
Bali	Indonesia	5,600	2,200
Cyprus	Mediterranean	3,570	1,400

Africa		km²	miles²
Madagascar	Indian Ocean	587,040	226,660
Socotra	Indian Ocean	3,600	1,400
Réunion	Indian Ocean	2,500	965
Tenerife	Atlantic Ocean	2,350	900
Mauritius	Indian Ocean	1,865	720

Oceania		km²	miles²
New Guinea	Indon./Papua NG	821,030	317,000
New Zealand (South)	New Zealand	150,500	58,100
New Zealand (North)	New Zealand	114,700	44,300
Tasmania	Australia	67,800	26,200
New Britain	Papua NG	37,800	14,600
New Caledonia	Pacific Ocean	19,100	7,400
Viti Levu	Fiji	10,500	4,100
Hawaii	Pacific Ocean	10,450	4,000
Bougainville	Papua NG	9,600	3,700
Guadalcanal	Solomon Is.	6,500	2,500
Vanua Levu	Fiji	5,550	2,100
New Ireland	Papua NG	3,200	1,200

North America		km²	miles²
Greenland	Atlantic Ocean	2,175,600	839,800
Baffin Is.	Canada	508,000	196,100
Victoria Is.	Canada	212,200	81,900
Ellesmere Is.	Canada	212,000	81,800
Cuba	Cuba	110,860	42,800
Newfoundland	Canada	110,680	42,700
Hispaniola	Atlantic Ocean	76,200	29,400
Banks Is.	Canada	67,000	25,900
Devon Is.	Canada	54,500	21,000
Melville Is.	Canada	42,400	16,400
Vancouver Is.	Canada	32,150	12,400
Somerset Is.	Canada	24,300	9,400
Jamaica	Caribbean Sea	11,400	4,400
Puerto Rico	Atlantic Ocean	8,900	3,400
Cape Breton Is.	Canada	4,000	1,500

South America		km²	miles²
Tierra del Fuego	Argentina/Chile	47,000	18,100
Falkland Is. (East)	Atlantic Ocean	6,800	2,600
South Georgia	Atlantic Ocean	4,200	1,600
Galapagos (Isabela)	Pacific Ocean	2,250	870

WORLD STATISTICS – CLIMATE

For each city, the top row of figures shows total rainfall in millimetres; the bottom row shows the average temperature in ° Celsius or centigrade. The total annual rainfall and average annual temperature are given at the end of the rows.

	Jan.	Feb.	Mar.	Apr.	May	June	July	Aug.	Sept.	Oct.	Nov.	Dec.	Total
Europe													
Berlin, Germany	46	40	33	42	49	65	73	69	68	49	46	43	603
Altitude 55 metres	1	0	4	9	14	17	19	18	15	9	5	1	9
London, UK	54	40	37	37	46	45	57	59	49	57	64	48	593
5 m	4	5	7	9	12	16	18	17	15	11	8	5	11
Málaga, Spain	61	51	62	46	26	5	1	3	29	64	64	62	474
33 m	12	13	16	17	19	29	25	26	23	20	16	13	18
Moscow, Russia	39	38	36	37	53	58	88	71	58	45	47	54	624
156 m	–13	–10	–4	6	13	16	18	17	12	6	–1	–7	4
Paris, France	56	46	35	42	57	54	59	64	55	50	51	50	619
75 m	3	4	8	11	15	18	20	19	17	12	7	4	12
Rome, Italy	71	62	57	51	46	37	15	21	63	99	129	93	744
17 m	8	9	11	14	18	22	25	25	22	17	13	10	16
Asia													
Bangkok, Thailand	8	20	36	58	198	160	160	175	305	206	66	5	1,397
2 m	26	28	29	30	29	29	28	28	28	28	26	25	28
Bombay (Mumbai), India	3	3	3	<3	18	485	617	340	264	64	13	3	1,809
11 m	24	24	26	28	30	29	27	27	27	28	27	26	27
Ho Chi Minh, Vietnam	15	3	13	43	221	330	315	269	335	269	114	56	1,984
9 m	26	27	29	30	29	28	28	28	27	27	27	26	28
Hong Kong, China	33	46	74	137	292	394	381	361	257	114	43	31	2,162
33 m	16	15	18	22	26	28	28	28	27	25	21	18	23
Tokyo, Japan	48	74	107	135	147	165	142	152	234	208	97	56	1,565
6 m	3	4	7	13	17	21	25	26	23	17	11	6	14
Africa													
Cairo, Egypt	5	5	5	3	3	<3	0	0	<3	<3	3	5	28
116 m	13	15	18	21	25	28	28	28	26	24	20	15	22
Cape Town, South Africa	15	8	18	48	79	84	89	66	43	31	18	10	508
17 m	21	21	20	17	14	13	12	13	14	16	18	19	17
Lagos, Nigeria	28	46	102	150	269	460	279	64	140	206	69	25	1,836
3 m	27	28	29	28	28	26	26	25	26	26	28	28	27
Nairobi, Kenya	38	64	125	211	158	46	15	23	31	53	109	86	958
1,820 m	19	19	19	19	18	16	16	16	18	19	18	18	18
Australia, New Zealand & Antarctica													
Christchurch, New Zealand	56	43	48	48	66	66	69	48	46	43	48	56	638
10 m	16	16	14	12	9	6	6	7	9	12	14	16	11
Darwin, Australia	386	312	254	97	15	3	<3	3	13	51	119	239	1,491
30 m	29	29	29	29	28	26	25	26	28	29	30	29	28
Mawson, Antarctica	11	30	20	10	44	180	4	40	3	20	0	0	362
14 m	0	–5	–10	–14	–15	–16	–18	–18	–19	–13	–5	–1	–11
Sydney, Australia	89	102	127	135	127	117	117	76	73	71	73	73	1,181
42 m	22	22	21	18	15	13	12	13	15	18	19	21	17
North America													
Anchorage, Alaska, USA	20	18	15	10	13	18	41	66	66	56	25	23	371
40 m	–11	–8	–5	2	7	12	14	13	9	2	–5	–11	2
Kingston, Jamaica	23	15	23	31	102	89	38	91	99	180	74	36	800
34 m	25	25	25	26	26	28	28	28	27	27	26	26	26
Los Angeles, USA	79	76	71	25	10	3	<3	<3	5	15	31	66	381
95 m	13	14	14	16	17	19	21	22	21	18	16	14	17
Mexico City, Mexico	13	5	10	20	53	119	170	152	130	51	18	8	747
2,309 m	12	13	16	18	19	19	17	18	18	16	14	13	16
New York, USA	94	97	91	81	81	84	107	109	86	89	76	91	1,092
96 m	–1	–1	3	10	16	20	23	23	21	15	7	2	11
Vancouver, Canada	154	115	101	60	52	45	32	41	67	114	150	182	1,113
14 m	3	5	6	9	12	15	17	17	14	10	6	4	10
South America													
Antofagasta, Chile	0	0	0	<3	<3	3	5	3	<3	3	<3	0	13
94 m	21	21	20	18	16	15	14	14	15	16	18	19	17
Buenos Aires, Argentina	79	71	109	89	76	61	56	61	79	86	84	99	950
27 m	23	23	21	17	13	9	10	11	13	15	19	22	16
Lima, Peru	3	<3	<3	<3	5	5	8	8	8	3	3	<3	41
120 m	23	24	24	22	19	17	17	16	17	18	19	21	20
Rio de Janeiro, Brazil	125	122	130	107	79	53	41	43	66	79	104	137	1,082
61 m	26	26	25	24	22	21	21	21	21	22	23	25	23

THE EARTH IN FOCUS

> Landsat image of the
San Francisco Bay area.
The narrow entrance to
the bay (crossed by the
Golden Gate Bridge)
provides an excellent
natural harbour. The
San Andreas Fault runs
parallel to the coastline.

THE UNIVERSE & SOLAR SYSTEM

RECENT ESTIMATES SUGGEST that around 12,5000 million years ago, the Universe was created in a huge explosion known as the 'Big Bang'. In the first 10^{-24} of a second the Universe expanded rapidly and the basic forces of nature, radiation and subatomic particles, came into being. The Universe has been expanding ever since. Traces of the original 'fireball' of radiation can still be detected, and most scientists accept the Big Bang theory of the origin of the Universe.

The Nearest Stars ▼	
The 20 nearest stars, excluding the Sun, with their distance from Earth in light-years.*	
Proxima Centauri	4.25
Alpha Centauri A	4.3
Alpha Centauri B	4.3
Barnard's Star	6.0
Wolf 359	7.8
Lalande 21185	8.3
Sirius A	8.7
Sirius B	8.7
UV Ceti A	8.7
UV Ceti B	8.7
Ross 154	9.4
Ross 248	10.3
Epsilon Eridani	10.7
Ross 128	10.9
61 Cygni A	11.1
61 Cygni B	11.1
Epsilon Indi	11.2
Groombridge 34 A	11.2
Groombridge 34 B	11.2
L789-6	11.2
A light-year equals approximately 9,500 billion km [5,900 billion miles].	

> The Lagoon Nebula is a huge cloud of dust and gas. Hot stars inside the nebula make the gas glow red.

GALAXIES

Almost a million years passed before the Universe cooled sufficiently for atoms to form. When a billion years had passed, the atoms had begun to form proto-galaxies, which are masses of gas separated by empty space. Stars began to form within the protogalaxies, as particles were drawn together, producing the high temperatures necessary to bring about nuclear fusion. The formation of the first stars brought about the evolution of the protogalaxies into galaxies proper, each containing billions of stars.

Our Sun is a medium-sized star. It is

Mercury ○   Venus ◐   Earth ◑   Mars ◔   Jupiter

PLANETARY DATA

	Mean distance from Sun (million km)	Mass (Earth = 1)	Period of orbit (Earth years)	Period of rotation (Earth days)	Equatorial diameter (km)	Escape velocity (km/sec)	Number of known satellites
Sun	–	332,946	–	25.38	1,392,000	617.5	–
Mercury	58.3	0.06	0.241	58.67	4,878	4.27	0
Venus	107.7	0.8	0.615	243.0	12,104	10.36	0
Earth	149.6	1.0	1.00	0.99	12,756	11.18	1
Mars	227.3	0.1	1.88	1.02	6,707	5.03	2
Jupiter	777.9	317.8	11.86	0.41	142,800	59.60	16
Saturn	1,427.1	95.2	29.46	0.42	120,000	35.50	20
Uranus	2,872.3	14.5	84.01	0.45	51,118	21.30	15
Neptune	4,502.7	17.2	164.79	0.67	49,528	23.3	8
Pluto	5,894.2	0.002	248.54	6.38	2,300	1.1	1

one of the billions of stars that make up the Milky Way galaxy, which is one of the millions of galaxies in the Universe.

THE SOLAR SYSTEM

The Solar System lies towards the edge of the Milky Way galaxy. It consists of the Sun and other bodies, including planets (together with their moons), asteroids, meteoroids, comets, dust and gas, which revolve around it.

The Earth moves through space in three distinct ways. First, with the rest of the Solar System, it moves around the centre of the Milky Way galaxy in an orbit that takes 200 million years.

As the Earth revolves around the Sun once every year, its axis is tilted by about 23.5 degrees. As a result, first the northern and then the southern hemisphere lean towards the Sun at different times of the year, causing the seasons experienced in the mid-latitudes.

The Earth also rotates on its axis every 24 hours, causing day and night. The movements of the Earth in the Solar System determine the calendar. The length of a year – one complete orbit of the Earth around the Sun – is 365 days, 5 hours, 48 minutes and 46 seconds. Leap years prevent the calendar from becoming out of step with the solar year.

> The diagram below shows the planets around the Sun. The sizes of the planets are relative but the distances are not to scale. Closest to the Sun are dense rocky bodies, known as the terrestrial planets. They are Mercury, Venus, Earth and Mars. Jupiter, Saturn, Uranus and Neptune are huge balls of gas. Pluto is a small, icy body.

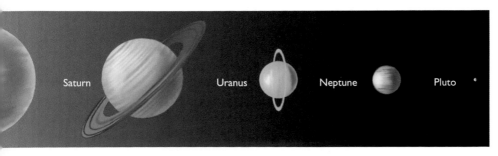

Saturn   Uranus   Neptune   Pluto

THE CHANGING EARTH

THE SOLAR SYSTEM was formed around 4.7 billion years ago, when the Sun, a glowing ball of gases, was created from a rotating disk of dust and gas. The planets were then formed from material left over after the creation of the Sun.

After the Earth formed, around 4.6 billion years ago, lighter elements rose to the hot surface, where they finally cooled to form a hard shell, or crust. Denser elements sank, forming the partly liquid mantle, the liquid outer core, and the solid inner core.

EARTH HISTORY

The oldest known rocks on Earth are around 4 billion years old. Natural processes have destroyed older rocks. Simple life forms first appeared on Earth around 3.5 billion years ago, though rocks formed in the first 4 billion years of Earth history contain little evidence of life. But

> Fold mountains, such as the Himalayan ranges which are shown above, were formed when two plates collided and the rock layers between them were squeezed upwards into loops or folds.

rocks formed since the start of the Cambrian period (the first period in the Paleozoic era), about 590 million years ago, are rich in fossils. The study of fossils has enabled scientists to gradually piece together the long and complex story of life on Earth.

THE PLANET EARTH

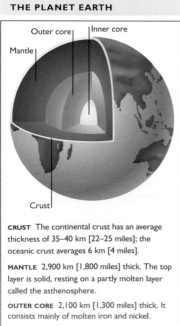

Outer core | Inner core
Mantle
Crust

CRUST The continental crust has an average thickness of 35–40 km [22–25 miles]; the oceanic crust averages 6 km [4 miles].

MANTLE 2,900 km [1,800 miles] thick. The top layer is solid, resting on a partly molten layer called the asthenosphere.

OUTER CORE 2,100 km [1,300 miles] thick. It consists mainly of molten iron and nickel.

INNER CORE (DIAMETER) 1,350 km [840 miles]. It is mainly solid iron and nickel.

ELEMENTS

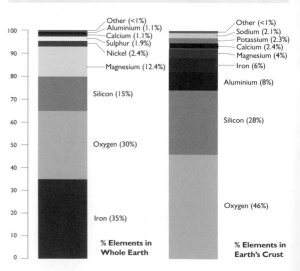

% Elements in Whole Earth

- Other (<1%)
- Aluminium (1.1%)
- Calcium (1.1%)
- Sulphur (1.9%)
- Nickel (2.4%)
- Magnesium (12.4%)
- Silicon (15%)
- Oxygen (30%)
- Iron (35%)

% Elements in Earth's Crust

- Other (<1%)
- Sodium (2.1%)
- Potassium (2.3%)
- Calcium (2.4%)
- Magnesium (4%)
- Iron (6%)
- Aluminium (8%)
- Silicon (28%)
- Oxygen (46%)

> The Earth contains about 100 elements, but eight of them account for 99% of the planet's mass. Iron makes up 35% of the Earth's mass, but most of it is in the core. The most common elements in the crust – oxygen and silicon – are often combined with one or more of the other common crustal elements, to form a group of minerals called silicates. The mineral quartz, which consists only of silicon and oxygen, occurs widely in such rocks as granites and sandstones.

PLATE BOUNDARIES

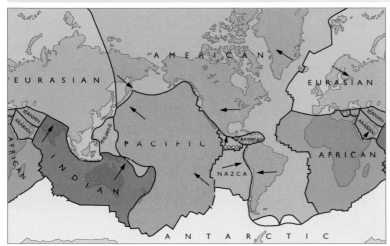

> The Earth's lithosphere is divided into six huge plates and several small ones. Ocean ridges, where plates are moving apart, are called constructive plate margins. Ocean trenches, where plates collide, are subduction zones. These are destructive plate margins. The map shows the main plates and the directions in which they are moving.

——— Plate boundaries

➤ Direction of plate movements

PACIFIC Major plates

THE DYNAMIC EARTH

The Earth's surface is always changing because of a process called plate tectonics. Plates are blocks of the solid lithosphere (the crust and outer mantle), which are moved around by currents in the partly liquid mantle. Around 250 million years ago, the Earth contained one super-continent called Pangaea. Around 180 million years ago, Pangaea split into a northern part, Laurasia, and a southern part, Gondwanaland. Later, these huge continents, in turn, also split apart and the continents drifted to their present positions. Ancient seas disappeared and mountain ranges, such as the Himalayas and Alps, were pushed upwards.

PLATE TECTONICS

In the early 1900s, two scientists suggested that the Americas were once joined to Europe and Africa. Together they proposed the theory of continental drift to explain the similarities between rock structures on both sides of the Atlantic. But no one could offer an explanation as to how the continents moved.

Evidence from the ocean floor in the 1950s and 1960s led to the theory of plate tectonics, which suggested that the lithosphere is divided into large blocks, or plates. The plates are solid, but they rest on the partly molten asthenosphere, within the mantle. Long ridges on the ocean floor were found to be the edges of plates which were moving apart, carried by currents in the asthenosphere. As the plates moved, molten material welled up from the mantle to fill the gaps. But at the ocean trenches, one plate is descending beneath another along what is called a subduction zone. The descending plate is melted and destroyed. This crustal destruction at subduction zones balances the creation of new crust along the ridges. Transform faults, where two plates are moving alongside each other, form another kind of plate edge.

GEOLOGICAL TIME SCALE

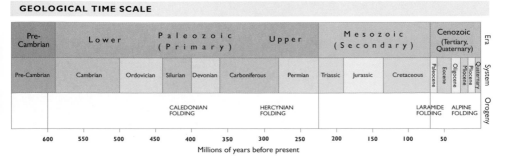

Pre-Cambrian	Lower	Paleozoic (Primary)		Upper		Mesozoic (Secondary)			Cenozoic (Tertiary, Quaternary)	Era
Pre-Cambrian	Cambrian	Ordovician	Silurian	Devonian	Carboniferous	Permian	Triassic	Jurassic	Cretaceous	Paleocene / Eocene / Oligocene / Miocene / Pliocene / Pleistocene / Quaternary	System
			CALEDONIAN FOLDING		HERCYNIAN FOLDING				LARAMIDE FOLDING / ALPINE FOLDING	Orogeny

| 600 | 550 | 500 | 450 | 400 | 350 | 300 | 250 | 200 | 150 | 100 | 50 |

Millions of years before present

EARTHQUAKES & VOLCANOES

PLATE TECTONICS HELP us to understand such phenomena as earthquakes, volcanic eruptions, and mountain building.

EARTHQUAKES

Earthquakes can occur anywhere, but they are most common near the edges of plates. They occur when intense pressure breaks the rocks along plate edges, making the plates lurch forward.

Major Earthquakes since 1900 ▾

Year	Location	Mag.	Deaths
1906	San Francisco, *USA*	8.3	503
1906	Valparaiso, *Chile*	8.6	22,000
1908	Messina, *Italy*	7.5	83,000
1915	Avezzano, *Italy*	7.5	30,000
1920	Gansu, *China*	8.6	180,000
1923	Yokohama, *Japan*	8.3	143,000
1927	Nan Shan, *China*	8.3	200,000
1932	Gansu, *China*	7.6	70,000
1934	Bihar, *India/Nepal*	8.4	10,700
1935	Quetta, *Pakistan*	7.5	60,000
1939	Chillan, *Chile*	8.3	28,000
1939	Erzincan, *Turkey*	7.9	30,000
1960	Agadir, *Morocco*	5.8	12,000
1964	Anchorage, *Alaska*	8.4	131
1968	North-east Iran	7.4	12,000
1970	North Peru	7.7	66,794
1976	Guatemala	7.5	22,778
1976	Tangshan, *China*	8.2	255,000
1978	Tabas, *Iran*	7.7	25,000
1980	El Asnam, *Algeria*	7.3	20,000
1980	South Italy	7.2	4,800
1985	Mexico City, *Mexico*	8.1	4,200
1988	North-west Armenia	6.8	55,000
1990	North Iran	7.7	36,000
1993	Maharashtra, *India*	6.4	30,000
1994	Los Angeles, *USA*	6.6	51
1995	Kobe, *Japan*	7.2	5,000
1997	North-east Iran	7.1	2,400
1998	Takhar, *Afghanistan*	6.1	4,200
1998	Rostaq, *Afghanistan*	7.0	5,000
1999	Izmit, *Turkey*	7.4	15,000
2001	Gujrat, *India*	7.9	20,000

> The earthquake that struck Kobe in January 1995 was the worst one experienced in Japan since 1923. Japan lies alongside subduction zones.

> The section between the Pacific and Indian oceans shows a subduction zone under the American plate, with spreading ocean ridges in the Atlantic and Indian oceans. East Africa may one day split away from the rest of Africa as plate movements pull the Rift Valley apart.

Earthquakes are common along the mid-ocean ridges, but they are a long way from land and cause little damage. Other earthquakes occur near land in subduction zones, such as those that encircle much of the Pacific Ocean. These earthquakes often trigger off powerful sea waves, called tsunamis. Other earthquakes occur along transform faults, such as the San Andreas fault in California, a boundary between the North American and Pacific plates. Movements along this fault cause periodic disasters, such as the earthquakes in San Francisco (1906) and Los Angeles (1994).

VOLCANOES & MOUNTAINS

Volcanoes are fuelled by magma (molten rock) from the mantle. Some volcanoes, such as in Hawaii, lie above 'hot spots' (sources of heat in the mantle). But most volcanoes occur either along the ocean ridges or above subduction zones, where

EARTHQUAKES

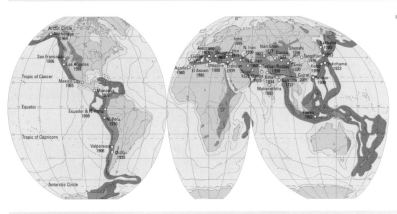

1976 ○   Selected major earthquakes & dates

▪   Mobile land areas

▪   Submarine zones of mobile land areas

☐   Stable land platforms

☐   Submarine extensions of land platforms

☐   Mid-oceanic volcanic ridges

☐   Oceanic platforms

VOLCANOES

▲   Land volcanoes active since 1700

──   Boundaries of tectonic plates

The maps show that the main earthquake zones follow plate edges. Most volcanoes are also in these zones, whereas some lie over 'hot spots', far from plate edges.

---

magma is produced when the descending plate is melted.

Volcanic mountains are built up gradually by runny lava flows or by exploded volcanic ash. Fold mountains occur when two plates bearing land areas collide and the plate edges are buckled upwards into fold mountain ranges. Plate movements also fracture rocks and block mountains are formed when areas of land are pushed upwards along faults or between parallel faults. Blocks of land sometimes sink down between faults, creating deep, steep-sided rift valleys.

> Volcanoes occur when molten magma reaches the surface under pressure through long vents. 'Quiet' volcanoes emit runny lava (called pahoehoe). Explosive eruptions occur when the magma is sticky. Explosive gases shatter the magma into ash, which is hurled upwards into the air.

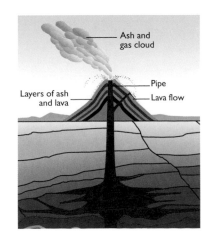

Ash and gas cloud

Pipe

Layers of ash and lava

Lava flow

WATER & ICE

A VISITOR FROM outer space might be forgiven for naming our planet 'Water' rather than 'Earth', because water covers more than 70% of its surface. Without water, our planet would be as lifeless as the Moon. Through the water cycle, fresh water is regularly supplied from the sea to the land. Most geographers divide the world's water into four main oceans: the Pacific, the Atlantic, the Indian and the Arctic. Together the oceans contain 97.2% of the world's water.

The water in the oceans is constantly on the move, even, albeit extremely slowly, in the deepest ocean trenches. The greatest movements of ocean water occur in the form of ocean currents. These are marked, mainly wind-blown

EXPLANATION OF TERMS

GLACIER A body of ice that flows down valleys in mountain areas. It is usually narrow and hence smaller than ice caps or ice sheets.

ICE AGE A period of Earth history when ice sheets spread over large areas. The most recent Ice Age began about 1.8 million years ago and ended 10,000 years ago.

ICEBERG A floating body of ice in the sea. About eight-ninths of the ice is hidden beneath the surface of the water.

ICE SHEET A large body of ice. During the last Ice Age, ice sheets covered large parts of the northern hemisphere.

OCEAN The four main oceans are the Pacific, the Atlantic, the Indian and the Arctic. Some

people classify a fifth southern ocean, but others regard these waters as extensions of the Pacific, Atlantic and Indian oceans.

OCEAN CURRENTS Distinct currents of water in the oceans. Winds are the main causes of surface currents.

SEA An expanse of water, but smaller than an ocean.

JANUARY TEMPERATURE AND OCEAN CURRENTS

(Northern Hemisphere – Winter)

ACTUAL SURFACE TEMPERATURE

°C
30
20
10
0
−10
−20
−30
−40

OCEAN CURRENTS
Cold   Warm   Speed (knots)
←- -   ←- -   Less than 0.5
←—   ←—   0.5 – 1.0
←—   ←—   Over 1.0

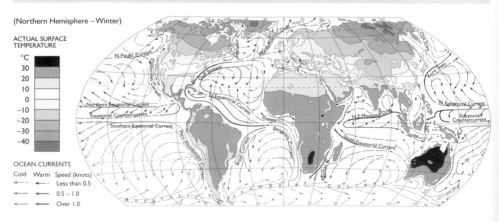

CROSS-SECTION OF ANTARCTICA

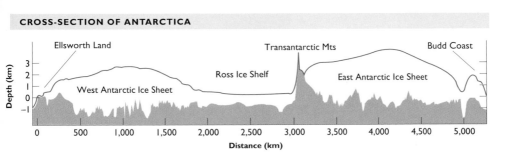

> This section across Antarctica shows the concealed land areas in brown, with the top of the ice in blue. The section is divided into the West and East Antarctic Ice Sheets. The vertical scale has been exaggerated.

movements of water on or near the surface. Other dense, cold currents creep slowly across the ocean floor. Warm and cold ocean currents help to regulate the world's climate by transferring heat between the tropics and the poles.

in several valley glaciers in numerous mountain areas.

Reports in the early 21st century sugg-ested global warming had begun to melt polar and glacier ice. If all the world's ice melted, sea level could rise by 100 m [330 ft], flooding islands and coastal areas and displacing tens of millions of people.

ICE

About 2.15% of the world's water is locked in two large ice sheets, several smaller ice caps and glaciers. The world's largest ice sheet covers most of Antarctica. The ice is up to 4,800 m [15,750 ft] thick and it represents 70% of the world's fresh water. The volume of ice is about nine times greater than that contained in the world's other ice sheet in Green-land. Besides these ice sheets, smaller ice caps are found in northern Canada, Iceland, Norway and Spitzbergen, and

Composition of Seawater ▾

The principal components of seawater, by percentage, excluding the elements of water itself.

Chloride (Cl)	55.04%	Potassium (K)	1.10%
Sodium (Na)	30.61%	Bicarbonate (HCO_3)	0.41%
Sulphate (SO_4)	7.69%	Bromide (Br)	0.19%
Magnesium (Mg)	3.69%	Strontium (Sr)	0.04%
Calcium (Ca)	1.16%	Fluorine (F)	0.003%

The oceans contain virtually every other element, the more important ones being lithium, rubidium, phosphorus, iodine and barium.

JULY TEMPERATURE AND OCEAN CURRENTS

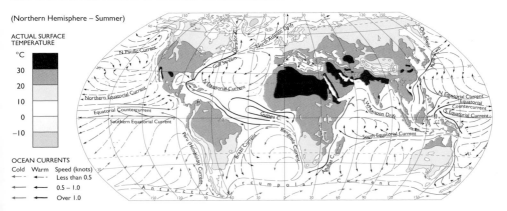

WEATHER & CLIMATE

WEATHER IS A description of the day-to-day state of the atmosphere. Climate, on the other hand, is weather in the long term: the seasonal pattern of temperature and precipitation averaged over time.

In some areas, the weather is so stable and predictable that a description of the weather is much the same as a statement of the climate. But in parts of the mid-latitudes, the weather changes from hour to hour. Changeable weather is caused mainly by low air pressure systems, called cyclones or depressions, which form along the polar front where warm subtropical air meets cold polar air.

The main elements of weather and climate are temperature and rainfall. Temperatures vary because the Sun heats the Earth unequally, with the most intense heating around the Equator. Unequal heating is responsible for the general circulation of the atmosphere and the main wind belts.

Rainfall occurs when warm air containing invisible water vapour rises. As the rising air cools, the capacity of the air to hold water vapour decreases and so the water vapour condenses into droplets of water or ice crystals, which collect together to form raindrops or snowflakes.

> Lightning occurs in clouds and also between the base of clouds and the ground. Lightning that strikes the ground can kill people or start forest fires.

> The rainfall map shows areas affected by tropical storms, which are variously called hurricanes, tropical cyclones, willy willies and typhoons. Strong polar winds bring blizzards in winter.

LIGHTNING

Lightning is a flash of light in the sky caused by a discharge of electricity in the atmosphere. Lightning occurs within cumulonimbus clouds during thunderstorms. Positive charges build up at the top of the cloud, while negative charges build up at the base. The charges are finally discharged as an electrical spark. Sheet lightning occurs inside clouds, while cloud to ground lightning is usually forked. Thunder occurs when molecules along the lightning channel expand and collide with cool molecules.

ANNUAL RAINFALL

mm
3,000
2,000
1,000
500
250

Paths of tropical storms and winter blizzards

BLIZZARDS November–March

HURRICANES August–October

CYCLONES June–November

TYPHOONS July–October

WILLY WILLIES January–March

GLOBAL WARMING

The Earth's climates have changed many times during its history. Around 11,000 years ago, much of the northern hemisphere was buried by ice. Some scientists believe that the last Ice Age may not be over and that ice sheets may one day return. Other scientists are concerned that air

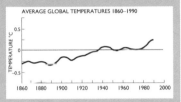

AVERAGE GLOBAL TEMPERATURES 1860–1990

pollution may be producing an opposite effect – a warming of the atmosphere. Since 1900, average world temperatures have risen by about 0.5°C [0.9°F] and increases are likely to continue. Global warming is the result of an increase in the amount of carbon dioxide in the atmosphere, caused by the burning of coal, oil and natural gas, together with deforestation. Short-wave radiation from the Sun passes easily through the atmosphere. But, as the carbon dioxide content rises, more of the long-wave radiation that returns from the Earth's surface is absorbed and trapped by the carbon dioxide. This creates a 'greenhouse effect', which will change the world's climates with, perhaps, disastrous environmental consequences.

CLIMATE

The world contains six main climatic types: hot and wet tropical climates; dry climates; warm temperate climates; cold temperate climates; polar climates; and mountain climates. These regions are further divided according to the character and amount of precipitation and special features of the temperature, notably seasonal variations. Regions with temperate climates include Mediterranean areas with hot, dry summers and mild, moist winters. The British Isles have a different type of temperate climate, with warm, rather than hot, summers and rain throughout the year.

CLIMATIC REGIONS

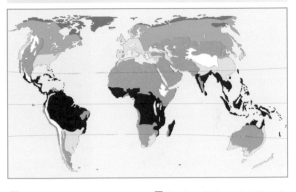

■ Tropical Climate (hot & wet)
■ Dry Climate (desert & steppe)
□ Temperate Climate (warm & wet)
▨ Continental Climate (cold & wet)
■ Polar Climate (very cold & wet)
□ Mountainous Areas (where altitude affects climate types)

WORLD CLIMATIC RECORDS

Highest Recorded Temperature
Al Aziziyah, Libya. 58°C [136.4°F] on 13 September 1922

Highest Mean Annual Temperature
Dallol, Ethiopia: 34.4°C [94°F] from 1960–66

Lowest Mean Annual Temperature
Polus, Nedostupnosti, Pole of Cold, Antarctica: –57.8°C [–72°F]

Lowest Recorded Temperature (outside poles)
Verkhoyansk, Siberia, Russia: –68°C [–90°F] on 6 February 1933

Windiest Place
Commonwealth Bay, Antarctica: gales often exceed 320 km/h [200 mph]

Longest Heatwave
Marble Bar, Western Australia: 162 days over 38°C [94°F], 23 October 1923 to 7 April 1924

Driest Place
Calama, northern Chile: no recorded rainfall in 400 years to 1971

Wettest Place (average)
Tututendo, Colombia: mean annual rainfall 11,770 mm [463 in]

Wettest Place (24 hours)
Cilaos, Réunion, Indian Ocean: 1,870 mm [73.6 in] from 15–16 March 1952

Wettest Place (12 months)
Cherrapunji, Meghalaya, north-east India: 26,470 mm [1,040 in], August 1860 to1861. Cherrapunji also holds the record for rainfall in one month: 2,930 mm [115 in] in July 1861

Heaviest Hailstones
Gopalganj, central Bangladesh: up to 1.02 kg [2.25 lbs] in April 1986, which killed 92 people

Heaviest Snowfall (continuous)
Bessans, Savoie, France: 1,730 mm [68 in] in 19 hours over the period 5–6 April 1969

Heaviest Snowfall (season/year)
Paradise Ranger Station, Mt Rainier, Washington, USA: 31,102 mm [1,224 in] fell from 19 February 1971 to 18 February 1972

11

Landforms & Vegetation

THE CLIMATE LARGELY determines the nature of soils and vegetation types throughout the world. The studies of climate and plant and animal communities are closely linked. For example, tropical climates are divided into tropical forest and tropical grassland climates. The tropical forest climate, which is hot and rainy throughout the year, is ideal for the growth of forests that contain more than half of the world's known plant and animal species. But tropical grassland, or savanna, climates have a marked dry season. As a result, the forest gives way to grassland, with scattered trees.

CLIMATE & SCENERY

The climate also helps to shape the land. Frost action in cold areas splits boulders apart, while rapid temperature changes in hot deserts make rock surfaces peel away like the layers of an onion. These are examples of mechanical weathering.

Chemical weathering usually results from the action of water on rocks. For example, rainwater containing dissolved carbon dioxide is a weak acid, which reacts with limestone. This chemical process is responsible for the erosion of the world's most spectacular caves.

Running water and glaciers play a major part in creating scenery, while in

> The tropical broadleaf forests are rich in plant and animal species. The extinction of many species because of deforestation is one of the great natural disasters of our time.

NATURAL VEGETATION

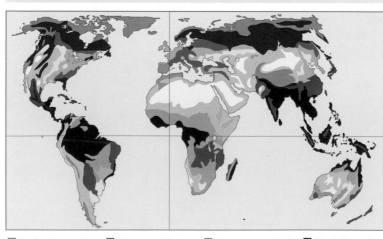

- ■ Tundra & mountain vegetation
- ■ Needleleaf evergreen forest
- ■ Broadleaf deciduous forest
- ■ Mixed needleleaf evergreen & broadleaf deciduous trees
- □ Mid-latitude grassland
- ■ Semi-desert scrub land
- ■ Evergreen broadleaf & deciduous trees & scrub
- □ Desert
- ■ Tropical grassland (savanna)
- ■ Tropical broadleaf & monsoon rainforest
- ■ Subtropical broadleaf & needleleaf forest

> Human activities, especially agriculture, have greatly modified plant and animal communities throughout the world. As a result, world vegetation maps show the natural 'climax vegetation'.of regions – that is, the kind of vegetation that would grow in a particular climatic area, had that area not been affected by human activities. For example, the climax vegetation of western Europe is broadleaf, deciduous forest, but most of the original forest, together with the animals which lived in it, was destroyed long ago.

DESERTIFICATION AND DEFORESTATION

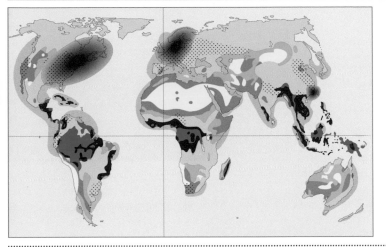

Pollution
- ☐ Polluted seas
- ▨ Main areas of sulphur & nitrogen emissions
- ▪ Areas of acid rain

Desertification
- ☐ Existing deserts
- ▪ Areas with a high risk of desertification
- ▪ Areas with a moderate risk of desertification

Deforestation
- ▪ Former areas of rainforest
- ▪ Existing rainforest

dry areas, wind-blown sand is a powerful agent of erosion. Most landforms seem to alter little in one person's lifetime. But geologists estimate that natural forces remove an average of 3.5 cm [1.4 in] from land areas every 1,000 years. Over millions of years, these forces reduce mountains to flat plains.

HUMAN INTERFERENCE

Climate also affects people, though air conditioning and central heating now make it possible for us live in comfort almost anywhere in the world.

However, human activities are damaging our planet. Pollution is poisoning rivers and seas, while acid rain, caused by air pollution, is killing trees and acidifying lakes. The land is also harmed by such things as nuclear accidents and the dumping of toxic wastes.

Some regions have been overgrazed or so intensively farmed that once fertile areas have been turned into barren deserts. The clearance of tropical forests means that some plant and animal species are disappearing before scientists have had a chance to study them.

MOULDING THE LAND

Powerful forces inside the Earth buckle rock layers to form fold mountain ranges. But even as they rise, the forces of erosion wear them away. On mountain slopes, water freezes in cracks in rocks. Because ice occupies more space than the equivalent amount of water, this 'frost action' shatters rocks, and the fragments tumble downhill. Some end up on or inside moving glaciers. Other rocks are carried away by running water. The glaciers and streams not only transport rock fragments, but they also wear out valleys and so add to their load. The eroded material breaks down into fragments of sand, silt and mud, much of which reaches the sea, where it piles up on the sea floor in layers. These layers eventually become compacted into sedimentary rocks, such as sandstones and shales. These rocks may eventually be squeezed up again by a plate collision to form new fold mountains, so completing a natural cycle of mountain building and destruction.

MAJOR FACTORS AFFECTING WEATHERING

	WEATHERING RATE		
	← SLOW		FAST →
Mineral solubility	low (e.g. quartz)	moderate (e.g. feldspar)	high (e.g. calcite)
Rainfall	low	moderate	heavy
Temperature	cold	temperate	hot
Vegetation	sparse	moderate	lush
Soil cover	bare rock	thin to moderate soil	thick soil

Weathering is the breakdown and decay of rocks in situ. It may be mechanical (physical), chemical or biological.

13

POPULATION

THE ADVENT OF agriculture around 10,000 years ago had a great impact on human society. People abandoned their nomadic way of life and settled in farming villages. With plenty of food, some people were able to pursue jobs unconnected with farming. These developments eventually led to rapid social changes, including the growth of early cities and the emergence of civilization.

THE POPULATION EXPLOSION

The social changes had a major effect on the world's population, which rose from around 8 million in 8000 BC, to about 300 million by AD 1000. The rate of population increase then began to accelerate further, passing the 1 billion mark in the 19th century, the 2 billion mark in the 1920s, and the 4 billion mark in the 1970s.

Today the world has a population of more than 6 billion and experts forecast that it will reach around 11 billion by 2200. However, they then predict that it will stabilize at this level or even begin to decline. Most of the expected increase will occur in developing countries in Africa, Asia and Latin America.

> Many cities in India, such as Mumbai (formerly called Bombay), have grown so quickly that they lack sufficient jobs and homes for their populations. As a result, slums now cover large areas.

POPULATION PYRAMIDS

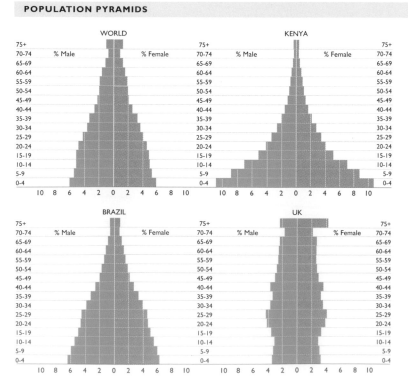

> The population pyramids compare the average age structures for the world with those of three countries at varying stages of development. Kenya, a developing country, had, until recently, one of the world's highest annual rates of population increase. As a result, a high proportion of Kenyans are aged under 15. Brazil has a much more balanced economy than Kenya's, and a lower rate of population increase. This is reflected in a higher proportion of people aged over 40. The UK is a developed country with a low rate of population growth, 0.3% per year between 1985–95, much lower than the world average of 1.6%. The UK has a far higher proportion of people over 60 years old.

The World's Largest Cities ▾

Early in the 21st century, for the first time ever, the majority of the world's population lives in cities. Below is a list of the 20 largest cities (in thousands) based on latest available figures.

1	Tokyo, *Japan*	26,836
2	São Paulo, *Brazil*	16,417
3	New York, *USA*	16,329
4	Shanghai, *China*	15,082
5	Mexico City, *Mexico*	15,048
6	Bombay (Mumbai), *India*	12,572
7	Los Angeles, *USA*	12,410
8	Beijing, *China*	12,362
9	Seoul, *South Korea*	11,641
10	Jakarta, *Indonesia*	11,500
11	Buenos Aires, *Argentina*	11,256
12	Calcutta, *India*	10,916
13	Tianjin, *China*	10,687
14	Osaka, *Japan*	10,601
15	Lagos, *Nigeria*	10,287
16	Cairo, *Egypt*	9,900
17	Rio de Janeiro, *Brazil*	9,888
18	Karachi, *Pakistan*	9,863
19	Paris, *France*	9,319
20	Manila, *Philippines*	9,280

This population explosion has been caused partly by better medical care, which has reduced child mortality and increased the average life expectancy at birth throughout the world. But it has also created problems. In some developing countries, nearly half of the people are children. They make no contribution to the economy, but they require costly education and health services. In richer countries, the high proportion of retired people is also a strain on the economy.

In the 21st century, for the first time in 10,000 years, the majority of people are no longer forced to rely on farming for their livelihood. Instead, nearly half of them live in cities where many of them enjoy a high standard of living. But rapid urbanization also creates problems, especially in the developing world, with the growth of slums and an increase in homelessness and crime.

POPULATION BY CONTINENT

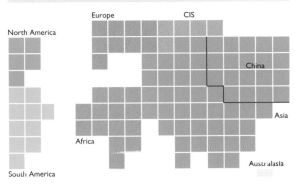

> The cartogram shows the populations of the continents in a diagrammatic way, with each square representing 1% of the world's population. For example, North America is represented by five squares, which means that it contains about 5% of the world's population, while Asia, the most populous continent even excluding the Asian part of the former USSR, is represented by 56 squares (China accounting for 19 of these). By contrast, Australasia is represented by less than half of a square because it contains only 0.45% of the world's population.

WORLD DEMOGRAPHIC EXTREMES

Fastest growing population; average annual % growth (1992–2000)		Slowest growing population; average annual % growth (1992–2000)	
1	Nigeria ... 5.09	1	Kuwait ... -1.39
2	Afghanistan ... 4.21	2	Ireland ... -0.24
3	Ivory Coast ... 3.54	3	St Kitts & Nevis ... -0.22
4	Oman ... 3.52	4	Bulgaria ... -0.13
5	Syria ... 3.51	5	Latvia ... -0.10

Youngest populations; % aged under 15 years (1996)		Oldest populations; % aged over 65 years (1996)	
1	West Bank/Gaza ... 51.7	1	Sweden ... 17.3
2	Uganda ... 48.6	2	Italy ... 16.1
3	Benin ... 48.4	3	Greece ... 15.9
=	Niger ... 48.4	=	Norway ... 15.9
5	Zambia ... 48.2	5	Belgium ... 15.8

Highest urban populations; % of population in urban areas (1996)		Lowest urban populations; % of population in urban areas (1996)	
1	Singapore ... 100.0	1	Bhutan ... 6.0
=	Bermuda ... 100.0	=	Rwanda ... 6.0
3	Macau ... 99.0	3	Burundi ... 8.0
4	Kuwait ... 97.0	4	Ethiopia ... 13.0
5	Hong Kong ... 95.0	=	Uganda ... 13.0

Most male populations; number of men per 100 women (1997)		Fewest male populations; number of men per 100 women (1997)	
1	Qatar ... 193.3	1	Latvia ... 84.3
2	United Arab Emirates ... 176.4	2	Ukraine ... 86.8
3	Bahrain ... 133.7	3	Russia ... 88.0
4	Saudi Arabia ... 125.1	5	Estonia ... 88.7
5	Oman ... 113.4	4	Belarus ... 88.8

LANGUAGES & RELIGIONS

ALL PEOPLE BELONG to one species, *Homo sapiens*, but within that species is a great diversity of cultures. Two of the main factors that give people an identity and sense of kinship with their neighbours are language and religion.

Definitions of languages vary and as a result estimates of the total number of languages in existence range from about 3,000 to 6,000. Many languages are spoken only by a small number of people. Papua New Guinea, for example, has only 4.2 million people but 869 languages.

The world's languages are grouped into families, of which the Indo-European is the largest. Indo-European languages are spoken in a zone stretching from

> Religion is a major force in South-east Asia. About 94% of the people in Thailand are Buddhists, and more than 40% of men over the age of 20 spend some time, if only a few weeks, serving as Buddhist monks. Confucianism, Islam, Hinduism, and Christianity are also practised in Thailand.

THE WORLD'S LANGUAGES

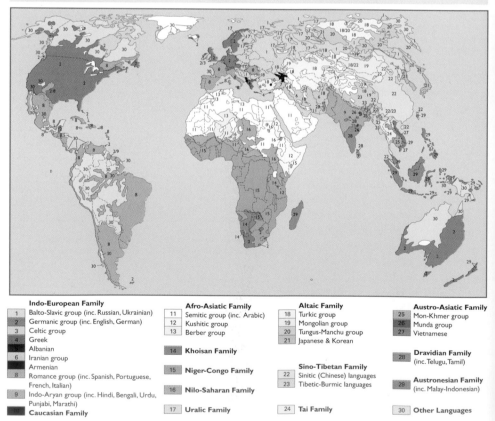

Indo-European Family

1	Balto-Slavic group (inc. Russian, Ukrainian)
2	Germanic group (inc. English, German)
3	Celtic group
4	Greek
5	Albanian
6	Iranian group
7	Armenian
8	Romance group (inc. Spanish, Portuguese, French, Italian)
9	Indo-Aryan group (inc. Hindi, Bengali, Urdu, Punjabi, Marathi)
10	**Caucasian Family**

Afro-Asiatic Family

11	Semitic group (inc. Arabic)
12	Kushitic group
13	Berber group

| 14 | **Khoisan Family** |

| 15 | **Niger-Congo Family** |

| 16 | **Nilo-Saharan Family** |

| 17 | **Uralic Family** |

Altaic Family

18	Turkic group
19	Mongolian group
20	Tungus-Manchu group
21	Japanese & Korean

Sino-Tibetan Family

| 22 | Sinitic (Chinese) languages |
| 23 | Tibetic-Burmic languages |

| 24 | **Tai Family** |

Austro-Asiatic Family

25	Mon-Khmer group
26	Munda group
27	Vietnamese

| 28 | **Dravidian Family** (inc. Telugu, Tamil) |

| 29 | **Austronesian Family** (inc. Malay-Indonesian) |

| 30 | **Other Languages** |

NATIVE SPEAKERS

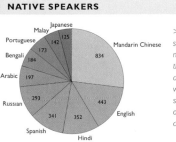

> The chart shows the native speakers of major languages in millions. Mandarin Chinese is the language of 834 million, as compared with English, which has 443 million speakers. However, many other people speak English as a second language.

Religious Adherents ▾

The world's major religions, with the number of adherents in millions (latest available year)

Christian	1,669
Roman Catholic	952
Protestant	337
Orthodox	162
Anglican	70
Other Christian	148
Muslim	915
Sunni	841
Shia	104
Hindu	663
Buddhist	312
Chinese folk	172
Ethnic/local	92
Jewish	18
Sikh	17

> Most languages have alphabetic systems of writing. The Greek alphabet uses some letters from the Roman alphabet, such as the A and B. Russians use the Cyrillic alphabet, which is based partly on Roman and partly on Greek letters. The Cyrillic alphabet is also used for Bulgarian and some central Asian languages. Serbs use either the Cyrillic or the Roman alphabet to write Serbo-Croat.

Europe, through south-western Asia into the Indian subcontinent. In addition, during the period of European colonization, they spread throughout North and South America and also to Australia and New Zealand. Today about two-fifths of the world's people speak an Indo-European language, as compared with one-fifth who speak a language belonging to the Sino-Tibetan language.

The Sino-Tibetan language family includes Chinese, which is spoken as a first language by more people than any other. English is the second most important first language, but it is more important than Chinese in international affairs and business, because so many people speak it as a second language.

RELIGIONS

Christianity is the religion of about a third of the world's population. Other major religions include Buddhism, Islam, Hinduism, Judaism, Chinese folk religions and traditional tribal religions.

Religion is a powerful force in human society, establishing the ethics by which people live. It has inspired great music, painting, architecture and literature, yet at the same time religion and language have contributed to conflict between people throughout history. Even today, the cause of many of the conflicts around the world are partly the result of linguistic and religious differences.

ALPHABETS

The Greek Alphabet

Α Β Γ Δ Ε Ζ Η Θ Ι Κ Λ Μ Ν Ξ Ο Π Ρ Σ Τ Υ Φ Χ Ψ Ω
A V/B G D E Z E TH I K L M N X O P R S T Y F CH PS O

The Cyrillic Alphabet

А Б В Г Д Е Ё Ж З И Й К Л М Н О П Р С Т У Ф Х Ц Ч Ш Щ Ю Я
A B V G D E YO ZH Z I Y K L M N O P R S T U F KH TS CH SH SHCH YU YA

AGRICULTURE & INDUSTRY

BECAUSE IT SUPPLIES so many basic human needs, agriculture is the world's leading economic activity. But its relative importance varies from place to place. In most developing countries, agriculture employs more people than any other activity. For example, the diagram at the bottom of this page shows that more than 90% of the people of Nepal are employed in farming.

Many farmers in developing countries live at subsistence level, producing barely enough to supply the basic needs of their families. Alongside the subsistence sector, some developing countries produce one or two cash crops that they export. Dependence on cash crops is precarious: when world commodity prices fall, the country is plunged into financial crisis.

In developed countries, by contrast, the proportion of people engaged in agriculture has declined over the last 200

> The cultivation of rice, one of the world's most important foods, is still carried out by hand in many areas. But the introduction of new strains of rice has greatly increased yields.

years. Yet, by using farm machinery and scientific methods, notably the selective breeding of crops and animals, the production of food has soared. For example, although agriculture employs only 3% of its workers, the United States is one of the world's top food producers.

INDUSTRIALIZATION

The Industrial Revolution began in Britain in the late 18th century and soon spread to mainland Europe and other parts of the world. Industries first arose in areas with supplies of coal, iron ore and cheap water power. But later, after oil and gas came into use as industrial fuels, factories could be set up almost anywhere.

The growth of manufacturing led to an increase in the number of industrial cities. The flight from the land was accompanied by an increase in efficiency in agriculture. As a result, manufacturing replaced agriculture as the chief source of

EMPLOYMENT

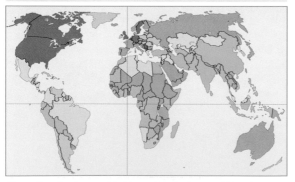

The number of workers employed in manufacturing for every 100 workers engaged in agriculture (latest available year)

- ▨ Under 10
- ▨ 10 – 50
- ☐ 50 – 100
- ☐ 100 – 200
- ▨ 200 – 500
- ▨ Over 500

DIVISION OF EMPLOYMENT

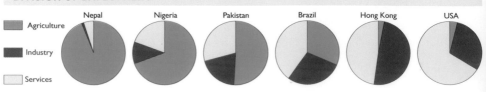

- Agriculture
- Industry
- Services

Nepal   Nigeria   Pakistan   Brazil   Hong Kong   USA

PATTERNS OF PRODUCTION

> *The table shows how the economy breaks down (in terms of the Gross Domestic Product for 1997) in a selection of industrialized countries. Agriculture remains important in some countries, though its percentage share has steadily declined since the start of the Industrial Revolution. Industry, especially manufacturing, accounts for a higher proportion, but service industries account for the greatest percentage of the GDP in most developed nations. The figures for Manufacturing are shown separately from Industry because of their importance in the economy.*

Country	Agriculture	Industry (excl. manufacturing)	Manufacturing	Services
Australia	3%	24%	12%	61%
Austria	1%	24%	14%	61%
Brazil	10%	28%	18%	44%
Denmark	4%	7%	20%	69%
Finland	5%	3%	28%	64%
France	2%	20%	13%	65%
Germany	1%	8%	24%	67%
Greece	17%	13%	23%	47%
Hungary	4%	24%	14%	58%
Ireland	8%	7%	3%	82%
Italy	3%	8%	21%	68%
Japan	1%	28%	19%	52%
Kuwait	0%	46%	9%	45%
Mexico	4%	18%	17%	61%
Netherlands	3%	21%	12%	64%
Norway	2%	24%	10%	64%
Singapore	0%	29%	17%	54%
Sweden	3%	8%	28%	61%
UK	2%	8%	23%	67%
USA	3%	10%	20%	67%

income and employment in industrialized countries, and rapidly widened the wealth gap between them and the poorer non-industrialized countries whose economies continued to rely on agriculture.

SERVICE INDUSTRIES

Eventually, the manufacturing sector became so efficient that it could supply most of the things that people wanted to buy. Trade between industrialized countries also increased, so widening the choice for consumers in the developed world. These factors led to a further change in the economies of developed countries, namely a reduction in the relative importance of manufacturing and the growth of the service sector.

Service industries include such activities as government, transport, insurance, finance, and even the writing of computer software. In the United States, service industries now account for about two-thirds of the Gross National Product (GNP), while in Japan they account for just over half. But the wealth of both countries still rests on their massive industrial production.

AGRICULTURE

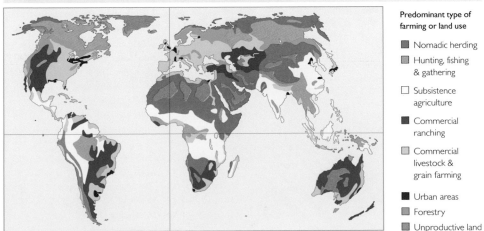

Predominant type of farming or land use

- ■ Nomadic herding
- ▨ Hunting, fishing & gathering
- □ Subsistence agriculture
- ■ Commercial ranching
- ▨ Commercial livestock & grain farming
- ■ Urban areas
- ▨ Forestry
- ▨ Unproductive land

TRADE & COMMERCE

TRADE HAS ALWAYS been an important human activity. It has widened the choice of goods available in any country, lowered prices and generally raised living standards. People regard any growth of world trade as a sign that the world economy is healthy, whereas a decline indicates a world recession.

Exports and imports are of two main kinds. Visible imports and exports include primary products, such as food and manufactures. Invisible imports and exports include services, such as banking, insurance, interest on loans, and money spent by tourists.

World trade, both visible and invisible, is dominated by the 29 members of the OECD (Organization for Economic Development), which includes the world's top trading nations, namely the United States, Japan, Germany, France, Italy and the United Kingdom, as well as Australia, New Zealand, Canada and Mexico. Hungary, Poland and South Korea joined in 1996.

> The new port of the historic Itulian city of Ravenna is linked to the Adriatic Sea by a canal. The port has large oil refining and petrochemical industries.

CHANGING EXPORTS

From the late 19th century to the 1950s, primary products, including farm products, minerals, natural fibres, timber and, in the latter part of this period, oil

The World's Largest Businesses ▼		
The world's largest businesses in 1997 by sales, in billions of US$.		
1	General Motors, *USA*	168.4
2	Ford Motor, *USA*	147.0
3	Mitsui, *Japan*	144.9
4	Mitsubishi, *Japan*	140.2
5	Itochu, *Japan*	135.5
6	Royal Dutch/Shell Group, *UK/Neths*	128.2
7	Marubeni, *Japan*	124.0
8	Exxon, *USA*	119.4
9	Summitomo, *Japan*	119.3
10	Toyota Motor, *Japan*	108.7
11	Wal-Mart Stores, *USA*	106.1
12	General Electric, *USA*	79.2
13	Nissho Iwai, *Japan*	78.9
14	Nippon Telegraph/Telephone, *Japan*	78.3
15	Intl. business Machines, *USA*	75.9
16	Hitachi, *Japan*	75.7
17	AT&T, *USA*	74.5
18	Nippon Life Insurance, *Japan*	72.6
19	Mobil, *USA*	72.3
20	Daimler-Benz, *Germany*	71.6

DEBT AND AID

International debtors and the development aid they receive (latest available year)

The provision of aid by rich countries to developing countries is part of international politics. But the grants made to developing countries are often dwarfed by the burden of debt which the countries are expected to repay. In 1990, the debts of Mozambique, one of the world's poorest countries, were estimated to be 75 times its entire earnings from exports.

Debt, US$ per capita

Aid, US$ per capita

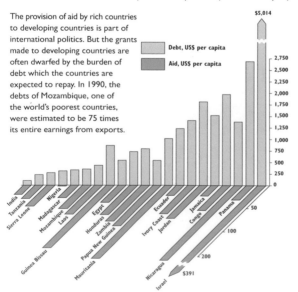

TRADED PRODUCTS

The character of world trade has greatly changed in the last 50 years. While primary products were once the leading commodities, world trade is now dominated by manufactured products. Cars are the single most valuable traded product, followed by vehicle parts and engines. The next most valuable goods are high-tech products such as data processing (computer) equipment, telecommunications equipment, and transistors. Other items include aircraft, paper and board, trucks, measuring and control instruments, and electrical machinery. Trade in most manufactured products is dominated by the OECD countries. For example, the leading vehicle exporter is Japan, which became the world's leading car manufacturer in the 1980s. The United States, Germany, the United Kingdom, France and Japan lead in the production of data processing equipment.

and natural gas, dominated world trade.

Many developing countries still remain dependent on exporting mineral ores, fossil fuels, or farm products such as cocoa or coffee whose prices fluctuate according to demand. But today, manufactured goods are the most important commodities in world trade. The OECD nations lead the world in exporting manufactured goods, though they are being challenged by a group of 'tiger economies' in eastern Asia, notably Singapore, Hong Kong and Taiwan. Other rapidly industrializing countries in Asia include Thailand, Malaysia and the Philippines. Despite a recession during the late 1990s, these countries, with their generally low labour costs, are able to produce manufactured goods that compete with similar goods made in the Western world.

Private companies carry on most of the world's trade. The small proportion handled by governments decreased recently with the collapse of Communist regimes in eastern Europe and the former Soviet Union.

SHARE OF WORLD TRADE

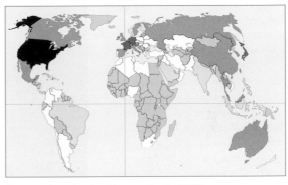

Percentage share of total world exports by value (1999)

- ■ Over 10%
- ■ 5 – 10%
- ■ 1 – 5%
- □ 0.5 – 1%
- □ 0.1 – 0.5%
- ▨ Under 0.1%

DEPENDENCE ON TRADE

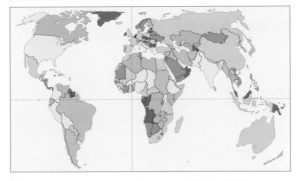

Value of exports as a percentage of Gross Domestic Product (1997)

- ■ Over 50% GDP
- ■ 40 – 50% GDP
- ▨ 30 – 40% GDP
- ▨ 20 – 30% GDP
- □ 10 – 20% GDP
- ▨ Under 10% GDP

Trade in Oil ▾

Major world trade in oil in millions of tonnes (1997)

Middle East to Asia (not Japan) 294.4	Mexico to USA 68.0
Middle East to Japan 218.1	W. Africa to W. Europe 40.1
Middle East to W. Europe 187.9	Western Europe to USA 32.9
S. and C. America to USA 132.1	Middle East to Africa 32.0
N. Africa to W. Europe 97.9	Middle East to South and Central America 27.8
CIS to Western Europe 90.8	
Middle East to USA 86.9	CIS to Central Europe 31.8
Canada to USA 72.7	Middle East to Central Europe 19.3
West Africa to USA 68.3	*Total world trade* 1,978.9

21

TRANSPORT & TRAVEL

ABOUT 200 YEARS ago, most people never travelled far from their birthplace. But adventurous travellers can now reach almost any part of the world.

Transport is concerned with moving goods and people around by land, water and air. Land transport was once laborious, and was dependent on pack animals or animal-drawn vehicles. But during the Industrial Revolution, railways played a vital role in moving bulky materials and equipment required by factories. They were also important in the opening up and development of remote areas around the world in North and South America, Africa, Asia and Australia

Today, however, motor vehicles have taken over many of the functions once served by railways. Unlike railways, motor vehicles provide a door-to-door service and, through the invention of heavy trucks, they can also carry large loads. In the late-1990s, about 90% of inland freight in Britain was carried by road, while car and van travel accounted for 86% of passenger travel, as compared with 6% by buses and coaches, 5% by rail and less than 1% by air.

> Traffic jams and vehicle pollution have affected cities throughout the world. Many of Bangkok's beautiful old canals have been filled in to provide extra roads to cope with the enormous volume of traffic in the city.

TRAVEL & TOURISM

Sea transport, which now employs huge bulk grain carriers, oil tankers and container ships, still carries most of the world's trade. But since the late 1950s, fewer passengers have travelled overseas by sea, because air travel is so much faster, though many former ocean liners now operate successfully as cruise ships.

Air travel has played a major part in the rapid growth of the tourist industry,

AIR TRAVEL

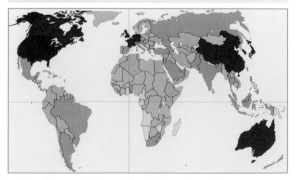

Number of passenger kilometres flown, in millions (1997). Passenger kilometres are the number of passengers (both international and domestic) multiplied by the distance flown by each passenger from airport of origin.

| ■ Over 100,000 | ☐ 10,000 – 50,000 | ☐ 500 – 1,000 |
| ■ 50,000 – 100,000 | ☐ 1,000 – 10,000 | ☐ Under 500 |

The World's Busiest Airports ▼
Total number of passengers, in thousands (1997)

#	Airport	Passengers
1	O'Hare Intl., *Chicago*	70,295
2	Hartsfield Atlanta Int., *Atlanta*	68,206
3	Dallas/Fort Worth Int., *Dallas*	60,489
4	Los Angeles Intl., *Los Angeles*	60,143
5	Heathrow, *London*	57,975
6	Haneda, *Tokyo*	49,302
7	San Francisco Intl., *San Francisco*	40,500
8	Frankfurt/Main, *Frankfurt*	40,263
9	Kimpo Intl., *Seoul*	36,757
10	Charles de Gaulle, *Paris*	35,294
11	Denver Intl., *Denver*	34,973
12	Miami Intl., *Miami*	34,533
13	Schiphol, *Amsterdam*	31,570
14	Metro Wayne County, *Detroit*	31,521
15	John F. Kennedy Intl., *New York*	31,229

The Longest Rail Networks ▼

Extent of rail network, in thousands of kilometres (latest available year)

1	USA	243.3
2	Russia	87.1
3	India	62.9
4	China	56.7
5	Germany	40.8
6	Argentina	34.2
7	France	31.9
8	Mexico	26.5
9	South Africa	25.9
10	Poland	23.4

which accounted for 7.5% of world trade by the 1990s. Travel and tourism have greatly increased people's understanding and knowledge of the world, especially in the OECD countries, which account for about 8% of world tourism.

Some developing countries have large tourist industries which have provided employment and led to improvements in roads and other facilities. In some cases, tourism plays a vital role in the economy. For example, in Kenya, tourism provides more income than any other activity apart from the production and sale of tea and coffee. However, too many tourists can damage fragile environments, such as the wildlife and scenery in national parks, and also harm local cultures.

THE IMPORTANCE OF TOURISM

Nations receiving the most from tourism, millions of US$ (1996)

1	USA	64,400
2	Spain	28,400
3	France	28,200
4	Italy	27,300
5	UK	20,400
6	Austria	15,100
7	Germany	13,200
8	Hong Kong	11,200
9	China	10,500
10	Switzerland	9,900

Number of tourist arrivals, millions (1996)

1	France	66,800
2	USA	49,038
3	Spain	43,403
4	Italy	34,087
5	UK	25,960
6	China	23,770
7	Poland	19,514
8	Mexico	18,667
9	Canada	17,610
10	Czech Republic	17,400

Fastest growing tourist destinations, % change in receipts (1994–95)

1	South Korea	49%
2	Czech Republic	27%
3	India	21%
4	Russia	19%
5	Philippines	18%
6	Turkey	17%
7	Thailand	15%
8	Poland	13%
9	China	12%
10	Israel	12%

Overseas travellers to the USA, thousands (1997)

1	Canada	13,900
2	Mexico	12,370
3	Japan	4,640
4	UK	3,350
5	Germany	1,990
6	France	1,030
7	Taiwan	885
8	Venezuela	860
9	South Korea	800
10	Brazil	785

THE WORLD'S VEHICLES

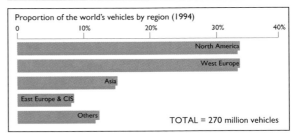

Proportion of the world's vehicles by region (1994)

North America
West Europe
Asia
East Europe & CIS
Others

TOTAL = 270 million vehicles

CAR OWNERSHIP

Number of people per car (1998)

- ■ Over 1,000
- ■ 25 – 100
- ■ 500 – 1,000
- ■ 5 – 25
- ■ 100 – 500
- □ Under 5

Two-thirds of the world's vehicles are found in the developed countries of Europe and North America. Car ownership is also high in Australia and New Zealand, as well as in Japan, the world's leading car exporter. Car transport is the most convenient form of passenger travel, but air pollution caused by exhaust fumes is a serious problem in many large cities.

INTERNATIONAL ORGANIZATIONS

IN THE LATE 1980s, people rejoiced at the collapse of Communist regimes in eastern Europe and the former Soviet Union, because this brought to an end the Cold War, a long period of hostility between East and West. But hope of a new era of peace was shattered when ethnic and religious rivalries led to civil war in Yugoslavia and in parts of the former Soviet Union.

In order to help maintain peace, many governments have formed international organizations to increase co-operation. Some, such as NATO (North Atlantic

> In the early 1990s, the United Nations peacekeeping mission worked to end the civil war in Bosnia-Herzegovina and also to bring aid to civilians affected by the fighting.

Treaty Organization), are defence alliances, while others aim to encourage economic and social co-operation. Some of the organizations such as the Red Cross are non-governmental organizations, or NGOs.

UN Contributions ▾

In 1996–97, the top ten contributing countries to the UN budget, which was US$2.6 billion, were as follows:

1	USA	25.0%
2	Japan	15.4%
3	Germany	9.0%
4	France	6.4%
5	UK	5.3%
6	Italy	5.2%
7	Russia	4.5%
8	Canada	3.1%
9	Spain	2.4%
10	Brazil	1.6%

UNITED NATIONS

The United Nations, the chief international organization, was formed in October 1945 and now has 188 member countries. The only independent nations that are not members are Switzerland, Taiwan and the Vatican City.

THE UNITED NATIONS

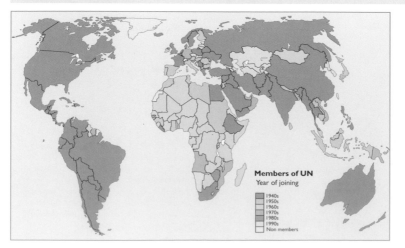

Members of UN
Year of joining

- 1940s
- 1950s
- 1960s
- 1970s
- 1980s
- 1990s
- Non members

> The membership of the UN had risen from 51 in 1945 to 188 by the end of 2000. The first big period of expansion came in the 1960s when many former colonies achieved their independence. The membership again expanded rapidly in the 1990s when new countries were formed from the former Soviet Union and Yugoslavia. The most recent addition, Palau, is a former US trust territory in the Pacific Ocean and joined in 1994.

The United Nations was formed at the end of World War II to promote peace, international co-operation and security, and to help solve economic, social, cultural and humanitarian problems. It promotes human rights and freedom and is a forum for negotiations between nations.

The main organs of the UN are the General Assembly, the Security Council, the Economic and Social Council, the Trusteeship Council, the International Court of Justice and the Secretariat.

The UN also operates 14 specialized agencies concerned with particular issues, such as agriculture, education, working conditions, communications and health. For example, UNICEF (the United Nations International Children's Fund), established in 1946 to deliver post-war relief to children, now aims to provide basic health care to children and mothers worldwide. The ILO (International Labour Organization) seeks to improve working conditions, while the FAO (Food and Agricultural Organization) aims at improving the production and distribution of food. The WTO (World Trade Organization) was set up as recently as January 1995 to succeed GATT (General Agreements on Tariffs and Trade).

THE UNITED NATIONS

THE GENERAL ASSEMBLY is the meeting of all member nations every September under a newly-elected president to discuss issues affecting development, peace and security.

THE SECURITY COUNCIL has 15 members, of which five are permanent. It is responsible for maintaining international peace.

THE SECRETARIAT consists of the staff and employees of the UN, including the Secretary-General (appointed for a five-year term), who is the UN's chief administrator.

THE ECONOMIC & SOCIAL COUNCIL works with the specialized agencies to implement UN policies on improving living standards, health, cultural and educational co-operation.

THE TRUSTEESHIP COUNCIL was designed to bring several dependencies to independence. This work is now complete.

THE INTERNATIONAL COURT OF JUSTICE, or World Court, deals with legal problems and helps to settle disputes. Its headquarters are at The Hague, in the Netherlands.

UN DEPARTMENTS

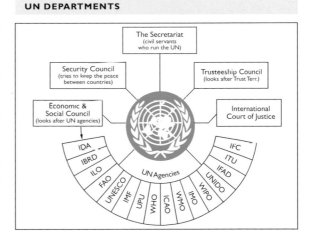

UN PEACEKEEPING MISSIONS

The United Nations tries to resolve international disputes in several ways. It sends unarmed observer missions to monitor cease-fires or supervise troop withdrawals, and the Security Council members also send peacekeeping forces.

The first of these forces was sent in 1948 to supervise the cease-fire between Arabs and Jews in disputed parts of Palestine and, since then, it has undertaken more than 30 other missions. The 'Blue Berets', as the 25,650 UN troops are called, must be impartial in any dispute

and they can fire only in self-defence. Hence, they can operate only with the support of both sides, which leaves them open to criticism when they are unable to prevent violence by intervening.

By the mid-1990s, the UN was involved in 15 world conflicts, was policing the boundary in partitioned Cyprus, and was seeking to enforce a peace agreement in Angola after 20 years of civil war. Other UN missions were in Tajikistan, Georgia, the Israeli-occupied Golan Heights, Haiti, Kuwait, southern Lebanon, the India–

Pakistan border, Liberia, Mozambique, Western Sahara and the former Yugoslavia. A force known as UNPROFOR (UN Protection Force) had been operating in Bosnia-Herzegovina and, by 1995, it accounted for 60% of the total UN peacekeeping budget. In February 1996, the Secretary-General of the UN approved the setting up of a new force, the United Nations Mission in Bosnia-Herzegovina (UNMIBH). Its main objective was to help create the right climate for the elections held in September 1996.

cludes the countries of East and Southeast Asia, as well as North America, plus Australia, New Zealand and Chile. APEC aims to create a free trade zone by 2020.

Together the United States, Canada and Mexico form NAFTA (North American Free Trade Agreement), which aims at eliminating trade barriers within 15 years of its foundation on 1 January 1994. Other economic groupings link the countries of Latin America.

Another economic group with more limited aims is OPEC (Organization of Petroleum Exporting Countries). It works to unify policies concerned with the sale of petroleum on world markets.

The central aim of the Colombo Plan is to provide economic development assistance for South and South-east Asia.

ECONOMIC ORGANIZATIONS

Over the last 40 years, many countries have joined common markets aimed at eliminating trade barriers and encouraging the free movement of workers and capital.

The best known of these is the European Union. Other organizations include ASEAN (the Association of South-east Asian Nations), which aims to reduce trade barriers between its ten members: Brunei, Burma, Cambodia, Indonesia, Laos, Malaysia, the Philippines, Singapore, Thailand and Vietnam.

APEC (the Asia-Pacific Co-operation Group) was founded in 1989 and in-

> The European Parliament, one of the branches of the EU, consists of 626 members. The number of members for each country is based mainly on population.

OTHER ORGANIZATIONS

Some organizations exist for consultation on matters of common interest. The Commonwealth of Nations grew out of the links created by the British Empire, while the OAS (Organization of American States) works to increase understanding throughout the Western hemisphere. The OAU (Organization of

THE EUROPEAN UNION

At the end of World War II (1939–45), many Europeans wanted to end the ancient emnities that had caused such destruction and rebuild the shattered continent. It was in this mood that Belgium, France, West Germany, Italy, Luxembourg and the Netherlands signed the Treaty of Paris in 1951. This set up the European Coal and Steel Community (ECSC), the forerunner of the European Union.

In 1957, through the Treaty of Rome, the same six countries created the European Economic Community (EEC) and the European Atomic Community (EURATOM). In 1967, the ECSC, the EEC and EURATOM merged to form the

single European Community (EC).

Another economic group, the European Free Trade Association (EFTA), was set up in 1960 by seven countries: Austria, Denmark, Norway, Portugal, Sweden, Switzerland and the United Kingdom. However, Denmark, Ireland and the UK left to become members of the EC in 1973, followed by Greece in 1981, Spain and Portugal in 1986, and Austria, Finland and Sweden in 1995. The expansion of the EC to 15 members left EFTA with just four members: Iceland, Liechtenstein, Norway and Switzerland.

In 1993, following the signing of the Maastricht Treaty, the EC was reconstituted

as the European Union (EU). The aims of the EU include economic and monetary union, a single currency for all 15 countries, and closer co-operation on foreign and security policies and also on home affairs. This step has led to a debate. Some people would like the EU to develop into a federal Europe, but others fear that this would lead to a loss of national identity. On 1 January 1999, 11 EU countries adopted the euro as their official currency, although euro coins and notes would not to come into use until 1 January 2002. On 1 January 2001, Greece also adopted the euro, leaving only Denmark, Sweden and the United Kingdom outside the euro zone.

AUSTRALIA'S NEW ROLE

Most of the people who settled in Australia between 1788 and the mid-20th century came from the British Isles. However, the strong ties between Australia and Britain were weakened after Britain joined the European Community in 1973. Since 1973, many Australians have argued that their world position has changed and that they are part of a Pacific community of nations, rather than an extension of Europe. Some want closer integration with ASEAN, the increasingly powerful economic group formed by seven South-east Asian nations. But in 1995, the prime minister of Malaysia, Dr Mahathir Mohamad, argued that Australia could not be regarded as Asian until at least 70% of its people were of ethnic Asian origin.

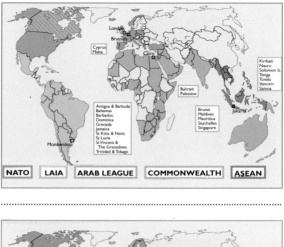

African Unity) has a similar role in Africa, while the Arab League is made up of Arabic-speaking North African and Middle Eastern states. The CIS (Commonwealth of Independent States) was formed in 1991 to maintain links between 12 of the former 15 republics in the Soviet Union.

NORTH–SOUTH DIVIDE

The deepest division in the world today is the divide between rich and poor nations. In international terms, this is called the North–South divide, because the North contains most of the world's developed countries, while the developing countries lie mainly in the South. The European Union recognizes this division and gives special trading terms to more than 60 former European dependencies, which form the ACP (African, Caribbean and Pacific) states. One organization containing a majority of developing countries is the Non-Aligned Movement. This Movement was created in 1961 during the Cold War as a political bloc allied neither to the East nor to the West. However, the aims of the 113 members who attended the movement's 11th gathering in 1995 were concerned mainly with economic matters. The 113 countries between them produce only about 7% of the world's gross output and they can speak for the poorer South.

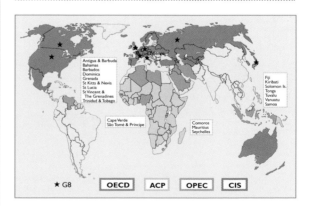

> The maps above show the membership of major international organizations. One important grouping shown on the bottom map is the Group of Eight (often called 'G8'). This group of eight leading industrial nations (comprising Canada, France, Germany, Italy, Japan, Russia, the United Kingdom and the United States) holds periodic meetings to discuss major problems, such as world recessions.

REGIONS IN THE NEWS

> The former Yugoslavia, a federation of six republics, split apart in 1991–92. Fearing Serb domination, Croatia, Slovenia, Macedonia and Bosnia-Herzegovina declared themselves independent. This left two states, Serbia and Montenegro, to continue as Yugoslavia. The presence in Croatia and Bosnia-Herzegovina of Orthodox Christian Serbs, Roman Catholic Croats and Muslims led to civil war and 'ethnic cleansing'. In 1995, the war ended when the Dayton Peace Accord affirmed Bosnia-Herzegovina as a single state partitioned into a Muslim-Croat Federation and a Serbian Republic. But the status of Kosovo, a former autonomous Yugoslav region, remained unresolved. Kosovo's autonomy was abolished in 1989 and Albanian-speaking, Muslim Kosovars came under direct Serbian rule. From 1995, support grew for the rebel Kosovo Liberation Army. War broke out, and NATO launched an offensive in 1999 that led to the withdrawal of Serbian troops from Kosovo. In 2000, President Slobodan Milosevic, whose policies were considered to be the cause of much of the ethnic conflict, was defeated in elections.

Population Breakdown ▾

Population totals and the proportion of ethnic groups (1995)

Yugoslavia **10,881,000**
  Serb 63%, Albanian 17%, Montenegrin 5%,
  Hungarian 3%, Muslim 3%
Serbia 6,017,200
  Kosovo *2,045,600*
  Vojvodina *2,121,800*
Montenegro 696,400

Bosnia-Herzegovina **4,400,000**
  Muslim 49%, Serb 31%, Croat 17%

Croatia **4,900,000**
  Croat 78%, Serb 12%

Slovenia **2,000,000**
  Slovene 88%, Croat 3%, Serb 2%

Macedonia (F.Y.R.O.M.) **2,173,000**
  Macedonian 64%, Albanian 22%, Turkish 5%,
  Romanian 3%, Serb 2%

- - - · - - International borders
- - - · - - Republic boundaries
- - - - - - Province boundaries
———— Line of the Dayton Peace Accord
▨ Muslim–Croat Federation
☐ Serbian Republic

> Since its establishment in 1948, the State of Israel has seldom been out of the news. During wars with its Arab neighbours in 1948–49, 1956, 1967 and 1973, it occupied several areas. The largest of the occupied territories, the Sinai peninsula, was returned to Egypt in 1979 following the signing of an Egyptian–Israeli peace treaty. This left three Israeli-occupied territories: the Gaza Strip, the West Bank bordering Jordan, and the Golan Heights, a militarily strategic area overlooking south-western Syria.

Despite the peace agreement with Egypt, conflict continued in Israel with the PLO (Palestine Liberation Organization), which claimed to represent Arabs in Israel and Palestinians living in exile. Finally, on 13 September 1993 Israel officially recognized the PLO, and Yasser Arafat, leader of the PLO, renounced terrorism and recognized the State of Israel. This led to an agreement signed by both sides in Washington, DC. In May 1994, limited Palestinian self-rule was established in the Gaza Strip and in parts of the occupied West Bank. A Palestinian National Authority (PNA) was created and took over from the Israeli military administration when Israeli troops withdrew from the Gaza Strip and the city of Jericho. On 1 July 1994 the Palestinian leader, Yasser Arafat, stepped on to Palestinian land for the first time in 25 years.

Many people hoped that these developments would eventually lead to the creation of a Palestinian state, which would co-exist in peace with its neighbour Israel. But groups on both sides sought to undermine the peace process. In November 1995, a right-wing Jewish student assassinated the Israeli prime minister, Yitzhak Rabin, who was succeeded by Símon Peres.

In 1996, a right-wing coalition led by Binyamin Netanyahu was elected to power. Peace talks with the PLO were halted, but, in 1999, the Labour Party leader Ehud Barak was elected prime minister. Barak revived negotiations with the PLO and Middle Eastern leaders aimed at exchanging 'land for peace'. But agreement, especially on the status of Jerusalem, proved elusive and fighting broke out in 2000. In 2001, Barak was defeated in elections by the right-wing Ariel Sharon.

THE NEAR EAST

Population Breakdown ▾

Population totals and the proportion of ethnic groups (1995)

Israel **5,696,000**
Jewish 82%, Arab Muslim 14%, Arab Christian 3%, Druse 2%
West Bank 973,500
Palestinian Arab 97% (Arab Muslim 85%, Christian 8%, Jewish 7%)
Gaza Strip 658,200
Arab Muslim 98%

Jordan **5,547,000**
Arab 99% (Palestinian Arab 50%)

Syria **14,614,000**
Arab 89%, Kurdish 6%

—·—·— 1949 Armistice Line

------ 1974 Cease-fire Lines (Golan Heights)

Efrata ● Main Jewish settlements in the West Bank and Gaza Strip

Halhul □ Main Palestinian Arab towns in the West Bank and Gaza Strip – under Palestinian control since May 1994 (Gaza and Jericho) and 28 September 1995 (West Bank)

WORLD FLAGS

 Afghanistan

 Albania

 Algeria

 Angola

 Argentina

 Armenia

 Australia

 Austria

 Azerbaijan

 Bahamas

 Bahrain

 Bangladesh

 Belarus

 Belgium

 Benin

 Bhutan

 Bolivia

 Bosnia-Herzegovina

 Botswana

 Brazil

 Bulgaria

 Burkina Faso

 Burma (Myanmar)

 Burundi

 Cambodia

 Cameroon

 Canada

 Central African Rep.

 Chad

 Chile

 China

 Colombia

 Congo

 Congo (Dem. Rep. of)

 Costa Rica

 Croatia

 Cuba

 Cyprus

 Czech Republic

 Denmark

 Djibouti

 Dominican Republic

 Ecuador

 Egypt

 El Salvador

 Equatorial Guinea

 Eritrea

 Estonia

 Ethiopia

 Finland

 France

Gabon

Georgia

Germany

Ghana

Greece

 Guatemala

 Guinea

 Guinea–Bissau

 Guyana

 Haiti

 Honduras

 Hong Kong

 Hungary

 Iceland

 India

 Indonesia

 Iran

 Iraq

 Ireland

 Israel

 Italy

 Ivory Coast

 Jamaica

 Japan

 Jordan

 Kazakstan

 Kenya

 Korea, North

 Korea, South

 Kuwait

 Kyrgyzstan

 Laos

 Latvia

 Lebanon

 Lesotho

 Liberia

 Libya

 Liechtenstein

 Lithuania

 Luxembourg

 Macedonia

 Madagascar

 Malawi

 Malaysia

 Mali

 Malta

 Mauritania

 Mexico

 Moldova

 Mongolia

 Morocco

 Mozambique

Namibia

Nepal

Netherlands

New Zealand

 Nicaragua

Niger

Nigeria

31

Norway
 Oman
 Pakistan
 Panama
 Papua New Guinea

 Paraguay
 Peru
 Philippines
 Poland
 Portugal

 Puerto Rico
 Qatar
 Romania
 Russia
 Rwanda

 São Tomé & Príncipe
 Saudi Arabia
 Senegal
 Sierra Leone
 Singapore

 Slovak Republic
 Slovenia
 Somalia
 South Africa
 Spain

 Sri Lanka
 Sudan
 Surinam
 Swaziland
 Sweden

 Switzerland
 Syria
 Taiwan
 Tajikistan
 Tanzania

 Thailand
 Togo
 Trinidad & Tobago
 Tunisia
 Turkey

 Turkmenistan
 Uganda
 Ukraine
 UAE
 United Kingdom

 USA
 Uruguay
 Uzbekistan
 Vatican City
Venezuela

 Vietnam
 Yemen
 Yugoslavia
Zambia
Zimbabwe

WORLD MAPS — GENERAL REFERENCE

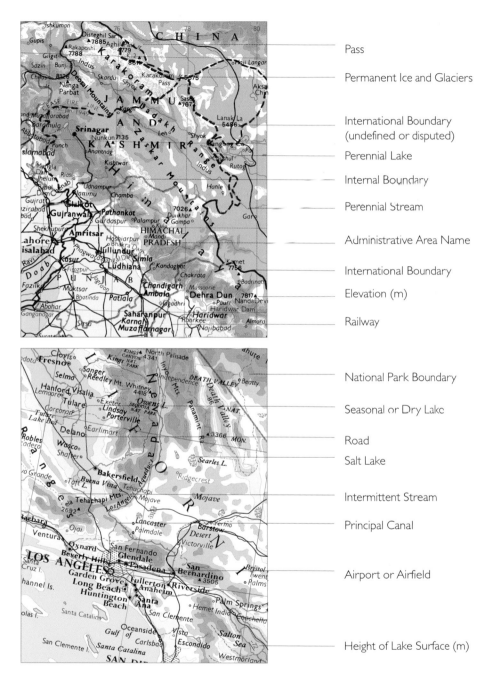

Pass

Permanent Ice and Glaciers

International Boundary
(undefined or disputed)

Perennial Lake

Internal Boundary

Perennial Stream

Administrative Area Name

International Boundary

Elevation (m)

Railway

National Park Boundary

Seasonal or Dry Lake

Road

Salt Lake

Intermittent Stream

Principal Canal

Airport or Airfield

Height of Lake Surface (m)

Settlements

Settlement symbols and type styles vary
according to the scale of each map and
indicate the importance of towns rather
than specific population figures.

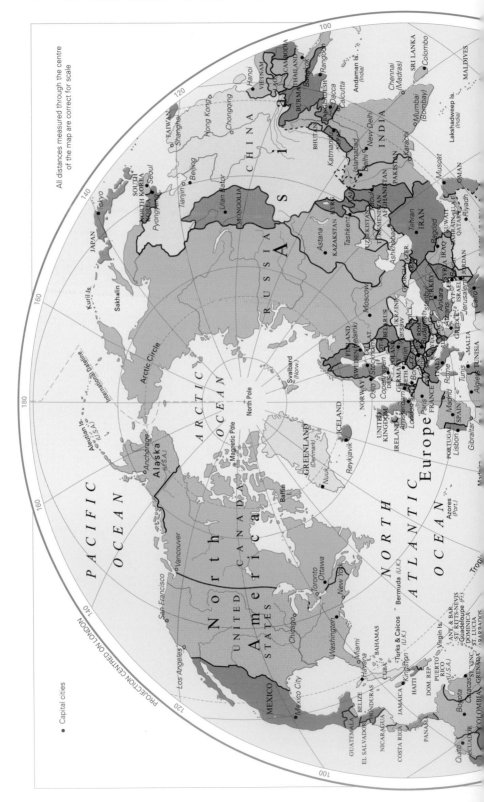

All distances measured through the centre of the map are correct for scale

PROJECTION CENTRED ON LONDON

• Capital cities

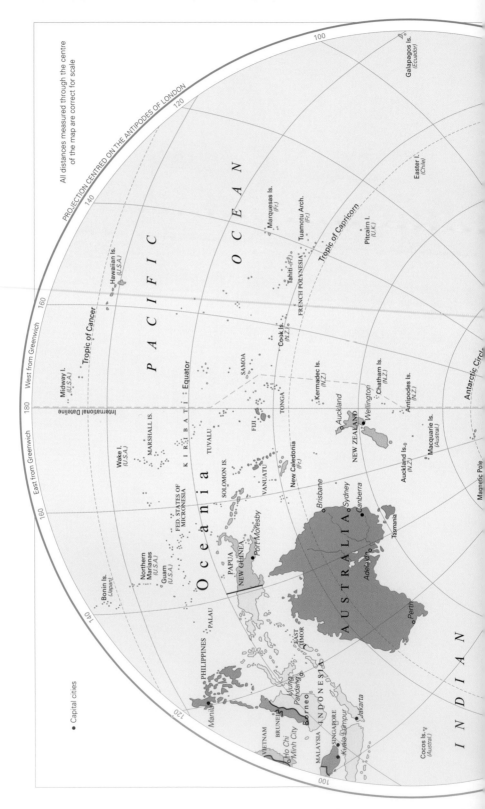

PROJECTION CENTRED ON THE ANTIPODES OF LONDON

All distances measured through the centre
of the map are correct for scale

• Capital cities

PACIFIC OCEAN

Galapagos Is.
(Ecuador)

Easter I.
(Chile)

Marquesas Is.
(Fr.)

Tuamotu Arch.
(Fr.)

Pitcairn I.
(U.K.)

Tropic of Capricorn

Tahiti *(Fr.)*

FRENCH POLYNESIA

Cook Is.
(N.Z.)

Antarctic Circle

Hawaiian Is.
(U.S.A.)

Tropic of Cancer

Midway I.
(U.S.A.)

West from Greenwich

Equator

SAMOA

Chatham Is.
(N.Z.)

Kermadec Is.
(N.Z.)

Antipodes Is.
(Austral.)

Auckland

Wellington

TONGA

International Dateline

Wake I.
(U.S.A.)

MARSHALL IS.

K I R I B A T I

FIJI

NEW ZEALAND

TUVALU

Macquarie Is.
(N.Z.)

Auckland Is.
(N.Z.)

Magnetic Pole

East from Greenwich

O c e a n i a

FED. STATES OF
MICRONESIA

SOLOMON IS.

VANUATU

New Caledonia
(Fr.)

Brisbane

Sydney
Canberra

Bonin Is.
(Japan)

Northern
Marianas
(U.S.A.)

Guam
(U.S.A.)

PAPUA
NEW GUINEA

Port Moresby

Tasmania

A U S T R A L I A

Adelaide

Perth

PHILIPPINES

PALAU

Manila

EAST
TIMOR

I N D I A N

VIETNAM

Ho Chi
Minh City

BRUNEI

Ujung
Pandang

Borneo

I N D O N E S I A

Jakarta

MALAYSIA
SINGAPORE
Kuala Lumpur

Cocos Is.
(Austral.)

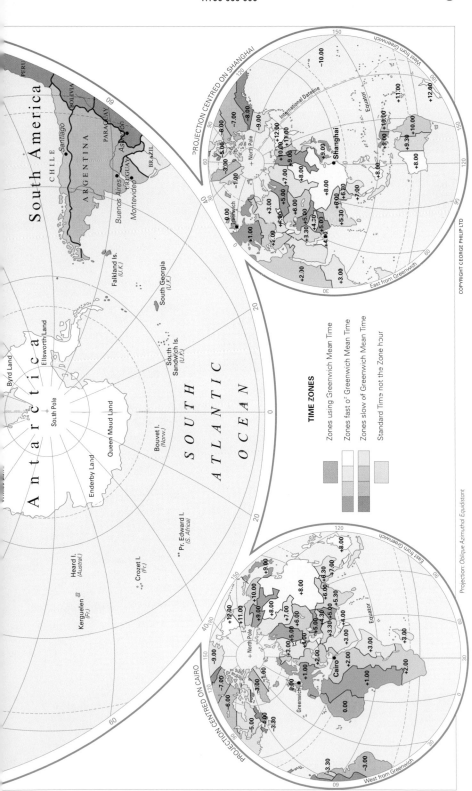

South America

CHILE · Santiago
BOLIVIA
PARAGUAY · Asunción
ARGENTINA
BRAZIL
Buenos Aires · URUGUAY
Montevideo

Falkland Is. (U.K.)
South Georgia (U.K.)
South Sandwich Is. (U.K.)

Antarctica
Byrd Land
Ellsworth Land
South Pole
Queen Maud Land
Enderby Land
Bouvet I. (Norw.)

SOUTH ATLANTIC OCEAN

** Pr. Edward I. (S. Africa)
Crozet I. (Fr.)
Heard I. (Austral.)
Kerguelen (Fr.)

TIME ZONES

Zones using Greenwich Mean Time
Zones fast of Greenwich Mean Time
Zones slow of Greenwich Mean Time
Standard Time not the Zone hour

PROJECTION CENTRED ON SHANGHAI
Shanghai
PROJECTION CENTRED ON CAIRO
Cairo
Greenwich

Projection: Oblique Azimuthal Equidistant

COPYRIGHT GEORGE PHILIP LTD

1: 20 000 000

100	0	100	200	300	400	500 miles
100	0	200	400	600	800 km

CARTOGRAPHY BY PHILIPS.

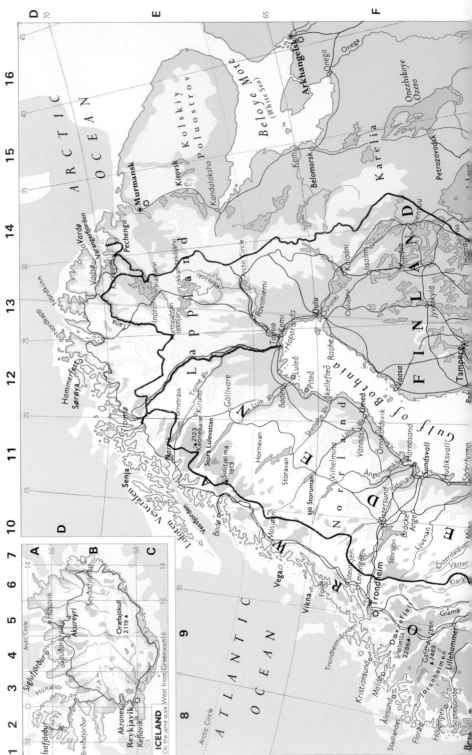

ARCTIC OCEAN

Kolskiy Poluostrov

Beloye More (White Sea)

Arkhangelsk

Onega

Onega

Onega

Onezhskoye Ozero

Kirovsk

Murmansk

Petrozavodsk

Kandalaksha

Kem

Belomorsk

Karelia

Pechenga

Nordkyn

Vardø

Vadsø

Varangerfjorden

Kirkenes

Kivijärvi

Inari

Inarinjärvi

Enare

Sortipahtam Tekojärvi

Nordkapp

Hammerfest

Sørøya

Sør

Lokkan tekojärvi

Kemijoki

L a p p l a n d

Arctic Circle

Rovaniemi

Kemijärvi

Kuusamo

Oulu

Kajaani

Iisalmi

Kuopio

Jyväskylä

Mänttä

F I N L A N D

Tampere

Tornio

Kemi

Haparanda

Rahe

Oulujoki

Oulujärvi

Nattavaara

Muonio

Inarjärvi

Torne älv

Gällivare

Kebnekaise 2123

Kiruna

Storuman

Tromsø

Senja

Narvik

Sulitjelma 1913

Storen Lulevattan

Hornavan

Storavan

Lule älv

Boden

Luleå

Piteå

Skellefteå

Skellefte älv

Vaasa

Gulf of Bothnia

Lofoten

Vesterålen

Vestfjorden

Bodø

Mo

Mosjøen

Vega

Vikna

N o r r l a n d

Vilhelmina

Vännäs

Umeå

Ume älv

Örnsköldsvik

Härnösand

Sundsvall

Angermanälven

Indalsälv

Hudiksvall

Söderhamn

Östersund

Storsjön

Brącke

Ange

Ljusnan

Trondheim

Steinkjer

Levanger

J A M T L A N D

Storlien

Västerdalälven

Österdalälven

Väster

Klarä

Kristiansund

Molde

Dovrefjell

Snøhetta 2286

Galdhøpiggen 2469

Jotunheimen

Glåma

O

Ålesund

Stadlandet

Florø

Høyanger

Sognefjorden

Lillehammer

ATLANTIC OCEAN

Arctic Circle

70   65

45   40   35   30   25   20   15   10

16   15   14   13   12   11   10

7   6   5   4   3   2   1

9   8

Iceland inset

A B C

Arctic Circle

Ísafjörður

Breiðafjörður

Húnaflói

Siglufjörður

Húsavik

Skjálfandi

Akureyri

Seyðisfjörður

Öræfajökull 2119

Akranes

Reykjavík

Keflavík

ICELAND
On the same scale   West from Greenwich 8

66   64

14   16   14

66   64   24

20   22

10

A B C

1 2 3 4 5 6 7

E F

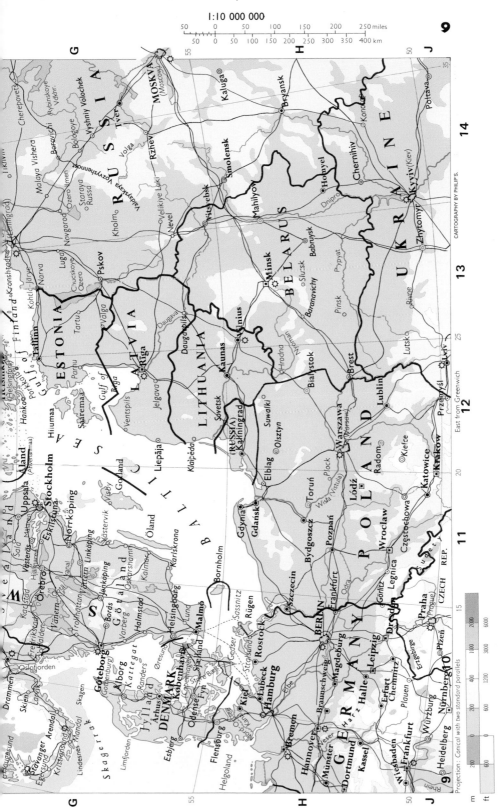

1:10 000 000

50   0   100   150   200   250 miles
50   0   50   100   150   200   250   300   350   400 km

G

H

J

CARTOGRAPHY BY PHILIP'S.

East from Greenwich

Projection : Conical with two standard parallels

R U S S I A

MOSKVA
(Moscow)

Cherepovets
Rybinskoye
Vdkhr.
Vyshniy Volochek
Bologoye
Bezhichi
Malaya Vishera
Tver
Kaluga
Bryansk
Pottava
Konotop
Chernihiv
Hoyel
Zhytomyr
Kyyiv (Kiev)
Lviv
Przhemyśl

U K R A I N E

Dnipro
Pyat
Lutsk
Rivne

Smolensk
Mahilyow
Babruysk
Slutsk
Baranovichy
Pinsk

B E L A R U S

Minsk

Vitsyebsk
Nevel
Velikiye Luki
Kholm

Pskov
Chudskoye
Ozero

E S T O N I A

Tallinn
Tartu
Pärnu

L A T V I A

Riga
Daugava
Daugavpils
Jelgava
Ventspils
Liepāja
Klaipėda

L I T H U A N I A

Vilnius
Kaunas
Sovetsk
(RUSSIA)
Kaliningrad

Hrodna
Białystok
Suwałki
Brest
Lublin
Olsztyn

Helsinki
(Helsingfors)
Gulf of Finland
Hanko
Kronshtadt
St Petersburg
(Leningrad)
Narva

G U L F   O F   B O T H N I A

Åland
(Ahvenanmaa)
Hiiumaa
Saaremaa
Gulf of Riga

Stockholm
Uppsala
Norrköping
Eskilstuna
Örebro
Göteborg

S W E D E N

Gotland
Visby
Öland
Kalmar
Karlskrona

B A L T I C   S E A

Bornholm
Rügen
Sassnitz
Stralsund
Rostock

Gdynia
Gdańsk
Elbląg
Toruń
Bydgoszcz
Poznań
Płock
Wisła (Vistula)
Łódź
Radom
Kielce

P O L A N D

Warszawa
(Warsaw)
Wrocław
Legnica
Częstochowa
Katowice
Kraków

Szczecin
Frankfurt
Odra
Görlitz

BERLIN
Magdeburg
Leipzig
Dresden
Chemnitz
Plauen

G E R M A N Y

Hamburg
Lübeck
Kiel
Bremen
Hannover
Braunschweig
Münster
Dortmund
Kassel
Erfurt
Würzburg
Frankfurt
Wiesbaden
Heidelberg
Nürnberg

DENMARK
København
(Copenhagen)
Odense
Århus
Ålborg
Esbjerg
Flensburg
Helgoland

Skagerrak
Kattegat
Jylland
Fyn
Sjælland

CZECH
REP.
Praha
(Prague)
Plzeň
Erzgebirge

m   ft
2000   6000
1000   3000
400   1200
200   600
0   0
200   600

14   13   12   11   10   9

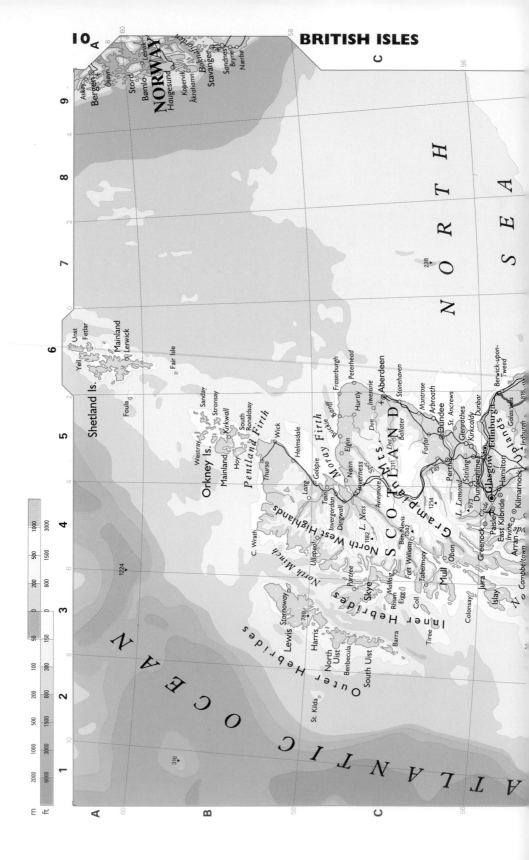

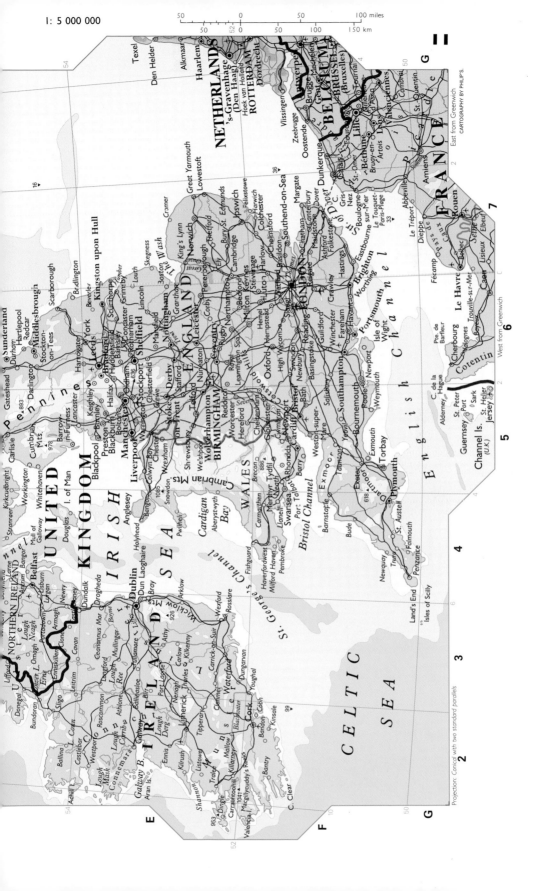

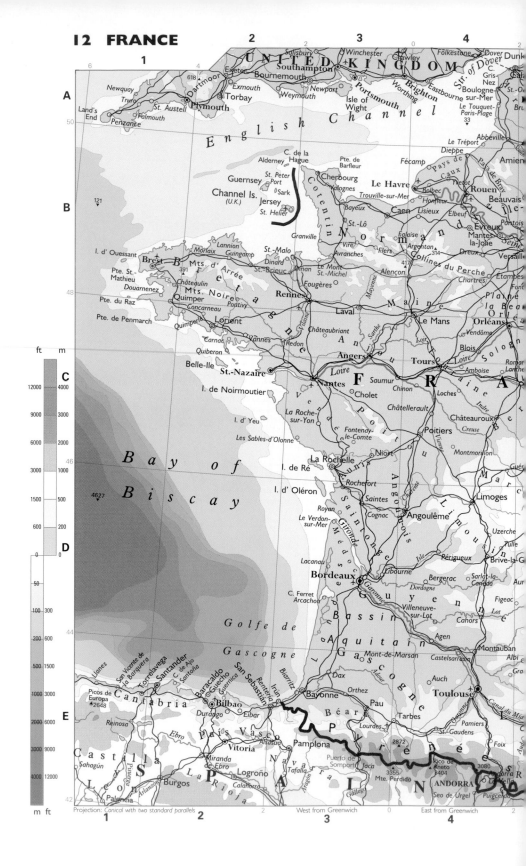

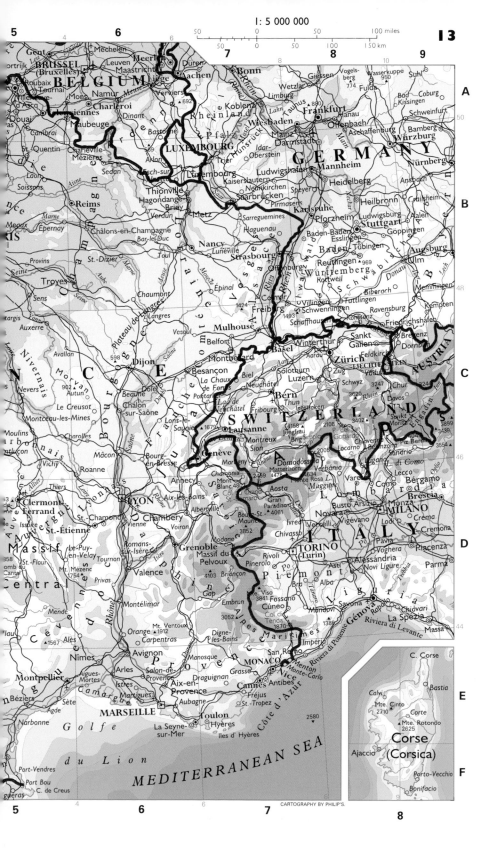

1: 5 000 000

50   0   50   100 miles
50   0   50   100   150 km

5   6   7   8   9

A

B

C

D

E

F

Gent • Mechelen • Meerhout
ortrijk **BRUSSEL** • Leuven • Maastricht • Düren • **Bonn** Vogels-berg Wasserkuppe Suhl
• Roubaix (Bruxelles) • Liège • Aachen 774 950
Tournai **BELGIUM** • Verviers Limburg Wetzlar Fulda Bad Coburg
Ath • Mons • Namur • 692 Koblenz Lahn Taunus Kissingen
Douai • Charleroi • Dinant **Rheinland** • Frankfurt Hanau Offenbach Schweinfurt Bamberg
Cambrai Maubeuge Bastogne **Pfalz** Wiesbaden Aschaffenburg Würzburg
St.-Quentin Charleville- **LUXEMBOURG** Idar- Mainz Darmstadt **G E R M A N Y** Nürnberg
Mézières Esch-sur- Oberstein Mannheim Ansbach
Laon Sedan Luxembourg Kaiserslautern Speyer Heidelberg Crailsheim
Soissons Thionville Saarbrücken Ludwigshafen Heilbronn Aalen
Hagondange Metz Pirmasens Karlsruhe Pforzheim Ludwigsburg **Stuttgart** Göppingen
Reims Briey Sarreguemines Baden-Baden Esslingen Augsburg
Épernay Verdun Haguenau Baden **Württemberg** Tübingen Ulm
Châlons-en-Champagne Nancy Strasbourg Offenburg Reutlingen 969 Donau
Bar-le-Duc Lunéville Villingen Schwäbische Memmingen
Provins St.-Dizier Toul Épinal Colmar Freiburg Schwenningen Tuttlingen Biberach Kempten
Troyes Chaumont 1424 Schaffhausen Ravensburg Friedrichshafen
Sens Langres 1493 Konstanz Bregenz
Auxerre Plateau de Langres Mulhouse Basel Winterthur Sankt **AUSTRIA**
Vesoul Belfort Gallen Dornbirn Feldkirch
Avallon Montbéliard Aarau Zürich Zug **LIECHTENSTEIN**
Nevers 598 Dijon Biel Solothurn Luzern Vaduz Chur
Morvan Besançon La Chaux- Neuchâtel Schwyz 3247 Inn
902 Dole de Fonds **Bern** 3620 Rhein Davos Engadin
Le Creusot Chalon- Pontarlier Thun Interlaken P. Gotthard St. 3402 3899
Montceau-les-Mines sur-Saône Lac de Lausanne **SWITZERLAND** Jungfrau Simplon Moritz 3439
Moulins Charolles Neuchâtel 1679 Fribourg Brig Locarno Bellinzona Sóndrio 3554
Autun Bourg- Montreux Chiavenna L. di Como
Vichy Mâcon en-Bresse **Genève** Sion 2005 Bernina
Roanne Martigny Rhône Domodóssola Verbánia Lecco
Charolles Annecy Mont Matterhorn 4634 Como Bérgamo Brescia
Thiers Aix-les-Bains 2469 Blanc 4478 Monte Rosa Varese Busto Arsizio Monza Crema
LYON Chambéry Aosta Ivrea Novara Vigévano **MILANO** Cremona
Clermont- St.-Chamond Voiron Albertville Gran Vercelli Pavia Lodi Piacenza
Ferrand St.-Étienne Grande Paradiso 4061 Bourg-St.- **TORINO** Voghera
Issoire Vienne Maurice 3852 Chivasso (Turin) Asti Alba Alessándria Novi Ligure Parma
Le-Puy- Romans- Modane **ITALY** Rívoli Pinerolo **Piemonte** Fréjus
Mt. Mézenc en-Velay Tournon sur-Isère 4103 Briançon Bra Ligúria La Spézia
St.-Flour 1754 Massif du Gap Mte. Viso Fossano Cúneo Mondoví Savona Génova Chiávari Massa
Privas Pelvoux 3841 Col di Riviera di Levante
Mende Embrun Tenda 1382 Impéria
Mt. Ventoux 3052 1870 Riviera di Ponente
Montélimar 1912 Digne- Alpes
Orange Carpentras les-Bains Maritimes San Remo
1567 Alès Nîmes Manosque Grasse **MONACO** Menton
Avignon Draguignan Cannes Nice Monte-Carlo
Montpellier Aigues- Arles Salon-de- Aix-en- Antibes Côte d'Azur
Béziers Mortes Isthes Provence Provence Fréjus
Agde Sète Martigues Aubagne St.-Tropez
Narbonne Golfe **MARSEILLE** Toulon Îles d' Hyères 2580
Port-Vendres du Lion La Seyne-
Port Bou sur-Mer Hyères
guéras C. de Creus **M E D I T E R R A N E A N   S E A**

C. Corse
Calvi Bastia
Mte. Cinto
2710 Corte
Mte. Rotondo
2625
Corse
(Corsica)
Ajaccio
Porto-Vecchio
Bonifacio

CARTOGRAPHY BY PHILIP'S.

5   6   7   8

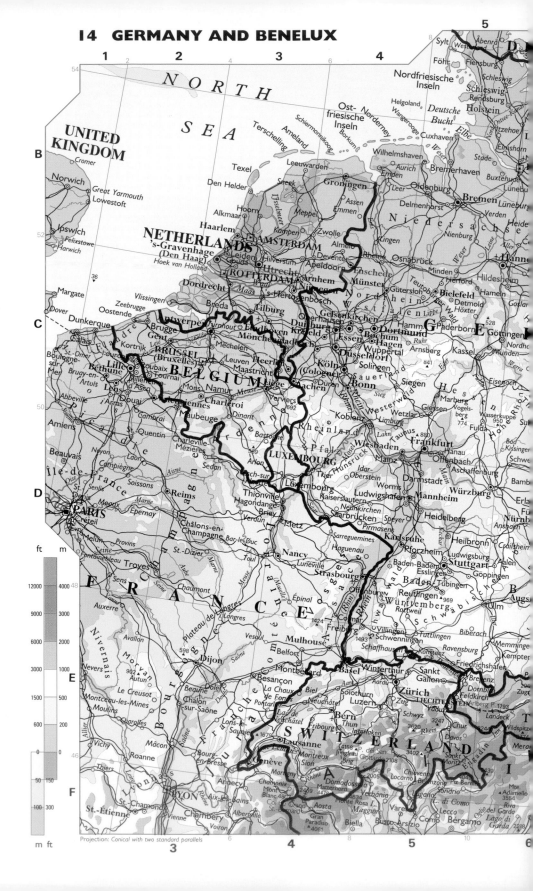

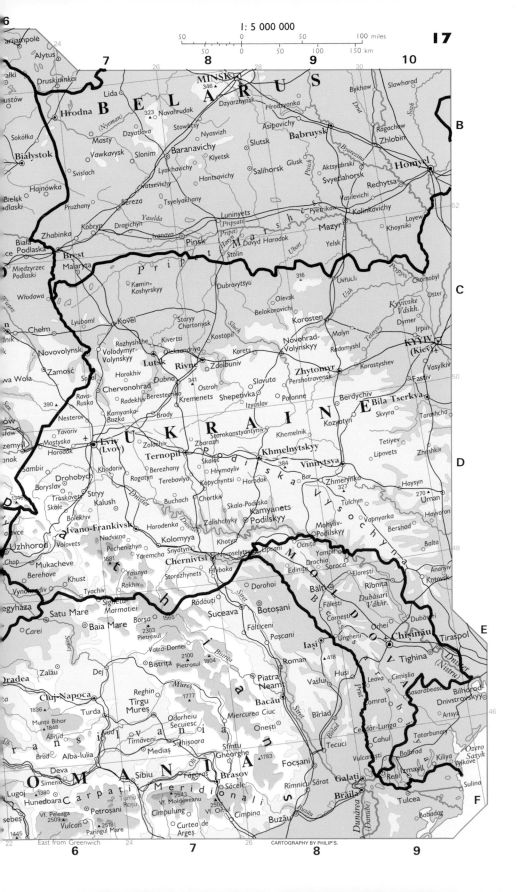

50   0   50   100 miles

50   0   50   100   150 km

7   8   9   10

arijampolė
24
Alytus

ałki

Druskininkai

ustów

Sokółka

Hrodna

B E L A R U S

MINSK
346

Lida

Navahrudak
323
(Nyoman)

Stowbtsy

Dzyarzhynsk

Hrodzyanka

Bykhaw   Slawharad

Dnu

B

Białystok

Masty

Dzyatlava

Nyasvizh

Asipovichy

Ragachew

Zhlobin

Svislach

Vawkavysk   Slonim

Baranavichy

Klyetsk

Slutsk

Babruysk

Byaresina

Homyel

Hajnówka

Pruzhany

Ivatsevichy

Lyakhavichy

Hantsavichy

Salihorsk

Glusk

Aktsyabrski

Svyetlahorsk

Rechytsa

52

Bielsk
dlaski

Bereza

Tsyelyakhany

Luninyets
(Pripyats)

Pyetrikaw

Kalinkavichy

Loyew

Biała
e Podlaska

Kobryn

Dragichyn

Yaselda

Ivanava

Pripet

Mazyr

Khoyniki

Międzyrzec
Podlaski

Zhabinka

Malaryta

Brest

Davyd Haradok

Stolin

Uvruch

Chornobyl

C

Włodawa

Kamin-
Kashyrskyy

Dubrovytsyu
316

Olevsk

Uzh

Ostei

Kyyivske
Vdskh.

Chełm

Lyuboml

Kovel

Staryy
Chartoriysk

Belokorovichi

Korosten

Malyn

Teterev

Irpin

KYYIV
(Kiev)

Dymer

Novovolynsk

Volodymyr-
Volynskyy

Rozhyshshe

Kivertsi

Kostopil

Korets

Novohrad-
Volynskyy

Radomyshl

Korostyshev

Fastiv

Vasylkiv

Zamość

Oleksandriya

Lutsk

Rivne

Zdolbuniv
341

Slavuta

Zhytomyr

Pershotravensk

Berdychiv

50

wa Wola

Sokal

Horokhiv

Dubno

Ostroh

Izyaslav

Polonne

Skvyra

Bila Tserkva

Tarashcha

Chervonohrad

Radekhiv

Berestechko

Kremenets

Shepetivka

Kozyatyn

E

Rava-
Ruska
390

Nesterov

Kamyanka-
Buzka

Brody

Starokonstyantyniv

Khmelnik

Tetiyev

Zhashkiv

sław
zemysl

Yavoriv

Mostyska

Zolochiv

Zbarazh

U K R A I N E

Lvi

Khmelnytskyy

Vinnytsya

Lipovets

Mostyska

Horodok

Lviv
(Lvov)

Ternopil

Skalat
384

Haysyn

Khodoriv

Berezhany

Hrymayliv

Bar

Zhmerynka
327

Uman
270

Drohobych

Rogatyn

Terebovlya

Kopychyntsi

Horodok

Tulchyn

Vapnyarka

Borysław

Truskavets

Stryy

Kalush

Buchach

Chortkiv

Skala-Podilska

Kamyanets

Bershad

Balta

Skole

Bolekhiv

Horodenka

Zalishchyky

Podilskyy

Mohyliv-
Podilskyy

48

346

Ivano-Frankivsk

Nadvirna

Pechenizhyn

Kolomyya

Khotyn

Ocnița

Yampil

Ananyiv

Kotovsk

Uzhhorod

Volovets

Yaremcha

Snyatyn

Chernivtsi

Noveselytsya

Lipsani

Drochia

Soroca

Chop

Mukacheve

Khust

1881

Yasinya

Storozhynets

Hlyboka

Edinita

Floresti

Ribnita

Berehove

Rakhiv

Dorohoi

Bălti

Dubăsari
Vdkhr.

Dubăsari

E

Vynohradiv

Tyachiv

Sighetu
Marmatiei

Rădăuţi
1565

Fălesti

Corneşti

Ocnei

Chişinău

Tiraspol

egyháza

Satu Mare

Borşa
2303
Pietrosul

Suceava

Botoşani

Ungheni

Tighina

Dniester
(Nistru)

Carei

Baia Mare

Vatra-Dornei
2100
Pietrosul
1804

Fălticeni

Paşcani

Iaşi
418

Roman

Huşi

Leova

Cimişlia

Basarabeasca

Bilhorod
Dnivstrovskyy

46

Zalău

Dej

Bistriţa

Piatra
Neamţ

Vaslui

Comrat

Artsyz

dradea

Cluj-Napoca
1836

Turda

Reghin

Tîrgu
Mureş
1777

Bacău

Bîrlad

Cahul

Ceadâr-Lunga

Tatarbunary

Ozero
Satyk

Muntii Bihor
1848

Aiud

Tîrnăveni

Odorheiu
Secuiesc

Miercurea Ciuc

Oneşti

Focşani

Bolhrad

Kiliya

Vylkove

Abrud

Mediaş

Sighişoara

Sfîntu
Gheorghe
1783

Izmayıl

Reni

Brad

Alba-Iulia

Tîrnaveni

Vulcaneşti

Deva

Sibiu

Făgăraş

Braşov

Săcele

Rîmnicu Sărat

Galati

Braila

Sulina

Simeria

Carpati
2543

Meridionali

Vf. Moldoveanu

Tulcea

F

Lugoj
1380

Hunedoara

Turnu
Roşu

Cîmpulung

Buzău

Dunărea (Danube)

Babadag

sebeş

Petroşani

Vf. Peleaga
2509

Vulcan
2518

Curtea de
Argeş

Cimpina
2507
Vf. Omul

Paringul Mare

1445

22

East from Greenwich
24
26

6   7   8   9

CARTOGRAPHY BY PHILIP'S.

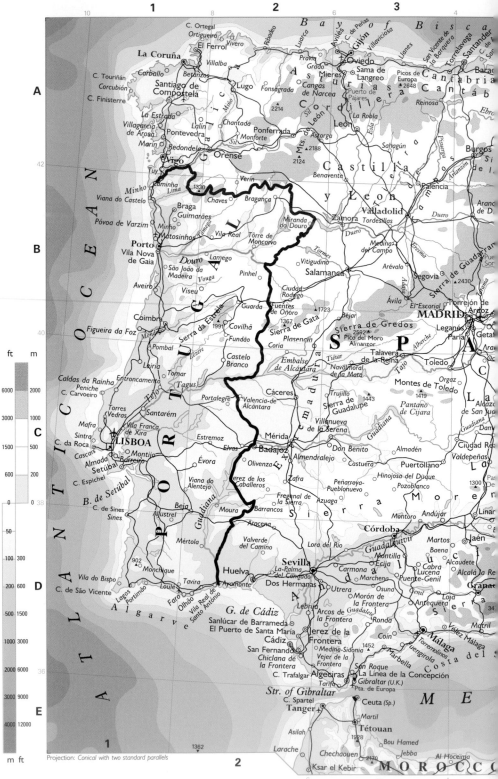

18 SPAIN AND PORTUGAL

10 1 8 2 6 3 4

Projection: Conical with two standard parallels

ft m

6000 2000
3000 1000
1500 500
600 200
0 0
50
100 300
200 600
500 1500
1000 3000
2000 6000
3000 9000
4000 12000

m ft

Spain and Portugal place names

A T L A N T I C   O C E A N

Bay of Biscay

B a y   o f   B i s c a y

C. Ortegal
Ortigueira
C. Touriñán
Corcubión
C. Finisterre
La Coruña
Villalba
El Ferrol
Vivero
Ribadeo
Luarca
Pravia
Gijón
Villaviciosa
Llanes
San Vicente de la Barquera
Torrelavega
Santander
Baracaldo
Carballo
Betanzos
Santiago de Compostela
Lugo
Fonsagrada
Grado
Mieres
Oviedo
Sama de Langreo
Cangas de Narcea
Picos de Europa 2648
Puerto de Pajares
Reinosa
Ebro
La Estrada
Villagarcia de Arosa
Pontevedra
Lalín
Chantada
Ponferrada
Astorga
La Robla
León
Sahagún
Palencia
Burgos
Marin
Redondela
Orense
Monforte
Sil
Mes de León 2188
2124
Benavente
Zamora
Tordesillas
Valladolid
Duero
Medina del Campo
Arévalo
Segovia
Sierra de Guadarrama
Aranda de D.
Vigo
Tuy
Minho
Caminha
Lima
Verín
1330
Chaves
Bragança
Miranda do Douro
Tormes
Salamanca
2430
Viana do Castelo
Braga
Guimarães
Vila Real
Torre de Moncorvo
Vitigudino
Ciudad Rodrigo
Fuentes de Oñoro
Béjar
Ávila
El Escorial
Torrejón de Ardoz
MADRID
Póvoa de Varzim
Minho
Matosinhos
Porto
Vila Nova de Gaia
Douro
Lamego
Pinhel
1723
Sierra de Gredos
2592 Pico del Moro Almanzor
Leganés
Getafe
Aveiro
São João da Madeira
Vouga
Viseu
Guarda
1367
Sierra de Gata
Coria
Plasencia
Talavera de la Reina
Toledo
Orgaz
Montes de Toledo
Coimbra
Figueira da Foz
Serra da Estrela 1991
Covilhã
Fundão
Navalmoral de la Mata
Tiétar
Tajo
Pombal
Leiria
Castelo Branco
Embalse de Alcântara
1419
La Alcázar de San Juan
Caldas da Rainha
Peniche
C. Carvoeiro
Entroncamento
Tomar
(Tagus)
Tejo
Portalegre
Cáceres
Trujillo
1443
Sierra de Guadalupe
Pantano de Cijara
Guadiana
Ciudad Real
Torres Vedras
Santarém
Valencia de Alcántara
Elvas
Villanueva de la Serena
Guadiana
Mafra
Vila Franca de Xira
Estremoz
Mérida
Don Benito
Almadén
Valdepeñas
Sintra
C. da Roca
Cascais
LISBOA
Montijo
Barreiro
Évora
Badajoz
Almendralejo
Castuera
Puertollano
1300
Moro
Almada
Setúbal
C. Espichel
Olivenza
Zafra
Peñarroya-Pueblonuevo
Pozoblanco
B. de Setúbal
C. de Sines
Sines
Viana do Alentejo
Jerez de los Caballeros
Fregenal de la Sierra
Azuaga
Sierra Morena
Montoro
Andújar
Linares
Beja
Guadiana
Moura
Barrancos
Aracena
Córdoba
Martos
Jaén
Allustrel
Mértola
Valverde del Camino
Lora del Río
Guadalquivir
Montilla
Baena
902
Monchique
Huelva
La Palma del Condado
Sevilla
Carmona
Écija
Cabra
Alcaudete
Alcalá la Real
Granada
Vila do Bispo
C. de São Vicente
Lagos
Portimão
Loulé
Tavira
Faro
Olhão
Vila Real de Santo António
Ayamonte
Dos Hermanas
Utrera
Morón de la Frontera
Osuna
Puente-Genil
Loja
Antequera
34
Algarve
Lebrija
Arcos de la Frontera
Guadalete
Ronda
Coín
Vélez Málaga
Matril
Sanlúcar de Barrameda
El Puerto de Santa María
Cádiz
Jerez de la Frontera
Medina-Sidonia
1452
Málaga
Torremolinos
Fuengirola
Costa del S.
San Fernando
Chiclana de la Frontera
Vejer de la Frontera
San Roque
Marbella
C. Trafalgar
Algeciras
La Línea de la Concepción
Gibraltar (U.K.)
Pta. de Europa
Tarifa
Str. of Gibraltar
C. Spartel
Ceuta (Sp.)
M E
Tanger
Martil
Tétouan
1928
Asilah
Bou Hamed
Jebba
Al Hoceima
1362
Larache
Chechaouen
2170
M O R O C C O
Ksar el Kebir

C O R D I L L E R A   C A N T Á B R I C A
A S T U R I A S
G A L I C I A
C A S T I L L A   y   L E Ó N
P O R T U G A L
E S P A Ñ A
E S T R E M A D U R A
La Mancha
Sierra Morena
Andalucía
Algarve

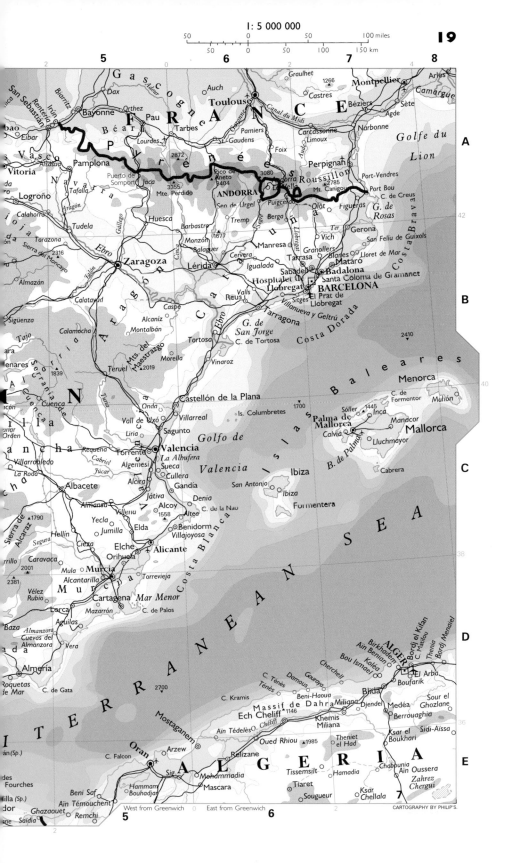

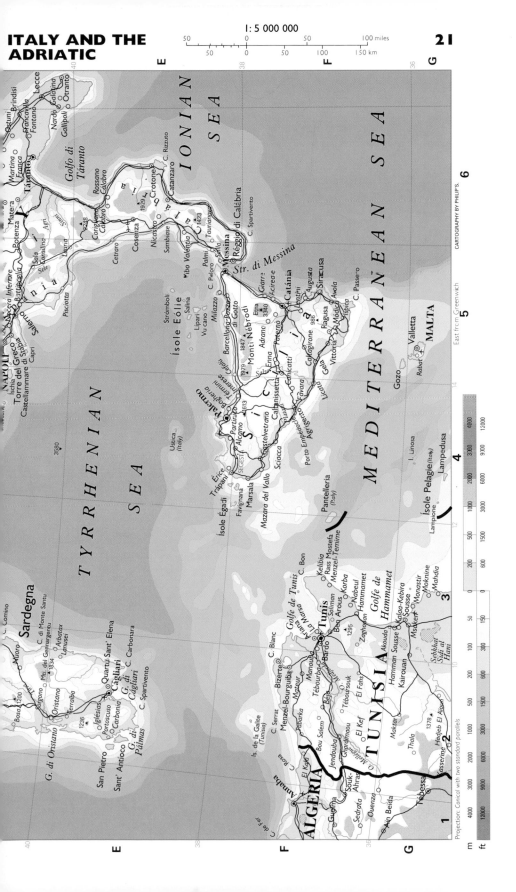

1: 5 000 000

CARTOGRAPHY BY PHILIP'S.

Projection: Conical with two standard parallels

East from Greenwich

TYRRHENIAN SEA

IONIAN SEA

MEDITERRANEAN SEA

ALGERIA

TUNISIA

Sardegna

Cagliari

Palermo

Sicilia

Catánia

Siracusa

MALTA

Valletta

Str. di Messina

Réggio di Calábria

Messina

Tunis

Bizerte

Kairouan

Sousse

Gozo

Rabat

Golfe de Tunis

Golfe de Hammamet

Isole Eólie

Isole Égadi

Monti Nébrodi

Etna 3340

Martina Franca

Táranto

Golfo di Táranto

Brindisi

Lecce

Otranto

Gallipoli

Nardò

Potenza

Matera

Cosenza

Catanzaro

Crotone

C. Rizzuto

C. Spartivento

NAPOLI

Pantelleria (Italy)

Isole Pelagie (Italy)

Lampedusa

Linosa

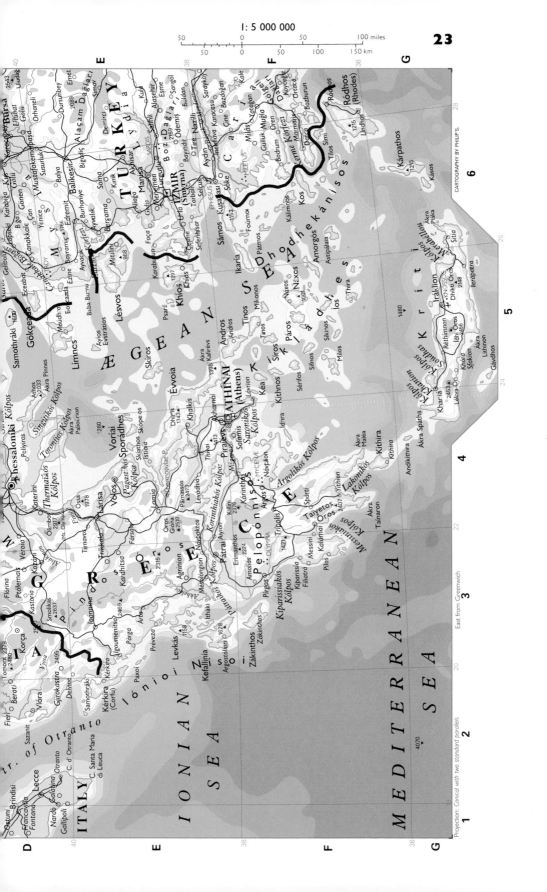

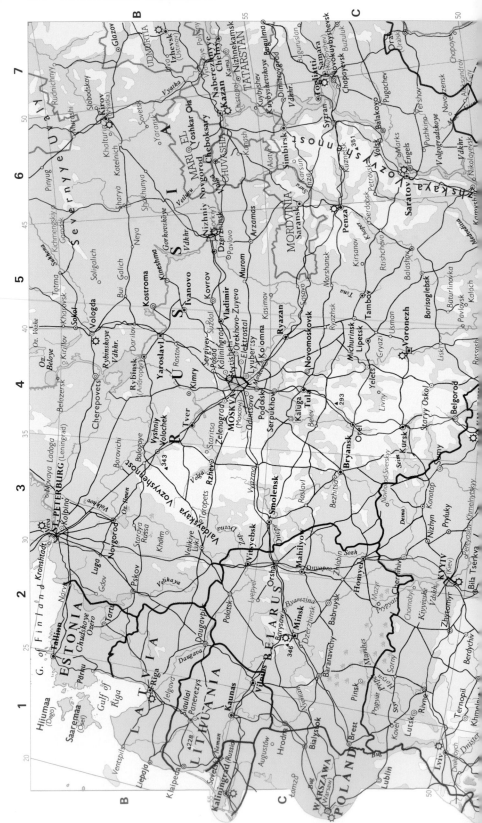

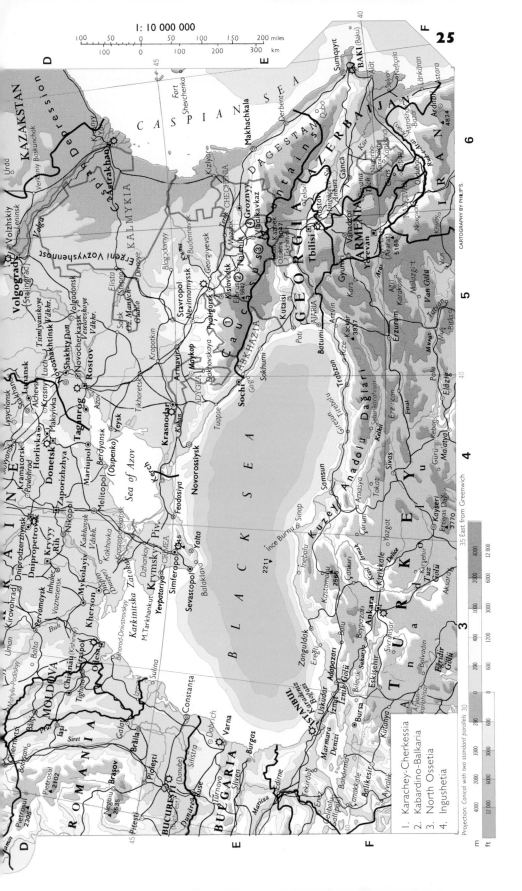

ATLANTIC OCEAN

GREENLAND

ARCTIC

Svalbard

ICELAND

Arctic Circle

Barents Sea

Novaya Zemlya

Kara Sea

NORWAY

Murmansk

Vorkuta

White Sea

Arkhangelsk

R U

Salekhard

North Sea

SWEDEN

FINLAND

ST. PETERSBURG

LONDON

UNITED KINGDOM

PARIS

FRANCE

GERMANY

Berlin

Warsaw

Nizhniy Novgorod

Perm

Yekaterinburg

Irtysh

Ob

E u r o p e

Prague

Vienna

Moscow

Kazan

Ufa

Chelyabinsk

Omsk

ITALY

Rome

Belgrade

UKRAINE

Volga

Samara

KAZAKSTAN

Astana

Pavlodar

Se

Danube

Odessa

Don

Volgograd

Rostov

Astrakhan

Karaganda

Mediterranean Sea

Athens

Black Sea

Bursa

ISTANBUL

Ankara

TURKEY

Izmir

Konya

Adana

GEORGIA

Tbilisi

Yerevan

ARMENIA

AZERBAIJAN

Baku

Caspian Sea

Aral Sea

L. Balkhash

UZBEKISTAN

Syrdarya

Tashkent

Alma Ata

Bishkek

KYRGYZSTAN

Samarkand

Kashi

LIBYA

Nicosia

CYPRUS Beirut

LEBANON

Aleppo

SYRIA

ISRAEL

Damascus

Euphrates

Mosul

Tabriz

TURKMENISTAN

Ashkhabad

Mashhad

TAJIKISTAN

Dushanbe

Ho

Alexandria

CAIRO

Suez

Jerusalem

Amman

JORDAN

Baghdad

IRAQ

Esfahan

TEHRĀN

IRAN

Herāt

Kābul

AFGHANISTAN

Islamabad

JAMMU & KASHMIR

Lahore

EGYPT

Nile

Aswân

Basra

KUWAIT

Kuwait

Shiraz

Zāhedān

Qandahār

Faisalabad

DELHI

SAUDI

Medina

Riyadh

BAHRAIN

Al Manāmah

Doha

QATAR

The Gulf

Indus

KARACHI

PAKISTAN

New Delhi

Jaipur

Lucknow

Kanpur

Varan

Aswân

Port Sudan

Jedda

Mecca

ARABIA

UNITED ARAB EMIRATES

Abu Dhabi

G. of Oman

Muscat

INDI

SUDAN

Khartoum

Red Sea

ERITREA

Saga

OMAN

Ahmadabad

Vadodara

Indore

Bhopal

Surat

Nag

YEMEN

Aden

G. of Aden

Arabian Sea

Socotra (Yemen)

MUMBAI (Bombay)

Pune

Hydera

ETHIOPIA

Addis Ababa

DJIBOUTI

SOMALI REP.

A f r i c a

Bangalore

CH Ma

UGANDA

L. Victoria

KENYA

Mogadishu

Lakshadweep Is. (India)

Madurai

SK

KONGO (DEM. REP. OF THE)

Nairobi

Equator

Colombo

MALDIVES

Male

I N D I A N   O C

TANZANIA

Mombasa

ZAMBIA

MALAWI

Dar es Salaam

SEYCHELLES

Victoria

Aldabra Is. (Seychelles)

Amirante Is. (Seychelles)

Chagos Arch. (U.K.)

Projection: Bonne

Hanoi ● Capital Cities

East from Greenwich

1: 67 000 000

| 200 | 0 | 200 | 400 | 600 | 800 | 1000 | 1200 miles |

| 200 | 0 | 400 | 800 | 1200 | 1600 | 2000 km |

B　　　　　　C　　　　　　D

140　　160　　180

OCEAN

New Siberian Is.

Laptev Sea

Wrangel I.

ALASKA (U.S.A.)

Bering Sea

Aleutian Is. (U.S.A.)

50

Gizhiga

·Khatanga

·Verkhoyansk

Okhotsk· ·Magadan

Petropavlovsk-Kamchatskiy

E

Lena

·Yakutsk

Sea of Okhotsk

S　I　A

40

Sakhalin

Komsomolsk

Angara

Krasnoyarsk· ·Bratsk

·Chita

L. Baikal

Khabarovsk·

Kuril Is.

Yuzhno-Sakhalinsk

Hokkaidō

·Sapporo

F

irsk

yokuznetsk

·Irkutsk ·Ulan Ude

Amur

·Hailar ·Qiqihar

·Blagoveshchensk

Vladivostok·

Honshū

30

·Ulan Bator

Harbin·

·Changchun

·Jilin

Sea of Japan

TŌKYŌ ·Yokohama

M　O　N　G　O　L　I　A

NORTH KOREA

JAPAN

Ürümqi

SHENYANG Anshan

Jinzhou

·Pyongyang

Kyōto

Nagoya

G

·Hami

·Baotou

BEIJING TIANJIN

Dalian·

SEOUL SOUTH KOREA

·Osaka

20

·Yumen

·Taiyuan

·Jinan

Pusan·

Hiroshima

Kitakyūshū

Bonin Is. (Japan)

·Lanzhou

Hwang-ho

·Xi'an

Yellow Sea

C　H　I　N　A

·Nanjing

SHANGHAI

·Wuhan

East China Sea

Volcano Is. (Japan)

ET

Chengdu

Yangtze

HANGZHOU

·Nanchang

·Fuzhou

Ryukyu Is.

Tropic of Cancer

·Lhasa

CHONGQING

·Changsha

Taipei

H

Thimphu

BHUTAN

·Kunming

GUANGZHOU

TAIWAN

adu ges

Brahmaputra

BANGLADESH

Si Kiang

HONG KONG

GUAM (U.S.A.)

10

na

DACCA

BURMA

Macau·

ITTA

Chittagong

(MYANMAR)

·Hanoi ·Haiphong

PHILIPPINES

FED. STATES OF MICRONESIA

Bay of Bengal

LAOS

·Vientiane

Hainan

Luzon

MANILA

PALAU

J

·Rangoon

THAILAND

VIETNAM

·Cebu

Andaman Is. (India)

BANGKOK

Phnom Penh

·Ho Chi Minh City

CAMBODIA

South China Sea

Palawan

Mindanao

·Davao

0

G. of Thailand

Zamboanga·

Sulu Sea

Nicobar Is. (India)

BRUNEI SABAH

Bandar Seri Begawan

Celebes Sea

·Manado

Halmahera

IRIAN JAYA

K

A

PEN. MALAYSIA

SARAWAK

M　A　L　A　Y　S　I　A

Kuala Lumpur

Ceram

Ambon·

·Medan

Str. of Malacca

SINGAPORE

Borneo

Celebes

AN

Sumatra

Banjarmasin

·Ujung Pandang

Banda Sea

Arafura Sea

·Palembang

Java Sea

I　N　D　O　N　E　S　I　A

Timor

L

JAKARTA

Semarang

Flores

·Bandung

·Surabaya

Java

Sumba

Timor Sea

AUSTRALIA

CARTOGRAPHY BY PHILIP'S.

12　　　　13　　　　14　　　　15　　　　16　　　　17

90　　　100　　　110　　　120　　　130　　　140

RUSSIA
1. Adygea
2. Karachey-Cherkessia
3. Kabardino-Balkaria
4. North Ossetia
5. Ingushetia
6. Chechenia
7. Dagestan
8. Mordvinia
9. Chuvashia
10. Mari El
11. Tatarstan
12. Udmurtia
13. Khakassia

GEORGIA
14. Naxçivan

AZERBAIJAN
15. Ajaria
16. Abkhazia

UKRAINE
17. Crimea

1: 20 000 000

100   0   100   200   300   400   500 miles

100   0   200   400   600   800 km

CARTOGRAPHY BY PHILIP'S

East from Greenwich

Projection: Conical Orthomorphic with two standard parallels

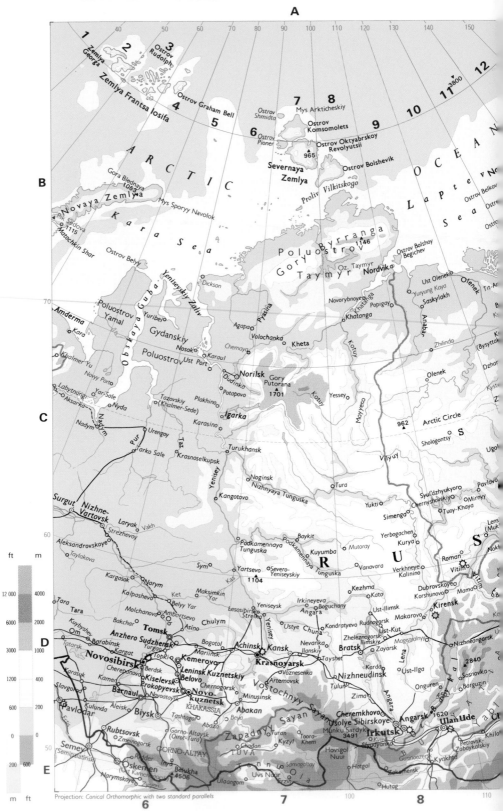

Projection: Conical Orthomorphic with two standard parallels

1 : 20 000 000

100   0   100   200   300   400   500 miles
100   0   200   400   600   800 km

B

C   Mys Dezhneva
(East C.)

Uelen

St. Lawrence I.
(U.S.A.)

14   170   15   16   60

Ostrov Henrietta
Ostrova Delong   Ostrov Jeanette

Ostrova   Ostrov Zhokhova

Ostrov Novaya Sibir

Ostrov Molly   Ostrov Bolshoy Lyakhovskiy
Lyakhovskiy

Ostrova Dmitriya Lapteva

Ostrov Vrangelya

Chukchi Sea

Ostrova Medvezhi

Nutepelmen

Vankarem

Amgu

1843

Enmelen

Providenya

Beringovskiy

Anadyrskiy Zaliv

Koryakskoye Nagorye

Bering Sea

D

Kamchatka

Poluostrov Kamchatka

Petropavlovsk-Kamchatskiy

E

Khrebet Sikhote Alin'

JAPAN

Hokkaidō   Sapporo   Hakodate

9   120   10   130   11   40

East from Greenwich   CARTOGRAPHY BY PHILIP'S.

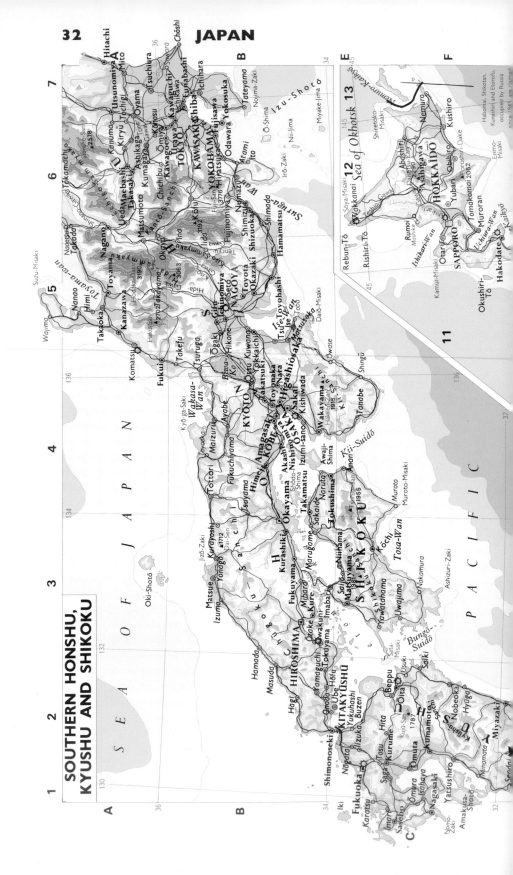

SOUTHERN HONSHU, KYUSHU AND SHIKOKU

Habomai, Shikotan,
Kunashiri and Etorofu,
occupied by Russia
since 1945, are claimed
by Japan

SEA OF JAPAN

Sea of Okhotsk

HOKKAIDO

SAPPORO

PACIFIC OCEAN

TOKYO
YOKOHAMA
KAWASAKI
NAGOYA
KYOTO
OSAKA
KOBE
HIROSHIMA
KITAKYUSHU
FUKUOKA
NAGASAKI

SHIKOKU
KYUSHU

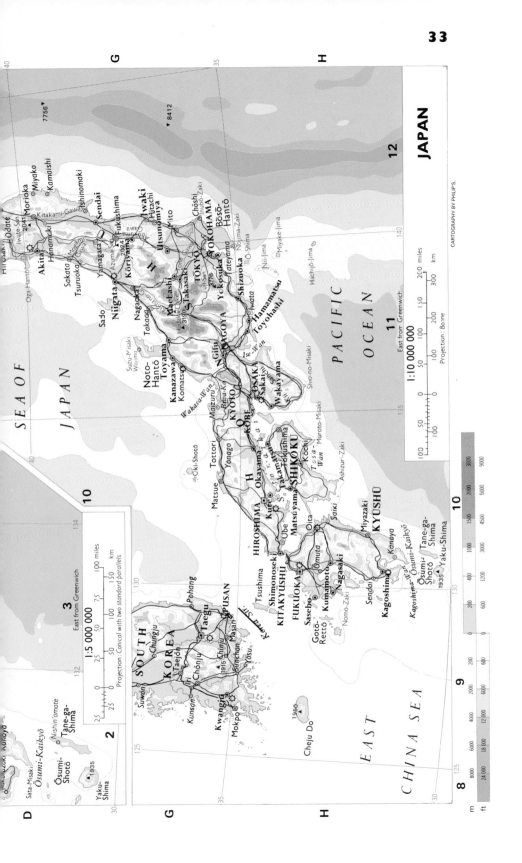

JAPAN

CARTOGRAPHY BY PHILIP'S.

1:10 000 000

East from Greenwich

Projection: Bonne

PACIFIC

OCEAN

SEA OF

JAPAN

EAST

CHINA SEA

SOUTH

KOREA

SHIKOKU

KYUSHU

1:5 000 000

East from Greenwich

Projection: Conical with two standard parallels

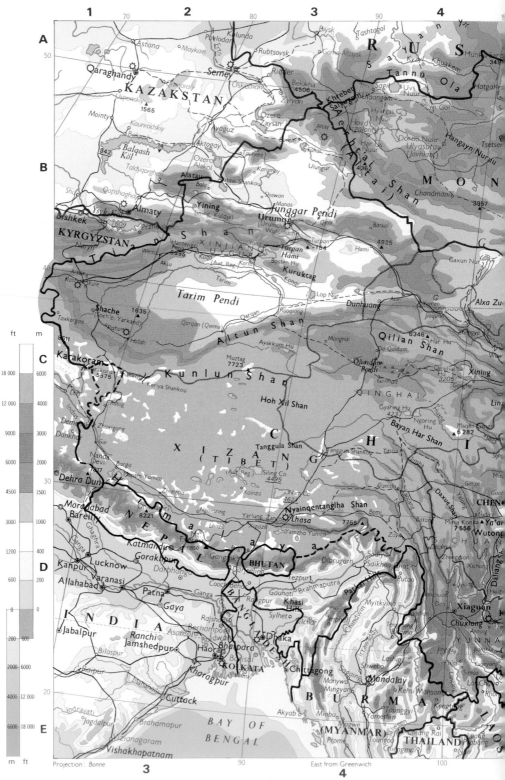

A

50

KAZAKSTAN

R U S

Astana   Pavlodar   Biysk   Tashtagol

Qaraghandy   Maykain   Rubtsovsk   Gorno-Altaysk

Semey   Oskemen   Rieder   Belükha ▲4506   Tannu Ola   Hatgal

Usponsky   1565   Qamaraly   Zyryan   Sagli   Uvs Nuur   Hyargas Nuur

Mointy   Kounradskiy   Ozero Zaysan   Altay   A L T A I

B

KYRGYZSTAN

Balqash Köl   342   Taldyqorghan   Karamay   4362   Chandmani   3957

Alatau   Dzungar Pendi   Ulungur

Bishkek   Yining (Ining, Kuldja)   Urumqi (Urumchi)   Wulumuchi   Barkol   Gaxun Nur

Almaty   Ysyk-köl   1609   T i e n   S h a n   XINJIANG   Turpan   Hami   4925   Xining

Neryn   Wensu   UYGUR   Bosten Hu   Kuruktag   Kong

Aksu   Korla   Tarim   Lop Nur   Dunhuang   Alxa Zu

Tarim Pendi

Shache (Soch'e, Yarkand)   1635   Qarqan (Qiemo)   Ruoqiang   Qilian Shan   6346   Har Hu

Taxkorgan   Hotan   Altun Shan   Ayakkum Hu   Mangnai   Da Qaidam

Karakoram   Muztag 7723   **Kunlun Shan**   Hoh Xil Shan   Qaidam Pendi   QINGHAI   3205   Xining

Keriya Shankou   Golmud   Lin

Gyaring Hu   Ngoring Hu   4237   **Bayan Har Shan**   6282   Magên

XIZANG (TIBET) (Aut. Reg.)   Tanggula Shan   Siling Co 4495   H

Nanda Devi ▲8221   Tangguia Shankou   Yushu   Garze

Dehra Dun   Zhaxigang   Nam Co 4627   Qamdo   Daxue Shan   CHEN

Moradabad   Bareilly   Dhankar   Barga   Zhongba   Xainza   Nyainqentanglha Shan 7755   Batang   Minya Konka 7556   Ya'an

Dhaulagiri ▲8221   **N E P A L**   Lhasa   Yamzho Yumco   Bomi   Zhongdian   Wutong

Katmandu   Everest 8860   Xigaze   Nyingchi   Degen

D

I N D I A

Kanpur   Lucknow   Gorakhpur   Gangtok   **BHUTAN**   Dibrugarh   Saikhoa Ghat   Putao   Xiaguan

Allahabad   Varanasi   Patna   Ghaghra   Cooch Behar   Tezpur   Brahmaputra   Myitkyina   Chuxiong   YUNNAN

Gaya   Ganga   Rangpur   Gauhati   Khasi Hills   Imphal

Jabalpur   Ranchi   Asansol   Berhampore   Rajshahi   Sylhet   Silchar   Chindwin   Tengchong

Jamshedpur   Bilaspur   Bhopara   **BANGLADESH**   Dhaka   Loshio   Yuanyang

Raipur   Haora   **KOLKATA**   Chittagong   Monywa   Shwebo   Kehsi Mansam

Kharagpur   Mingyan   **Mandalay**   Kengtung

E

Indravati   Cuttack   **B U R M A**   Taunggyi   Mimbu   Yamethin

Jagdalpur   Brahamapur   **BAY OF BENGAL**   Akyab   Tougoo   Chiang Rai

Vizianagaram   **(MYANMAR)**   Magwe   Prome   **THAILAND**   Chiang Mai

Vishakhapatnam

ft   m
18 000   6000
12 000   4000
9000   3000
6000   2000
4500   1500
3000   1000
1200   400
600   200
0   0
200   600
2000   6000
4000   12 000
6000   18 000
m   ft

1: 20 000 000

100   0   100   200   300   400   500 miles

100   0   200   400   600   800 km

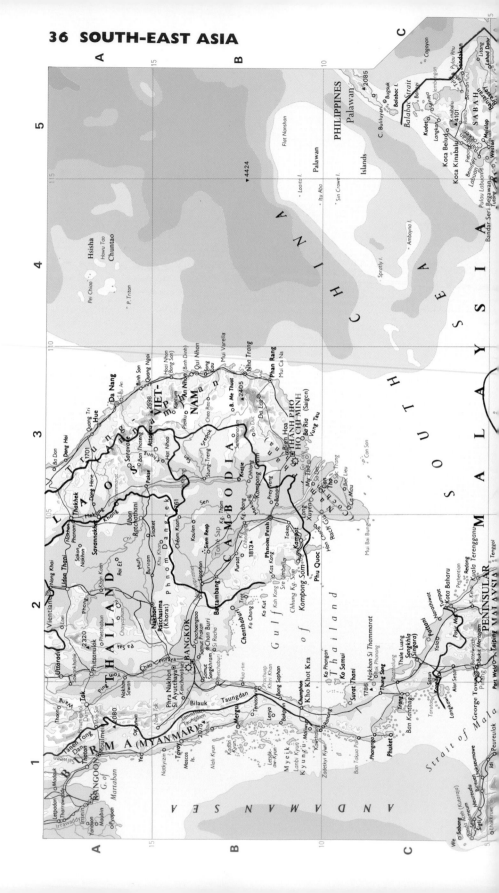

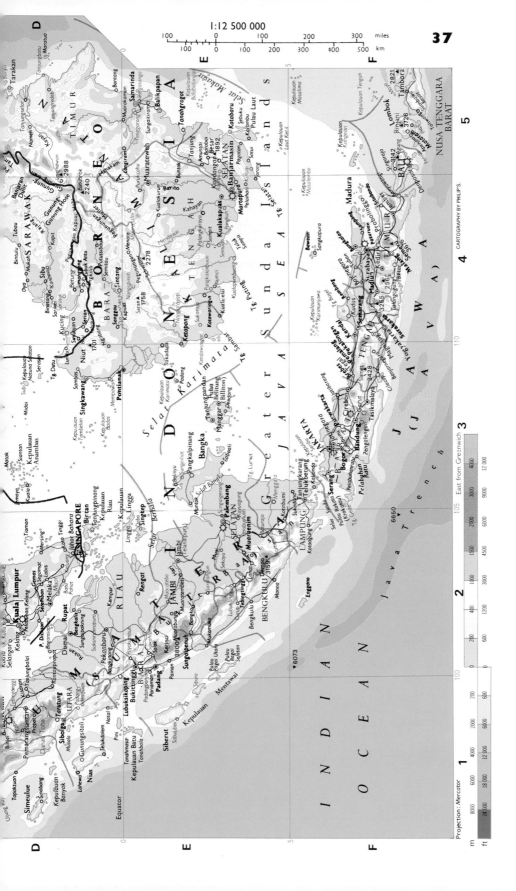

1:12 500 000

100   0   100   200   300   miles
100 0 100 200 300 400 500 km

CARTOGRAPHY BY PHILIPS.

Projection: Mercator

East from Greenwich

m
ft

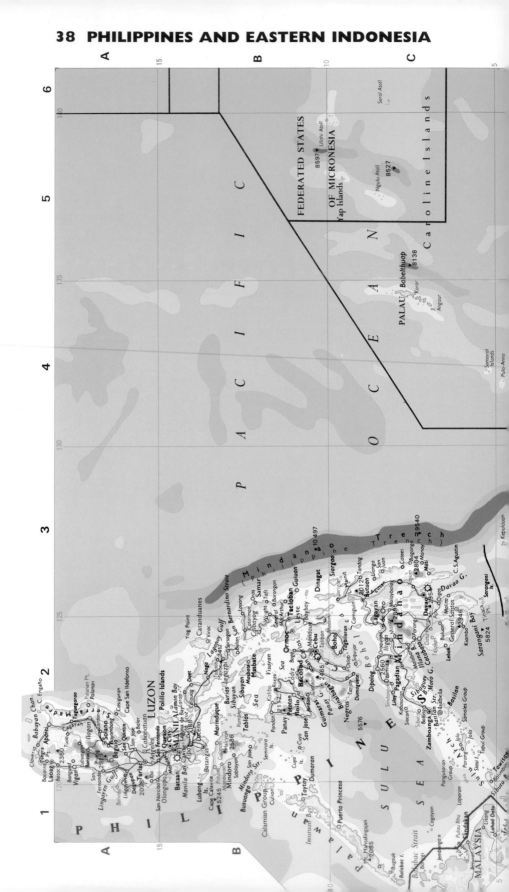

1:12 500 000

100   0   100   200   300   miles
100   0   100   200   300   400   500   km

PAPUA NEW GUINEA

CARTOGRAPHY BY PHILIP'S

East from Greenwich

Projection Mercator

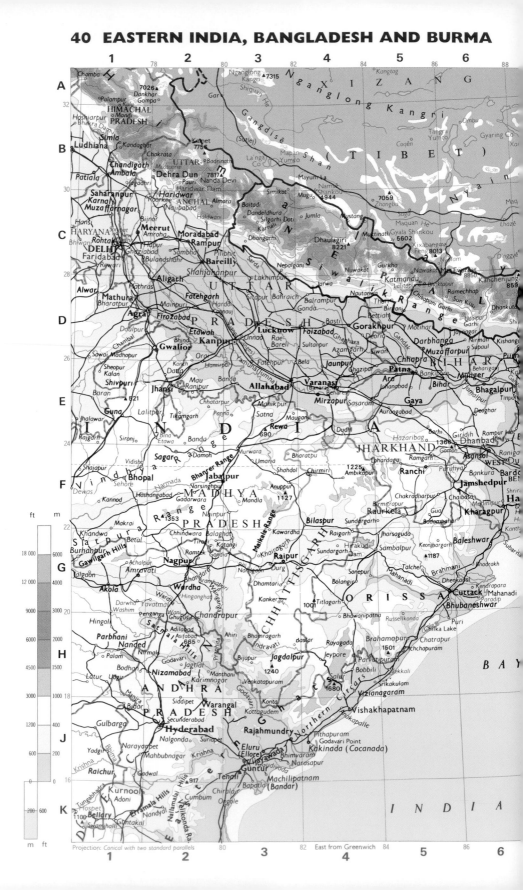

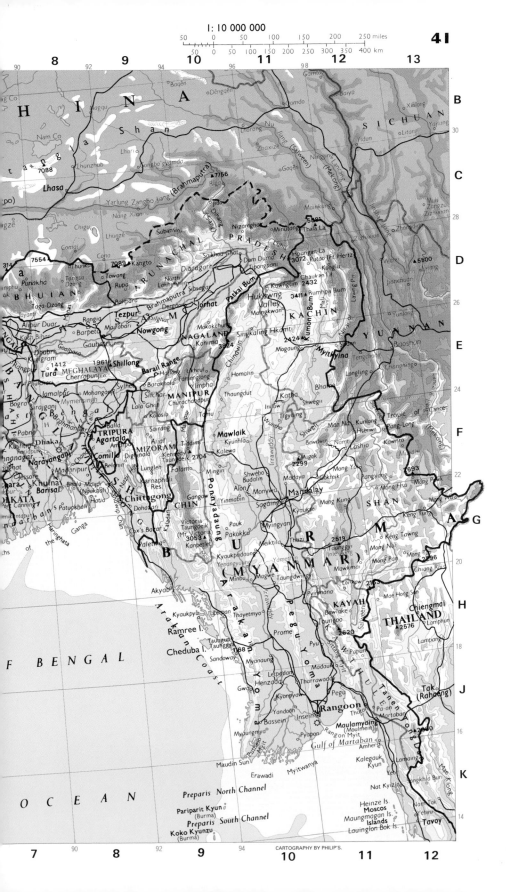

1:10 000 000

CARTOGRAPHY BY PHILIP'S.

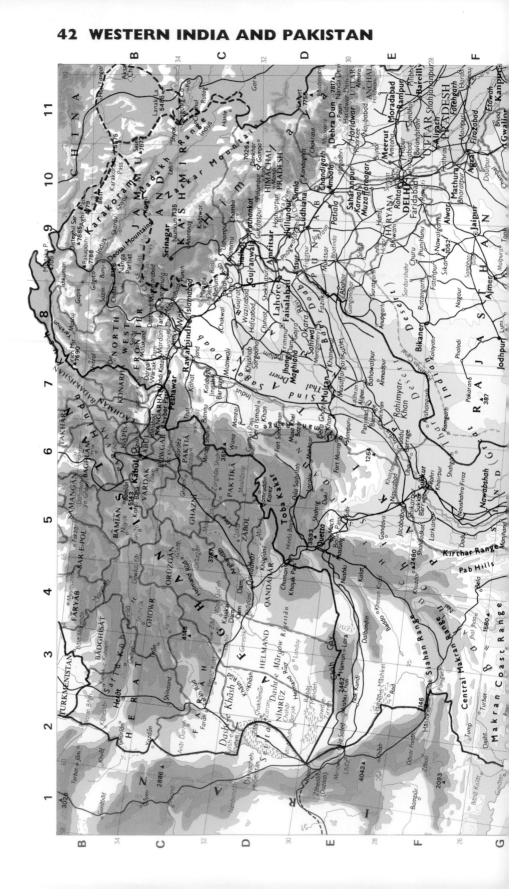

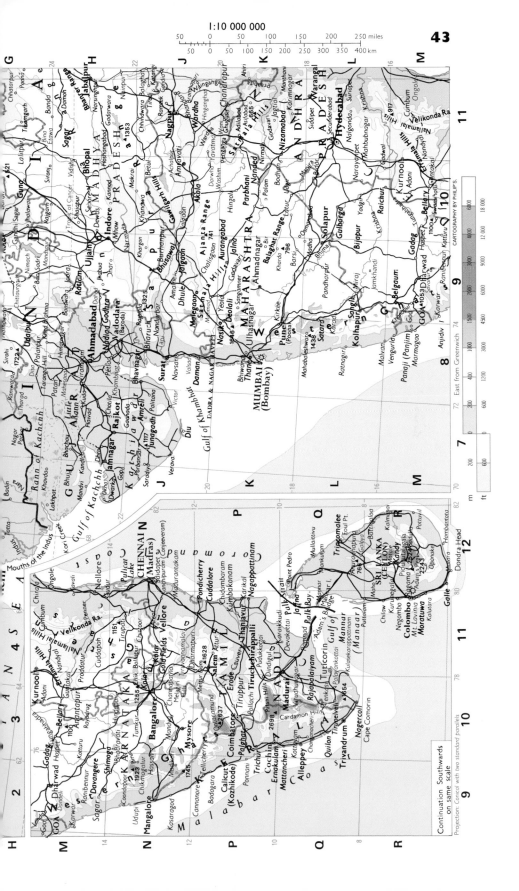

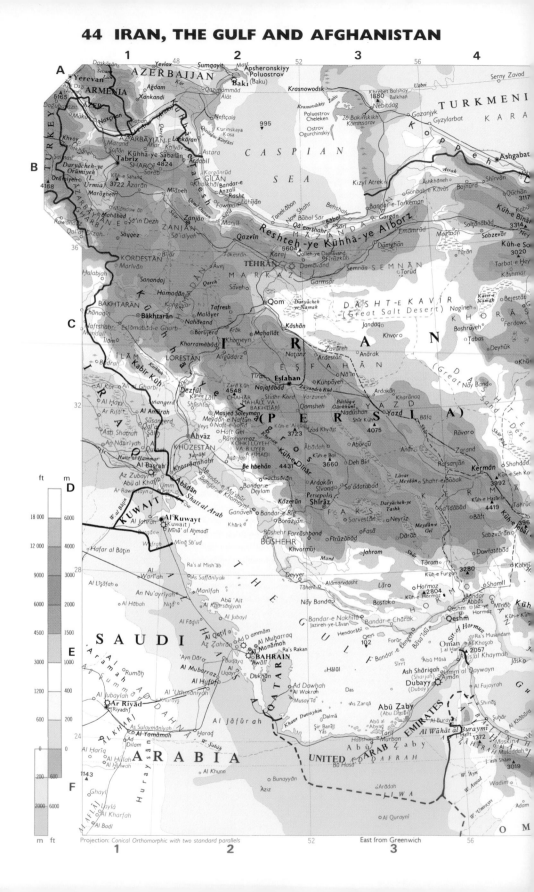

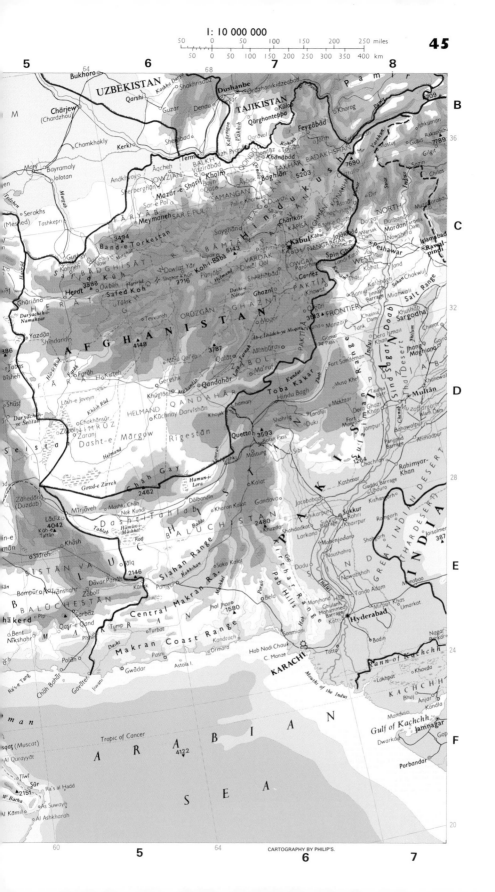

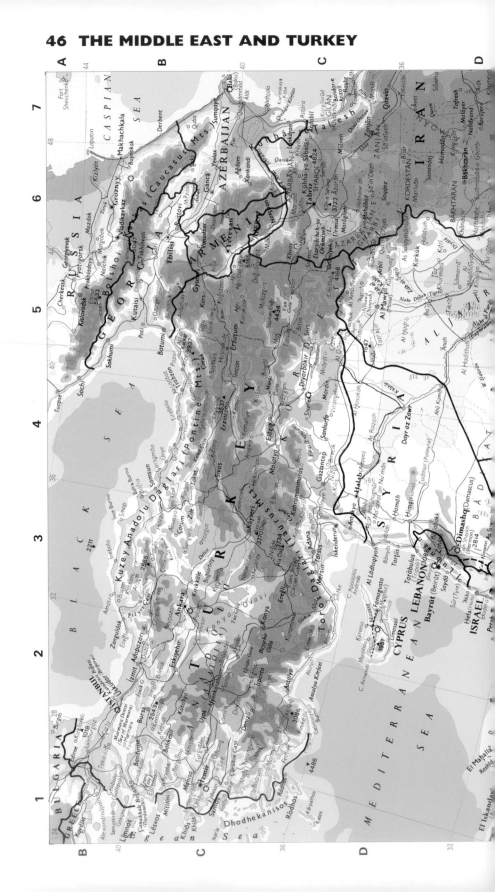

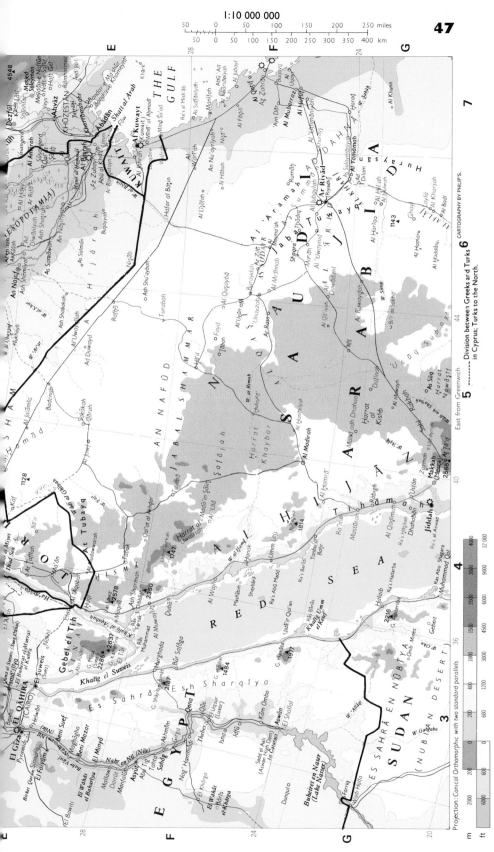

1:10 000 000

50   0   50   100   150   200   250 miles
50   0   50   100   150   200   250   300   350   400 km

East from Greenwich

CARTOGRAPHY BY PHILIP'S.

Division between Greeks and Turks
in Cyprus; Turks to the North.

Projection: Conical Orthomorphic with two standard parallels

THE GULF

KHŪZESTĀN

4548 Masjed
Soleimān

Deẓfūl

Kārūn L.

Shaṭṭ al Arab

Ahvaz

Ābādān

Al Kuwayt
Kuwait

KUWAIT

MESOPOTAMIA

IRAQ

An Nafūd

AL ḤIJĀZ

EGYPT

SINAI

Gebel el Tîh

RED SEA

SUDAN

Es Saḥrâ en Nûbîya
(NUBIAN DESERT)

Bûḥeiret en Naser
(Lake Nasser)

EL QÂHIRA
(CAIRO)

El Gîza

AN NAFŪD

JABAL SHAMMAR

Ar Riyāḍ
(Riyadh)

Al 'Aramah

SUM ṬADĀ

Najd

SAUDI ARABIA

AD DAHNA

AL HASA

AS SUMMAN

Makkah
(Mecca)

Jiddah

NAJD

m   ft
2000   6000
             4000   12 000
             3000   9000
             2000   6000
             1500   4500
             1000   3000
             600   1200
             400   600
200   600
0   0

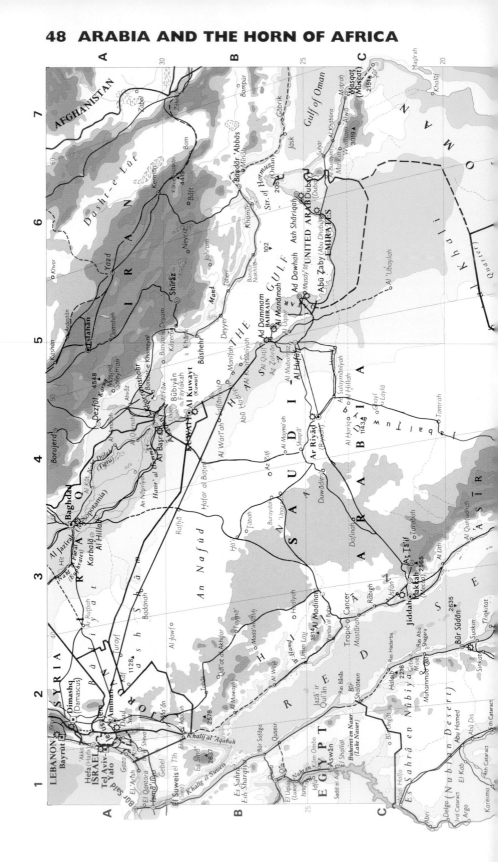

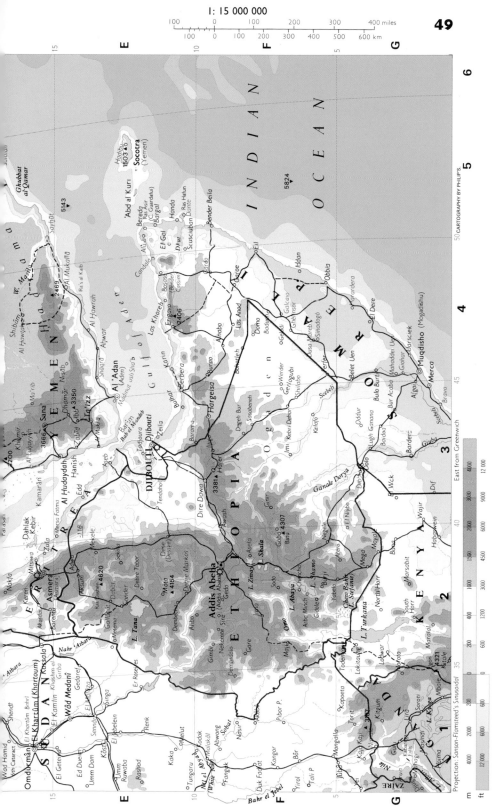

1 : 15 000 000

```
100        0        100       200       300      400 miles
100    0    100   200   300   400   500   600 km
```

CARTOGRAPHY BY PHILIP'S

Projection: Sanson-Flamsteed's Sinusoidal

East from Greenwich

I N D I A N   O C E A N

Socotra (Yemen)
1503
'Abd al Kuri
5824

S O M A L I A

Muqdisho (Mogadishu)
Merca

Y E M E N
5143
2469
Sana'
3666
Al Hudaydah
3350
Ta'izz

E R I T R E A
Asmera
4620
4154

D J I B O U T I
Djibouti

E T H I O P I A
Addis Abeba (Adis Abeba)
3381
4307

S U D A N
El Khartûm (Khartoum)
Wâd Medanî

K E N Y A
L. Turkana
4321

U G A N D A

ZAIRE

m ft

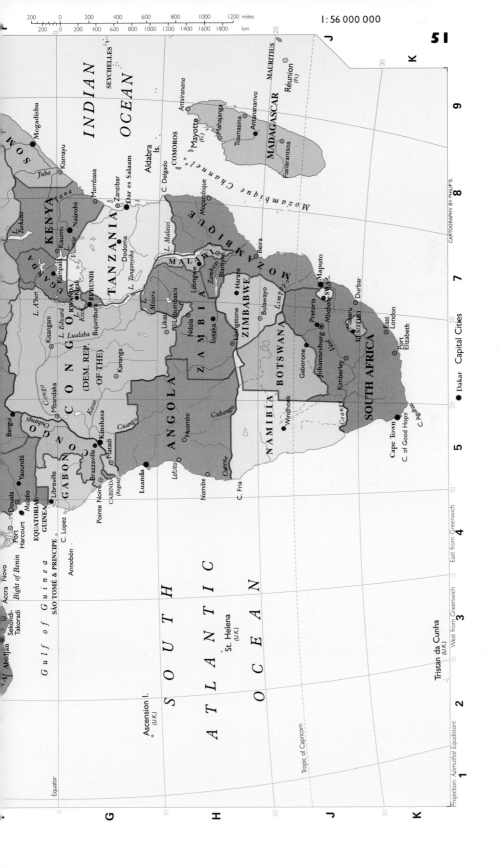

200   0   200   400   600   800   1000   1200 miles
200   0   200   400   600   800   1000   1200 1400 1600 1800   km

1 : 56 000 000

CARTOGRAPHY BY PHILIP'S.

INDIAN OCEAN

SEYCHELLES

MAURITIUS
Réunion (Fr.)

Antsiranana
Mahajanga
Toamasina
Antananarivo

MADAGASCAR

Fianarantsoa

Mayotte (Fr.)

COMOROS

Aldabra Is.

C. Delgado

Mogadishu

Kismayu

Juba

Mombasa

Zanzibar
Dar es Salaam

KENYA

L. Turkana

Kisumu
Nairobi
L. Victoria

UGANDA

Kampala

L. Albert

L. Edward

RWANDA
Kigali

BURUNDI
Bujumbura

L. Tanganyika

TANZANIA

Dodoma

L. Malawi

MALAWI

Lilongwe
Blantyre

CONGO (DEM. REP. OF THE)

Kisangani

Mbandaka

Lualaba

Kasai

Likasi
Lubumbashi

Kananga

Ndola
Luanshya

ZAMBIA

Lusaka

Zambezi

Harare
Livingstone

Bulawayo

ZIMBABWE

Limpopo

Beira

MOZAMBIQUE

Mozambique Channel

Maputo

SWAZ.
Mbabane

Pretoria
Johannesburg
Mabane
Maseru
LESOTHO

BOTSWANA

Gaborone

Kimberley

Durban

East London

SOUTH AFRICA

Port Elizabeth

Cape Town
C. of Good Hope

Vaal

Orange

NAMIBIA

Windhoek

Cubango

Okavango

Cunene

Namibe

C. Fria

ANGOLA

Lobito

Luanda

CABINDA (Angola)

Pointe Noire
Brazzaville
Kinshasa
Matadi

Cuango

Kwai

CONGO

GABON

Libreville

C. Lopez

Port Gentil

EQUATORIAL GUINEA

Malabo
Douala
Yaoundé

Bangui

Ubangi

Congo

Annobón

SÃO TOMÉ & PRINCIPE

Bight of Benin

Gulf of Guinea

Accra Novo
Accra
Sekondi-Takoradi

Abidjan

Equator

SOUTH ATLANTIC OCEAN

Ascension I. (U.K.)

St. Helena (U.K.)

West from Greenwich

East from Greenwich

Tristan da Cunha (U.K.)

Tropic of Capricorn

Projection: Azimuthal Equidistant

● Dakar   Capital Cities

G   H   J   K

1   2   3   4   5   7   8   9

J   K

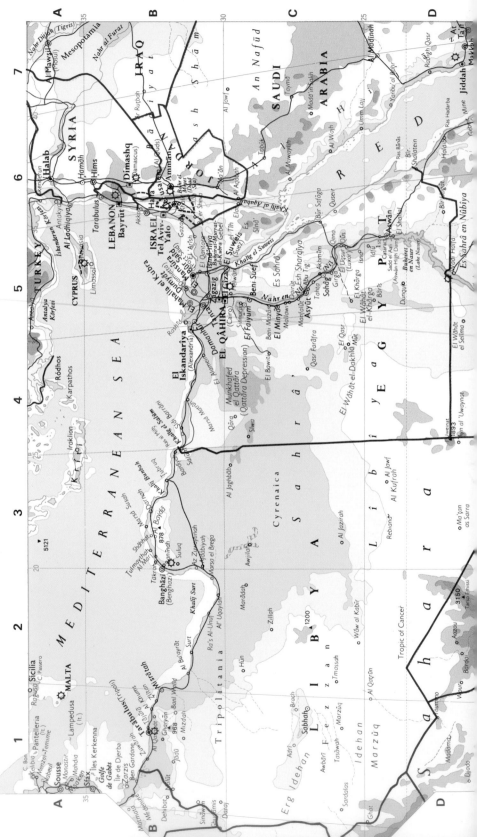

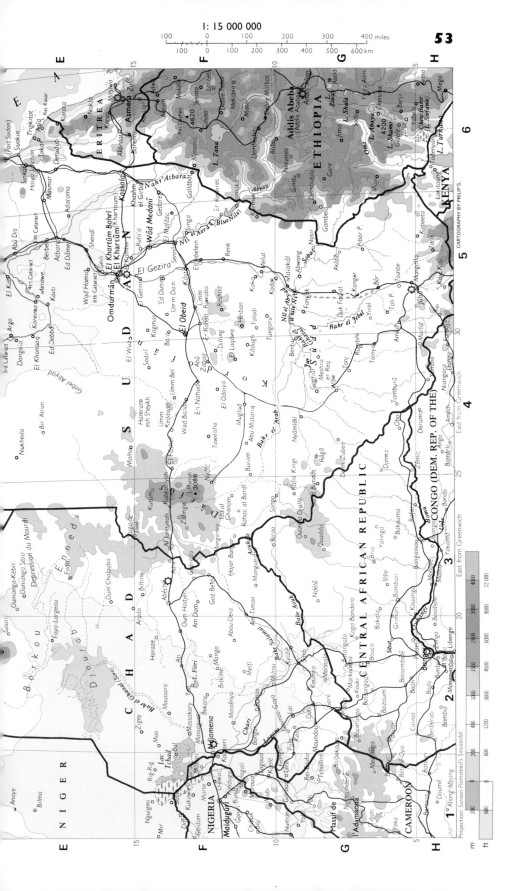

1: 15 000 000

100   0   100   200   300   400 miles

100 0 100 200 300 400 500 600 km

CARTOGRAPHY BY PHILIP'S.

Projection Sanson-Flamsteed's Sinusoidal

E R I T R E A

Asmera

ETHIOPIA

Addis Abeba
(Addis Ababa)

KENYA

L. Turkana

L. Tana

S U D A N

El Khartûm Bahri
El Khartûm (Khartoum)
Omdurmân

Wâd Medanî

El Gezira

El Obeid

Nîl el Abyad
(White Nile)

Bahr el Jebel

C H A D

N'Djamena

Lac Tchad

NIGERIA

Maiduguri

CAMEROON

CENTRAL AFRICAN REPUBLIC

CONGO (DEM. REP. OF THE)

Bangui

N I G E R

Depression du Mourdi

Ennedi

Borkou

East from Greenwich

m   ft

4000   12 000
3000   9000
2000   6000
1500   4500
1000   3000
600   1200
400   1200
0   0
600

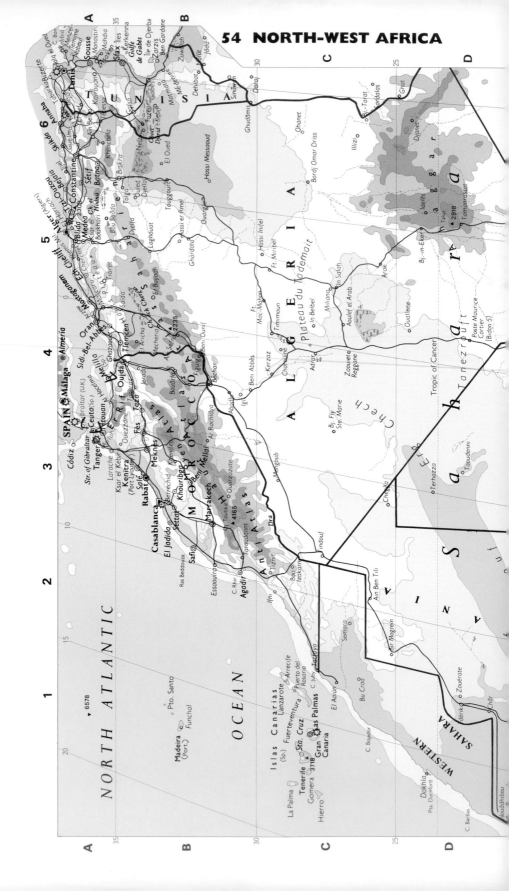

NORTH ATLANTIC OCEAN

SPAIN

Cádiz
Málaga
Almería
Str. of Gibraltar
Gibraltar (UK)
Ceuta (Sp.)
Tanger
Tetouan
Larache
Ksar el Kebir
Kenitra (Port Lyautey)
Rabat
Salé
Casablanca
El Jadida
Safi
Essaouira
Agadir
Ifni
Tiznit
C. Rhir
Ras Bedouza
C. Juby
Tarfaya
El Aaiun
Semara
Dakhla
Ras Durnford
C. Bojador
C. Barbas
Nouâdhibou
derikh
Châr

EL RIF
Chechaouen
Ouezzane
Fès
Meknès
Taza
Settat
Berrechid
Khouribga
Beni Mellal
Marrakech
Taroudant
Ouarzazate
Al Rachidiya

MOYEN ATLAS
HAUT ATLAS
Anti Atlas
4165
Toubkal
Garoudann
Boù I-Izakarn

MOROCCO
Oujda
Tlemcen
2235
Sidi-Bel-Abbès
Oran
Mostaganem
Alger (Algiers)
Blida
Medea
Miliana
El Asnam
(Chlef)
Ksar el Chellala
Tiaret
Relizane
Ghazaouet
Nedroma
Saïda
El Bayadh
Mecheria
Aïn Sefra
Béchar
Abadla
Figuig
Bou Arfa
Boudenib

ALGERIA

TUNISIA
Tunis
Bizerte
Sousse
Monastir
Mahdia
Sfax
Îles Kerkenna
Golfe de Gabès
Gabès
Île de Djerba
Zarzis
Ben Gardane
Médenine
Tataouine
Matmata
Dehibat
Zuwarah
Al-Oued
Kairouan
Sbeïtla
Kasserine
Gafsa
Tozeur
Nefta
Chott Djerid
El Oued
Touggourt
Ouargla
Ghardaïa
Laghouat
Djelfa
Bou Saâda
M'Sila
Batna
Biskra
Khenchela
Tébessa
Sétif
Constantine
Skikda
Annaba
C. Bon
Menzel Bourguiba

Ghdamis
Sinawin
Daraj
Ghât
Bordj Omar Driss
Illizi
Djanet
Amguid
Idelès
Tamanrasset
2918
Tahat
In Ekker
Bj.-in-Eker
Poste Maurice Cortier (Bidon 5)
Ouallene
Aoulef el Arab
In Salah
In Belbel
Timimoun
Adrar
Reggane
Zaouiet Reggane
Kerzaz
Beni Abbès
Bj. Fly
Ste. Marie
Chenachane
Tindouf
Hassi Messaoud
El Golea
Ft. Miribel
Hassi Inifel
Ft. Mac-Mahon
Hassi er Rmel
Ghardaïa
Laghouat
Metlili
Ft. Flatters

SAHARA

Plateau du Tademaît
Tropic of Cancer
Erg Chech
Hamada du Dra
Tanezrouft
Erg Iguidi

WESTERN SAHARA
Sr. Mogrein
Bu Crâa
Bir Moghrein
Ain Ben Tili
Chegga
Terhazza
Taoudenni
Tioudenni
Zouérate

Madeira (Port.)
Funchal
Pto. Santo

Islas Canarias (Sp.)
Lanzarote
Arrecife
Fuerteventura
Puerto del Rosario
Sta. Cruz
Tenerife
Gran Canaria
Las Palmas
La Palma
Gomera
Hierro
3718
6578

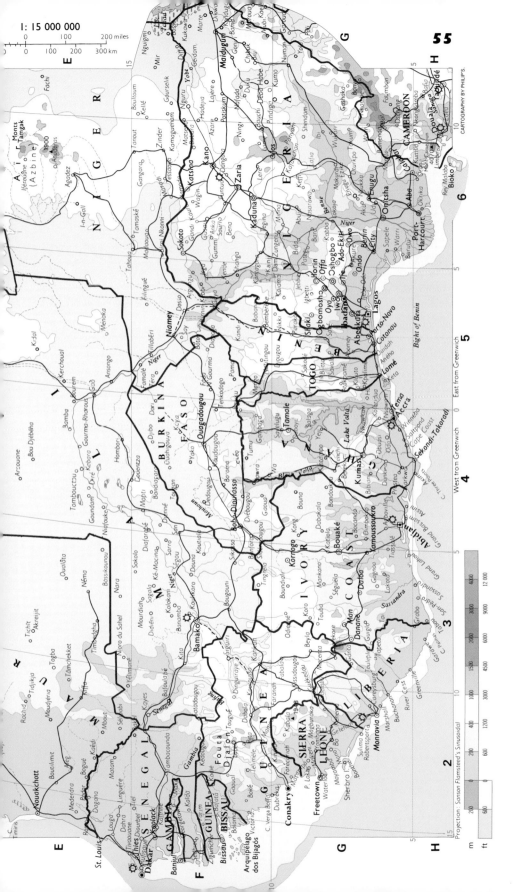

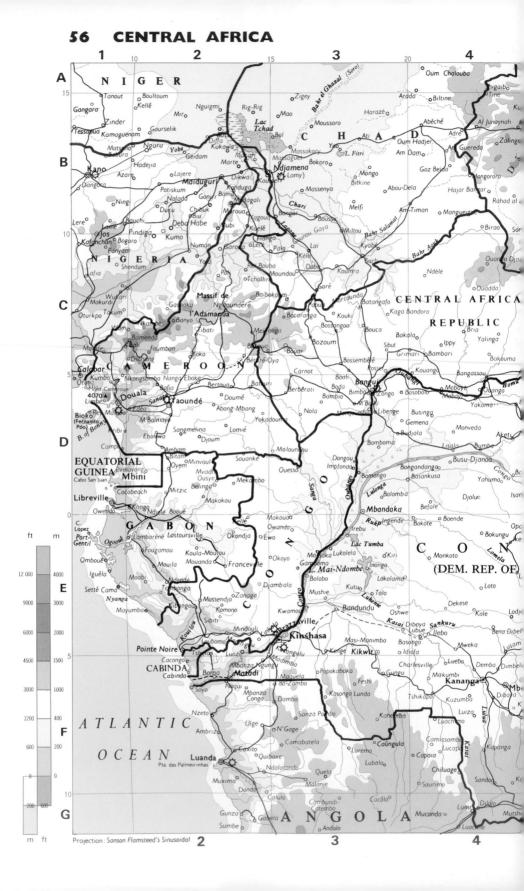

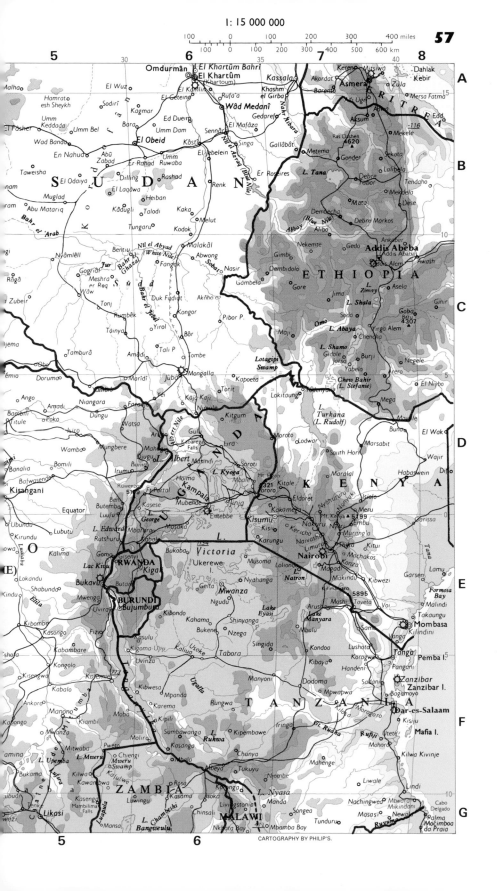

5   6   7   8

30   35   40

A

15

B

10

C

5

D

0

E

E)

F

10

G

5   6

CARTOGRAPHY BY PHILIP'S.

Omdurmân
El Khartûm Bahri
El Khartûm
(Khartoum)
Kassala
Akordat Mitsiwa
Kerena
Asmera
Dahlak Kebir
El Wuz
El Khartûm
El Kâmlin
El Geteina
Rufa'a
Khashm
el Girba
Gedaref
Adi Ugri
Zula
Mersa Fatma
Hamrat
esh Sheykh
Sodirî
Kagmar
Wâd Medanî
Sennâr
El Mafâza
Barentu
Aksum
Edd
Umm
Keddada
Bara
Ed Dueim
Umm Dam
Singa
Gallâbât
Mekele
-116
Umm Bel
El Obeid
Kôsti
El Jebelein
Metema
Gonder
Sekota
Ras Dashen
4620
Lalibela
Wad Banda
En Nahud
Abu
Zabad
Umm
Ruwaba
Er Rahad
Rashad
Renk
Er Roseires
L. Tana
Debre
Tabor
Tendaho
Taweisha
El Odaiya
Drilling
Kâdugli
Heiban
Talodi
Kaka
Melut
Debre Markos
Mota
Mekdela
Dese
Muglad
El Laqôwa
Tungaru
Kodok
(Blue Nile)
Abbay
Alibo
Abu Matariq
Nyâmlêll
Ntl el Abyad
White Nile
Malakâl
Bentiu
Abwong
Nasir
Dembidolo
Nekemte
Gedo
Ankober
Awash
Addis Abeba
(Addis Ababa)
Gôj Aleni
Gogrial
Meshra
er Req
Fangak
Gambēla
Gimbi
Gore
ETHIOPIA
L. Zwaiy
Asela
Râga
Wâw
Tonj
Duk Fadiat
Kongor
Pibor P.
Maji
Soda
Jima
L. Shala
Goba
Batu
4307
Gihir
Rumbēk
Yirol
Bôr
Omo
L. Abaya
Yirga Alem
Chencha
Tamburâ
Amadi
Tali P
Tombe
L. Shamo
Gidole
Jorso
Burji
Negele
Toinya
Mongalla
Kapoeta
Chew Bahir
(L. Stefanie)
El Niybo
Dorumo
Maridi
Jûba
Lotagipi
Swamp
Atero
Mega
Moyale
El Wak
Niangara
Faradje
Torit
Lakitaung
Kajo Kaji
Nimule
Kitgum
Moroto
Lodwar
L. Turkana
(L. Rudolf)
Bunia
Wajir
Mungbere
Gulu
Lira
South Horr
Marsabit
Habaswein
Dungu
Watsa
Soroti
Mt Moroto
Maralal
Garba
Dif
Kisangani
Mahagi
Kaparega
Falls
Albert Nile
Mbale
321
Kitale
Eldoret
Nyahururu
Isiolo
Butembo
Hoima
5119
L. Kyoga
Kakamega
Nakuru
Nyeri
Meru
Mt Kenya 5199
Equator
Kasese
Mubende
Jinja
Kisumu
Kericho
Naivasha
Limuru
Thika
Kitui
Garissa
Ubundu
Lubutu
George
Entebbe
Kisii
Konza
Nairobi
Machakos
Kirundu
Kalima
L. Edward
Mbarara
Masaka
Karungu
Magadi
Kibwezi
Lamu
Kindu
Bukavu
Gisenyi
Lac Kivu
RWANDA
Kigali
Bukoba
Victoria L.
Ukerewe
I.
Musoma
Loliondo
L.
Natron
Makindu
Garsen
Lokandu
Butare
Nyahanga
Kilimanjaro
5895
Arusha
Voi
Formosa
Bay
Malindi
Shabunda
BURUNDI
Bujumbura
Uvira
Mwanza
Ngudu
Lake
Eyasi
Moshi
Taveta
Takaungu
Mombasa
Kilindini
Ebita
Mwenga
Kahama
Bukene
Shinyanga
Mbulu
Same
Vanga
Pemba I.
Kibombo
Fizi
Kasulu
Kigoma-Ujiji
Usoke
Nzega
Singida
Kondoa
Korogwe
Tanga
Kasongo
Kabambare
Uvinza
Tabora
Manyoni
Dodoma
Kibaya
Handeni
Pangani
Kongolo
Kasanga
Kibwesa
Mpanda
Kilosa
Mpwapwa
Sabaki
Zanzibar
Zanzibar I.
Kabalo
Katemie
772
Karema
Rungwa
Iringa
Morogoro
Bagamoyo
Kisiju
Manono
Kiambi
Kipili
TANZANIA
Dar-es-Salaam
Ankoro
Moba
Molira
Sumbawanga
Chunya
Mahenge
Mafia I.
Kongolo
Mwazia
Pweto
Chiengi
Kasanga
Mbeya
Tukuyu
Njombe
Kilwa Kivinje
Mitwaba
L. Mweru
Kalulu
Rosa
Isoka
Manda
Songea
Nachingwea
Mtwara
Bukama
Kawambwa
Kasama
Kalunga
L. Nyasa
Tunduru
Masasi
Mikindani
Palma
Moçimboa
da Praia
Likasi
Mansa
Chinsali
Livingstonia
Mbamba Bay
Newala
Ruvuma
Cabo
Delgado
ZAMBIA
L. Bangweulu
MALAWI
Nkhata Bay
SUDAN
UGANDA
KENYA
ERITREA

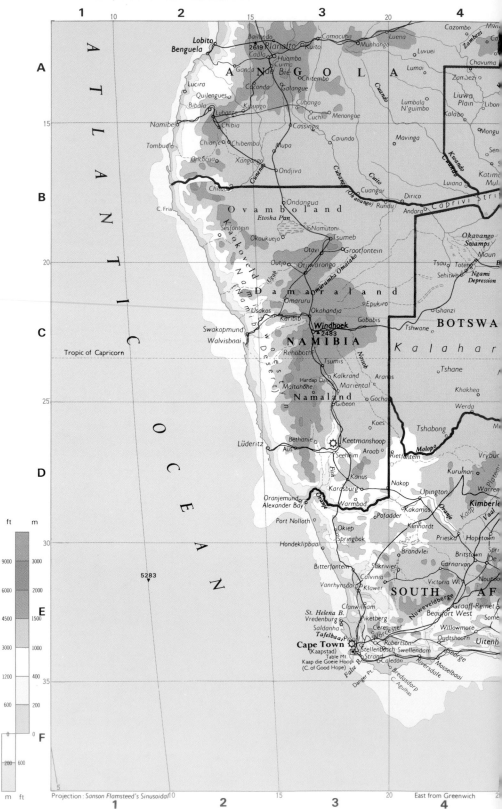

ATLANTIC OCEAN

ANGOLA

Lobito
Benguela
Lucira
Quilengues
Bibala
Namibe
Tombua
Ondcócua

Balhnbo
Cadla
2619 Planalto
Ganda Nova Bié
Huambo
Cuima
Cóconda
Salangue
Luhanda
Kipungo
Chibia
Chianje
Chibemba
Xangongo

Camacupa
Kuito
Munhango
Cubango
Menongue
Cuchi
Cassinga
Mupa
Ondjiva

Cazombo
Luena
Lumai
Lumbala
N'guimbo
Kalabo

Mwi
Ca

Zambezi

Chavuma
Zam.Sezi
Liuwa
Plain
Libon
Mongu
Sen
Mavinga

Katima
Mul.

Cuando

Cutio
Cuangar
Dirico
Andara

Cubango (Okavango) Rundu
Caiundo

Kwando

Caprivi Stri

Ovamboland
C. Fria
Sesfontein
Okaukuejo
Etosha Pan
Ondangua
Namutoni
Tsumeb
Grootfontein
Otavi
Outjo
Otjiwarongo
Omatako
Tsau
Sehitwa
Toteng
Maun
Okavango
Swamps
Ngami
Depression

Damaraland
Usakos
Omaruru
Karibib
Okahandja
Epukiro
Gobabis
Tshwane
Ghanzi

BOTSWA

Kaokoveld
Swakopmund
Walvisbaai
Windhoek
2483
NAMIBIA
Rehoboth
Tsumis
Nossob
Kalahar

Namib Desert (Woesteyn)

Tropic of Capricorn

Namaland
Hardap Da
Maltahöhe
Mariental
Kalkrand
Araras
Gibeon
Gocha
Koes
Werda
Tshabong
Khakhea
Shane
Me

Lüderitz
Bethanie
Aus
Seeheim
Keetmanshoop
Aroab
Rietfontein
Kolop

Fish
Kanus
Karasburg
Nakop
Upington
Kuruman
Kimberle

Oranjemund
Alexander Bay
Warmbad
Pofadder
Kakamas
Orange
Kadp
Vaal
Warren

Port Nolloth
Okiep
Springbok
Kenhardt
Prieska
Hopetown
Vryhur

5283
Hondeklipbaai
Bitterfontein
Brandvlei
Britstown
De
Carnarvon
Spr

Vanrhynsdorp
Calvinia
Klawer
Sukrivier
Victoria W.
Noupo

Clanwilliam
Nuweveldberge
Graaff-Reinet
SOUTH
AF

St. Helena B.
Vredenburg
Saldanha
Piketberg
Ceres
Beaufort West
Willowmore
Oudtshoorn
Some

Tafelbaai
Cape Town
(Kaapstad)
Stellenbosch
Swellendam
Worcester
Robertson
Uitenh

Table Mt.
Kaap die Goeie Hoop
(C. of Good Hope)
Strand
Caledon
Riversdale
Mosselbaai

False B
Bredasdorp
C. Aguhas
Danger Pt.

ft m
9000 3000
6000 2000
4500 1500
3000 1000
1200 400
600 200
0 0
200 600
m ft

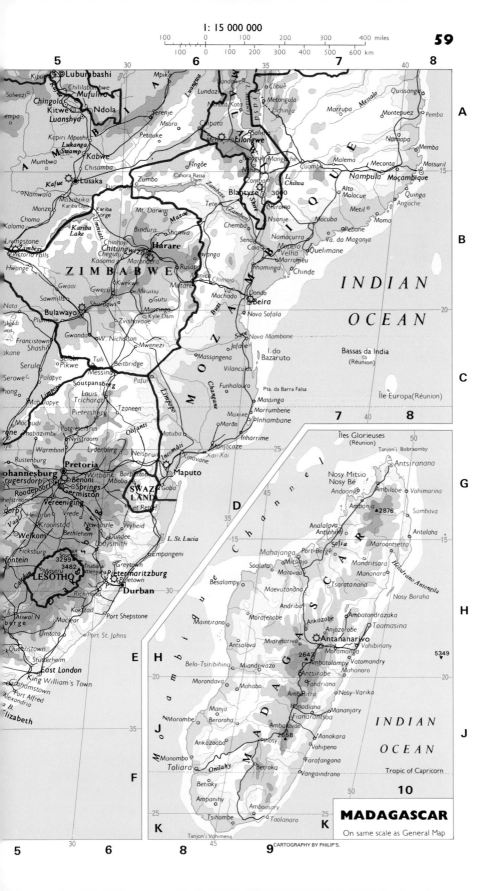

1: 15 000 000

100   100   200   300   400 miles

100   0   100   200   300   400   500   600 km

INDIAN

OCEAN

Bassas da India
(Réunion)

Île Europa (Réunion)

Îles Glorieuses
(Réunion)

Tanjon'i Bobraomby

Nosy Mitsio
Nosy Bé

Andoany

Ambanja ▲2876

Antsiranana

Vohimarina

Sambava

Antalaha

Maroantsetra

Mandritsara

Mananara

Nosy Boraha

Toamasina

Ambatondrazaka

Anjozorobe

Ankazobe

Antananarivo

Miandrivazo

Moramanga

Vatomandry

▲2642 Ambatolampy

Antsirabe

Mahanoro

Fandriana

Nosy-Varika

Ambositra

Fianarantsoa

Mananjary

Ambalavao

▲2658

Ihosy

Manakara

Vohipeno

Betroka

Farafangana

Vangaindrano

Tropic of Capricorn

Betioky

Ampanihy

Amboasary

Tsihombe

Taolanaro

Tanjon'i Vohimena

ZIMBABWE

LESOTHO

MOZAMBIQUE

SWAZILAND

MADAGASCAR

On same scale as General Map

CARTOGRAPHY BY PHILIP'S.

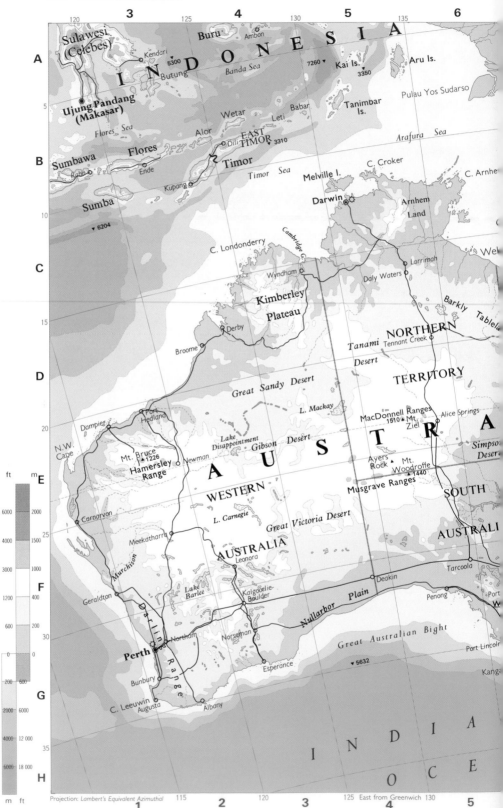

3 120 **4** 125 **5** 130 **6** 135

A
Sulawesi (Celebes)
Buru
Ambon
INDONESIA
Kendari
5300
Butung
Banda Sea
7260
Kai Is.
3350
Aru Is.
Pulau Yos Sudarso

Ujung Pandang (Makasar)
Wetar
Leti
Babar
Tanimbar Is.
Arafura Sea

Flores Sea
Alor
Dili
EAST TIMOR
3310
C. Croker
C. Arnhe

B
Sumbawa
Flores
Ende
Timor
Timor Sea
Melville I.
Darwin
Arnhem Land

Raba
Kupang
Sumba
6204

C. Londonderry
Cambridge G.
Larrimah
Wel

C
Wyndham
Daly Waters
Barkly Tablela

Kimberley Plateau
NORTHERN

15
Derby
Tanami Desert
Tennant Creek

Broome
TERRITORY

D
Great Sandy Desert
L. Mackay
MacDonnell Ranges
1510 Mt. Ziel
Alice Springs

Port Hedland
Lake Disappointment
Gibson Desert
AUSTRA

20
Dampier
Mt. Bruce 1226
Newman
Ayers Rock
Mt. Woodroffe 1440
Simpso Deser

N.W. Cape
Hamersley Range
AUST
Musgrave Ranges
SOUTH

E
WESTERN

Carnarvon
L. Carnegie
Great Victoria Desert
AUSTRALI

25
Meekatharra
AUSTRALIA
Leonora
Tarcoola

F
Murchison
Lake Barlee
Kalgoorlie-Boulder
Deakin
Penong
Port

Geraldton
Nullarbor Plain
Lincoln

30
Northam
Norseman
Great Australian Bight
Port Lincoln

Perth
Darling Range
Esperance
5632
Kanga

Bunbury

G
C. Leeuwin Augusta
Albany

35
INDIA

H
OCE

Projection: *Lambert's Equivalent Azimuthal*   115   **2**   120   **3**   125 East from Greenwich 130   **5**
1   **4**

ft   m
6000   2000
4000   1500
3000   1000

1200   400
600   200
0   0
200   600
2000   6000
4000   12 000
6000   18 000
m   ft

1:20 000 000

100   0   100   200   300   400   500 miles

100   0   200   400   600   800 km

7   145   8   150   9   155   10   160   11

Mount Hagen 4508 Mt. New Britain 9140 Mt. Bougainville SOLOMON
Wilhelm Lae Balbi ISLANDS
PAPUA NEW GUINEA Choiseul Santa Isabel B
Fly Owen Stanley Range Solomon New Malaita
Gulf of Sea Georgia
Papua Port D'Entrecasteaux Arch. Honiara 2331
Torres Strait Moresby Guadalcanal 10
C. York Louisiade San Cristobal
Cape Archipelago Rennell
Weipa York C
Peninsula C o r a l   S e a

Cooktown 15
Mitchell Cairns **P** **A** **C** **I** **F** **I** **C** D
Normanton 1611 Bartle Frere Coral
Forsayth Sea Chesterfield Is.
Townsville Islands 20
Mount Isa Charters Towers Territory **O** **C** **E** **A** **N** E
Hughenden Mackay
Winton Tropic of Capricorn
QUEENSLAND Rockhampton 25
I A Longreach Gladstone
Yaraka Bundaberg F
Charleville Maryborough
Quilpie Roma Gympie
Cunnamulla **BRISBANE** Lord Howe G
Thargomindah Dirrabandi Toowoomba Ipswich (Austr.)
Gold 734
Walgett Coast 30
Bourke Lismore
Tamworth Round Taree
NEW SOUTH Mt. 1615
Broken Hill Cobar Dubbo Lord Howe G
WALES **Newcastle** Orange Bathurst
York Pirie **SYDNEY** 35
Murray Mildura Goulburn **Wollongong** T a s m a n   S e a
Adelaide Wagga Wagga Shellharbour
Murray **Canberra**
Shepparton Albury 2237 CAPITAL TERRITORY
Horsham Bombala 40
VICTORIA C. Howe
Ballarat **Bendigo**
Mount Gambier **Geelong** **MELBOURNE** H
Warrnambool
Bass Strait Furneaux Group 5267
King I.
Burnie Launceston J
1617
Mt.Ossa
TASMANIA **Hobart**
S.E. Cape

CARTOGRAPHY BY PHILIP'S.

140   7   8   150   9   10   160   11   165

145

SOUTH AUSTRALIA

Projection: Bonne

East from Greenwich

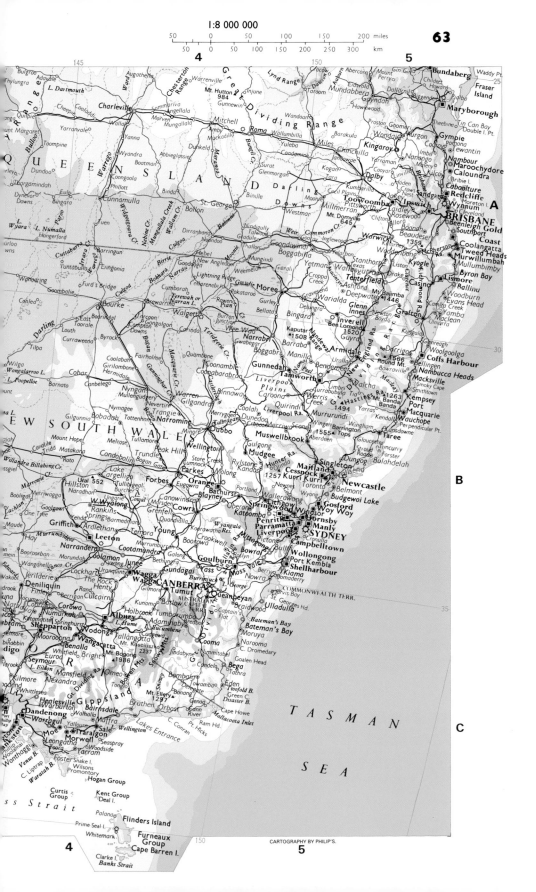

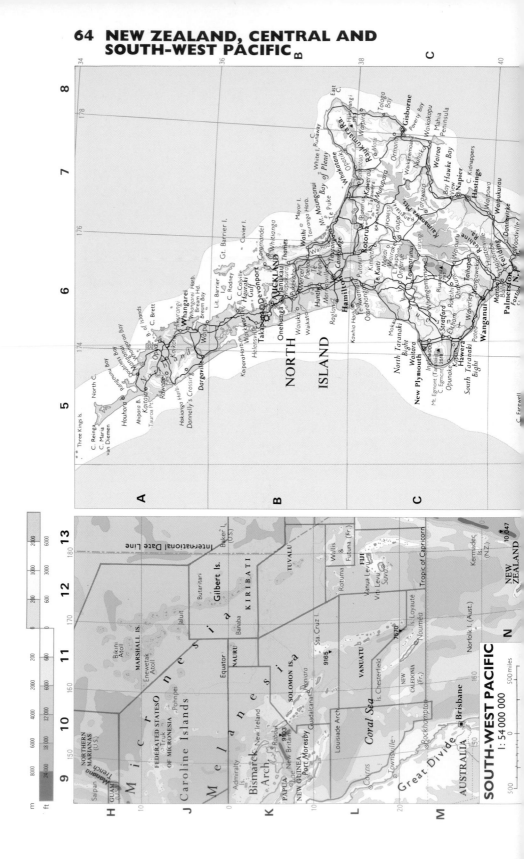

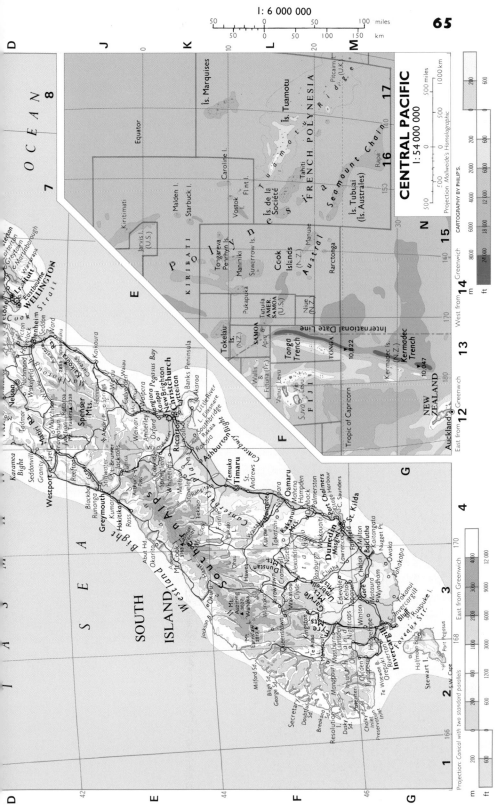

ICELAND

Reykjavik

Denmark Strait

Cape Farewell

Nuuk

G R E E N L A N D
(KALAALLIT NUNAAT)
(Denmark)

NEWFOUNDLAND

St. John's

St. Pierre
Channel St. Pierre Et Miquelon (Fr.)

PRINCE
EDWARD
ISLAND

NOVA SCOTIA

Halifax

Davis Strait

Baffin
Bay

Labrador

QUEBEC

Charlottetown

St. Lawrence

Québec

Baffin Island

Hudson Strait

N U N A V U T

Hudson Bay

Eastmain

ONTARIO

A R C T I C

O C E A N

Queen Elizabeth Is.

Ellesmere I.

Victoria I.

Back

Dubawnt

C A N A D A

Nelson

L. Winnipeg

MANITOBA

Churchill

SASKATCHEWAN

Regina (P)

Beaufort

Sea

Great Bear L.

Great Slave L.

Yellowknife

NORTHWEST TERRITORIES

Athabasca

L. Athabasca

Edmonton

Saskatchewan

International Date Line

Arctic Circle

Mackenzie

Liard

Peace

ALBERTA

Calgary

BRITISH

COLUMBIA

Fraser

Vancouver

WASHINGTON

YUKON
TERRITORY

Whitehorse

Juneau

Skeena

Victoria

A L A S K A
(USA)

Porcupine

Yukon

Fairbanks

Anchorage

Gulf of Alaska

Kodiak I.

RUSSIA

Asia

St. Lawrence

Bering Strait

Bering

Sea

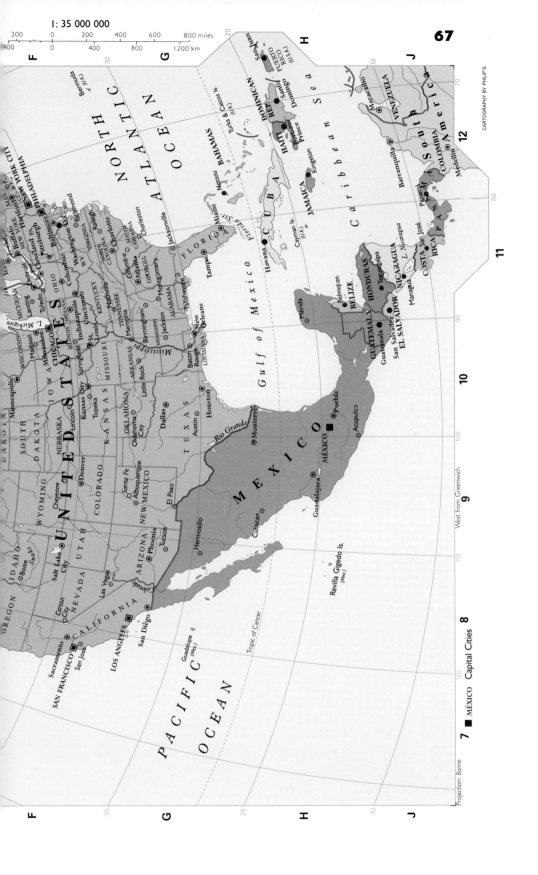

1 : 35 000 000

200   0   200   400   600   800 miles
400   0   400   800   1200 km

CARTOGRAPHY BY PHILIP'S.

Projection: Bonne

■ MÉXICO   Capital Cities

PACIFIC OCEAN

UNITED STATES

OREGON
IDAHO
Snake
Boise
NEVADA
Carson City
Sacramento
SAN FRANCISCO
San José
CALIFORNIA
Los Angeles
San Diego
Guadalupe (Mex.)
Tropic of Cancer

WYOMING
UTAH
Salt Lake City
Colorado
ARIZONA
Phoenix
Tucson
Las Vegas

Cheyenne
Denver
COLORADO
Santa Fe
Albuquerque
NEW MEXICO
El Paso

SOUTH DAKOTA
NEBRASKA
Lincoln
KANSAS
Topeka
Kansas City
OKLAHOMA
Oklahoma City

WISCONSIN
Minneapolis
Madison
Milwaukee
IOWA
MICHIGAN
L. Michigan
CHICAGO
ILLINOIS
INDIANA
Springfield
Indianapolis
St. Louis
MISSOURI
KENTUCKY
TENNESSEE
Nashville
Memphis
ARKANSAS
Little Rock
Mississippi
Jackson
ALABAMA
Birmingham
Montgomery
GEORGIA
TEXAS
Dallas
Austin
Houston
LOUISIANA
Baton Rouge
New Orleans
Tallahassee
FLORIDA
Tampa
Miami

Buffalo
NEW YORK CITY
PHILADELPHIA
N.J.
Baltimore
Pittsburgh
Cleveland
OHIO
Toledo
Lansing
Detroit
Columbus
Cincinnati
Washington D.C.
Richmond
VIRGINIA
W.V.
Raleigh
NORTH CAROLINA
Charlotte
SOUTH CAROLINA
Columbia
Charleston
Atlanta
Jacksonville

NORTH ATLANTIC OCEAN

Bermuda (U.K.)

MEXICO

Hermosillo
Culiacán
Rio Grande
Monterrey
Guadalajara
MÉXICO
Puebla
Acapulco
Mérida

Revilla Gigedo Is. (Mex.)

Gulf of Mexico

BAHAMAS
Nassau
Turks & Caicos Is. (U.K.)
CUBA
Havana
Florida Str.
Cayman Is. (U.K.)
JAMAICA
Kingston

Caribbean Sea

San Juan
PUERTO RICO (U.S.A.)
DOMINICAN REP.
Santo Domingo
HAITI
Port-au-Prince

Belmopan
BELIZE
GUATEMALA
Guatemala
HONDURAS
Tegucigalpa
EL SALVADOR
San Salvador
NICARAGUA
Managua
L. Nicaragua
COSTA RICA
San José
PANAMA
Panamá
COLOMBIA
Medellín
VENEZUELA
Maracaibo
Barranquilla

South America

West from Greenwich

F   G   H   J

7   8   9   10   11   12

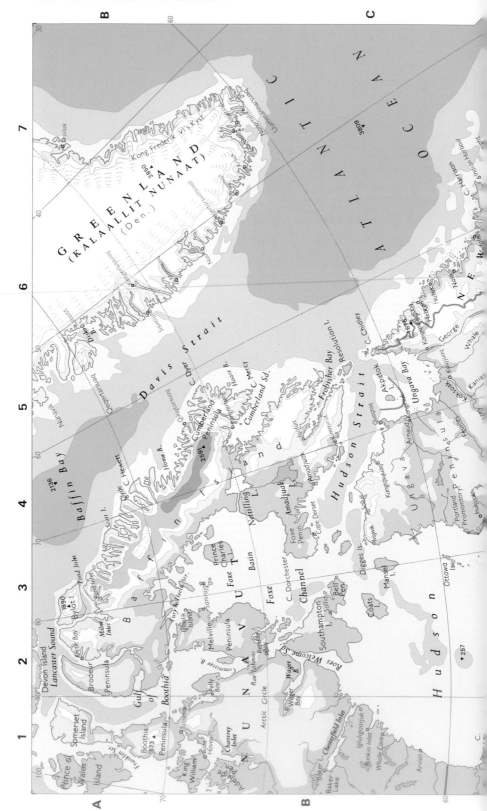

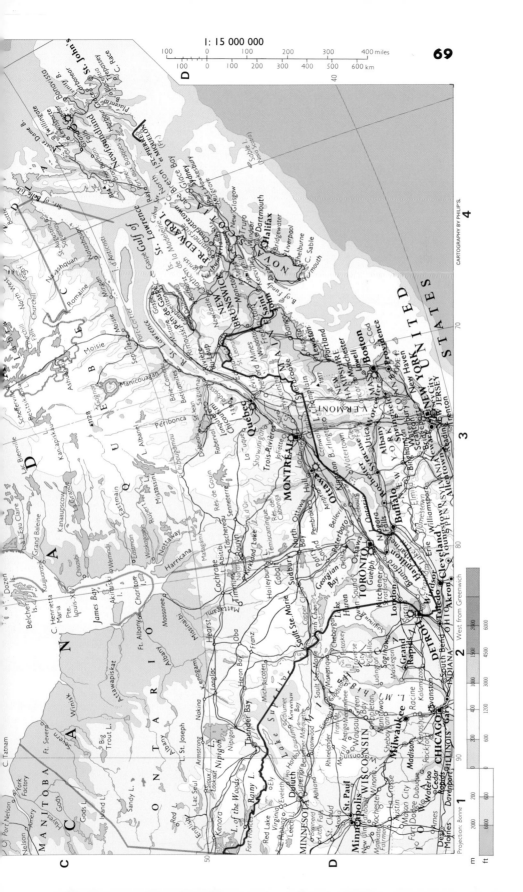

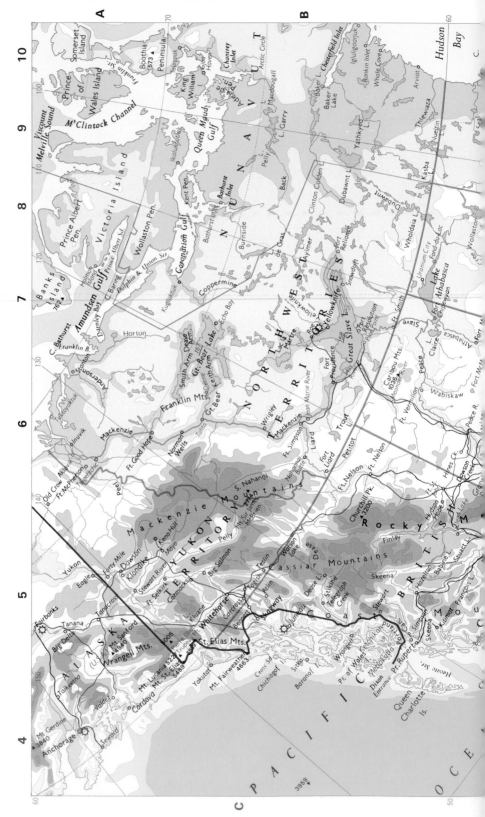

71

1: 15 000 000

| 100 | 0 | 100 | 200 | 300 | 400 miles |

| 100 | 0 | 100 | 200 | 300 | 400 | 500 | 600 km |

CARTOGRAPHY BY PHILIP'S.

ONTARIO

MANITOBA

SASKATCHEWAN

ALBERTA

UNITED STATES

NORTH DAKOTA

SOUTH DAKOTA

MINNESOTA

WIS.

MONTANA

WYOMING

NEBRASKA

Winnipeg

St. Boniface

Minneapolis

St. Paul

Omaha

Sioux City

Sioux Falls

Regina

Saskatoon

Moose Jaw

Prince Albert

Edmonton

Calgary

Lethbridge

Vancouver

Victoria

Seattle

Tacoma

Spokane

WASHINGTON

OREGON

Selkirk Mts.

Brooks Range

Fairbanks

College

Anchorage

Seward

Kodiak

Nome

Barrow

Juneau

Whitehorse

GULF OF ALASKA

BERING SEA

PACIFIC OCEAN

ALEUTIAN IS.

West from Greenwich

Projection : Bonne

ALASKA
1:30 000 000

| 100 | 0 | 100 | 200 | 300 miles |

| 100 | 0 | 100 | 200 | 300 | 400 km |

m			ft
2000			6000
600			2000
200			600
0			0
600			1500
1200			3000
1500			4500
3000			9000

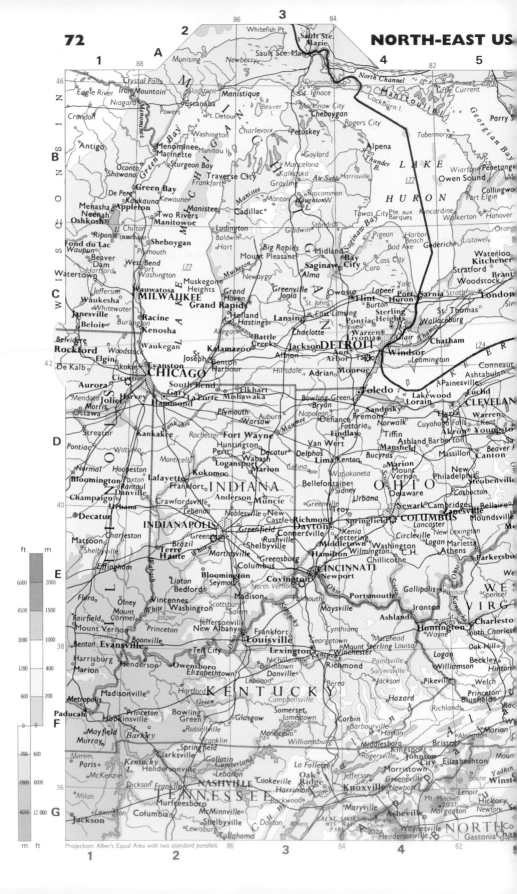

A full-page map of the North-East US.

ft   m
6000 2000
4500 1500
3000 1000
1200   400
600   200
0   0
200   600
2000 6000
4000 12 000
m   ft

Projection: Alber's Equal Area with two standard parallels

1 : 6 000 000

50   0   50   100 miles

50   0   50   100   150   km

6   78   7   76   8   74   9   72   10

MONTREAL
Lachine Granby   Sherbrooke
Magog   Coaticook Richardson
Lakes
Pembroke Coulonge Hawkesbury   St. Jean   Colebrook
Fort   Ottawa   Beauharnois   Cowansville   Island Pond   B
Eganville   Buckingham   Newport   St. Albans   Lancaster   Berlin
Renfrew Hull   Cornwall   Malone   Winooski St.   Mt.
Arnprior Ottawa   Massena Plattsburg   Montpelier Johnsbury Washington 144
Barry's   Carleton Massena   Montpelier Barre   1917
Bay   Place   Prescott Ogdensburg   Canton   VERMONT   Conway
Smiths Falls   Brockville   Potsdam   Middlebury   Laconia
Bracebridge   Perth   Champlain   R.   Rochester
Gravenhurst Bancroft   Kingston Gouverneur   Saranac Lakes   Rutland   Lebanon   Dover
Marmora   Watertown   Ticonderoga L.   Claremont Concord   Portsmouth
Lindsay Belleville   Lowville   George Glens   Springfield   Manchester Newburyport
Simcoe Trenton   Lake Pleasant   Falls Falls   Keene   Haverhill C. Ann
Peterborough Picton   Adirondack Mts   Saratoga Springs   Nashua Lawrence
Cobourg   1629   Glens Hudson   Amsterdam Brattleboro   Lowell Salem
Oshawa   75 LAKE ONTARIO   Oswego Rome   Utica Gloversville Schenectady   MASS.   Cambridge BOSTON
TORONTO   Fulton Oneida   Albany Troy   Greenfield   Worcester Quincy
Niagara Rochester   Syracuse   Pittsfield Northampton   Springfield   Brockton
Falls Newark Auburn   Cortland   Catskill   Chicopee   Taunton
Buffalo Batavia Geneva   Cayuga Oneonta   Catskill Hudson   Hartford Providence Fall River
West Seneca   Seneca Penn Yan   NEW YORK   Kingston   New Britain CONN. New Bedford
Dunkirk   Canandaigua   Ithaca   1281 Poughkeepsie   Waterbury Meriden   Martha's
Bath   Johnson City Catskill   Newburgh Danbury New Newport Vineyard
Salamanca   Hornell Corning   Endicott Binghamton Mts   Middletown Haven   New London
Olean Wellsville   Elmira   Delaware R.   Bridgeport Stamford   Long Island
Jamestown Bradford   Sayre   Kingston   Yonkers Mount Riverhead
Warren   Towanda Wellsboro Susquehanna Scranton Dunmore   Paterson Vernon
Coudersport 759   Carbondale   Jersey City   NEW YORK
Kane   Emporium   Nanticoke Wilkes   Newark
Ridgway St. Marys   Williamsport   Barre   Elizabeth Long Branch
Du   Lock   Bloomsburg Berwick Hazelton   New Brunswick Asbury Park
Bois   Haven   Sunbury Shenandoah   New Brunswick
Clearfield   PENNSYLVANIA   Pottsville Mt. Easton   NEW 40
Punxsutawney   State College Lewistown Blue Mt.   Allentown Bethlehem   Trenton JERSEY
PITTSBURGH Indiana Altoona   Reading   Morristown
Penn Hills 956   Harrisburg   Lebanon   Pottstown
Greensburg Johnstown   Carlisle York Lancaster PHILADELPHIA   Camden
Connellsville   Chambersburg Hanover   Chester Wilmington   E
Uniontown   Hagerstown Westminster Newark   Vineland Atlantic City
Cumberland Potomac Martinsburg   Frederick Columbia   Bridgeton   Ocean City
Keyser Romney   BALTIMORE Towson   MARYLAND   Millville
Winchester   Annapolis   Dover   Cape May
Elkins Franklin Front Royal   Arlington   Easton C. Henlopen
1482   Luray WASHINGTON D.C.   DELAWARE   Seaford   A
Harrisonburg   Culpeper Alexandria   Cambridge Salisbury
Staunton Orange   Lexington Park   Snow Hill
Waynesboro   Fredericksburg   Potomac
Clifton Buena Vista   Rappahannock   West Accomac   F
Forge   VIRGINIA Charlottesville   Point   Cape Charles
Lynchburg   Lakeside   Charles
Bedford   Richmond   Williamsburg
Roanoke Farmville Petersburg   Hampton Charles
John H. Kerr   Colonial Heights   Newport News Virginia Beach
Danville Reservoir Emporia Roanoke Nottoway   Portsmouth Norfolk
Eden   Oxford Henderson   Franklin Winton   Elizabeth Chesapeake
High Burlington Graham   Edenton Albemarle Sd.   City   Currituck Sd.
Point   Durham   Manteo
Lexington Chapel Hill   Rocky Mount Williamston
Asheboro Sanford Raleigh Wilson   Greenville
Smithfield   Washington   Pamlico   G
CAROLINA   Dunn Goldsboro Kinston New Bern   Pamlico Sound Hatteras
Albemarle   New Bern
80   6   78   West from Greenwich   76

Continuation Eastwards

CANADA
Edmundston
Fort
Kent Van
Eagle Buren Grand
Lake   Caribou Falls
St. John   Presque Isle   A
Eagle L. Chamberlain   Houlton
Chesuncook Patten   46
46   Mt. Katahdin 1605
Moosehead   Chiputneticook
L.   Lakes
Greenville   Millinocket
Richardson   Mattawamkeag B
Lakes Rangeley   Lincoln
Dover   East-
MAINE   Foxcroft   port
Farmington   Bangor Old Town
Rumford   Skowhegan Brewer Machias
Berlin Augusta   Waterville   Ellsworth
Mt. Washington   Belfast   Mt. Desert
1917   Gardiner   Rockland
Conway   Auburn Lewiston   44
NEW HAMPSHIRE Brunswick Bath   68
Laconia Westbrook Portland   C
Saco
Rochester Biddeford
Dover Portsmouth
Haverhill
70   10   11

Continuation
Eastwards
On same scale

CARTOGRAPHY BY PHILIP'S.

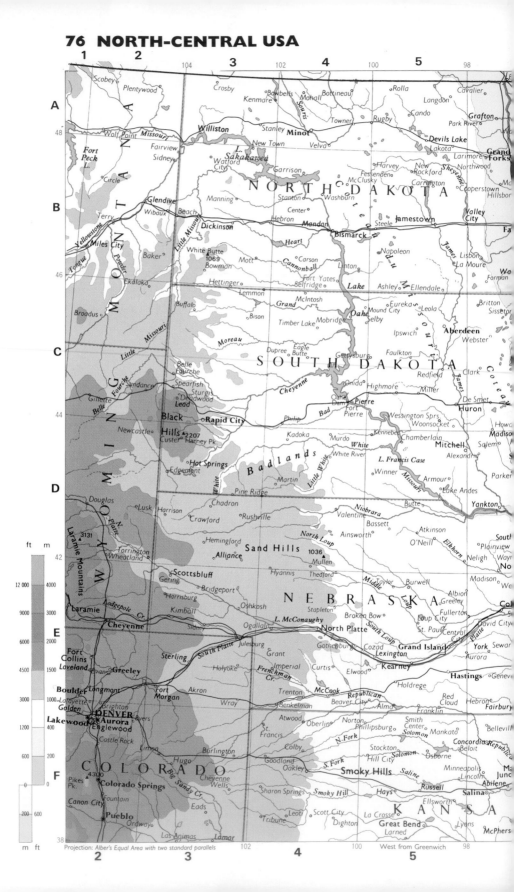

Projection: Alber's Equal Area with two standard parallels
West from Greenwich

1: 6 000 000

50   0   50   100 miles

50   0   50   100 150 km

CARTOGRAPHY BY PHILIP'S.

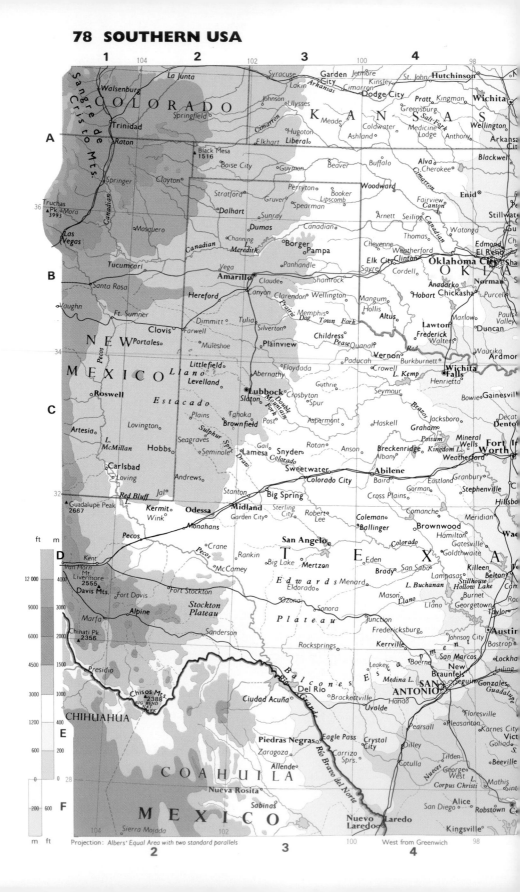

1: 6 000 000

50   0   50   100 miles
50 0 50 100 150 km

A

B

C

D

E

F

MISSOURI

Yates
Center Iola
Chanute Nevada Camdenton Rolla Steelville Murphysboro Marion
do Center Stockton Lebanon Salem Ironton Perryville Carbondale
Howard Fort Scott Buffalo Jackson Fredericktown Anna
Fredonia Girard Lamar Greenfield Marshfield Houston Cape Girardeau Metropolis
Parsons Pittsburg Bolivar Van Charleston Cairo Paducah
Sedan Independence Carthage Springfield Ozark Poplar Bluff Buren Sikeston Mayfield
Coffeyville Joplin Aurora West Plains Dexter New Madrid Hickman Union City
Bartlesville Miami Neosho Monett Cassville Doniphan Malden Tiptonville
Vinita Lake O' Bull Shoals Gainesville Pocahontas Corning Kennett McKenzie
Claremore The Cherokees Jay Berryville L. Norfork Caruthersville Dyersburg
Tulsa Pryor Rogers Siloam Harrison L. Black Blytheville Humboldt
Wagoner Springdale Mountain White Paragould Osceola TENNESSEE
Haskell Stilwell Fayetteville Home Walnut Ridge Covington Jackson
Okmulgee Marshall Mountain Jonesboro Ripley Bolivar Henderson
Muskogee Boston Mts. View Batesville Trumann West
Sallisaw Clinton Little Red Newport Wynne Memphis
Eufaula Van Buren Clarksville Heber Springs Augusta St. Forrest MEMPHIS
Stigler Ft. Smith Russellville Searcy Francis City Holly Sprs.
McAlester Poteau Booneville McGehee Hernando
Wilburton Ouachita Mts. ARKANSAS Conway Tunica Senatobia New Albany
Heavener Waldron L. Lonoke Marianna Helena Oxford
Coalgate Mena Ouachita Little Rock Stuttgart West Helena Batesville Tupelo
Atoka Broken Hot Springs Benton Clarksdale Charleston
Antlers Bow Sheridan Aberdeen
Durant Lake Malvern Rison Rosedale Grenada West Point
Idabel Arkadelphia Pine Bluff Dumas McGehee Cleveland Winona Columbus
De Queen Nashville Fordyce Monticello Indianola Greenwood Ackerman Starkville
Paris Millwood Warren Lake Village Louisville Macon
Bonham L. Prescott Camden Greenville Belzoni Kosciusko
Clarksville Hope Hampton Hamburg MISSISSIPPI Philadelphia
Texarkana Magnolia Ouachita Crossett Yazoo City Canton
Commerce Atlanta El Dorado Lake Greenville Meridian
Mount Linden Haynesville Providence Big Black Forest
Springs Pleasant Homer Farmerville Yazoo
Quitman Pittsburg Marshall Minden Bayville Vicksburg Jackson Quitman
DALLAS Gilmer Jefferson Shreveport Ruston Monroe Tallulah
Terrell Longview Bossier Jonesboro Winnsboro Bay Sprs.
Cedar Tyler Kilgore City Columbia St. Port Hazlehurst Laurel
Creek Res. Henderson Carthage Mansfield Joseph Gibson Waynesboro
Athens Coushatta Brookhaven Monticello
Jacksonville Tenaha Winnfield Natchitoches Jena Natchez McComb Hattiesburg
Fairfield Palestine Center Colfax Columbia
Nacogdoches Toledo Many Catahoula L. Lucedale
Crockett Bend Pineville Wiggins
Centerville Lufkin San Reservoir Alexandria Marksville Bogalusa
Groveton Augustine Leesville LOUISIANA Picayune Biloxi
Madisonville Livingston Oakdale St. Francisville Amite Gulfport
Bryan L. Woodville De Ridder Ville New Roads Baton Slidell Mississippi Sd.
Navasota Huntsville Livingston Platte Rouge Hammond L.
Brenham L. Kountze Silsbee Eunice Opelousas Maurepas Pontchartrain NEW ORLEANS
Bellville Conroe Cleveland Sulphur Lake Crowley Plaquemine Metairie Chandeleur
HOUSTON Conroe Orange Charles Lafayette Donaldsonville Sd.
Liberty Calcasieu New Iberia Morgan City Pointe a la Chandeleur
Rosenberg Pasadena Beaumont L. Abbeville Franklin Houma Hache Is.
Richmond Port Arthur Sabine Grand L. Salvador Breton Sd. Mississippi
Wharton Baytown Cameron White Thibodaux River
Angleton Galveston B. L. Vermilion B. Marsh Burrs Delta
Bay City Galveston Atchafalaya B. I. Barataria B. Isles Dernieres B.

GULF   OF

MEXICO

Continuation
Southwards
on same scale

Kingsville
Hebbronville Falfurrias Sarita Padre
Zapata I.
Salado Falcon L. Raymondville Laguna Madre
MEXICO Rio Grande Edinburg
City McAllen Harlingen
San
Benito
Brownsville

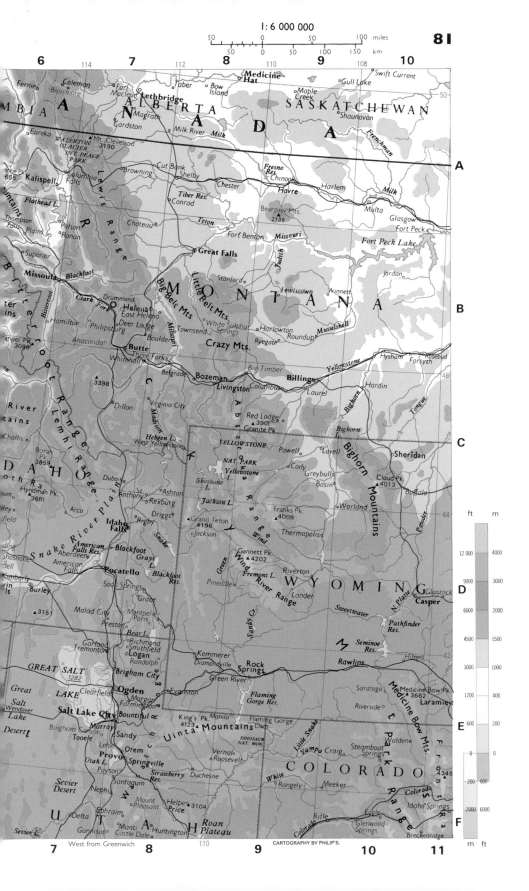

1 : 6 000 000

50   0   50   100 miles

50   0   50   100   150 km

6   114   7   112   8   110   9   108   10

CANADA

Fernie · Coleman · Blairmore · Taber · Bow Island · Medicine Hat · Gull Lake · Swift Current

MBIA · **ALBERTA** · **SASKATCHEWAN** · A

Fort Macleod · **Lethbridge** · Shaunavon

Eureka · Magrath · Milk River · Milk · Frenchman

Cardston

WATERTON GLACIER INT'L PEACE PARK · Mt. Cleveland 3190

Kalispell · Columbia Falls · Browning · Cut Bank · Shelby · Chester · Fresno Res. · Chinook · Havre · Harlem · Milk

hoe Pk 655

Flathead L. · Conrad · Tiber Res. · Havre · Malta · Glasgow

Thompson Falls · Plains · Polson · Ronan · Chateau · Teton · Fort Benton · Bearpaw Mts. 2108 · Fort Peck

Superior · Missouri · Fort Peck Lake

ter · **Missoula** · Blackfoot · **Great Falls** · Fort Peck Lake

Missoula · Blackfoot

Bitterroot · Clark Fork · Drummond · **Helena** · Stanford · Lewistown · Winnett · Jordan · B

per Pk 3096 · Hamilton · Philipsburg · East Helena · Deer Lodge · Townsend · White Sulphur Springs · Harlowton · Roundup · Musselshell

Anaconda · Boulder · Crazy Mts. · Ryegate · Hysham · Rosebud · Forsyth

Butte · Three Forks · Big Timber · Yellowstone

Whitehall · Belgrade · **Bozeman** · Livingston · Columbus · **Billings** · Hardin · Tongue

3398 · Dillon · Virginia City · Laurel · Bighorn

IDAHO · Madison · Red Lodge · 3901 · Granite Pk. · Bighorn · **Sheridan** · C

Challis · Hebgen L. · West Yellowstone · **YELLOWSTONE** · Powell · Lovell · Cloud Pk. 4013 · Buffalo

Borah Pk 3859 · Dubois · **NAT. PARK** · Yellowstone L. · Cody · Greybull · Greybulla Basin · Worland

Hyndman Pk 3681 · Ashton · Shoshone L. · Jackson L. · Franks Pk. 4009 · Thermopolis

Arco · Rexburg · Driggs · Grand Teton 4196 · Jackson · Powder

Idaho Falls · Rigby · Snake · Gannett Pk. 4202 · Riverton

American Falls Res. · Blackfoot · Grays L. · Fremont L. · Lander · **WYOMING** · Glenrock · **Casper** · D

Aberdeen · American Falls · Blackfoot Res. · Pinedale · Sandy Cr. · Sweetwater · N. Platte

Pocatello · Soda Springs · Grace · Pathfinder Res.

Burley · 3151 · Malad City · Montpelier · Paris · Seminoe Res. · Hanna

Garland · Tremonton · Richmond · Smithfield · Kemmerer · **Rock Springs** · **Rawlins** · Saratoga · Medicine Bow Pk. 3662 · **Laramie**

GREAT SALT · 1282 · **Logan** · Diamondville · Green River · Riverside

Clearfield · **Brigham City** · Flaming Gorge Res. · Little Snake · Walden

Salt Lake · **Ogden** · Morgan · Evanston · Flaming Gorge Dam

Salt Lake City · Bountiful · Farmington · King's Pk. 4123 · Manila · **Uinta Mountains** · DINOSAUR NAT. MON. · Yampa · Craig · Steamboat Springs

Desert · Murray · Sandy · Vernal · Roosevelt · White · Rangely · Meeker · **COLORADO**

Tooele · Lehi · Orem · Springville · Strawberry Res. · Duchesne · 4345 · Colorado Springs · Idaho Springs

Provo · Payson · Santaquin · Helper 3104 · Price · Roan Plateau · Rifle · Eagle · Glenwood Springs · Breckenridge

Sevier Desert · Nephi · Mount Pleasant

UTAH · Delta · Ephraim · Manti · Castle Dale · Huntington · Roan Plateau · Colorado · Glenwood Springs

Sevier L. · Gunnison

ft	m
12 000	4000
9000	3000
6000	2000
4500	1500
3000	1000
1200	400
600	200
0	0
200	600
2000	6000

m ft

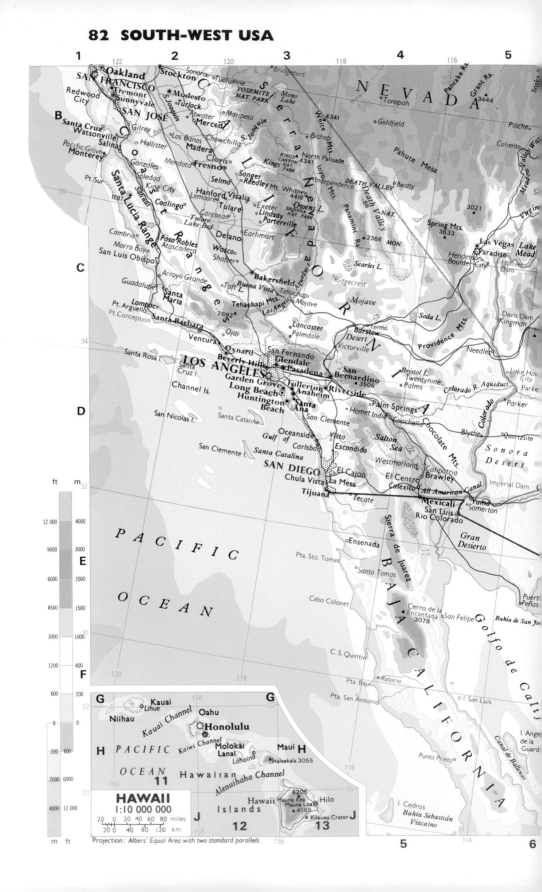

1 122 **2** 120 **3** 118 **4** 116 **5**

Oakland · Stockton · Sonora · Tuolumne · Bridgeport

SAN FRANCISCO · Modesto · Turlock · YOSEMITE NAT. PARK · Mono Lake · Tonopah · Pancake Ra. · Grant Ra.

A N E V A D A 3444

Redwood City · Fremont · Sunnyvale · Mariposa · Atwater · Merced · S. Joaquin · White · 4341

SAN JOSÉ

B Santa Cruz · Gilroy · Los Banos · Chowchilla · Bishop · Goldfield · Pioche

Watsonville · Salinas · Madera · North Palisade 4341 · Independence · Caliente

Pacific Grove · Hollister · Mendota · Clovis · Sanger · **Fresno** · KINGS CANYON NAT. PARK · Kings Ra. · Pahute Mesa

Monterey · Gonzales · Selma · Reedley · Mt Whitney 4418 · DEATH VALLEY · Beatty · Meadow Valley Wa.

Soledad · King City · Lemoore · Visalia · Exeter · SEQUOIA NAT. PARK · Death Valley · 3021

Santa Lucia Range 1787 · Salinas · Coalinga · Hanford · Tulare · Lindsay · Owens L. · Panamint Ra. · V. R. Virgin

C Cambria · Paso Robles · Corcoran · Porterville · 3366 MON. · Spring Mts. 3633

Morro Bay · Atascadero · Arroyo Grande · Tulare Lake Bed · Earlimart · Las Vegas · Lake Mead

San Luis Obispo · Delano · Searles L. · Paradise · Hoover Dam

Guadalupe · Shafter · Wasco · Ridgecrest · Henderson · Boulder City

Santa Maria · Taft · Buena Vista · **Bakersfield** · Tehachapi · Mojave · Soda L. · Davis Dam

Lompoc · Pt. Arguello · Tehachapi Mts. 2692 · Los Angeles Aqueduct · Mojave · Providence Mts. · Kingman

Pt. Conception · **Santa Barbara** · Ojai · Lancaster · Barstow · Needles

34 Santa Rosa I. · Ventura · Palmdale · Victorville · Desert · Bristol L. · Lake Hav. City

Oxnard · San Fernando · Termo · Parke

LOS ANGELES · Beverly Hills · Glendale · Pasadena · San Bernardino 3505 · Twentynine Palms · Colorado R. Aqueduct · Parker

Santa Cruz I. · Garden Grove · Fullerton · Riverside · Palm Springs · Colorado

D Channel Is. · Long Beach · Anaheim · Santa Ana · Hemet · Indio · Coachella · Blythe · Quartzsite

San Nicolas I. · Santa Catalina · Huntington Beach · San Clemente · Palm Springs · Chocolate Mts. · Sonora Desert

Oceanside · Vista · Salton Sea · Cahpatria · Imperial Dam

Gulf of · Carlsbad · Escondido · Westmorland · Brawley

Santa Catalina · **SAN DIEGO** · El Cajon · El Centro

San Clemente I. · Chula Vista · La Mesa · Calexico · All American Canal · Yuma

Tijuana · Tecate · **Mexicali** · San Luis · Somerton

Rio Colorado

E P A C I F I C · Ensenada · Gran Desierto

Pta. Sto. Tomas · Santo Tomas · Puert Peñas

O C E A N · Cabo Colonet · Cerro de la Encantada 3078 · San Felipe · Bahia de San Jo

C. S. Quintin · B A J A

F 120 118 · Pta. Baja · Rosario · I. San Luis

Pta. San Antonio · 116 · I. Ange de la Guard

G Kauai · Lihue · Oahu · **Honolulu** · 158 · G

Niihau · Kauai Channel · Kaiwi Channel

H P A C I F I C · Molokai · Lanai · Maui · H

O C E A N · Lahaina · Haleakala 3055 · 116

H a w a i i a n

Alenuihaha Channel

11

Hawaii · Mauna Kea 4206 · Hilo · J

HAWAII · Mauna Loa 4169 · Kilauea Crater

1:10 000 000 · Islands

20 0 20 40 60 80 miles
20 0 40 80 120 km

12 **13**

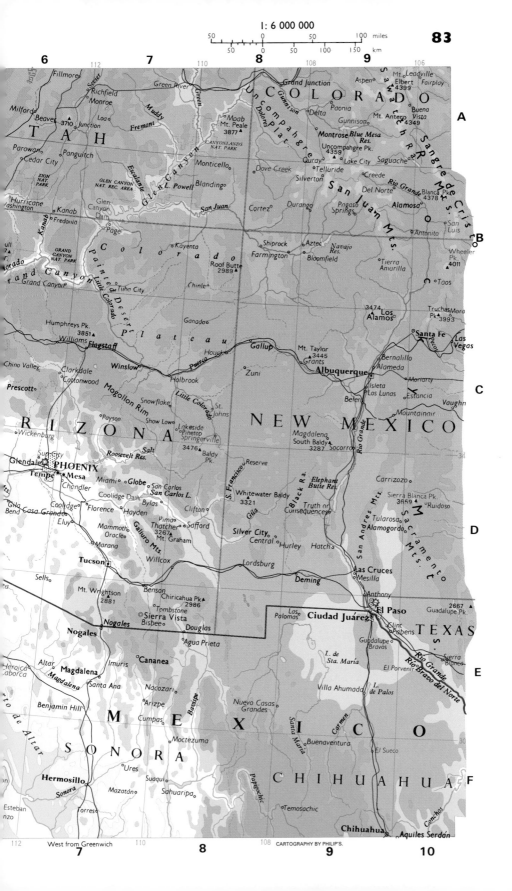

1 : 6 000 000

50   0   50   100   miles

50   0   50   100   150   km

6   112   **7**   110   **8**   108   **9**   106

Fillmore

Richfield
Monroe

Milford
Beaver
3710
Loa
Junction
Fremont
Green River
Green
Grand Junction
COLORADO
Aspen
Mt. Elbert
4399
Leadville
Fairplay
A

Delta
Paonia
Buena
Vista
4349

Parowan
Cedar City
Panguitch
Escalante
Monticello
Moab
Mt. Peale
3877
CANYONLANDS
NAT. PARK
Montrose
Uncompahgre Plateau
Blue Mesa
Res.
Mt. Antero
4349
Gunnison

ZION
NAT.
PARK
GLEN CANYON
NAT. REC. AREA.
Glen Canyon
L. Powell
Blanding
Dove Creek
Uncompahgre Pk.
4359
Ouray
Lake City
Saguache

Hurricane
Washington
Kanab
Fredonia
Page
Glen
Canyon
Dam
San Juan
Cortez
Silverton
Durango
San Juan Mts.
Telluride
Creede
Del Norte
Rio Grande
Alamosa
San
Luis
B

GRAND
CANYON
NAT. PARK
Kayenta
Roof Butte
2989
Shiprock
Aztec
Navajo
Res.
Bloomfield
Pagosa
Springs
Blanca Pk.
4378
Antonito

Grand Canyon
Little Colorado
Painted Desert
Tuba City
Chinle
Farmington
Tierra
Amarilla
Taos

Humphreys Pk.
3851
P l a t e a u
Ganado
3474
Los
Alamos
Truchas
Pk. 3993
Mora

Williams
Flagstaff
Winslow
Holbrook
Houck
Gallup
Mt. Taylor
3445
Grants
Santa Fe
Pecos
Las
Vegas
C

Chino Valley
Clarkdale
Cottonwood
Snowflake
Little Colorado
Zuni
Bernalillo
Alameda
Albuquerque

Prescott
Payson
Mogollon Rim
Show Low
Lakeside
Pinetop
Springerville
St.
Johns
Isleta
Los Lunas
Belen
Estancia
Moriarty
Vaughn

Wickenburg
A R I Z O N A
3476
Baldy
Pk.
NEW MEXICO
Magdalena
South Baldy
3287
Socorro
Mountainair
34

Glendale
Sun City
PHOENIX
Mesa
Roosevelt Res.
Salt
Reserve
S. Francisco
Whitewater Baldy
3321
Elephant
Butte Res.
Carrizozo
Sierra Blanca Mts.

Tempe
Miami
Globe
San Carlos
San Carlos L.
Gila
Truth or
Consequences
Black Ra.
Sierra Blanca Pk.
3659
Ruidoso
D

Chandler
Coolidge
Florence
Bylas
Clifton
Silver City
Central
Hurley
Hatch
Tularosa
Alamogordo
Sacramento Mts.

Casa
Grande
Coolidge Dam
Hayden
Thatcher
Safford
Mt. Graham
3267
San Andres Mts.

Eloy
Mammoth
Oracle
Galiuro Mts.
Lordsburg
Deming
Las Cruces
Mesilla

Marana
Tucson
Willcox
Benson
Anthony
Guadalupe Pk.
2667
E

Sells
Mt. Wrightson
2881
Chiricahua Pk.
2986
Tombstone
Las
Palomas
Ciudad Juárez
El Paso
Clint
Fabens
TEXAS

Nogales
Sierra Vista
Bisbee
Douglas
Guadalupe
Bravos
Rio Grande
Sierra
Blanca

Nogales
Agua Prieta
L. de
Sta. María
Rio Bravo del Norte

Heroica
Caborca
Altar
Magdalena
Imuris
Cananea
El Porvenir
Villa Ahumada
L. de
Palos
El Sueco

Santa Ana
Benjamin Hill
Nacozari
Nuevo Casas
Grandes
Buenaventura
F

M E X I C O
Arizpe
Carmen
Santa María
Conchos

S O N O R A
Cumpas
Moctezuma
C H I H U A H U A

Hermosillo
Ures
Suaqui
Sahuaripa
Bavispe
Temosachic
Chihuahua
Aquiles Serdán

Sonora
Mazatán
Torres

1:15 000 000

100   0   100   200   300   400 miles
100   0   100   200   300   400   500   600 km

6   7   8   9

UNITED STATES

Marshall
Dallas
Shreveport
Monroe
Birmingham
Columbia
Atlanta
Augusta
C. Royal
Charleston
A
Tyler
Vicksburg
Jackson
Meridian
Montgomery
Macon
Natchez
Alabama
Columbus
Savannah
Alexandria
Hattiesburg
Dothan
Albany
Altamaha
Beaumont
Lake Charles
Baton Rouge
Mobile
Pensacola
Tallahassee
Jacksonville
Port Arthur
Lafayette
Galveston
Atchafalaya
New Orleans
C. San Blas
Apalachee B.
Daytona Beach
gorda I.
de del Norte
Mississippi Delta
Orlando
C. Canaveral
christi
Tampa
Lakeland
Palm Beach
Grand Bahama
B
St. Petersburg
Sarasota
L. Okeechobee
Fort Lauderdale

GULF OF MEXICO

Miami
C. Sable
Key West
Andros I.
25
Tropic of Cancer
Florida Str.
C. Catoche
La Habana
Matanzas
Sagua la Grande
Progreso
El Cuyo
Pinar del Río
(Havana)
Cárdenas
Colón
Sta. Clara
Marianao
Caibarién
C
Temax
El Díaz
Puerto Morelos
C. San Antonio
G. de Batabanó
Sancti Spíritus
Ciego de Ávila
Mérida
Valladolid
I. de Cozumel
I. de Juventud
Cienfuegos
Trinidad
Jucaro
Peto
Campeche
Golfo de
Vigía Chico
20
Campeche
Felipe
Carillo Puerto
Grand Cayman (U.K.)
ruz
Ciudad del Carmen
Yucatan
cotalpan
Laguna de Terminos
Ciudad Chetumal
Coatzacoalcos
Corozal
Ambergris Cay
Villahermosa
Belize
Turneffe Is.
D
de
antepec
Belmopan
BELIZE
Golfo de Honduras
Tuxtla
Gutierrez
Middlesex
Pto. Barrios
Chiapa
San Cristobal
GUATEMALA
Pto. Cortés
Tela
Trujillo
Iriona
de
Huixtla
4217
La Ceiba
L. Caratasca
15
antepec
Guatemala
Zacapa
Pedro Sula
HONDURAS
C. Gracias á Dios
Sta. Ana
Sta. Rosa
Comayagua
Tegucigalpa
Jinotega
Puerto Cabezas
San Salvador
San Vicente
Nacaome
Matagalpa
Providencia (Col.)
EL SALVADOR
San Miguel
Juticalpa
El Gallo
San José
G. de Fonseca
NICARAGUA
San Andrés (Col.)
E
Sonsonate
Chinandega
León
Bluefields
Managua
Masaya
Granada
L. Nicaragua
COSTA RICA
Limón
10
Pen. de Nicoya
Colón
PANAMA
Panama
Puntarenas
San José
Chitré
La Palma
El Real
Coiba
Pen. de Azuero
Arch. de las Perlas
G. de Panama
F

West from Greenwich   90   CARTOGRAPHY BY PHILIP'S.   85

6

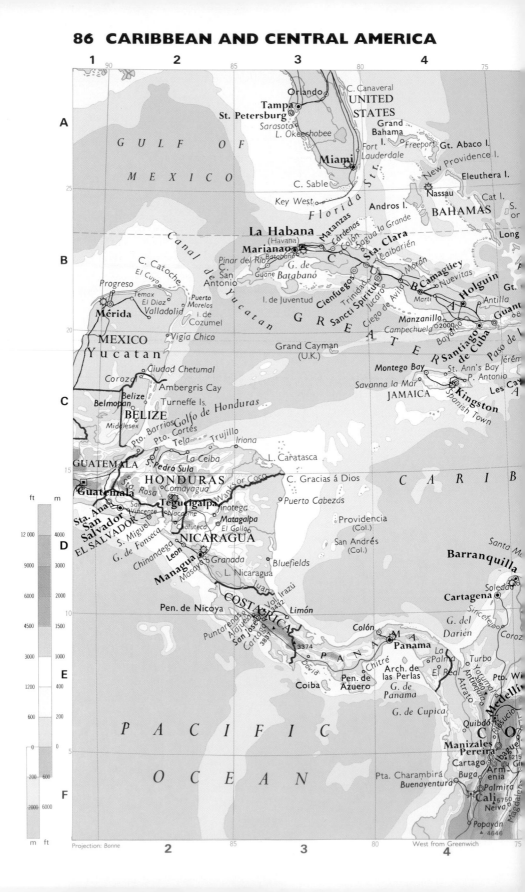

1   **2**   **3**   **4**

90   85   80   75

A

Orlando • C. Canaveral
UNITED
Tampa • **STATES**
St. Petersburg •
Sarasota • Grand
L. Okeechobee • Bahama
Freeport • Gt. Abaco I.
Miami • Fort I. New Providence I.
Lauderdale Eleuthera I.

GULF OF

MEXICO

25

C. Sable Nassau
Key West BAHAMAS Cat I.
Florida Str. Andros I. S. or
La Habana Matanzas Long
(Havana) Cárdenas Sagua la Grande
Marianao Colón **Sta. Clara** Caibarién
Pinar del Río C. G. de Caibarién Morón **Camagüey**
C. Catoche San Batabanó C Nuevitas
El Cuyo Antonio Guane I. de Juventud **Cienfuegos** Trinidad U **Holguin**
Progreso Puerto Sancti Spiritus Ciego de Ávila Martí Antilla
Témax Morelos I. de G R Manzanillo A Gt.
El Diaz Cozumel E E Campechuela 2000 **Santiago** **Guant**
Mérida Valladolid A de Cuba Paso de l
T Grand Cayman R Bay Jérém
MEXICO (U.K.) Montego Bay St. Ann's Bay
Yucatan Vigía Chico Savanna la Mar P. Antonio Les Cay
Corozal Ciudad Chetumal **JAMAICA** **Kingston** A
Ambergris Cay Spanish Town
Belize Turneffe Is.
Belmopan Middlesex **BELIZE** Barrios Golfo de Honduras
Pto. Cortés
GUATEMALA Pto. Tela Trujillo Iriona *C A R I B*
S. Rosa La Ceiba L. Caratasca
S. Pedro Sula
Guatemala Sta. **HONDURAS** Wanks or Coco C. Gracias á Dios
Sta. Ana Comayagua
San **Tegucigalpa** Jinotega Puerto Cabezas
Vincente Nacaome Matagalpa Providencia
San San El Gallo (Col.)
Salvador Miguel **NICARAGUA** San Andrés
EL SALVADOR G. de Fonseca Choluteca (Col.)
Chinandega **Managua** Masoya Bluefields **Barranquilla** Santa Me
Leon Granada
L. Nicaragua Soledad
Juan **Cartagena**
Pen. de Nicoya **COSTA RICA** Vol. Irazú Sincelejo Coroz
Puntarenas Alajuela Limón Colón Turbo
San José Cartago 3374 G. del Darién La
Coiba Pen. de **Panama** Palma El Real
Azuero Chitré Arch. de Pto. W
Coiba las Perlas
G. de David P A N A
G. de Panama
G. de Cupica **Medellín**
Quibdó C O
Pta. Charambirá **Manizales**
Buenaventura **Pereira**
Cartago
Buga Arm
enia
Palmira
Cali Gi
Neiva
Popayán 4646

B

20

C

15

D

E

10

F

5

P A C I F I C

O C E A N

Projection: Bonne   West from Greenwich

2   85   **3**   80   **4**   75

ft | m
12 000 | 4000
9000 | 3000
6000 | 2000
4500 | 1500
3000 | 1000
1200 | 400
600 | 200
0 | 0
200 | 600
2000 | 6000
m | ft

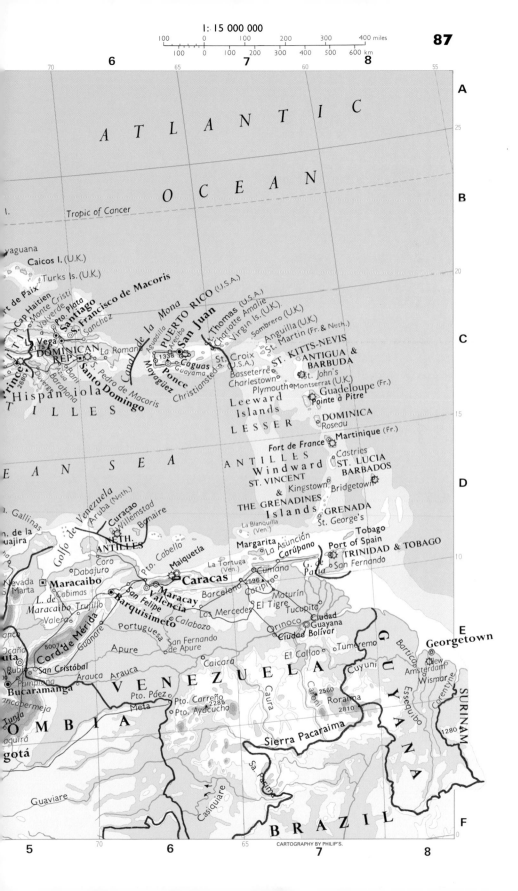

1: 15 000 000

100   0   100   200   300   400 miles

100 0 100 200 300 400 500 600 km

A T L A N T I C

O C E A N

Tropic of Cancer

A

B

C

D

E

F

yaguana

Caicos I. (U.K.)

Turks Is. (U.K.)

ort de Paix

Cap Haitien

Monte Cristi

Volverde

Pto. Plata

Santiago

S. Francisco de Macoris

Sanchez

L. Vega

175?

DOMINICAN

REP.

La Romana

S. Pedro de Macoris

Santo Domingo

Prince

2680?

Azua

Bani

Barahona

Duverge

Hispaniola

T I L L E S

A N T I L L E S

E A N   S E A

Canal de la Mona

PUERTO RICO (U.S.A.)

Aguadilla

Arecibo

San Juan

1338

Caguas

Guayama

Mayagüez

Ponce

St. Croix

(U.S.A.)

Christiansted

Thomas (U.S.A.)

Charlotte Amalie

Virgin Is. (U.K.)

Sombrero (U.K.)

Anguilla (U.K.)

St. Martin (Fr. & Neth.)

ST. KITTS-NEVIS

Basseterre

Charlestown

Plymouth

ANTIGUA &

BARBUDA

St. John's

Montserrat (U.K.)

Guadeloupe (Fr.)

Pointe à Pitre

DOMINICA

Roseau

Fort de France

Martinique (Fr.)

Castries

ST. LUCIA

BARBADOS

Bridgetown

Leeward

Islands

L E S S E R

A N T I L L E S

Windward

ST. VINCENT

& Kingstown

THE GRENADINES

Islands

GRENADA

St. George's

La Blanquilla

(Ven.)

Tobago

Port of Spain

TRINIDAD & TOBAGO

San Fernando

a. Gallinas

n. de la

uajira

Golfo de Venezuela

Aruba (Neth.)

Curacao

Willemstad

Bonaire

NETH.

ANTILLES

Coro

Dabajuro

Pto. Cabello

Maiquetia

Margarita

La Asunción

Carúpano

Cumaná

G. de

Paria

Nevada

Sta. Marta

Maracaibo

Cabimas

L. de

Maracaibo

Trujillo

Valera

Cord. de Mérida

5007

San Cristóbal

Rubio

Pamplona

Bucaramanga

ancabermeja

Tunja

O M B I A

aquirá

gotá

Guaviare

San Felipe

Valencia

Maracay

Caracas

2596

Barcelona

Las Mercedes

El Tigre

Maturín

Tucupita

Orinoco

Ciudad

Guayana

Ciudad Bolívar

Cotopi

Barquisimeto

Calabozo

Portuguesa

San Fernando

de Apure

Apure

Guanare

Meta

Arauca

Arauca

Caicara

V E N E Z U E L A

El Callao

Tumeremo

Pto. Páez

Pto. Carreño

Pto. Ayacucho

2285

Caura

El Callao

Roraima

2560

2810

Sierra Pacaraima

Casiquiare

Sa. Parima

B R A Z I L

Cuyuni

G U Y A N A

Barti

Cuni

Essequibo

Georgetown

New

Amsterdam

Wismar

orenyne

1280

SURINAM

CARTOGRAPHY BY PHILIP'S.

70   6   65   7   60   8   55

70   5   6   65   7   8

25

20

15

10

0

1 : 35 000 000

200   0   200   400   600   800 miles
400   0   400   800   1200 km

89

CARTOGRAPHY BY PHILIP'S

Projection: *Lambert's Azimuthal Equal Area*

60 West from Greenwich 50

■ LIMA   Capital Cities

PACIFIC

OCEAN

Tropic of Capricorn

San Félix (Chile)

San Ambrosio (Chile)

Arch. de Juan Fernández (Chile)

Iquique

Antofagasta

Viña del Mar
Valparaíso
SANTIAGO
Talca
Concepción
Valdivia
Puerto Montt

Gulf of Penas

C H I L E

San Miguel de Tucumán
Salta
San Juan
Mendoza
Córdoba
Santa Fe
Paraná
Rosario

Santa Cruz
Sucre

BOLIVIA

Paraguay
Pilcomayo

PARAGUAY

Asunción

Corrientes
Resistencia

Salado

A R G E N T I N A

BUENOS AIRES
La Plata
Mar del Plata
Bahía Blanca
Colorado
Negro
Chubut
Medano

Comodoro Rivadavia
Gulf of San Jorge

Punta Arenas
Magellan's Str.
Tierra del Fuego
C. Horn

MINAS GERAIS
ESPÍRITO SANTO
Vitória
Campos
Belo Horizonte
Juiz de Fora
Niterói
RIO DE JANEIRO
Ribeirão Prêto
Campinas
SÃO PAULO
Curitiba
MATO GROSSO DO SUL
Paraná
PARANÁ
SANTA CATARINA
RIO GRANDE DO SUL
Porto Alegre
Pelotas

URUGUAY
Montevideo
Río de la Plata

SOUTH

ATLANTIC

OCEAN

FALKLAND IS. (U.K.)
West Falkland
East Falkland
Stanley

South Georgia (U.K.)

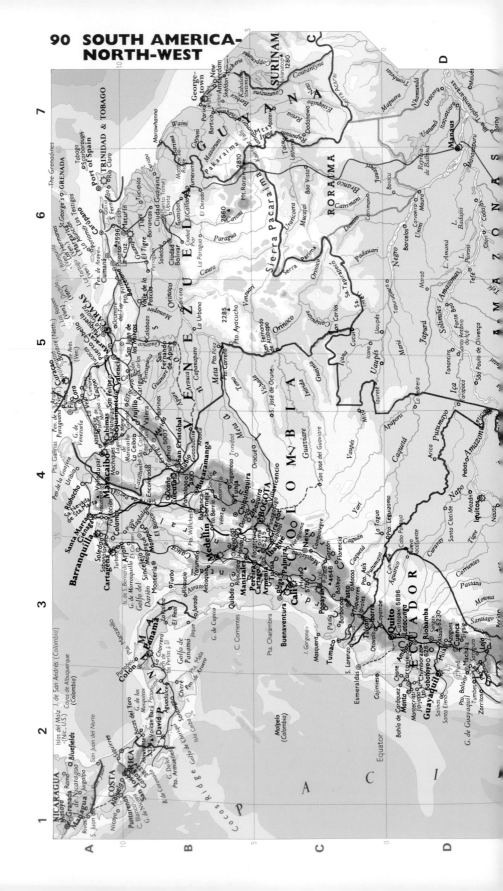

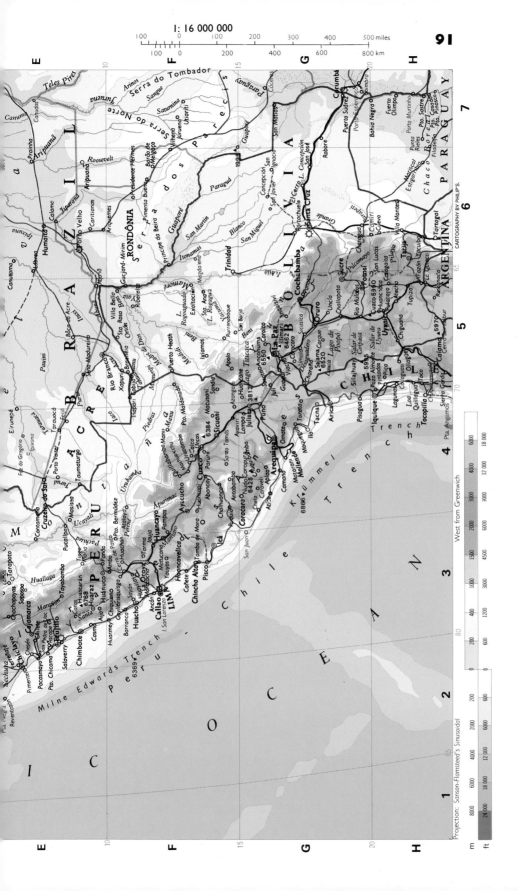

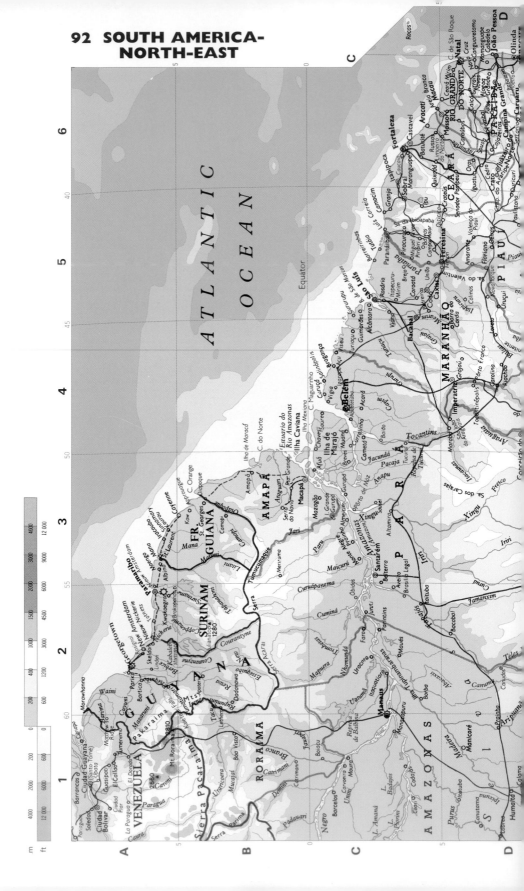

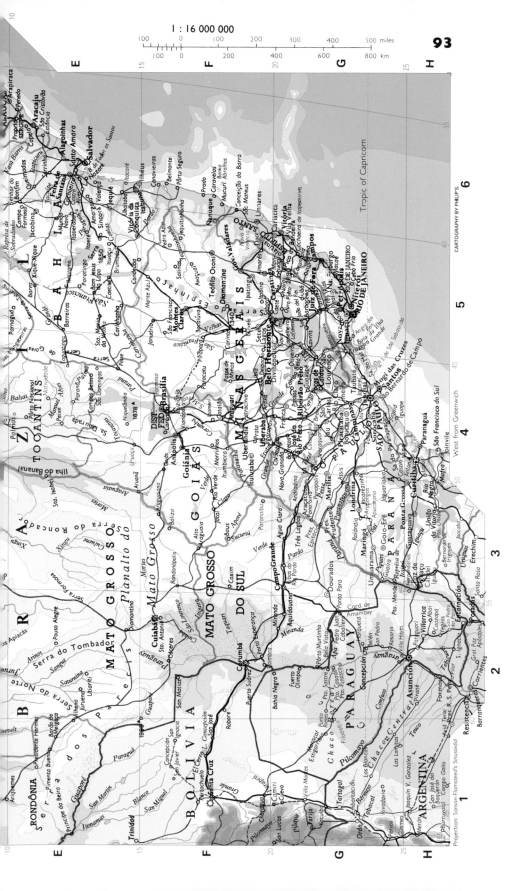

1 : 16 000 000

100   100   200   300   400   500 miles

100   0   200   400   600   800 km

CARTOGRAPHY BY PHILIPS.

Tropic of Capricorn

West from Greenwich

Projection: Sanson-Flamsteed's Sinusoidal

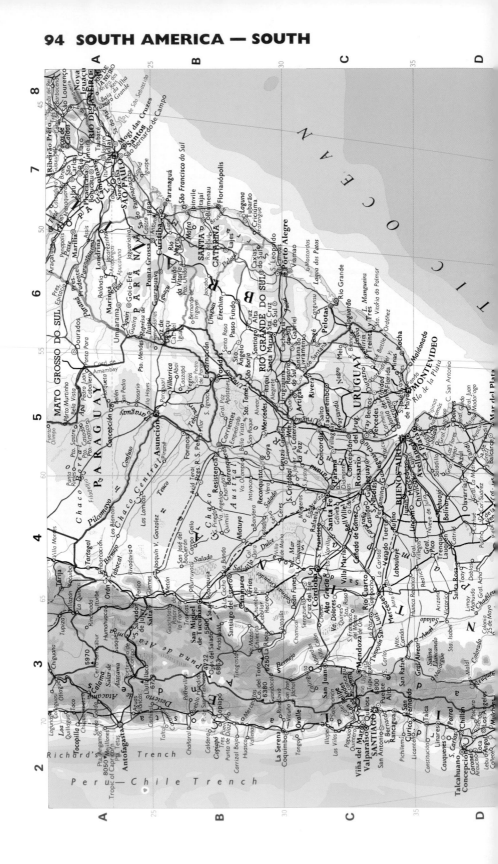

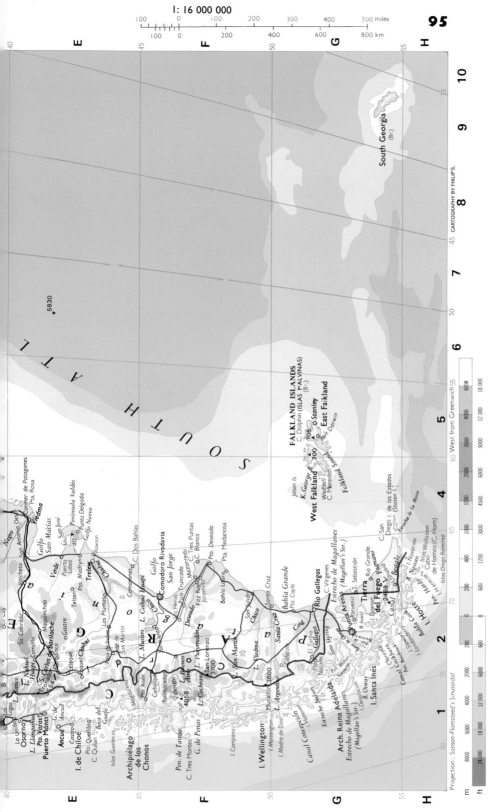

95

1: 16 000 000

| 100 | 0 | 100 | 200 | 300 | 400 | 500 miles |
| 100 | 0 | 200 | 400 | 600 | 800 km |

SOUTH ATL

South Georgia (Br.)

FALKLAND ISLANDS (ISLAS MALVINAS)
C. Dolphin
K. George B.
Weddell
C. Meredith Sd.
West Falkland
Stanley
705
700
East Falkland
Darwin
Jason Is.
Falkland

CARTOGRAPHY BY PHILIP'S.

60 West from Greenwich 95

La Unión
L. Ranco
Osorno
L. Llanquihue
Pto. Varas
Puerto Montt
Ancud
I. de Chiloé
Castro
Pto. Quellón
C. Quilán
Islas Guaitecas
Archipiélago de los Chonos
Pen. de Taitao
C. Tres Montes
G. de Penas
I. Wellington
I. Mornington
I. Madre de Dios
Arch. Reina Adelaida
Estrecho de Magallanes (Magellan's Str.)

Negro
San Antonio Oeste
Viedma
Carmen de Patagones
Pta. Rosa
Golfo San Matías
San José
Peninsula Valdés
Punta Delgada
Golfo Nuevo
Rawson
C. Dos Bahías
C. Tres Puntas
C. Blanco
Pto. Deseado
Pta. Medanosa
Golfo San Jorge
Comodoro Rivadavia
Camarones
Trelew
Puerto Lobos
Verde

Mazorredo
Deseado
Fitz Roy
Jaramillo
Bahía Laura
San Julián
Santa Cruz
Bahía Grande
Pto. Coyle
C. Vírgenes
Río Gallegos
Estrecho de Magallanes (Magellan's Str.)
Punta Arenas
Oroveni
C. San Sebastián
Río Grande
Tierra del Fuego
Ushuaia
Camar
C. San Diego
I. de los Estados (Staten I.)
Estrecho de Le Maire
B. Nassau
Islas Wollaston
Cabo de Hornos (C. Horn)
Islas Diego Ramírez

Projection: Sanson-Flamsteed's Sinusoidal

| m | 8000 | 6000 | 4000 | 2000 | 1500 | 1000 | 400 | 200 | 0 | 200 | 600 |
| ft | 24,000 | 18,000 | 12,000 | 6000 | 4500 | 3000 | 1200 | 600 | 0 | 600 | 6000 9000 12,000 18,000 |

5830

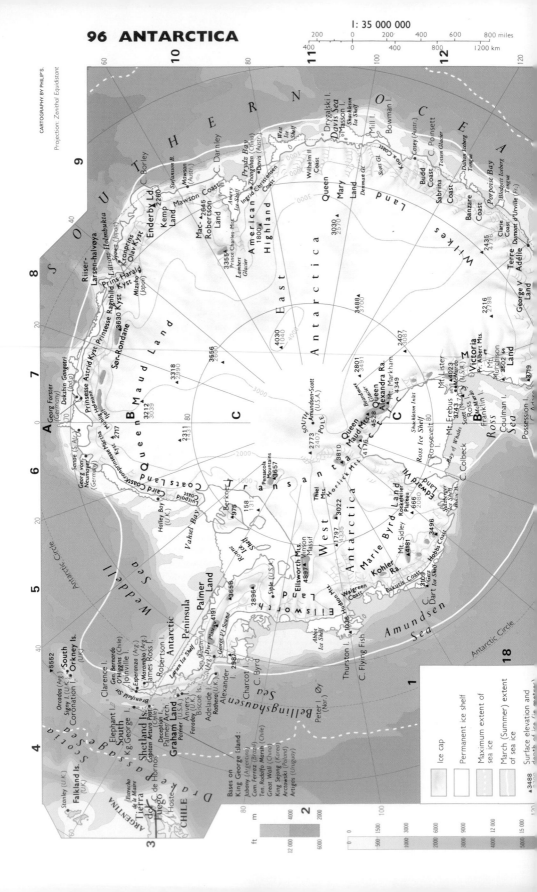

1 : 35 000 000

CARTOGRAPHY BY PHILIP'S.

Projection: Zenithal Equidistant

Legend:

- Ice cap
- Permanent ice shelf
- Maximum extent of sea ice
- March (Summer) extent of sea ice
- ▲3488 Surface elevation and depth of ice (in metres)

Bases on King George Island:
Jubany (Argentina)
Cam. Ferraz (Brazil)
Ten. Rodolfo Marsh (Chile)
Great Wall (China)
King Sejong (Korea)
Arctowski (Poland)
Artigas (Uruguay)

Index to Map Pages

The index contains the names of all principal places and features shown on the maps. Physical features composed of a proper name (Erie) and a description (Lake) are positioned alphabetically by the proper name. The description is positioned after the proper name and is usually abbreviated:

Erie, L. **72** **C5**

Where a description forms part of a settlement or administrative name however, it is always written in full and put in its true alphabetical position:

Lake Charles   **79**   **D7**

Names beginning St. are alphabetized under Saint, but Sankt, Sint, Sant, Santa and San are all spelt in full and are alphabetized accordingly.

The number in bold type which follows each name in the index refers to the number of the map page where that feature or place will be found. This is usually the largest scale at which the place or feature appears.

The letter and figure which are in bold type immediately after the page number give the grid square on the map page, within which the feature is situated.

Rivers carry the symbol ⤳ after their names. A solid square ■ follows the name of a country while an open square ☐ refers to a first order administrative area.

A

A Coruña = La
  Coruña **18** **A1**
Aachen **14** **C4**
Aalborg =
  Ålborg **9** **G9**
Aalen **14** **D6**
Aarau **13** **C8**
Aare ⤳ **13** **C8**
Aarhus = Århus **9** **G10**
Aba **55** **G6**
Ābādān **47** **E7**
Ābādeh **44** **D3**
Abadla **54** **B4**
Abaetetuba . . . **92** **C4**
Abakan **30** **D7**
Abancay **91** **F4**
Abarqū **44** **D3**
Abashiri **32** **F12**
Abay **29** **E8**
Abaya, L. **53** **G6**
Abbay = Nîl el
  Azraq ⤳ . . . **53** **E5**
Abbeville **12** **A4**
Abbieglassie . . **63** **A5**
Abbot Ice Shelf **96** **B2**
Abbottabad . . . **42** **B8**
Abd al Kūrī . . . **49** **E5**
Abéché **53** **F3**
Abeokuta **55** **G5**
Abercorn =
  Mbala **57** **F6**
Abercorn **63** **A5**
Aberdeen,
  Australia **63** **B5**
Aberdeen, *U.K.* **10** **C5**
Aberdeen,
  S. Dak., U.S.A. **76** **C5**

Aberdeen,
  Wash., U.S.A. **80** **B2**
Aberystwyth . . **11** **E4**
Abidjan **55** **G4**
Abilene **78** **C4**
Abitibi L. **69** **D3**
Abkhaz
  Republic ☐ =
  Abkhazia ☐ . **25** **E5**
Abkhazia ☐ . . **25** **E5**
Abminga **62** **A1**
Åbo = Turku . **9** **F12**
Abohar **42** **D9**
Aboméy **55** **G5**
Abong-Mbang . **56** **D2**
Abou-Deïa **53** **F2**
Abri **52** **D5**
Abrolhos, Banka **93** **F6**
Abrud **17** **E6**
Absaroka Range **81** **C9**
Abū al Khaşīb . **47** **E6**
Abū 'Alī **47** **E7**
Abu 'Arīsh **49** **D3**
Abu Dhabi =
  Abū Ẓaby . . **44** **E3**
Abû Dis **53** **E5**
Abu Hamed . . . **53** **E5**
Abū Kamāl **46** **D5**
Abū Madd, Ra's **47** **F4**
Abu Matariq . . **53** **F4**
Abu Rudeis . . . **47** **E3**
Abu Tig **52** **C5**
Abû Zabad **53** **F4**
Abū Ẓaby **44** **E3**
Abuja **55** **G6**
Abukuma-
  Gawa ⤳ . . . **33** **G12**
Abunã **91** **E5**
Abunã ⤳ **91** **E5**

Abut Hd. **65** **E4**
Abwong **53** **G5**
Acaponeta **84** **C3**
Acapulco **84** **D5**
Acarigua **90** **B5**
Accra **55** **G4**
Aceh ☐ **36** **D1**
Achalpur **43** **J10**
Achill I. **11** **E1**
Achinsk **30** **D7**
Acireale **21** **F5**
Acklins I. **86** **B5**
Aconcagua,
  Cerro **94** **C3**
Aconquija, Mt. . **94** **B3**
Açores, Is. dos
  = Azores . . . **50** **C1**
Acraman, L. . . . **62** **B2**
Acre = 'Akko . . **46** **D3**
Acre ☐ **91** **E4**
Acre ⤳ **91** **E5**
Ad Dahnā **47** **F7**
Ad Dammām . . **47** **F7**
Ad Dawhah . . . **44** **E2**
Ad Dilam **47** **G6**
Ad Dīwānīyah . **47** **E6**
Ada **79** **B5**
Adaja ⤳ **18** **B3**
Adam **44** **F4**
Adamaoua,
  Massif de l' . **53** **G1**
Adamawa
  Highlands =
  Adamaoua,
  Massif de l' . **53** **G1**
Adamello, Mte. . **20** **A3**
Adaminaby . . . **63** **C4**
Adam's Bridge **43** **Q11**
Adams Mt. **80** **B3**

Adana **46** **C3**
Adapazarı **46** **B2**
Adarama **53** **E5**
Adare, C. **96** **B15**
Adaut **39** **F4**
Adavale **63** **A3**
Adda ⤳ **20** **B2**
Addis Ababa =
  Addis Abeba **53** **G6**
Addis Abeba . . **53** **G6**
Addis Alem . . . **53** **G6**
Adelaide **62** **B2**
Adelaide I. **96** **A3**
Adelaide Pen. . **70** **B10**
Adélie, Terre . . **96** **A14**
Adélie Land =
  Adélie, Terre **96** **A14**
Aden = Al
  'Adan **49** **E4**
Aden, G. of . . . **49** **E4**
Adi **39** **E4**
Adi Ugri **53** **E6**
Adige ⤳ **20** **B4**
Adilabad **43** **K11**
Adirondack Mts. **73** **C8**
Admer **54** **D6**
Admiralty I. . . . **71** **C6**
Admiralty Is. . . **64** **K9**
Ado-Ekiti **55** **G6**
Adonara **39** **F2**
Adoni **43** **M10**
Adour ⤳ **12** **E3**
Adra **18** **D4**
Adrano **21** **F5**
Adrar **54** **C4**
Adré **53** **F3**
Adri **52** **C1**
Adriatic Sea . . . **20** **C5**
Adua **39** **E3**

Adwa

Adwa 53 F6
Adzhar
  Republic □ =
  Ajaria □ 25 E5
Ægean Sea ... 23 E5
Aerhtai Shan .. 34 B4
Afghanistan ■ . 45 C6
Afgoi 49 G3
'Afif 47 G5
Afognak I. 71 C4
Afuá 92 C3
Afyonkarahisar 46 C2
Agadès =
  Agadez 55 E6
Agadez 55 E6
Agadir 54 B3
Agapa 30 B6
Agartala 41 F8
Agats 39 F5
Agboville 55 G4
Agde 13 E5
Agen 12 D4
Agra 42 F10
Agri → 21 D6
Ağrı Dağı 46 C6
Ağrı Karakose . 46 C5
Agrigento 21 F4
Agrinion 23 E3
Água Clara .. 93 G3
Agua Prieta ... 84 A3
Aguadas 90 B3
Aguadilla 87 C6
Aguarico → .. 90 D3
Aguas Blancas 94 A3
Aguascalientes 84 C4
Aguilas 19 D5
Agulhas, C. ... 58 E4
Agung 37 F5
Agusan → ... 38 C3
Ahaggar 54 D6
Ahar 46 C6
Ahipara B. 64 A5
Ahiri 43 K12
Ahmadabad ... 43 H8
Ahmadnagar .. 43 K9
Ahmadpur ... 42 E7
Ahmedabad =
  Ahmadabad . 43 H8
Ahmednagar =
  Ahmadnagar 43 K9
Ahvāz 47 E7
Ahvenanmaa =
  Åland 9 F11
Aḥwar 49 E4
Aigues-Mortes . 13 E6
Aihui 35 A7
Aija 91 E3
Aiken 75 C7
Aimere 39 F2
Aimorés 93 F5
Ain Banaiyan .. 44 F2
Aïn Beïda 54 A6
Aïn Ben Tili .. 54 C3
Aïn-Sefra 54 B4
Ainabo 49 F4
Aïr 55 E6
Aisne → 13 B5
Aiud 17 E6
Aix-en-Provence 13 E6
Aix-la-Chapelle
  = Aachen .. 14 C4
Aix-les-Bains .. 13 D6
Aiyion 23 E4
Aizawl 41 F9
Ajaccio 13 F8
Ajanta Ra. 43 J9
Ajari Rep. =
  Ajaria □ 25 E5
Ajaria □ 25 E5

Ajdâbiyah 52 B3
Ajka 16 E3
'Ajmān 44 E3
Ajmer 42 F9
Ajo, C. de 18 A4
Akaroa 65 E5
Akashi 32 B4
Akelamo 39 D3
Aketi 56 D4
Akharnaí 23 E4
Akhelöös → .. 23 E3
Akhisar 23 E6
Akhmīm 52 C5
Akimiski I. 69 C2
Akita 33 G12
Akjoujt 55 E2
'Akko 46 D3
Akkol 29 E8
Aklavik 70 B6
Akmolinsk =
  Astana 29 D8
Akobo → 53 G5
Akola 43 J10
Akordat 53 E6
Akpatok I. 68 B4
Akreïjit 55 E3
Akron 72 D5
Aksai Chin ... 42 B11
Aksaray 46 C3
Aksarka 28 C7
Akşehir 46 C2
Aksu 34 B3
Aksum 53 F6
Aktogay 29 E8
Aktsyabrski ... 17 B9
Aktyubinsk =
  Aqtöbe 29 D6
Aku 55 G6
Akure 55 G6
Akyab = Sittwe 41 G9
Al 'Adan 49 E4
Al Aḥsā 47 F7
Al Amādīyah .. 46 C5
Al Amārah 47 E6
Al 'Aqabah 47 E3
Al 'Aramah ... 47 F6
Al Ashkhara .. 45 F4
Al Badī' 47 G6
Al Başrah 47 E6
Al Bayḍā 52 B3
Al Bu'ayrāt al
  Ḥasūn 52 B2
Al Fallūjah 46 D5
Al Fāw 47 E7
Al Fujayrah ... 44 E4
Al Hābah 47 F6
Al Haddār 47 G6
Al Hāmad 47 E4
Al Ḥamar 47 G6
Al Ḥamrā' 47 F4
Al Ḥarīq 47 G6
Al Ḥasakah ... 46 C5
Al Ḥawrah 49 E4
Al Ḥayy 47 D6
Al Ḥijāz 47 F4
Al Ḥillah, Iraq . 47 D6
Al Ḥillah,
  Si. Arabia .. 47 G6
Al Hindīyah ... 47 D6
Al Hoceïma ... 54 A4
Al Ḥudaydah .. 49 E3
Al Ḥufūf 47 F7
Al Ḥulwah 47 G6
Al Ittihad =
  Madīnat ash
  Sha'b 49 E3
Al Jāfūrah 47 F7
Al Jaghbūb ... 52 C3
Al Jahrah 47 E6

Al Jalāmīd 47 E4
Al Jawf, Libya . 52 D3
Al Jawf,
  Si. Arabia ... 47 E4
Al Jazirah, Iraq 46 D5
Al Jazirah, Libya 52 C3
Al Jubayl 47 F7
Al Jubaylah ... 47 F6
Al Junaynah .. 53 F3
Al Khābūra ... 44 F4
Al Khalīl 47 E3
Al Kharfah 47 G6
Al Kharj 47 F6
Al Khasab 44 E4
Al Kufrah 52 D3
Al Kūt 47 D6
Al Kuwayt 47 E7
Al Lādhiqīyah . 46 D3
Al Luḥayyah .. 49 D3
Al Madīnah ... 47 F4
Al Majma'ah .. 47 F6
Al Manāmah .. 44 E2
Al Marj 52 B3
Al Mawṣil 46 C5
Al Midhnab ... 47 F6
Al Mish'āb 47 E7
Al Mubarraz .. 47 F7
Al Muḥarraq .. 44 E2
Al Mukallā ... 49 E4
Al Mukhā 49 E3
Al Musayyib .. 47 D6
Al Muwaylih .. 47 F3
Al Qaḍīmah ... 47 G4
Al Qā'iyah 47 F5
Al Qāmishli ... 46 C5
Al Qaṣabát ... 52 B1
Al Qaṣīm 47 F5
Al Qaṭīf 47 F7
Al Qaṭrūn 52 D2
Al Qayṣūmah . 47 E6
Al Quaisūmah . 47 E6
Al Quds =
  Jerusalem .. 47 E3
Al Qurayyāt .. 45 E4
Al Qurnah 47 E6
Al 'Ulā 47 F4
Al Uqaylah ash
  Sharqīgah .. 52 B2
Al Uqayr 47 F7
Al 'Uthmānīyah 47 F7
Al 'Uwaynid ... 47 F6
Al 'Uwayqīlah . 47 E5
Al 'Uyūn 47 F5
Al Wakrah 44 E2
Al Wari'āh 47 F6
Al Yamāmah .. 47 F6
Alabama □ ... 74 C4
Alabama → .. 74 D4
Alaçam Dağları 23 E7
Alagoa Grande 92 D6
Alagoas □ 93 D6
Alagoinhas ... 93 E6
Alajuela 86 D3
Alamosa 83 B10
Åland 9 F11
Alania = North
  Ossetia □ ... 25 E5
Alanya 46 C2
Alapayevsk ... 29 D7
Alaşehir 23 E7
Alaska □ 71 B4
Alaska, G. of . 71 C5
Alaska Peninsula 71 C4
Alaska Range . 71 B4
Alataw Shankou 34 B3
Alatyr 24 C6
Alausi 90 D3
Alawoona 62 B3
Alba 20 B2

Alba-Iulia 17 E6
Albacete 19 C5
Albacutya, L. .. 62 C3
Albania ■ ... 23 D3
Albany,
  Australia 60 H2
Albany, Ga.,
  U.S.A. 75 D5
Albany, N.Y.,
  U.S.A. 73 C9
Albany, Oreg.,
  U.S.A. 80 C2
Albany → ... 69 C2
Albardón 94 C3
Albemarle 75 B7
Alberche → .. 18 C3
Albert, L. 62 C2
Albert L. 57 D6
Albert Nile → . 57 D6
Albertville 13 D7
Albi 12 E5
Albina 92 A3
Alborán 18 E4
Ålborg 9 G9
Alborz, Reshteh-
  ye Kūhhā-ye . 44 B3
Albuquerque .. 83 C9
Albury 63 C4
Alcalá de
  Henares 18 B4
Alcalá la Real . 18 D4
Alcamo 21 F4
Alcaníz 19 B5
Alcântara 92 C5
Alcântara,
  Embalse de . 18 C2
Alcantarilla ... 19 D5
Alcaraz, Sierra
  de 19 C4
Alcaudete 18 D3
Alcázar de San
  Juan 18 C4
Alchevsk 25 D4
Alcira 19 C5
Alcoy 19 C5
Aldabra Is. 51 G8
Aldan → 31 C10
Alderney 11 G5
Aleg 55 E2
Alegrete 94 B5
Aleisk 29 D9
Aleksandriya =
  Oleksandriya 17 C8
Aleksandrovskoye
  .... 29 C8
Alemania 94 B3
Alençon 12 B4
Aleppo = Ḥalab 46 C4
Alès 13 D6
Alessándria .. 20 B2
Ålesund 8 F9
Aleutian Is. ... 71 C2
Alexander Arch. 71 C6
Alexander I. ... 96 A3
Alexandra,
  Australia 63 C4
Alexandra, N.Z. 65 F3
Alexandria = El
  Iskandarīya .. 52 B4
Alexandria,
  Canada 71 C7
Alexandria,
  Romania 22 C5
Alexandria,
  S. Africa 59 E5
Alexandria, La.,
  U.S.A. 79 D7
Alexandria, Va.,
  U.S.A. 73 E7

Alexandrina, L. 62 C2
Alexandroúpolis 22 D5
Alga 29 E6
Algarve 18 D1
Algeciras 18 D3
Algemesi 19 C5
Alger 54 A5
Algeria ■ 54 C5
Alghero 21 D2
Algiers = Alger 54 A5
Algoa B. 59 E5
Alhucemas = Al
Hoceïma .. 54 A4
'Alī al Gharbī .. 47 D6
'Alī Khēl 42 C6
Aliağa 23 E6
Alibo 53 G6
Alicante 19 C5
Alice Springs .. 60 E5
Aligarh 42 F11
Aligūdarz 46 D7
Alipur 42 E7
Alipur Duar ... 41 D7
Aliwal North .. 59 E5
Aljustrel 18 D1
Alkmaar 14 B3
All American
Canal 82 D5
Allahabad 40 E3
Allanmyo 41 H10
Allegheny → . 73 D5
Allegheny
Plateau 73 F5
Allentown 73 D8
Alleppey 43 Q10
Aller → 14 B5
Allier → 13 C5
Allora 63 A5
Alma Ata =
Almaty 29 E8
Almada 18 C1
Almadén 18 C3
Almansa 19 C5
Almanzor, Pico
del Moro ... 18 B3
Almanzora → . 19 D5
Almaty 29 E8
Almazán 19 B4
Almeirim 92 C3
Almelo 14 B4
Almendralejo .. 18 C2
Almería 19 D4
Almora 42 E11
Alnwick 10 D6
Alon 41 F10
Alor 39 F2
Alor Setar ... 36 C2
Alps 14 E5
Alsace 13 B7
Alsask 71 C9
Alsásua 19 A4
Alta Gracia ... 94 C4
Altagracia ... 90 A4
Altai = Aerhtai
Shan 34 B4
Altamira 92 C3
Altamura 21 D6
Altanbulag ... 35 A5
Altay 34 B3
Altea 19 C5
Alto Araguaia . 93 F3
Alto Molocue .. 59 B7
Alton 77 F9
Alton Downs .. 62 A2
Altoona 73 D6
Altun Shan ... 34 C3
Alùla 49 E5
Alusi 39 F4
Alvarado 85 D5

Alvear 94 B5
Alvie 62 C3
Alwar 42 F10
Alxa Zuoqi 35 C5
Am Dam 53 F3
Am-Timan 53 F3
Amâdi, Sudan . 53 G5
Amadi,
Dem. Rep. of the Congo
.... 57 D5
Amadjuak 68 B3
Amadjuak L. .. 68 B3
Amagasaki 32 B4
Amakusa-Shotō 32 C2
Amaliás 23 F3
Amalner 43 J9
Amambay,
Cordillera de 94 A5
Amangeldy ... 29 D7
Amapá 92 B3
Amapá □ 92 B3
Amarante 92 D5
Amargosa 93 E6
Amarillo 78 B3
Amaro, Mte. .. 20 C5
Amasra 46 B3
Amasya 46 B3
Amazon =
Amazonas → 92 C3
Amazonas □ .. 90 D6
Amazonas → . 92 C3
Ambala 42 D10
Ambalavao ... 59 J9
Ambam 56 D2
Ambanja 59 G9
Ambartsevo ... 29 D9
Ambato 90 D3
Ambatolampy . 59 H9
Ambatondrazaka 59 H9
Amberg 15 D6
Ambergris Cay 85 D7
Amberley 65 E5
Ambikapur 40 F4
Ambilobé 59 G9
Ambo 91 F3
Amboise 12 C4
Ambon 39 E3
Ambositra 59 J9
Amboyna I. ... 36 C4
Ambriz 56 F2
Amby 63 A4
Amchitka I. ... 71 C1
Amderma 28 C7
Ameca 84 C4
Ameland 14 B3
American
Highland 96 B10
American
Samoa ■ ... 65 L13
Americus 75 C5
Amery 71 C10
Amery Ice Shelf 96 A10
Ames 77 D8
Amherst, Burma 41 J11
Amherst,
Canada 69 D4
Amiata, Mte. .. 20 C3
Amiens 12 B5
Amirante Is. ... 26 K9
'Ammān 47 E3
Amorgós 23 F5
Amoy = Xiamen 35 D6
Ampanihy 59 J8
Ampenan 37 F5
Amper → 15 D6
Amravati 43 J10
Amreli 43 J7
Amritsar 42 D9
Amroha 42 E11

Amsterdam ... 14 B3
Amstetten 15 D8
Amudarya → . 29 E6
Amundsen Gulf 70 A7
Amundsen Sea 96 B1
Amuntai 37 E5
Amur → 31 D12
Amurang 39 D2
Amuri Pass ... 65 E5
Amyderya =
Amudarya → 29 E6
An Nafūd 47 E5
An Najaf 47 D6
An Nhon 36 B3
An Nu'aynyah . 47 F7
Anabar → 30 B9
Anaconda 81 B7
Anadolu 46 C2
'Ānah 46 D5
Anaheim 82 D4
Anakapalle ... 40 J4
Analalava 59 G8
Anambas,
Kepulauan .. 37 D3
Anambas Is. =
Anambas,
Kepulauan .. 37 D3
Anamur 46 C3
Anan 32 C4
Anantnag 42 C9
Ananyiv 17 E9
Anápolis 93 F4
Anār 44 D3
Anārak 44 C3
Anatolia =
Anadolu ... 46 C2
Añatuya 94 B4
Anaye 53 E1
Anchorage ... 71 B5
Ancohuma,
Nevada, ... 91 G5
Ancón 91 F3
Ancona 20 C4
Ancud 95 E2
Ancud, G. de .. 95 E2
Andalgalá 94 B3
Andalucía □ .. 18 D3
Andalusia 74 D4
Andalusia =
Andalucía □ . 18 D3
Andaman Is. .. 27 H13
Andaman Sea . 36 B1
Andara 58 B4
Anderson 72 D3
Anderson → .. 70 B7
Andes = Andes,
Cord. de los . 91 G4
Andes, Cord. de
los 91 G4
Andhra
Pradesh □ .. 43 L11
Andijon 29 E8
Andikíthira ... 23 G4
Andizhan =
Andijon 29 E8
Andkhvoy 45 B6
Andoany 59 G9
Andorra ■ ... 19 A6
Andorra La Vella 19 A6
Andreanof Is. .. 71 C2
Andrewilla ... 62 A2
Ándria 20 D6
Andriba 59 H9
Andropov =
Rybinsk 24 B4
Ándros 23 F5
Andros I. 86 B4
Andújar 18 C3
Andulo 56 G3

Aného 55 G5
Aneto, Pico de . 19 A6
Angamos, Punta 94 A2
Ang'angxi 35 B7
Angara → 30 D7
Angarsk 30 D8
Angaston 62 B2
Ånge 8 F11
Angeles 38 A2
Angellala 63 A4
Angermanälven →
.... 8 F11
Angers 12 C3
Anglesey 11 E4
Ango 57 D5
Angola ■ 58 A3
Angoulême ... 12 D4
Angoumois ... 12 D4
Angra dos Reis 94 A8
Angren 29 E8
Anguilla ■ ... 87 C7
Anhui □ 35 C6
Anhwei □ =
Anhui □ 35 C6
Anjidiv I. 43 M9
Anjou 12 C3
Anjozorobe ... 59 H9
Anju 35 C7
Anka 55 F6
Ankang 35 C5
Ankara 46 C3
Ankazoabo ... 59 J8
Ankazobe 59 H9
Ankoro 57 F5
Ann Arbor ... 72 C4
Annaba 54 A6
Annan 11 D5
Annapolis 73 E7
Annecy 13 D7
Anning 34 D5
Anniston 74 C5
Annobón 51 G4
Annuello 62 B3
Anqing 35 C6
Ansbach 14 D6
Anshan 35 B7
Anshun 35 D5
Ansirabe 59 H9
Ansongo 55 E5
Ansudu 39 E5
Antabamba ... 91 F4
Antakya 46 C4
Antalaha 59 G10
Antalya 46 C2
Antalya Körfezi 46 C2
Antananarivo . 59 H9
Antarctic Pen. . 96 A4
Antarctica .... 96 C
Antequera ... 18 D3
Anti Atlas 54 C3
Antibes 13 E7
Anticosti, I. d' . 69 D4
Antigua &
Barbuda ■ .. 87 C7
Antilla 86 B4
Antioquia 90 B3
Antofagasta .. 94 A2
Antofagasta de
la Sierra ... 94 B3
Antongila,
Helodrano . 59 H9
Antonina 94 B7
Antrim 11 D3
Antsalova 59 H8
Antsiranana .. 59 G9
Antsohihy 59 G9
Antwerp =
Antwerpen . 14 C3
Antwerpen 14 C3

Anupgarh 42 E8
Anvers =
  Antwerpen .. 14 C3
Anvers I. 96 A3
Anxi 34 B4
Anxious B. 62 B1
Anyang 35 C6
Anzhero-
  Sudzhensk .. 29 D9
Ánzio 20 D4
Aomori 33 F12
Aoraki
  Mt. Cook 65 E4
Aosta 20 B1
Aoudéras 55 E6
Aoulef el Arab . 54 C5
Apalachicola → 74 E5
Apaporis → .. 90 D5
Aparri 38 A2
Apeldoorn .. 14 B3
Apennines =
  Appennini .. 20 B3
Apia 65 L13
Apiacás, Serra
  dos 91 E7
Aplao 91 G4
Apo, Mt. 38 C3
Apollonia =
  Marsá Susah 52 B3
Apolo 91 F5
Apoteri 90 C7
Appalachian
  Mts. 73 F5
Appennini 20 B3
Appleton 72 B1
Approuague .. 92 B3
Aprília 20 D4
Apucarana 94 A6
Apure → 90 B5
Apurimac → . 91 F4
Aqabah = Al
  'Aqabah 47 E3
'Aqabah, Khalīj
  al 47 E3
Āqcheh 45 B6
Aqîq .... 53 'E6
Aqmola =
  Astana 29 D8
Aqrah 46 C5
Aqtöbe 29 D6
Aquidauana .. 93 G2
Aquitain, Bassin 12 D3
Ar Rachidiya .. 54 B4
Ar Ramādī 46 D5
Ar Raqqah 46 D4
Ar Rass 47 F5
Ar Rifā'ī 47 E6
Ar Riyād 47 F6
Ar Ruṭbah 46 D5
Ar Ruwaydah . 47 G6
Ara 40 E5
'Arab, Bahr el → 53 G4
'Arab, Shatt al → 47 E7
Arabian Desert
  = Es Sahrâ'
  Esh Sharqîya 52 C5
Arabian Gulf =
  Gulf, The ... 44 E2
Arabian Sea ... 26 H10
Araç 46 B3
Aracaju 93 E6
Aracataca 90 A4
Aracati 92 C6
Araçatuba 93 G3
Aracena 18 D2
Araçuaí 93 F5
Arad 16 E5
Arada 53 F3
Arafura Sea ... 39 F4
Aragón □ 19 B5

Aragón → 19 A5
Araguacema .. 92 D4
Araguaia → .. 92 D4
Araguari 93 F4
Araguari → .. 92 B4
Arak 54 C5
Arakan Coast .. 41 H9
Arakan Yoma . 41 H10
Araks = Aras,
  Rūd-e → ... 46 B7
Aral 29 E7
Aral Sea 29 E6
Aral Tengizi =
  Aral Sea 29 E6
Aralsk = Aral .. 29 E7
Aralskoye More
  = Aral Sea .. 29 E6
Aran I. 10 D2
Aran Is. 11 E2
Aranda de
  Duero 18 B4
Aranjuez 18 B4
Aranos 58 C3
Araouane 55 E4
Arapgir 46 C4
Arapiraca 93 D6
Arapongas .. 94 A6
Araranguá 94 B7
Araraquara .. 93 G4
Ararat 62 C3
Ararat, Mt. =
  Ağrı Dağı ... 46 C6
Araripe,
  Chapada do . 92 D6
Aras, Rūd-e → 46 B7
Arauca 90 B4
Arauca → 90 B5
Arauco 94 D2
Araxá 93 F4
Araya, Pen. de . 90 A6
Arbatax 21 E2
Arbīl 46 C6
Arbroath 10 C5
Arcachon 12 D3
Archangel =
  Arkhangelsk . 28 C5
Arcila = Asilah 54 A3
Arckaringa ... 62 A1
Arckaringa
  Cr. → 62 A2
Arcos de la
  Frontera 18 D3
Arcot 43 N11
Arcoverde ... 92 D6
Arctic Bay 68 A2
Arctic Red River 70 B6
Arda → 22 D6
Ardabīl 46 C7
Ardahan 46 B5
Ardakān =
  Sepīdān 44 D3
Ardenne 14 D3
Ardennes =
  Ardenne 14 D3
Ardestān 44 C3
Ardlethan ... 63 B4
Ardmore 78 B5
Ardrossan 62 B2
Arecibo 87 C6
Areia Branca . 92 C6
Arendal 9 G9
Arequipa 91 G4
Arero 53 H6
Arévalo 18 B3
Arezzo 20 C3
Argamakmur .. 37 E2
Arganda 18 B4
Argentan 12 B3
Argentário, Mte. 20 C3

Argentina ■ ... 94 D3
Argentina Is. .. 96 A3
Argentino, L. .. 95 G2
Argeş → 22 B6
Arghandab → 42 D4
Argo 53 E5
Argolikós
  Kólpos 23 F4
Árgos 23 F4
Argostólion ... 23 E3
Argungu 55 F5
Århus 9 G10
Arica, Chile .. 91 G4
Arica, Colombia 90 D4
Aridh 47 F6
Arinos → 91 F7
Aripuanã 91 E6
Aripuanã → .. 90 E6
Ariquemes ... 91 E6
Arizona 94 D3
Arizona □ 83 C7
Arjona 90 A3
Arkalyk =
  Arqalyk 29 D7
Arkansas □ ... 79 B7
Arkansas → .. 79 C8
Arkansas City . 78 A5
Arkhangelsk ... 28 C5
Arklow 11 E3
Arkticheskiy,
  Mys 30 A7
Arlanzón → .. 18 A3
Arlberg P. 14 E6
Arles 13 E6
Arlington, Va.,
  U.S.A. 73 E7
Arlington,
  Wash., U.S.A. 80 A2
Arlon 14 D3
Armagh 11 D3
Armavir 25 D5
Armenia 90 C3
Armenia ■ 25 E5
Armidale 63 B5
Armstrong ... 69 C2
Arnaud → 68 B3
Arnauti, C. ... 46 D3
Arnhem 14 C3
Arnhem, C. ... 60 C6
Arnhem Land . 60 C5
Arno → 20 C3
Arno Bay 62 B2
Arnsberg 14 C5
Aroab 58 D3
Arqalyk 29 D7
Arrabury 62 A3
Arrah = Ara .. 40 E5
Arran 10 D4
Arras 13 A5
Arrecife 54 C2
Arrée, Mts. d' . 12 B2
Arrowtown ... 65 F3
Árta 23 E3
Arthur → 62 D3
Arthur's Pass .. 65 E4
Artigas 94 C5
Artois 12 A5
Artsyz 17 E9
Artvin 46 B5
Aru, Kepulauan 39 F4
Aru Is. = Aru,
  Kepulauan .. 39 F4
Arua 57 D6
Aruanã 93 E3
Aruba ■ 87 D6
Arumpo 62 B3
Arunachal
  Pradesh □ .. 41 C10
Arusha 57 E7

Aruwimi → ... 56 D4
Arviat 70 B10
Arxan 35 B6
Arys 29 E7
Arzamas 24 B5
Arzew 54 A4
'As Saffānīyah . 47 E7
As Samāwah .. 47 E6
As
  Sulaymānīyah,
  Iraq 46 D6
As
  Sulaymānīyah,
  Si. Arabia ... 47 F6
As Summān .. 47 F6
As Sūq 47 G5
As Suwaydā' .. 46 D4
As Suwayh ... 45 F4
As Şuwayrah .. 47 D6
Asahigawa ... 32 F12
Asansol 40 F6
Ascension I. ... 51 G2
Aschaffenburg . 14 D5
Aschersleben .. 15 C6
Áscoli Piceno .. 20 C4
Ascope 91 E3
Aseb 49 E3
Asela 53 G6
Asenovgrad ... 22 C5
Ash Shām,
  Bādiyat 47 D4
Ash Shāmīyah . 47 E6
Ash Shāriqah . 44 E3
Ash Shaṭrah .. 47 E6
Ash Shaykh, J. 46 D3
Ash Shu'aybah . 47 F6
Ash Shu'bah .. 47 E6
Ashburton ... 65 E4
Ashcroft 71 C7
Asheville 75 B6
Ashford,
  Australia 63 A5
Ashford, U.K. .. 11 F7
Ashgabat 29 F6
Ashikaga 32 A6
Ashizuri-Zaki . 32 C3
Ashkhabad =
  Ashgabat ... 29 F6
Ashmyany ... 17 A7
Ashqelon 47 E3
Ashtabula ... 72 D5
Ashuanipi, L. . 69 C4
Asia, Kepulauan 39 D4
Asifabad 43 K11
Asike 39 F6
Asilah 54 A3
Asinara 20 D2
Asinara, G. dell' 20 D2
Asino 29 D9
Asipovichy ... 17 B9
'Asīr □ 48 D3
Asir, Ras 49 E5
Asmara =
  Asmera 53 E6
Asmera 53 E6
Aspiring, Mt. .. 65 F3
Assam □ 41 D9
Assen 14 B4
Assini 55 G4
Assiniboia ... 71 D9
Assiniboine → 71 D10
Assis 94 A6
Assisi 20 C4
Astana 29 D8
Asti 20 B2
Astipálaia ... 23 F6
Astorga 18 A2
Astoria 80 B2
Astrakhan ... 25 D6
Astrakhan-Bazàr 25 F6

Asturias □ 18 A3
Asunción 94 B5
Aswân 52 D5
Aswân High
Dam = Sadd
el Aali 52 D5
Asyût 52 C5
At Ṭafilah 47 E3
At Ṭā'if 48 C3
Atacama,
Desierto de . 94 A3
Atacama, Salar
de 94 A3
Atakpamé 55 G5
Atalaya 91 F4
Atami 32 B6
Atapupu 39 F2
Atâr 54 D2
Atasu 29 E8
Atauro 39 F3
Atbara 53 E5
'Atbara ➜ .. 53 E5
Atbasar 29 D7
Athabasca ... 71 C8
Athabasca ➜ . 70 C8
Athabasca, L. . . 70 C8
Athens =
Athínai 23 F4
Athens, Ala.,
U.S.A. 74 B4
Athens, Ga.,
U.S.A. 75 C6
Athínai 23 F4
Athlone 11 E3
Áthos 23 D5
Athy 11 E3
Ati 53 F2
Atico 91 G4
Atlanta 75 C5
Atlantic City .. 73 E8
Atlas Mts. =
Haut Atlas .. 54 B3
Atrak =
Atrek ➜ 44 B3
Atrek ➜ 44 B3
Attawapiskat ➜ 69 C2
Attock 42 C8
Attopeu 36 B3
Attur 43 P11
Atuel ➜ 94 D3
Atyraū 29 E6
Aubagne 13 E6
Aube ➜ 13 B5
Auburn 74 C5
Auburn Ra. ... 63 A5
Aubusson 12 D5
Auch 12 E4
Auckland 64 B6
Aude ➜ 13 E5
Augathella ... 63 A4
Augsburg 14 D6
Augusta, Italy . 21 F5
Augusta, Ga.,
U.S.A. 75 C7
Augusta, Maine,
U.S.A. 73 B11
Aunis 12 C3
Auponhia 39 E3
Aurangabad,
Bihar, India . 40 E5
Aurangabad,
Maharashtra,
India 43 K9
Aurich 14 B4
Aurillac 12 D5
Aurora, Colo.,
U.S.A. 76 F2
Aurora, Ill.,
U.S.A. 72 D1

Aus 58 D3
Auschwitz =
Oświęcim ... 16 C4
Austin, Minn.,
U.S.A. 77 D8
Austin, Tex.,
U.S.A. 78 D5
Austral Is. =
Tubuai Is. ... 65 M16
Austral
Seamount
Chain 65 M16
Australia ■ ... 60 E6
Australian
Capital
Territory □ .. 63 C4
Austria ■ 15 E8
Autun 13 C6
Auvergne 13 D5
Auvergne, Mts.
d' 13 D5
Auxerre 13 C5
Avallon 13 C5
Aveiro, Brazil . 92 C2
Aveiro, Portugal 18 B1
Āvej 46 D7
Avellaneda 94 C5
Avellino 21 D5
Aversa 21 D5
Avezzano 20 C4
Aviá Terai 94 B4
Aviemore 10 C5
Avignon 13 E6
Ávila 18 B3
Avilés 18 A3
Avoca ➜ 62 C3
Avola 21 F5
Avranches 12 B3
'Awālī 44 E2
Awash 49 F3
Awatere ➜ ... 65 D6
Awbārī 52 C1
Awjilah 52 C3
Axim 55 H4
Axiós ➜ 23 D4
Ayabaca 90 D3
Ayabe 32 B4
Ayacucho,
Argentina ... 94 D5
Ayacucho,
Peru 91 F4
Ayaguz 29 E9
Ayamonte 18 D2
Ayaviri 91 F4
Āybak 45 B7
Aydın 23 F6
Ayers Rock ... 60 F5
Áyios Evstrátios 23 E5
Aylmer, L. 70 B8
Ayn Dār 47 F7
Ayn Zālah 46 C5
Ayr 10 D4
Aytos 22 C6
Ayu, Kepulauan 39 D4
Ayutla 84 D5
Ayvacık 23 E6
Ayvalık 23 E6
Az Zahrān ... 47 F7
Az Zarqā 46 D4
Az-Zilfi 47 F6
Az Zubayr 47 E6
Az Zuwaytīnah 52 B3
Azamgarh 40 D4
Azärbayjan =
Azerbaijan ■ . 25 E6
Āzarbāyjān-e
Gharbī □ ... 46 C6
Āzarbāyjān-e
Sharqī □ 46 C6

Azare 55 F7
Azbine = Aïr .. 55 E6
Azerbaijan ■ .. 25 E6
Azerbaijchan =
Azerbaijan ■ . 25 E6
Azogues 90 D3
Azores 50 C1
Azov 25 D4
Azov, Sea of .. 25 D4
Azovskoye More
= Azov, Sea
of 25 D4
Azovy 28 C7
Azúa 87 C5
Azuaga 18 C3
Azuero, Pen. de 86 E3
Azul 94 D5

B

Ba Don 36 A3
Ba Ria 36 B3
Bab el Mandeb 49 E3
Baba Burnu ... 23 E6
Babadag 22 B7
Babadayhan .. 29 F7
Babaeski 22 D6
Babahoyo 90 D3
Babana 55 F5
Babar 39 F3
Babo 39 E4
Bābol 44 B3
Bābol Sar 44 B3
Baboua 56 C2
Babruysk 17 B9
Babura 55 F6
Babuyan Chan. 38 A2
Babylon 47 D6
Bacabal 92 C5
Bacan,
Kepulauan . 39 E3
Bacan, Pulau .. 39 E3
Bacarra 38 A2
Bacău 17 E8
Bachelina 29 D7
Back ➜ 70 B9
Backstairs
Passage 62 C2
Bacolod 38 B2
Bad Ischl 15 E7
Bad Kissingen . 14 C6
Bad Lands 76 D3
Badagara 43 P9
Badajoz 18 C2
Badalona 19 B7
Badalzai 42 E4
Badampahar .. 40 F6
Badanah 47 E5
Badarinath ... 42 D11
Badas 36 D4
Badas,
Kepulauan .. 37 D3
Baddo ➜ 42 E4
Bade 39 F5
Baden 15 D9
Baden-Baden .. 14 D5
Baden-
Württemberg □
.... 14 D5
Badgastein ... 15 E7
Bādghīsāt □ .. 42 B3
Badin 43 G6
Baduen 49 F4
Baena 18 D3
Baeza 18 D4
Bafatá 55 F2

Baffin B. 68 A4
Baffin I. 68 B3
Bafia 56 D2
Bafing ➜ 55 F2
Bafoulabé 55 F2
Bāfq 44 D3
Bafra 46 B3
Bāft 44 D4
Bafwasende ... 57 D5
Bagamoyo 57 F7
Baganga 38 C3
Bagansiapiapi . 37 D2
Bagdarin 30 D9
Bagé 94 C6
Baghdād 46 D6
Bagheria 21 E4
Baghlān 42 A6
Baghlān □ 45 C7
Baguio 38 A2
Bahamas ■ ... 86 A4
Baharampur .. 40 E7
Bahawalpur ... 42 E7
Bahía =
Salvador ... 93 E6
Bahía □ 93 E5
Bahía Blanca . 94 D4
Bahía de
Caráquez ... 90 D2
Bahía Laura ... 95 F3
Bahía Negra .. 91 H7
Bahr Aouk ➜ . 56 C3
Bahr
Salamat ➜ .. 53 G2
Bahraich 40 D3
Bahrain ■ 44 E2
Baia Mare 17 E6
Baïbokoum ... 53 G2
Baidoa 49 G3
Baie Comeau . 69 D4
Ba'iji 46 D5
Baikal, L. =
Baykal, Oz. .. 30 D8
Baile Atha Cliath
= Dublin ... 11 E3
Băileşti 22 B4
Bailundo 58 A3
Bā'ir 47 E4
Baird Mts. 71 B3
Bairnsdale ... 63 C4
Baitadi 40 C3
Baiyin 35 C5
Baja 16 E4
Baja, Pta. 84 B1
Baja California . 84 A1
Bajimba, Mt. .. 63 A5
Bakala 56 C4
Bakchar 29 D9
Bakel 55 F2
Baker, L. 70 B10
Baker I. 66 J13
Baker Lake ... 70 B10
Baker Mt. 80 A3
Baker's Dozen
Is. 69 C3
Bakersfield ... 82 C3
Bākhtarān 46 D6
Bakı 25 E6
Bakony Forest =
Bakony
Hegyseg 16 E3
Bakony Hegyseg 16 E3
Bakouma 56 C4
Baku = Bakı .. 25 E6
Baky = Bakı .. 25 E6
Balabac I. 36 C5
Balabac Str. ... 36 C5
Balabalangan,
Kepulauan .. 37 E5

Balaghat Ra. . . 43 K10
Balaguer 19 B6
Balaklava,
  Australia 62 B2
Balaklava,
  Ukraine 25 E3
Balakovo 24 C6
Balashov 24 C5
Balasore =
  Baleshwar . . 40 G6
Balaton 16 E3
Balbina, Represa
  de 90 D7
Balchik 22 C7
Balclutha 65 G3
Baleares, Is. . . . 19 C7
Balearic Is. =
  Baleares, Is. . 19 C7
Baler 38 A2
Baleshwar 40 G6
Bali, Cameroon 55 G7
Bali, Indonesia 37 F5
Bali □ 37 F5
Balikeşir 23 E6
Balikpapan 37 E5
Balimbing 38 C1
Balipara 41 D9
Baliza 93 F3
Balkan Mts. =
  Stara Planina 22 C4
Balkh 45 B6
Balkhash =
  Balqash 29 E8
Balkhash, Ozero
  = Balqash Köl 29 E8
Balla 41 E8
Ballarat 62 C3
Ballater 10 C5
Ballina, Australia 63 A5
Ballina, Ireland 11 D2
Ballinasloe 11 E2
Ballymena 11 D3
Balmaceda 95 F2
Balmoral 62 C3
Balonne → . . . 63 A4
Balqash 29 E8
Balqash Köl . . . 29 E8
Balrampur 40 D4
Balranald 62 B3
Balsas → 84 D4
Balta 17 D9
Bălţi 17 E8
Baltic Sea 9 G11
Baltimore 73 E7
Baluchistan □ . 42 F4
Balya 23 E6
Bam 44 D4
Bama 53 F1
Bamako 55 F3
Bamba 55 E4
Bambari 56 C4
Bamberg 14 D6
Bambili 57 D5
Bamenda 55 G7
Bāmiān □ 42 B5
Bampūr 45 E5
Ban Don =
  Surat Thani . 36 C1
Ban Mê Thuột =
  Buon Me
  Thuot 36 B3
Banaba 64 K11
Banalia 57 D5
Banam 36 B3
Banamba 55 F3
Bananal, I. do . 93 E3
Banaras =
  Varanasi . . . 40 E4
Band-e
  Torkestän . . . 45 C6

Banda,
  Kepulauan . . 39 E3
Banda Aceh . . . 36 C1
Banda Banda,
  Mt. 63 B5
Banda Elat 39 F4
Banda Is. =
  Banda,
  Kepulauan . . 39 E3
Banda Sea 39 F3
Bandanaira . . . 39 E3
Bandar =
  Machilipatnam 40 J3
Bandār 'Abbās 44 E4
Bandar-e Anzalī 46 C7
Bandar-e
  Bushehr =
  Būshehr 44 D2
Bandar-e Chārak 44 E3
Bandar-e
  Deylam 47 E7
Bandar-e
  Khomeynı . . 47 E7
Bandar-e
  Lengeh 44 E3
Bandar-e
  Ma'shur 47 E7
Bandar-e
  Nakhīlū 44 E3
Bandar-e Rīg . . 44 D2
Bandar-e
  Torkeman . . . 44 B3
Bandar
  Maharani =
  Muar 37 D2
Bandar
  Penggaram =
  Batu Pahat . . 37 D2
Bandar Seri
  Begawan . . . 36 D5
Bandawe 59 A6
Bandeira, Pico
  da 93 G5
Bandera 94 B4
Bandiagara . . . 55 F4
Bandırma 23 D7
Bandon 11 F2
Bandundu 56 E3
Bandung 37 F3
Banff, Canada . 71 C8
Banff, U.K. 10 C5
Banfora 55 F4
Bang Saphan . . 36 B1
Bangalore 43 N10
Bangassou 56 D4
Banggai,
  Kepulauan . . 39 E2
Banggi, P. 36 C5
Banghāzī 52 B3
Bangka, P.,
  Sulawesi,
  Indonesia . . . 39 D3
Bangka, P.,
  Sumatera,
  Indonesia . . . 37 E3
Bangka, Selat . 37 E3
Bangkinang . . . 37 D2
Bangko 37 E2
Bangkok 36 B2
Bangladesh ■ . 41 E7
Bangong Co . . 42 B11
Bangor, Down,
  U.K. 11 D4
Bangor,
  Gwynedd,
  U.K. 11 E4
Bangor, U.S.A. . 73 B11
Bangued 38 A2
Bangui 56 D3

Bangweulu, L. . 57 G6
Bani 87 C5
Banī Walīd 52 B1
Banīnah 52 B3
Bāniyās 46 D3
Banja Luka 20 B6
Banjarmasin . . 37 E4
Banjul 55 F1
Bankipore 40 E5
Banks I. 70 A7
Banks Pen. . . . 65 E5
Banks Str. 62 D4
Bankura 40 F6
Banningville =
  Bandundu . . 56 E3
Bannu 42 C7
Banská Bystrica 16 D4
Banswara 43 H9
Bantry 11 F2
Banu 42 B6
Banyak,
  Kepulauan . . 37 D1
Banyo 55 G7
Banzare Coast . 96 A13
Banzyville =
  Mobayi 56 D4
Baoding 35 C6
Baoji 35 C5
Baoshan 34 D4
Baotou 35 B6
Bapatla 40 K3
Ba'qūbah 46 D6
Bar,
  Montenegro, Yug.
  . . . . 22 C2
Bar, Ukraine . . 17 D8
Bar-le-Duc 13 B6
Barabai 37 E5
Barabinsk 29 D8
Baracaldo 19 A4
Baracoa 86 B5
Barahona 87 C5
Barail Range . . 41 E9
Barakhola 41 E9
Barakpur 41 F7
Barakula 63 A5
Baramula 42 B9
Baran 43 G10
Baranavichy . . . 17 B8
Baranof I. 71 C6
Barão de
  Melgaço 91 F6
Barapasi 39 E5
Barat Daya,
  Kepulauan . . 39 F3
Barbacena 93 G5
Barbacoas 90 C3
Barbados ■ . . . 87 D8
Barbastro 19 A6
Barberton 59 D6
Barcellona Pozzo
  di Gotto 21 E5
Barcelona, Spain 19 B7
Barcelona,
  Venezuela . . 90 A6
Barcelos 90 D6
Bardai 52 D2
Barddhaman . . 40 F6
Bardejov 16 D5
Bardera 49 G3
Bardi, Ra's 47 F4
Bardīyah 52 B4
Bareilly 42 E11
Barentu 53 E6
Barfleur, Pte. de 12 B3
Barga 34 C3
Bargal 49 E5
Barhi 40 E5
Bari 20 D6

Bari Doab 42 D8
Barīm 49 E3
Barinas 90 B4
Baring, C. 70 B8
Bârîs 52 D5
Barisal 41 F8
Barisan, Bukit . 37 E2
Barito → 37 E4
Barkly Tableland 60 D6
Barlee, L. 60 F2
Barletta 20 D6
Barmedman . . . 63 B4
Barmer 42 G7
Barmera 62 B3
Barnato 63 B4
Barnaul 29 D9
Barnsley 11 E6
Barnstaple 11 F4
Baro 55 G6
Baroda =
  Vadodara . . . 43 H8
Barpeta 41 D8
Barquísimeto . . 90 A5
Barra, Brazil . . 93 E5
Barra, U.K. 10 C3
Barra do Corda 92 D4
Barra do Piraí . 93 G5
Barra Falsa, Pta.
  da 59 C7
Barraba 63 B5
Barrackpur =
  Barakpur . . . 41 F7
Barraigh =
  Barra 10 C3
Barranca, Lima,
  Peru 91 F3
Barranca,
  Loreto, Peru . 90 D3
Barrancabermeja
  . . . . 90 B4
Barrancas 90 B6
Barrancos 18 C2
Barranqueras . . 94 B5
Barranquilla . . . 90 A4
Barras 92 C5
Barreiras 93 E5
Barreirinhas . . . 92 C5
Barreiro 18 C1
Barreiros 92 D6
Barretos 93 G4
Barrier Ra. 62 B3
Barrington Tops 63 B5
Barringun 63 A4
Barrow 71 A4
Barrow-in-
  Furness 11 D5
Barry 11 F5
Barsi 43 K9
Barsoi 40 E6
Barstow 82 C4
Bartica 90 B7
Bartın 46 B3
Bartle Frere . . . 61 D8
Bartlesville 79 A6
Barysaw 17 A9
Bāsa'idū 44 E3
Basankusa 56 D3
Basarabeasca . 17 E9
Basel 13 C7
Bashi Channel . 35 D7
Bashkir Republic
  =
  Bashkortostan □
  . . . . 29 D6
Bashkortostan □ 29 D6
Basilan 38 C2
Basilan Str. . . . 38 C2
Basildon 11 F7
Basim =
  Washim 43 J10

Basingstoke ... 11 F6
Basle = Basel . 13 C7
Basoka 56 D4
Basongo 56 E4
Basque
 Provinces =
 País Vasco □ 19 A4
Basra = Al
 Başrah 47 E6
Bass Str. 61 H8
Bassano 71 C8
Bassano del
 Grappa 20 B3
Bassas da India 59 C7
Bassein 41 J10
Basseterre 87 C7
Bassikounou .. 55 E3
Bastak 44 E3
Bastar 40 H3
Basti 40 D4
Bastia 13 E8
Bastogne 14 C3
Bata 56 D1
Bataan 38 B2
Batabanó 86 B3
Batabanó, G. de 86 B3
Batac 38 A2
Batagoy 31 C11
Batamay 31 C10
Batang 34 C4
Batangafo 56 C3
Batangas 38 B2
Batanta 39 E4
Bateman's B. . 63 C5
Batemans Bay . 63 C5
Bath 11 F5
Bathurst,
 Australia 63 B4
Bathurst,
 Canada 69 D4
Bathurst, C. .. 70 A7
Bathurst Harb. . 62 D4
Bathurst Inlet .. 70 B9
Batinah 44 F4
Batlow 63 C4
Batman 46 C5
Batna 54 A6
Baton Rouge .. 79 D8
Batouri 56 D2
Battambang ... 36 B2
Battipáglia 21 D5
Battle Creek .. 72 C3
Battle Harbour . 69 C5
Battleford 71 C9
Batu 49 F2
Batu, Kepulauan 37 E1
Batu Is. = Batu,
 Kepulauan .. 37 E1
Batu Pahat ... 37 D2
Batuata 39 F2
Batumi 25 E5
Baturaja 37 E2
Baturité 92 C6
Bau 37 D4
Baubau 39 F2
Bauchi 55 F6
Bauer, C. 62 B1
Baukau 39 F3
Bauru 93 G4
Baús 93 F3
Bautzen 15 C8
Bavaria =
 Bayern □ ... 15 D6
Bawdwin 41 F11
Bawean 37 F4
Bawku 55 F4
Bawlake 41 H11
Bay, L. de 38 B2
Bay City 72 C4

Bay View 64 C7
Bayamo 86 B4
Bayan Har Shan 34 C4
Bayan Hot =
 Alxa Zuoqi .. 35 C5
Bayanaūyl 29 D8
Bayanhongor .. 35 B5
Bayázeh 44 C3
Baybay 38 B2
Bayburt 46 B5
Bayern □ 15 D6
Bayeux 12 B3
Bayındır 23 E6
Baykal, Oz. ... 30 D8
Baykit 30 C7
Baykonur =
 Bayqongyr . 29 E7
Bayombong ... 38 A2
Bayonne 12 E3
Bayovar 91 E2
Bayqongyr .. 29 E7
Bayram-Ali =
 Bayramaly .. 29 F7
Bayramaly ... 29 F7
Bayramiç 23 E6
Bayreuth 15 D6
Bayrūt 46 D3
Baytown 79 E6
Baza 19 D4
Bazaruto, I. do . 59 C7
Beachport 62 C2
Beagle, Canal . 95 G3
Beardmore
 Glacier 96 C14
Béarn 12 E3
Beauce, Plaine
 de la 12 B4
Beaudesert ... 63 A5
Beaufort 36 C5
Beaufort Sea .. 66 B6
Beaufort West . 58 E4
Beaumont 79 D6
Beaune 13 C6
Beauvais 12 B5
Beauval 71 C9
Beaver 71 B5
Beaver →..... 71 C9
Beawar 42 F9
Bečej 22 B3
Béchar 54 B4
Bedford 11 E6
Beenleigh 63 A5
Be'er Sheva ... 47 E3
Beersheba =
 Be'er Sheva . 47 E3
Befale 56 D4
Bega 63 C4
Behbehān 47 E7
Behshahr 44 B3
Bei Jiang →.. 35 D6
Bei'an 35 B7
Beibei 35 D5
Beihai 35 D5
Beijing 35 C6
Beilpajah 63 B3
Beinn na
 Faoghla =
 Benbecula .. 10 C3
Beira 59 B6
Beirut = Bayrūt 46 D3
Beitbridge ... 59 C6
Beja, Portugal . 18 C2
Béja, Tunisia . 54 A6
Bejaia 54 A6
Béjar 18 B3
Bejestān 44 C4
Békéscsaba ... 16 E5
Bela, India 40 E4
Bela, Pakistan . 42 F5

Bela Crkva 22 B3
Bela Vista 94 A5
Belarus ■ 24 C2
Belau = Palau ■ 38 C4
Belawan 37 D1
Belaya Tserkov
 = Bila Tserkva 17 D10
Belcher Is. 69 C3
Belém 92 C4
Belén 94 A5
Belet Uen 49 G4
Belev 24 C4
Belfast 11 D4
Belfort 13 C7
Belgaum 43 M9
Belgium ■ 14 C3
Belgorod 24 C4
Belgorod-
 Dnestrovskiy
 = Bilhorod-
 Dnistrovskyy 25 D3
Belgrade =
 Beograd 22 B3
Beli Drim → .. 22 C3
Belinga 56 D2
Belinyu 37 E3
Beliton Is. =
 Belitung 37 E3
Belitung 37 E3
Belize ■ 85 D7
Belize City 85 D7
Belkovskiy,
 Ostrov 30 B11
Bell Bay 62 D4
Bell Peninsula . 68 B2
Bell Ville 94 C4
Bella Unión ... 94 C5
Bella Vista 94 B5
Bellary 43 M10
Bellata 63 A4
Belle-Ile 12 C2
Belle Isle 69 C5
Belle Isle, Str. of 69 C5
Belleville,
 Canada 69 D3
Belleville, U.S.A. 77 F10
Bellin =
 Kangirsuk ... 68 C4
Bellingen 63 B5
Bellingham ... 80 A2
Bellingshausen
 Sea 96 A2
Bellinzona ... 13 C8
Belluno 20 A4
Belmont 63 B5
Belmonte 93 F6
Belmopan 85 D7
Belo Horizonte . 93 F5
Belo-Tsiribihina 59 H8
Beloit 77 D10
Belokorovichi . 17 C9
Belomorsk ... 28 C4
Belonia 41 F8
Belorussia ■ =
 Belarus ■ ... 24 C2
Belovo 29 D9
Beloye, Ozero . 24 A4
Beloye More .. 28 C4
Belozersk 24 A4
Beltana 62 B2
Belterra 92 C3
Beltsy = Bălţi . 17 E8
Belukha 29 E9
Beluran 36 C5
Belyy, Ostrov . 28 B8
Belyy Yar 29 D9
Bembéréke ... 55 F5
Bemidji 77 B7
Ben Gardane . 52 B1

Ben Lomond,
 N.S.W.,
 Australia 63 B5
Ben Lomond,
 Tas., Australia 62 D4
Ben Nevis 10 C4
Bena 55 F6
Bena Dibele .. 56 E4
Benagerie 62 B3
Benalla 63 C4
Benambra, Mt. 63 C4
Benares =
 Varanasi 40 E4
Benavente ... 18 A3
Benbecula .. 10 C3
Benbonyathe .. 62 B2
Bend 80 C3
Bender Beila . 49 F5
Bendery =
 Tighina 17 E9
Bendigo 63 C3
Benevento 20 D5
Bengal, Bay of . 41 J7
Bengbu 35 C6
Benghazi =
 Banghāzī ... 52 B3
Bengkalis 37 D2
Bengkulu 37 E2
Bengkulu □ ... 37 E2
Benguela 58 A2
Beni 57 D5
Beni →...... 91 F5
Beni Abbès ... 54 B4
Beni Mazâr ... 52 C5
Beni Mellal ... 54 B3
Beni Ounif ... 54 B4
Beni Suef 52 C5
Benidorm 19 C5
Benin ■ 55 G5
Benin, Bight of 55 H5
Benin City 55 G6
Benjamin
 Constant 90 D4
Benoni 59 D5
Bent 44 E4
Benteng 39 F2
Benton Harbor 72 C2
Benue →..... 55 G6
Benxi 35 B7
Beo 38 D3
Beograd 22 B3
Beppu 32 C2
Berati 23 D2
Berau, Teluk .. 39 E4
Berber 53 E5
Berbera 49 E4
Berbérati 56 D3
Berbice → ... 90 B7
Berdichev =
 Berdychiv ... 17 D9
Berdsk 29 D9
Berdyansk ... 25 D4
Berdychiv ... 17 D9
Berebere 39 D3
Bereda 49 E5
Berehove 17 D6
Berekum 55 G4
Berestechko ... 17 C7
Bereza 17 B7
Berezhany ... 17 D7
Berezina =
 Byarezina → 17 B10
Berezniki 28 D6
Berezovo 28 C7
Berga 19 A6
Bergama 23 E6
Bérgamo 20 B2
Bergen 8 F9
Bergerac 12 D4

Berhala, Selat .	37	E2
Berhampore =		
Baharampur .	40	E7
Berhampur =		
Brahamapur .	40	H5
Bering Sea	71	C1
Bering Strait ..	71	B3
Berja	19	D4
Berkeley	80	G2
Berkner I.	96	B4
Berlin	15	B7
Bermejo →,		
Formosa,		
Argentina ...	94	B5
Bermejo →,		
San Juan,		
Argentina ...	94	C3
Bermuda ■ ...	67	F13
Bern	13	C7
Bernardo de		
Irigoyen	94	B6
Bernburg	15	C6
Berne = Bern .	13	C7
Bernina, Piz ..	13	C8
Beroroha	59	J9
Beroun	16	D2
Berrechid	54	B3
Berri	62	B3
Berry, Australia	63	B5
Berry, France ..	12	C5
Bershad	17	D9
Bertoua	56	D2
Berwick-upon-		
Tweed	10	D6
Besalampy	59	H8
Besançon	13	C7
Besar	37	E5
Besni	46	C4
Bessarabiya ...	17	E9
Bessarabka =		
Basarabeasca	17	E9
Bessemer	74	C4
Betanzos	18	A1
Bétaré Oya	56	C2
Bethanien	58	D3
Bethel	71	B3
Bethlehem,		
S. Africa	59	D5
Bethlehem,		
U.S.A.	73	D8
Béthune	13	A5
Bethungra	63	B4
Betioky	59	J8
Betroka	59	J9
Betsiamites ...	69	D4
Bettiah	40	D5
Betul	43	J10
Betung	37	D4
Beverley	11	E6
Beverly Hills ..	82	C3
Beyla	55	G3
Beyneu	29	E6
Beypazarı	46	B2
Beyşehir Gölü .	46	C2
Bezhitsa	24	C3
Béziers	13	E5
Bezwada =		
Vijayawada .	40	J3
Bhachau	43	H7
Bhadrakh	40	G6
Bhadravati	43	N9
Bhagalpur	40	E6
Bhakra Dam ...	42	D10
Bhamo	41	E11
Bhandara	43	J11
Bhanrer Ra. ...	43	H11
Bharat =		
India ■	43	J10
Bharatpur	42	F10

Bhatpara	41	F7
Bhaunagar =		
Bhavnagar ..	43	J8
Bhavnagar	43	J8
Bhawanipatna .	40	H3
Bhilsa = Vidisha	43	H10
Bhilwara	43	G9
Bhima →	43	L10
Bhimavaram ..	40	J3
Bhind	42	F11
Bhiwandi	43	K8
Bhiwani	42	E10
Bhola	41	F8
Bhopal	43	H10
Bhubaneshwar	40	G5
Bhuj	43	H6
Bhumiphol Dam		
= Phumiphon,		
Khuan	36	A1
Bhusaval	43	J9
Bhutan ■	41	D8
Biafra, B. of =		
Bonny, Bight		
of	56	D1
Biak	39	E5
Biała Podlaska .	17	B6
Białogard	16	A2
Białystok	17	B6
Biaro	39	D3
Biarritz	12	E3
Bibala	58	A2
Biberach	14	D5
Bibiani	55	G4
Bida	55	G6
Bidar	43	L10
Biddeford	73	C10
Bidon 5 = Poste		
Maurice		
Cortier	54	D5
Bié, Planalto de	58	A3
Biel	13	C7
Bielefeld	14	B5
Biella	20	B2
Bielsk Podlaski	17	B6
Bielsko-Biała ..	16	D4
Bien Hoa	36	B3
Bienne = Biel .	13	C7
Bienville, L. ...	69	C3
Big Horn Mts. =		
Bighorn Mts. .	81	C10
Big Spring	78	C3
Big Trout L. ...	69	C2
Biğa	23	D6
Bigadiç	23	E7
Biggar	71	C9
Biggenden	63	A5
Bighorn → ...	81	B10
Bighorn Mts. ..	81	C10
Bihać	20	B5
Bihar	40	E5
Bihar □	40	E5
Bihor, Munţii ..	17	E6
Bijagós,		
Arquipélago		
dos	55	F1
Bijapur,		
Karnataka,		
India	43	L9
Bijapur, Mad. P.,		
India	40	H3
Bījār	46	D6
Bijeljina	20	B7
Bijnor	42	E11
Bikaner	42	E8
Bikini Atoll	64	H11
Bila Tserkva ...	17	D10
Bilara	42	F8
Bilaspur	40	F4
Bilauk Taungdan	36	B1

Bilbao	19	A4
Bilbo = Bilbao .	19	A4
Bilecik	46	B2
Bilhorod-		
Dnistrovskyy	25	D3
Bilir	31	C11
Billings	81	C9
Billiton Is. =		
Belitung	37	E3
Bilma	53	E1
Biloxi	79	D9
Biltine	53	F3
Bima	39	F1
Bimbo	56	D3
Bina-Etawah ..	43	G11
Binalbagan ...	38	B2
Binalong	63	B4
Bīnālūd, Kūh-e	44	B4
Binatang	37	D4
Binda	63	A4
Bindle	63	A4
Bindura	59	B6
Bingara, N.S.W.,		
Australia ...	63	A5
Bingara,		
Queens.,		
Australia	63	A3
Bingham		
Canyon	81	E7
Binghamton ...	73	C8
Bingöl	46	C5
Binh Dinh = An		
Nhon	36	B3
Binh Son	36	A3
Binjai	37	D1
Binnaway	63	B4
Binongko	39	F2
Bintan	37	D2
Bintulu	37	D4
Bintuni	39	E4
Binzert = Bizerte	54	A6
Bioko	56	D1
Bir	43	K9
Bir Autrun	53	E4
Bir Mogrein ...	54	C2
Bîr Ungât	52	D5
Bira	39	E4
Birao	53	F3
Birchip	62	C3
Birecik	46	C4
Bireuen	36	C1
Bîrlad	17	E8
Bîrlad →	17	F8
Birmingham,		
U.K.	11	E6
Birmingham,		
U.S.A.	74	C4
Birmitrapur ...	40	F5
Birni Nkonni ..	55	F6
Birnin Kebbi ..	55	F5
Birr	11	E3
Birrie →	63	A4
Birsk	29	D6
Birur	43	N9
Bisa	39	E3
Biscay, B. of ..	12	D2
Biscoe Bay	96	B17
Biscoe Is.	96	A3
Bishkek	29	E8
Biskra	54	B6
Bislig	38	C3
Bismarck	76	B4
Bismarck Arch.	64	K9
Bissagos =		
Bijagós,		
Arquipélago		
dos	55	F1
Bissau	55	F1
Bistriţa	17	E7

Bistriţa →	17	E8
Bitam	56	D2
Bitkine	53	F2
Bitlis	46	C5
Bitola	22	D3
Bitolj = Bitola .	22	D3
Bitter L. =		
Buheirat-		
Murrat-el-		
Kubra	52	B5
Bitterfontein ..	58	E3
Bitterroot Range	81	B6
Biu	53	F1
Biwa-Ko	32	B5
Biysk	29	D9
Bizerte	54	A6
Bjelovar	20	B6
Black Forest =		
Schwarzwald	14	D5
Black Hills	76	D3
Black Sea	25	E3
Black Volta →	55	G4
Blackball	65	E4
Blackburn	11	E5
Blackpool	11	E5
Blackwater → .	11	E2
Blagodarnoye =		
Blagodarnyy	25	D5
Blagodarnyy ..	25	D5
Blagoevgrad ..	22	C4
Blagoveshchensk		
....	31	D10
Blairmore	71	D6
Blanc, Mont ...	13	D7
Blanca, B.	95	D4
Blanca Peak ...	83	B10
Blanche, C. ...	62	B1
Blanche, L. ...	62	A2
Blanes	19	B7
Blantyre	59	B6
Blayney	63	B4
Blednaya, Gora	28	B7
Blenheim	65	D5
Blida	54	A5
Bligh Sound ..	65	F2
Blitta	55	G5
Blodgett Iceberg		
Tongue	96	A13
Bloemfontein ..	59	D5
Bloemhof	59	D5
Blois	12	C4
Bloomington,		
Ill., U.S.A. ...	77	E10
Bloomington,		
Ind., U.S.A. ..	72	E2
Blue Mts., Oreg.,		
U.S.A.	80	C4
Blue Mts., Pa.,		
U.S.A.	73	D7
Blue Nile = Nîl		
el Azraq → .	53	E5
Blue Ridge Mts.	75	A7
Bluefields	86	D3
Bluff	65	G3
Blumenau	94	B7
Bo	55	G2
Bo Duc	36	B3
Bo Hai	35	C6
Boa Vista	90	C6
Boatman	63	A4
Bobadah	63	B4
Bobbili	40	H4
Bobo-Dioulasso	55	F4
Bóbr →	16	B2
Bobraomby,		
Tanjon' i	59	G9
Bobruysk =		
Babruysk ...	17	B9
Bôca do Acre ..	91	E5

Name	Page	Grid
Boca Raton	75	F7
Bocaiúva	93	F5
Bocanda	55	G4
Bocaranga	56	C3
Bochnia	16	D5
Bochum	14	C4
Boda	56	D3
Bodaybo	30	D9
Boden	8	E12
Bodensee	13	C8
Bodhan	43	K10
Bodø	8	E10
Bodrog →	16	D5
Bodrum	23	F6
Boende	56	E4
Boffa	55	F2
Bogalusa	79	D9
Bogan Gate	63	B4
Boggabilla	63	A5
Boggabri	63	B5
Bogo	38	B2
Bogong, Mt	63	C4
Bogotá	90	C4
Bogotol	29	D9
Bogra	41	E7
Bogué	55	E2
Bohemian Forest = Böhmerwald	15	D7
Bohena Cr. →	63	B4
Böhmerwald	15	D7
Bohol	38	C2
Bohol Sea	38	C2
Bohotleh	49	F4
Boise	80	D5
Boise City	78	A2
Bojador C.	54	C2
Bojana →	22	D2
Bojnūrd	44	B4
Boké	55	F2
Bokhara →	63	A4
Bokoro	53	F2
Bokote	56	E4
Bokungu	56	E4
Bol	53	F1
Bolama	55	F1
Bolan Pass	42	E5
Bolbec	12	B4
Bole	34	B3
Bolekhiv	17	D6
Bolekhov = Bolekhiv	17	D6
Bolesławiec	16	C2
Bolgrad = Bolhrad	17	F9
Bolhrad	17	F9
Bolinao C.	38	A1
Bolívar, Argentina	94	D4
Bolívar, Colombia	90	C3
Bolivia ■	91	G6
Bollon	63	A4
Bolobo	56	E3
Bologna	20	B3
Bologoye	24	B3
Bolomba	56	D3
Bolong	38	C2
Bolsena, L. di	20	C3
Bolshereche	29	D8
Bolshevik, Ostrov	30	B8
Bolshoi Kavkas = Caucasus Mountains	25	E5
Bolshoy Atlym	28	C7
Bolshoy Begichev, Ostrov	30	B9
Bolshoy Lyakhovskiy, Ostrov	31	B12
Bolton	11	E5
Bolu	46	B2
Bolvadin	46	C2
Bolzano	20	A3
Bom Despacho	93	F4
Bom Jesus da Lapa	93	E5
Boma	56	F2
Bomaderry	63	B5
Bombala	63	C4
Bombay	43	K8
Bomboma	56	D3
Bomili	57	D5
Bomongo	56	D3
Bomu →	56	D4
Bon, C.	52	A1
Bonaire	87	D6
Bonang	63	C4
Bonavista	69	D5
Bondo	56	D4
Bondoukou	55	G4
Bone, Teluk	39	E2
Bonerate	39	F2
Bonerate, Kepulauan	39	F2
Bong Son = Hoai Nhon	36	B3
Bongandanga	56	D4
Bongor	53	F2
Bonifacio	13	F8
Bonn	14	C4
Bonney, L.	62	C3
Bonny, Bight of	56	D1
Bonoi	39	E5
Bontang	37	D5
Bonthain	39	F1
Bonthe	55	G2
Bontoc	38	A2
Boolaboolka L.	62	B3
Booligal	63	B3
Boonah	63	A5
Boorindal	63	B4
Boorowa	63	B4
Boothia, Gulf of	68	A2
Boothia Pen.	70	A10
Booué	56	E2
Bor, Serbia, Yug.	22	B4
Bôr, Sudan	53	G5
Borama	49	F3
Borås	9	G10
Borāzjān	44	D2
Borba	90	D7
Borda, C.	62	C2
Bordeaux	12	D3
Bordertown	62	C3
Bordj Fly Ste. Marie	54	C4
Bordj-in-Eker	54	D6
Bordj Omar Driss	54	C6
Bordj-Tarat	54	C6
Borger	78	B3
Borisoglebsk	24	C5
Borisov = Barysaw	17	A9
Borja	90	D3
Borkou	53	E2
Borkum	14	B4
Borley, C.	96	A9
Borneo	37	D4
Bornholm	9	G11
Boromo	55	F4
Borongan	38	B3
Borovichi	24	B3
Borşa	17	E7
Borūjerd	46	D7
Boryslav	17	D6
Bosa	21	D2
Bosanska Gradiška	20	B6
Bosaso	49	E4
Boshan	35	C6
Boshrūyeh	44	C4
Bosna →	20	B7
Bosna i Hercegovina = Bosnia-Herzegovina ■	20	B6
Bosnia-Herzegovina ■	20	B6
Bosnik	39	E5
Bosobolo	56	D3
Bosporus = Karadeniz Boğazı	22	D7
Bossangoa	56	C3
Bossembélé	53	G2
Bosso	53	F1
Bosten Hu	34	B3
Boston, U.K.	11	E6
Boston, U.S.A.	73	C10
Botany B.	63	B5
Bothnia, G. of	8	F12
Bothwell	62	D4
Botletle →	58	C4
Botoşani	17	E8
Botswana ■	58	C4
Botucatu	94	A7
Bou Djébéha	55	E4
Bou Izakarn	54	C3
Bouaké	55	G3
Bouar	56	C3
Bouârfa	54	B4
Bouca	56	C3
Bougie = Bejaia	54	A6
Bougouni	55	F3
Boulder	76	E2
Boulder Dam = Hoover Dam	82	B5
Boulogne-sur-Mer	12	A4
Boultoum	55	F7
Bouna	55	G4
Boundiali	55	G3
Bourbonnais	13	C5
Bourem	55	E4
Bourg-en-Bresse	13	C6
Bourg-St.-Maurice	13	D7
Bourges	12	C5
Bourgogne	13	C6
Bourke	63	B4
Bournemouth	11	F6
Bousso	53	F2
Boutilimit	55	E2
Bowen Mts.	63	C4
Bowman I.	96	A12
Bowmans	62	B2
Bowral	63	B5
Bowraville	63	B5
Boyne →	11	E3
Boyni Qara	45	B6
Boz Dağlan	23	E7
Bozburun	23	F7
Bozcaada	23	E6
Bozdoğan	23	F7
Bozeman	81	C8
Bozen = Bolzano	20	A3
Bozoum	56	C3
Bra	20	B1
Brač	20	C6
Bracciano, L. di	20	C4
Brach	52	C1
Bräcke	8	F11
Brad	17	E6
Bradenton	75	F6
Bradford	11	E6
Braemar	62	B2
Braga	18	B1
Bragança, Brazil	92	C4
Bragança, Portugal	18	B2
Brahamapur	40	H5
Brahmanbaria	41	F8
Brahmani →	40	G6
Brahmaputra →	41	F7
Braidwood	63	C4
Bräila	17	F8
Branco →	90	D6
Brandenburg = Neubrandenburg	15	B7
Brandenburg	15	B7
Brandenburg □	15	B7
Brandon	71	D10
Brandvlei	58	E4
Braniewo	16	A4
Bransfield Str.	96	A4
Brantford	69	D2
Branxholme	62	C3
Brasiléia	91	F5
Brasília	93	F4
Braşov	17	F7
Brassey, Banjaran	36	D5
Bratislava	16	D3
Bratsk	30	D8
Braunau	15	D7
Braunschweig	14	B6
Brava	49	G3
Bravo del Norte, R. → = Grande, Rio →	79	F5
Brawley	82	D5
Bray	11	E3
Bray, Pays de	12	B4
Brazil ■	93	E4
Brazos →	79	E6
Brazzaville	56	E3
Brčko	20	B7
Breaksea Sd.	65	F2
Bream B.	64	A6
Bream Hd.	64	A6
Brechin	11	F5
Brecon	11	F5
Breda	14	C3
Bredasdorp	58	E4
Bredbo	63	C4
Bregenz	14	E5
Brejo	92	C5
Bremen	14	B5
Bremerhaven	14	B5
Bremerton	80	B2
Brenner P.	15	E6
Bréscia	20	B3
Breslau = Wrocław	16	C3
Bressanone	20	A3
Brest, Belarus	17	B6
Brest, France	12	B1
Brest-Litovsk = Brest	17	B6
Bretagne	12	B2
Brett, C.	64	A6
Brewarrina	63	A4
Brezhnev = Naberezhnyye Chelny	29	D6
Bria	56	C4
Briançon	13	D7
Bribie I.	63	A5
Bridgeport	73	D9

Bridgetown	...	87	D8	Bucharest =				Bûr Sa'îd	.....	52	B5	Bydgoszcz	....	16	B3
Bridgewater	...	69	D4	București	...	22	B6	Bûr Sûdân	....	53	E6	Byelarus =			
Bridgewater, C.	62	C3	Buckie	....	10	C5	Burao	......	49	F4	Belarus ■	..	24	C2
Bridlington	....	11	D6	Buckleboo	...	62	B2	Buraydah	...	47	F6	Byelorussia =			
Bridport	......	62	D4	București	....	22	B6	Buraymī, Al				Belarus ■	...	24	C2
Brig	....	13	C7	Budalin	....	41	F10	Wāhāt al	....	44	E3	Bykhaw	......	17	B10
Brigham City	..	81	E7	Budapest	...	16	E4	Burcher	......	63	B4	Bykhov =			
Bright	....	63	C4	Budd Coast	..	96	A12	Burdur	....	46	C2	Bykhaw	.....	17	B10
Brighton,				Bude	....	11	F4	Burdwan =				Bylot I.	....	68	A3
Australia	....	62	C2	Budennovsk	..	25	E5	Barddhaman	40	F6	Byrd, C.	......	96	A3
Brighton, U.K.	.	11	F6	Budgewoi	....	63	B5	Burgas	....	22	C6	Byrock	......	63	B4
Bríndisi	......	21	D6	Budjala	....	56	D3	Burgersdorp	..	59	E5	Byron Bay	....	63	A5
Brinkworth	....	62	B2	Buenaventura	.	90	C3	Burgos	......	18	A4	Byrranga, Gory	30	B8
Brisbane	......	63	A5	Buenos Aires	..	94	C5	Burgundy =				Byrranga Mts. =		
Brisbane →	..	63	A5	Buenos Aires, L.	95	F2	Bourgogne	..	13	C6	Byrranga,			
Bristol,				Buffalo	....	73	C6	Burhaniye	...	23	E6	Gory	....	30	B8
U.K.	....	11	F5	Bug → =				Burhanpur	...	43	J10	Bytom	....	16	C4
Bristol,				Buh →	.....	25	D3	Burias	....	38	B2	Bytów	....	16	A3
U.S.A.	......	75	A6	Bug →	......	16	B5	Buriram	....	36	A2				
Bristol B.	.....	71	C3	Buga	....	90	C3	Burji	....	53	G6				
Bristol Channel	11	F4	Bugel, Tanjung	37	F4	Burkina Faso ■	55	F4				
Britstown	.....	58	E4	Bugsuk	......	36	C5	Burlington,				C			
Brittany =				Bugun Shara	..	35	B5	Iowa, U.S.A.	.	77	E9				
Bretagne	....	12	B2	Buguruslan	...	29	D6	Burlington, N.C.,				Ca Mau = Quan		
Brive-la-				Buh →	......	25	D3	U.S.A.	......	75	A8	Long	....	36	C3
Gaillarde	....	12	D4	Buheirat-Murrat-				Burlington, Vt.,				Caála	....	58	A3
Brixen =				el-Kubra	....	52	B5	U.S.A.	......	73	B9	Cabanatuan	...	38	A2
Bressanone	.	20	A3	Buir Nur	......	35	B6	Burlyu-Tyube	..	29	E8	Cabedelo	.....	92	D7
Brlik	....	29	E8	Bujumbura	...	57	E5	Burma ■	....	41	G11	Cabimas	......	90	A4
Brno	....	16	D3	Bukama	......	57	F5	Burnie	....	62	D4	Cabinda	......	56	F2
Brocken	......	14	C6	Bukavu	......	57	E5	Burnley	....	11	E5	Cabinda □	....	56	F2
Brodeur Pen.	..	68	A2	Bukene	....	57	E6	Burnside →	...	70	B9	Cabinet Mts.	..	81	B6
Brodnica	.....	16	B4	Bukhara =				Burqān	....	47	E6	Cabo Blanco	..	95	F3
Brody	....	17	C7	Bukhoro	....	29	F7	Burqin	....	34	B3	Cabo Frio	....	93	G5
Broken Hill =				Bukhoro	....	29	F7	Burra	....	62	B2	Cabo Pantoja	..	90	D3
Kabwe	....	59	A5	Bukittinggi	....	37	E2	Burren Junction	63	B4	Cabonga,			
Broken Hill	....	62	B3	Bukoba	......	57	E6	Burrendong				Réservoir	...	69	D3
Bronte Park	...	62	D4	Bula	....	39	E4	Dam	....	63	B4	Caboolture	....	63	A5
Brooks Ra.	....	71	B5	Bulahdelah	...	63	B5	Burrinjuck Res.	.	63	C4	Cabora Bassa		
Brooloo	......	63	A5	Bulan	....	38	B2	Burruyacú	...	94	B4	Dam =			
Broome	......	60	D3	Bulandshahr	..	42	E10	Bursa	....	23	D7	Cahora Bassa		
Brown, Pt.	....	62	B1	Bulawayo	....	59	C5	Burtundy	.....	62	B3	Dam	....	59	B6
Brownsville	...	78	G5	Buldan	....	23	E7	Buru	....	39	E3	Cabot Str.	....	69	D5
Brownwood	...	78	D4	Bulgan	....	35	B5	Burundi ■	....	57	E6	Cabra	....	18	D3
Bruay-en-Artois	13	A5	Bulgaria ■	....	22	C5	Burutu	....	55	G6	Cabrera	......	19	C7
Bruce, Mt.	....	60	E2	Bulgroo	......	63	A3	Bury St.				Cabriel →	....	19	C5
Bruck an der				Bulgunnia	....	62	B1	Edmunds	...	11	E7	Čačak	....	22	C3
Mur	....	15	E8	Bulhar	....	49	E3	Buşayyah	.....	47	E6	Cáceres, Brazil	.	91	G7
Bruges =				Buli, Teluk	....	39	D3	Būshehr	.....	44	D2	Cáceres, Spain	.	18	C2
Brugge	.....	14	C2	Buliluyan, C.	..	36	C5	Būshehr □	....	44	D2	Cachimbo, Serra		
Brugge	....	14	C2	Bulli	....	63	B5	Bushire =				do	....	93	D2
Brumado	.....	93	E5	Bulloo →	...	63	A3	Būshehr	....	44	D2	Cachoeira	.....	93	E6
Brunei = Bandar				Bulloo Downs	.	62	A3	Businga	......	56	D4	Cachoeira de		
Seri Begawan	36	D5	Bulloo L.	.....	62	A3	Busra ash Shām	46	D4	Itapemirim	..	93	G5
Brunei ■	...	36	D4	Bulls	....	64	D6	Busto Arsízio	..	20	B2	Cachoeira do		
Brunner, L.	...	65	E4	Bulo Burti	....	49	G4	Busu-Djanoa	..	56	D4	Sul	....	94	C6
Brunswick =				Bulsar = Valsad	43	J8	Busuanga	....	38	B1	Cacólo	......	56	G3
Braunschweig	14	B6	Bulukumba	...	39	F2	Buta	....	57	D4	Caconda	.....	58	A3
Brunswick	....	75	D7	Bulun	....	30	B10	Butare	....	57	E5	Cacongo	.....	56	F2
Brunswick, Pen.				Bumba	....	56	D4	Butaritari	.....	64	J12	Cadibarrawirracanna,		
de	....	95	G2	Bumhpa Bum	.	41	D11	Butembo	.....	57	D5	L.	....	62	A2
Brusque	.....	94	B7	Buna	....	57	D7	Butha Qi	.....	35	B7	Cadiz, Phil.	...	38	B2
Brussel	....	14	C3	Bunbah, Khalīj	.	52	B3	Buton	....	39	E2	Cádiz, Spain	..	18	D2
Brussels =				Bunbury	.....	60	G2	Butte	....	81	B7	Cádiz, G. de	..	18	D2
Brussel	....	14	C3	Buncrana	....	11	D3	Butterworth	...	36	C2	Cadney Park	..	62	A1
Bruthen	......	63	C4	Bundaberg	...	63		Butuan	....	38	C3	Caen	....	12	B3
Bruxelles =				Bundi	....	43	G9	Butung = Buton	39	E2	Caeté	....	93	F5
Brussel	....	14	C3	Bundoran	....	11	D2	Buturlinovka	..	24	C5	Caetité	....	93	E5
Bryan	....	79	D5	Bungo-Suidō	..	32	C3	Buxtehude	...	14	B5	Cagayan →	.	38	A2
Bryan, Mt.	....	62	B2	Bunia	....	57	D6	Buy	....	24	B5	Cagayan de Oro	38	C2
Bryansk	......	24	C3	Bunji	....	42	B9	Büyük				Cágliari	......	21	E2
Bu Craa	......	54	C2	Buntok	....	37	E4	Menderes →	23	F6	Cágliari, G. di	.	21	E2
Buapinang	...	39	E2	Bunyu	....	37	D5	Büyükçekmece	22	D7	Caguas	....	87	C6
Buayan	......	38	C3	Buol	....	39	D2	Buzău	....	17	F8	Cahora Bassa		
Bucak	....	46	C2	Buon Me Thuot	36	B3	Buzău →	...	17	F8	Dam	....	59	B6
Bucaramanga	.	90	B4	Buorkhaya, Mys	31	B11	Buzen	....	32	C2	Cahors	....	12	D4
Buchach	......	17	D7	Buqayq	......	47	F7	Buzi →	...	59	B6	Cahuapanas	..	91	E3
Buchanan	....	55	G2	Bur Acaba	...	49	G3	Buzuluk	......	29	D6	Cahul	....	17	F9
Buchans	......	69	D5	Bûr Safâga	...	52	C5	Byarezina →	17	B10				

Caia 59 B7
Caibarién 86 B4
Caicara 90 B5
Caicó 92 D6
Caicos Is. 87 B5
Caird Coast ... 96 B5
Cairns 61 D8
Cairo = El
 Qâhira 52 B5
Cairo 79 A9
Caiundo 58 B3
Caiza 91 H5
Cajamarca 91 E3
Cajàzeiras 92 D6
Calabar 55 H6
Calábria □ ... 21 E6
Calafate 95 G2
Calahorra 19 A5
Calais 12 A4
Calama, *Brazil* . 91 E6
Calama, *Chile* . 94 A3
Calamar,
 Bolívar,
 Colombia ... 90 A4
Calamar,
 Vaupés,
 Colombia ... 90 C4
Calamian Group 38 B1
Calamocha 19 B5
Calang 36 D1
Calapan 38 B2
Călăraşi 22 B6
Calatayud 19 B5
Calauag 38 B2
Calavite, C. ... 38 B2
Calbayog 38 B2
Calca 91 F4
Calcutta 41 F7
Caldas da
 Rainha 18 C1
Caldera 94 B2
Caldwell 80 D5
Caledon 58 E3
Caledon ⟶ ... 59 E5
Calgary 71 C8
Cali 90 C3
Calicut 43 P9
California □ ... 82 B3
California, G. de 84 B2
Calingasta 94 C3
Callabonna, L. . 62 A3
Callao 91 F3
Caloundra 63 A5
Caltagirone .. 21 F5
Caltanissetta .. 21 F5
Calulo 56 G2
Calunda 58 A4
Calvi 13 E8
Calviá 19 C7
Calvinia 58 E3
Camabatela .. 56 F3
Camacupa 58 A3
Camagüey 86 B4
Camaná 91 G4
Camargo 91 H5
Camargue 13 E6
Camarones ... 95 E3
Cambay =
 Khambhat . 43 H8
Cambay, G. of =
 Khambat, G.
 of 43 J8
Cambodia ■ .. 36 B3
Cambrai 13 A5
Cambrian Mts. 11 E5
Cambridge, *N.Z.* 64 B6
Cambridge, *U.K.* 11 E7
Cambridge,
 U.S.A. 73 C10

Cambridge Bay
 = Ikaluktutiak 70 B9
Cambridge G. . 60 C4
Cambundi-
 Catembo 56 G3
Camden, *Ark.,*
 U.S.A. 79 C7
Camden, *N.J.,*
 U.S.A. 73 E8
Cameroon ■ .. 56 C2
Cameroun, Mt. 56 D1
Cametá 92 C4
Caminha 18 B1
Camira Creek .. 63 A5
Camissombo .. 56 F4
Camocim 92 C5
Camopi ⟶ ... 92 B3
Campana, I. .. 95 F1
Campánia □ .. 21 D5
Campbell Town 62 D4
Campbellton .. 69 D4
Campbelltown . 63 B5
Campbeltown . 10 D4
Campeche 85 D6
Campeche, B. de 85 D6
Camperdown .. 62 C3
Campina Grande 92 D6
Campinas 94 A7
Campo 56 D1
Campo Belo ... 93 G4
Campo Formoso 93 E5
Campo Grande 93 G3
Campo Maíor . 92 C5
Campo Mourão 93 G3
Campoalegre .. 90 C3
Campobasso .. 20 D5
Campos 93 G5
Campos Belos . 93 E4
Campuya ⟶ .. 90 D4
Camrose 71 C8
Çan 23 D6
Can Tho 36 B3
Canada ■ 70 C8
Cañada de
 Gómez 94 C4
Çanakkale 23 D6
Çanakkale
 Boğazı 23 D6
Cananea 84 A2
Canarias, Is. ... 54 C1
Canary Is. =
 Canarias, Is. .. 54 C1
Canavieiras ... 93 F6
Canbelego 63 B4
Canberra 63 C4
Candala 49 E4
Candelo 63 C4
Candia =
 Iráklion 23 G5
Canea = Khaniá 23 G5
Canelones 94 C5
Cañete, *Chile* .. 94 D2
Cañete, *Peru* .. 91 F3
Cangas de
 Narcea 18 A2
Canguaretama . 92 D6
Canguçu 94 C6
Canicattì 21 F4
Canigou, Mt. .. 12 E5
Canipaan 36 C5
Çankırı 46 B3
Cann River ... 63 C4
Cannanore 43 P9
Cannes 13 E7
Canoas 94 B6
Canora 71 C9
Canowindra ... 63 B4
Cantabria □ ... 18 A4

Cantabrian Mts.
 = Cantábrica,
 Cordillera ... 18 A3
Cantábrica,
 Cordillera ... 18 A3
Cantal, Plomb
 du 13 D5
Canterbury ... 11 F7
Canterbury □ . 65 E4
Canterbury
 Bight 65 F4
Canterbury
 Plains 65 E4
Canton =
 Guangzhou .. 35 D6
Canton 72 D5
Canudos 91 E7
Canutama 91 E6
Cap-Haïtien ... 87 C5
Cap St.-Jacques
 = Vung Tau . 36 B3
Capaia 56 F4
Capanaparo ⟶ 90 B5
Cape Barren I. . 62 D4
Cape Breton I. . 69 D4
Cape Coast ... 55 G4
Cape Dorset .. 68 B3
Cape Girardeau 79 A9
Cape Jervis .. 62 C2
Cape Town ... 58 E3
Cape Verde
 Is. ■ 50 E1
Cape York
 Peninsula ... 61 C7
Capela 93 E6
Capim ⟶ 92 C4
Capraia 20 C2
Capri 21 D5
Caprivi Strip .. 58 B4
Captain's Flat . 63 C4
Caquetá ⟶ ... 90 D5
Caracal 22 B5
Caracas 90 A5
Caracol 93 D5
Caradoc 62 B3
Carajás, Serra
 dos 92 D3
Carangola 93 G5
Caransebeş ... 17 F6
Caratasca, L. .. 86 C3
Caratinga 93 F5
Caraúbas 92 D6
Caravaca 19 C5
Caravelas 93 F6
Caraveli 91 G4
Carballo 18 A1
Carbonara, C. . 21 E2
Carbondale ... 79 A9
Carbonear 69 D5
Carbonia 21 E2
Carcassonne .. 12 E5
Carcross 70 B6
Cardamon Hills 43 Q10
Cárdenas 86 B3
Cardiff 11 F5
Cardigan B. ... 11 E4
Cardston 71 D8
Carei 17 E6
Careysburg ... 55 G2
Carhué 94 D4
Caria 23 F7
Cariacica 93 G5
Caribbean Sea . 86 D5
Cariboo Mts. .. 71 C7
Carinda 63 B4
Carinhanha ... 93 E5
Carinthia □ =
 Kärnten □ .. 15 E7
Caripito 90 A6

Caritianas 91 E6
Carlisle 11 D5
Carlow 11 E3
Carlsbad 78 C1
Carmacks 70 B6
Carman 71 D10
Carmarthen ... 11 F4
Carmaux 12 D5
Carmelo 94 C5
Carmen 90 B3
Carmen de
 Patagones .. 95 E4
Carmona 18 D3
Carnac 12 C2
Carnarvon,
 Australia 60 E1
Carnarvon,
 S. Africa ... 58 E4
Carnegie, L. ... 60 F3
Carnic Alps =
 Karnische
 Alpen 20 A4
Carniche Alpi =
 Karnische
 Alpen 20 A4
Carnot 56 D3
Carnot, C. 62 B2
Carolina 92 D4
Caroline I. 65 K15
Caroline Is. ... 64 J10
Caroní ⟶ 90 B6
Caroníe =
 Nébrodi,
 Monti 21 F5
Caroona 63 B5
Carpathians ... 16 D5
Carpaţii
 Meridionali .. 17 F7
Carpentaria, G.
 of 60 C6
Carpentras 13 D6
Carpi 20 B3
Carpolac =
 Morea 62 C3
Carrara 20 B3
Carrauntoohill . 11 E2
Carrick-on-Suir 11 E3
Carrieton 62 B2
Carrizal Bajo .. 94 B2
Çarşamba 46 B4
Carson City .. 80 F4
Cartagena,
 Colombia ... 90 A3
Cartagena,
 Spain 19 D5
Cartago,
 Colombia ... 90 C3
Cartago,
 Costa Rica .. 86 E3
Carterton 65 D6
Carthage 79 A6
Cartwright 68 C5
Caruaru 92 D6
Carúpano 90 A6
Carvoeiro 90 D6
Carvoeiro, C. .. 18 C1
Casablanca ... 54 B3
Cascade Ra. .. 80 B3
Cascais 18 C1
Cascavel 94 A6
Cáscina 20 C3
Caserta 20 D5
Casiguran 38 A2
Casilda 94 C4
Casino 63 A5
Casiquiare ⟶ . 90 C5
Casma 91 E3
Caspe 19 B5
Casper 81 D10

Caspian Sea

Caspian Sea . . 29 E6
Cassinga 58 B3
Castellammare
di Stábia 21 D5
Castellón de la
Plana 19 C5
Castelo Branco 18 C2
Castelsarrasin . . 12 D4
Castelvetrano . 21 F4
Casterton 62 C3
Castilla La
Mancha □ . . 18 C4
Castilla y
Leon □ 18 A3
Castlebar 11 E2
Castleblaney . . 11 D3
Castlemaine . . 63 C3
Castlereagh → 63 B4
Castres 12 E5
Castries 87 D7
Castro 95 E2
Castro Alves . 93 E6
Castuera 18 C3
Cat I. 86 B4
Catacáos 91 E2
Catalão 93 F4
Çatalca 22 D7
Catalonia =
Cataluña □ . . 19 B6
Cataluña □ . . 19 B6
Catamarca . . . 94 B3
Catanduanes . . 38 B2
Catanduva 93 G4
Catánia 21 F5
Catanzaro 21 E6
Catarman 38 B2
Cateel 38 C3
Catoche, C. . . . 85 C7
Catrimani 90 C6
Catskill Mts. . . 73 C8
Cauca → 90 B4
Caucaia 92 C6
Caucasus
Mountains . . 25 E5
Caúngula 56 F3
Cauquenes 94 D2
Caura → 90 B6
Cauvery → . . 43 P11
Caux, Pays de . 12 B4
Cavan 11 D3
Cavendish 62 C3
Caviana, I. 92 B3
Cavite 38 B2
Cawndilla L. . . . 62 B3
Cawnpore =
Kanpur 40 D3
Caxias 92 C5
Caxias do Sul . 94 B6
Caxito 56 F2
Cayambe 90 C3
Cayenne 92 A3
Cayman Is. ■ . . 67 H11
Cazombo 58 A4
Ceadâr-Lunga . 17 E9
Ceanannus Mor 11 E3
Ceará =
Fortaleza 92 C6
Ceará □ 92 D6
Ceará Mirim . . 92 D6
Cebollar 94 B3
Cebu 38 B2
Cecil Plains . . 63 A5
Cedar L. 71 C10
Cedar Rapids . 77 E9
Cedro 92 D6
Ceduna 62 B1
Cefalù 21 E5
Ceglèd 16 E4
Celaya 84 C4

Celebes =
Sulawesi □ . 39 E2
Celebes Sea . . . 39 D2
Celje 20 A5
Celle 14 B6
Celtic Sea 11 F2
Central,
Cordillera . . . 90 C3
Central African
Rep. ■ 56 C4
Central Makran
Range 42 F4
Cephalonia =
Kefallinía . . . 23 E3
Ceram = Seram 39 E3
Ceram Sea =
Seram Sea . . 39 E3
Ceres, Argentina 94 B4
Ceres, S. Africa 58 E3
Cerignola 20 D5
Cerigo = Kíthira 23 F4
Çerkeş 46 B3
Çerkeşköy 22 D6
Cervera 19 B6
Cesena 20 B4
Česka Republika
= Czech
Rep. ■ 16 D2
České
Budějovice . 16 D2
Ceskomoravská
Vrchovina . . . 16 D2
Çeşme 23 E6
Cessnock 63 B5
Cetinje 22 C2
Cetraro 21 E5
Ceuta 18 E3
Cévennes 13 D5
Ceyhan 46 C3
Ceylon = Sri
Lanka ■ 43 R12
Chachapoyas . . 91 E3
Chachran 42 E7
Chad ■ 53 E2
Chad, L. =
Tchad, L. . . 53 F1
Chadileuvú → 94 D3
Chadyr-Lunga =
Ceadâr-Lunga 17 E9
Chagai Hills . . 42 E3
Chagos Arch. . 27 K11
Chāh Bahār . . . 45 E5
Chāh Gay Hills 45 D6
Chahar Burjak . 42 D3
Chaibasa 40 F5
Chakhānsūr . . . 42 D3
Chakradharpur . 40 F5
Chakwal 42 C8
Chala 91 G4
Chalcis =
Khalkís 23 E4
Chalhuanca . . . 91 F4
Chalisgaon 43 J9
Chalky Inlet . . . 65 G2
Challapata 91 G5
Chalon-sur-
Saône 13 C6
Châlons-en-
Champagne . 13 B6
Chaman 42 D5
Chamba, India . 42 C10
Chamba,
Tanzania . . . 59 A7
Chambal → . . 42 F11
Chambéry 13 D6
Chamical 94 C3
Chamonix-Mont
Blanc 13 D7
Champagne . . . 13 B6

Champaign . . . 72 D1
Champlain, L. . 73 B9
Chañaral 94 B2
Chandigarh . . . 42 D10
Chandler 62 A1
Chandmani . . . 34 B4
Chandpur 41 F8
Chandrapur . . . 43 K11
Chang Jiang → 35 C7
Changanacheri 43 Q10
Changane → . 59 C6
Changchiak'ou
= Zhangjiakou 35 B6
Ch'angchou =
Changzhou . . 35 C6
Changchun . . . 35 B7
Changde 35 D6
Changhai =
Shanghai . . . 35 C7
Changjiang . . . 35 E5
Changsha 35 D6
Changting 35 D6
Changzhi 35 C6
Changzhou . . . 35 C6
Channapatna . . 43 N10
Channel Is. . . . 11 G5
Chantada 18 A2
Chanthaburi . . 36 B2
Chantrey Inlet . 70 B10
Chanute 79 A6
Chao Phraya → 36 B2
Chao'an 35 D6
Chaoyang 35 D6
Chapala, L. de . 84 C4
Chapayevsk . . . 24 C6
Chapra =
Chhapra 40 E5
Châr 54 D2
Chara 31 D9
Charadai 94 B5
Charagua 91 G6
Charaña 91 G5
Chardara 29 E7
Chardzhou =
Chärjew 29 F7
Charente → . . 12 D3
Chari → 53 F1
Chārīkār 42 B6
Chärjew 29 F7
Charleroi 14 C3
Charles, C. . . . 73 F8
Charleston, S.C.,
U.S.A. 75 C8
Charleston,
W. Va., U.S.A. 72 E5
Charlesville . . . 56 F4
Charleville 63 A4
Charleville-
Mézières . . . 13 B6
Charlotte 75 B7
Charlotte Amalie 87 C7
Charlottesville . 73 E6
Charlottetown . 69 D4
Charlton 62 C3
Charolles 13 C6
Charouine 54 C4
Charters Towers 61 E8
Chartres 12 B4
Chascomús . . . 94 D5
Châteaubriant . 12 C3
Châteaulin 12 B1
Châteauroux . . 12 C4
Châtellerault . . 12 C4
Chatham, N.B.,
Canada 69 D4
Chatham, Ont.,
Canada 69 D2
Chatham, U.K. . 11 F7
Chatrapur 40 H5

Chattahoochee →
. . . . 74 D5
Chattanooga . . 74 B5
Chauk 41 G10
Chaukan La . . 41 D11
Chaumont 13 B6
Chaves, Brazil . 92 C4
Chaves, Portugal 18 B2
Chavuma 58 A4
Cheb 16 C1
Cheboksary . . . 24 B6
Chech, Erg . . . 54 D4
Chechenia □ . . 25 E6
Checheno-
Ingush
Republic =
Chechenia □ 25 E6
Chechnya =
Chechenia □ 25 E6
Cheduba I. 41 H9
Cheepie 63 A4
Chegga 54 C3
Chegutu 59 B6
Chehalis 80 B2
Cheju Do 35 C7
Chekiang =
Zhejiang □ . 35 D7
Cheleken 29 F6
Chelforó 95 D3
Chelkar =
Shalqar 29 E6
Chelkar Tengiz,
Solonchak . . 29 E7
Chelm 17 C6
Chelmno 16 B4
Chelmsford . . . 11 F7
Cheltenham . . . 11 F5
Chelyabinsk . . 29 D7
Chemnitz 15 C7
Chen Xian 35 D6
Chenab → . . . 42 D7
Chencha 53 G6
Chenchiang =
Zhenjiang . . . 35 C6
Chengde 35 B6
Chengdu 35 C5
Chengjiang . . . 34 D5
Ch'engtu =
Chengdu . . . 35 C5
Chennai =
Madras 43 N12
Cheo Reo 36 B3
Cheom Ksan . . 36 B2
Chepén 91 E3
Chepes 94 C3
Cher → 12 C4
Cherbourg 12 B3
Cherchell 54 A5
Cherdyn 28 C6
Cherepanovo . . 29 D9
Cherepovets . . 24 B4
Chergui, Chott
ech 54 B5
Cherikov =
Cherykaw . . 17 B10
Cherkasy 24 D3
Cherlak 29 D8
Chernaya 30 B6
Chernigov =
Chernihiv . . . 24 C3
Chernihiv 24 C3
Chernivtsi 17 D7
Chernobyl =
Chornobyl . . 17 C10
Chernovtsy =
Chernivtsi . . 17 D7
Chernyakhovsk 28 D3
Cherquenco . . . 94 D2
Cherrapunji . . . 41 E8

Cherven 17 B9
Chervonohrad . 17 C7
Cherykaw 17 B10
Chesapeake ... 73 F7
Chesapeake B. . 73 E7
Cheshskaya
  Guba 28 C5
Chester, U.K. ... 11 E5
Chester, U.S.A. 73 E8
Chesterfield ... 11 E6
Chesterfield, Is. 64 L10
Chesterfield Inlet 70 B10
Chesterton Ra. 63 A4
Cheviot Hills .. 10 D5
Chew Bahir ... 53 H6
Cheyenne 76 E2
Cheyenne ➝ . 76 C4
Chhapra 40 E5
Chhatarpur ... 43 G11
Chhattisgarh
  □ 40 G3
Chhindwara ... 43 H11
Chhlong 36 B3
Chi ➝ 36 A2
Chiamussu =
  Jiamusi 35 B8
Chiange 58 B2
Chiapa ➝ 85 D6
Chiávari 20 B2
Chiavenna 20 A2
Chiba 32 B7
Chibemba 58 B2
Chibia 58 B2
Chibougamau . 69 D3
Chibuk 53 F1
Chicacole =
  Srikakulam .. 40 H4
Chicago 72 D2
Chichagof I. .. 71 C6
Chichibu 32 A6
Chickasha 78 B5
Chiclana de la
  Frontera 18 D2
Chiclayo 91 E3
Chico ➝ 80 F3
Chico ➝,
  Chubut,
  Argentina ... 95 E3
Chico ➝,
  Santa Cruz,
  Argentina ... 95 F3
Chicoutimi 69 D3
Chidambaram . 43 P11
Chidley, C. 68 B4
Chiemsee 15 E7
Chiengi 57 F5
Chiese ➝ 20 B3
Chieti 20 C5
Chiguana 91 H5
Chihli, G. of =
  Bo Hai 35 C6
Chihuahua 84 B3
Chiili 29 E7
Chik Bollapur .. 43 N10
Chikmagalur .. 43 N9
Chilapa 84 D5
Chilas 42 B9
Chilaw 43 R11
Childers 63 A5
Chile ■ 94 D2
Chilete 91 E3
Chililabombwe 59 A5
Chilin = Jilin .. 35 B7
Chilka L. 40 H5
Chillán 94 D2
Chiloé, I. de ... 95 E2
Chilpancingo .. 84 D5
Chiluage 56 F4
Chilwa, L. 59 B7

Chimbay 29 E6
Chimborazo ... 90 D3
Chimbote 91 E3
Chimkent =
  Shymkent ... 29 E7
Chimoio 59 B6
Chin □ 41 F9
China ■ 35 C5
Chinan = Jinan 35 C6
Chinandega .. 85 E7
Chincha Alta .. 91 F3
Chinchilla 63 A5
Chinchou =
  Jinzhou 35 B7
Chinde 59 B7
Chindwin ➝ .. 41 G10
Chingola 59 A5
Ch'ingtao =
  Qingdao 35 C7
Chinguetti 54 D2
Chinhoyi 59 B6
Chiniot 42 D8
Chinju 35 C7
Chinnampo ... 35 C7
Chinon 12 C4
Chinsali 57 G6
Chióggia 20 B4
Chíos = Khíos . 23 E6
Chipata 59 A6
Chiquián 91 F3
Chiquinquira . 90 B4
Chirchiq 29 E7
Chirmiri 40 F4
Chiromo 59 B7
Chisamba 59 A5
Chisapani Garhi 40 D5
Chişinău 17 E9
Chistopol 24 B7
Chita 30 D9
Chitado 58 B2
Chitembo 58 A3
Chitral 42 B7
Chitré 86 E3
Chittagong 41 F8
Chittagong □ .. 41 E8
Chittaurgarh .. 43 G9
Chittoor 43 N11
Chiusi 20 C3
Chivasso 20 B1
Chivilcoy 94 B4
Chkalov =
  Orenburg ... 29 D6
Choele Choel .. 95 D3
Chojnice 16 B3
Cholet 12 C3
Choluteca 85 E7
Choma 59 B5
Chomutov 16 C1
Chon Buri 36 B2
Chone 90 D3
Chŏngjin 35 B7
Chŏngju 35 C7
Chongqing ... 35 D5
Chŏnju 35 C7
Chonos, Arch.
  de los 95 F2
Chop 17 D6
Chornobyl 17 C10
Chortkiv 17 D7
Chorzów 16 C4
Chos-Malal ... 94 D2
Chōshi 32 B7
Choszczno 16 B2
Chotila 43 H7
Choybalsan .. 35 B6
Christchurch .. 65 E5
Christiana 59 D5
Christmas I. =
  Kiritimati ... 65 J15

Chu = Shu 29 E8
Ch'uanchou =
  Quanzhou ... 35 D6
Chubut ➝ 95 E3
Chudskoye, Oz. 24 B2
Chūgoku-Sanchi 32 B3
Chula Vista ... 82 D4
Chulucanas ... 90 E2
Chulym ➝ ... 29 D9
Chumbicha ... 94 B3
Chumphon 36 B1
Chuna ➝ 30 D7
Chunchŏn ... 35 C7
Chungking =
  Chongqing .. 35 D5
Chunya 57 F6
Chuquibamba . 91 G4
Chuquicamata . 94 A3
Chur 13 C8
Churachandpur 41 E9
Churchill 70 C10
Churchill ➝,
  Man., Canada 70 C10
Churchill ➝,
  Nfld., Canada 69 C4
Churchill, C. .. 70 C10
Churchill Falls . 69 C4
Churchill L. ... 71 C9
Churu 42 E9
Chushal 42 C11
Chusovoy 28 D6
Chuvash
  Republic □ =
  Chuvashia □ 24 B6
Chuvashia □ .. 24 B6
Cicero 72 D2
Ciechanów 16 B5
Ciego de Avila . 86 B4
Ciénaga 90 A4
Cienfuegos ... 86 B3
Cieszyn 16 D4
Cieza 19 C5
Cijara, Pantano
  de 18 C3
Cilician Gates P. 46 C3
Cill Chainnigh =
  Kilkenny 11 E3
Cimişlia 17 E9
Cimone, Mte. .. 20 B3
Cîmpina 17 F7
Cîmpulung ... 17 F7
Cinca ➝ 19 B6
Cincar 20 C6
Cincinnati 72 E3
Çine 23 F7
Cinto, Mte. 13 E8
Circle 71 B5
Cirebon 37 F3
Citlaltépetl 84 D5
Città di Castello 20 C4
Ciudad Bolívar 90 B6
Ciudad
  Chetumal ... 85 D7
Ciudad del
  Carmen 85 D6
Ciudad Delicias
  = Delicias .. 84 B3
Ciudad Guayana 90 B6
Ciudad Juárez . 84 A3
Ciudad Madero 84 C5
Ciudad Mante . 84 C5
Ciudad Obregón 84 B3
Ciudad Real .. 18 C4
Ciudad Rodrigo 18 B2
Ciudad Trujillo
  = Santo
  Domingo ... 87 C6
Ciudad Victoria 84 C5
Civitanova
  Marche 20 C4

Civitavécchia .. 20 C3
Cizre 46 C5
Clanwilliam .. 58 E3
Clare 62 B2
Clarence ➝,
  Australia 63 A5
Clarence ➝,
  N.Z. 65 E5
Clarence, I. ... 95 G2
Clarence I. 96 A4
Clarie Coast ... 96 A13
Clarke I. 62 D4
Clarksdale ... 79 B8
Clarksville ... 74 A4
Claveria 38 A2
Clear, C. 11 F2
Clearwater ... 75 F6
Clearwater Mts. 81 B6
Clermont-
  Ferrand ... 13 D5
Cleveland,
  Australia 63 A5
Cleveland,
  U.S.A. 72 D5
Clifden 65 G2
Clifton 63 A5
Clifton Hills .. 62 A2
Clinton, Canada 71 C7
Clinton, N.Z. .. 65 G3
Clinton, U.S.A. 77 E9
Clinton Colden
  L. 70 B9
Clones 11 D3
Clonmel 11 E3
Clovis 78 B2
Cluj-Napoca .. 17 E6
Clunes 62 C3
Clutha ➝ 65 G3
Clyde 65 F3
Clyde ➝ 10 D4
Clyde, Firth of . 10 D4
Clyde River ... 68 A4
Coari 90 D6
Coast Mts. 70 C7
Coast Ranges . 80 F2
Coats I. 68 B2
Coats Land ... 96 B5
Coatzacoalcos . 85 D6
Cobalt 69 D3
Cobar 63 B4
Cóbh 11 F2
Cobham 62 B3
Cobija 91 F5
Cobourg 69 D3
Cobram 63 C4
Cóbué 59 A6
Coburg 15 C6
Cocanada =
  Kakinada ... 40 J4
Cochabamba .. 91 G5
Cochin 43 Q10
Cochin China =
  Nam-Phan .. 36 B3
Cochrane 69 D2
Cochrane, L. .. 95 F2
Cockburn 62 B3
Cockburn, Canal 95 G2
Coco ➝ 86 D3
Cocobeach ... 56 D1
Cod, C. 73 C10
Codajás 90 D6
Codó 92 C5
Cœur d'Alene . 80 B5
Coffeyville ... 79 A6
Coffin B. 62 B2
Coffin Bay
  Peninsula ... 62 B2
Coffs Harbour . 63 B5
Cognac 12 D3

Cohuna 63 C3
Coiba, I. 86 E3
Coig → 95 G3
Coihaique ... 95 F2
Coimbatore ... 43 P10
Coimbra, *Brazil* 91 G7
Coimbra,
  Portugal 18 B1
Coín 18 D3
Cojimies 90 C3
Colac 62 C3
Colatina 93 F5
Colbeck, C. 96 B17
Colbinabbin ... 63 C3
Colchester 11 F7
Colebrook 62 D4
Coleman ... 71 D8
Coleraine,
  Australia 62 C3
Coleraine, *U.K.* 11 D3
Coleridge, L. .. 65 E4
Colesberg 59 E5
Colhué Huapi, L. 95 F3
Colima 84 D4
Colinas 92 D5
Coll 10 C3
Collaguasi 91 H5
Collarenebri ... 63 A4
Collingwood .. 64 D5
Colmar 13 B7
Colo → 63 B5
Cologne = Köln 14 C4
Colomb-Béchar
  = Béchar .. 54 B4
Colômbia ... 93 G4
Colombia ■ .. 90 C4
Colombo 43 R11
Colón, *Cuba* ... 86 B3
Colón, *Panama* 85 F9
Colonia 94 C5
Colonia Dora . 94 B4
Colonsay 10 C3
Colorado □ ... 83 A10
Colorado →,
  Argentina ... 95 D4
Colorado →,
  N. Amer. 82 E5
Colorado
  Plateau 83 B7
Colorado
  Springs 76 F2
Columbia, *Mo.,*
  U.S.A. 77 F8
Columbia, *S.C.,*
  U.S.A. 75 B7
Columbia,
  Tenn., U.S.A. 74 B4
Columbia → .. 80 B1
Columbia,
  District of □ . 73 E7
Columbia Basin 80 B4
Columbretes, Is. 19 C6
Columbus, *Ga.,*
  U.S.A. 74 C5
Columbus,
  Miss., U.S.A. 74 C3
Columbus, *Ohio,*
  U.S.A. 72 E4
Colville → 71 A4
Colville, C. ... 64 B6
Colwyn Bay .. 11 E5
Comácchio 20 B4
Comallo 95 E2
Comilla 41 F8
Comino, C. 21 D2
Committee B. . 68 B2
Commonwealth
  B. 96 A14
Commoron
  Cr. → 63 A5

Communism Pk.
  =
  Kommunizma,
  Pik 29 F8
Como 20 B2
Como, L. di ... 20 B2
Comodoro
  Rivadavia ... 95 F3
Comorin, C. ... 43 Q10
Comoro Is. =
  Comoros ■ . 51 H8
Comoros ■ ... 51 H8
Comox 71 D7
Compiègne ... 13 B5
Compton Downs 63 B4
Comrat 17 E9
Conakry 55 G2
Conara Junction 62 D4
Concarneau ... 12 C2
Conceição da
  Barra 93 F6
Concepción,
  Bolivia 91 G6
Concepción,
  Chile 94 D2
Concepción,
  Paraguay ... 94 A5
Concepción, L. 91 G6
Concepción del
  Oro 84 C4
Concepción del
  Uruguay 94 C5
Conchos → .. 84 B3
Concord, *N.C.,*
  U.S.A. 75 B7
Concord, *N.H.,*
  U.S.A. 73 C10
Concordia,
  Argentina ... 94 C5
Concórdia, *Brazil* 90 D5
Condamine ... 63 A5
Condeúba 93 E5
Condobolin ... 63 B4
Conegliano ... 20 B4
Confuso → ... 94 B5
Congo ■ 56 E3
Congo → 56 F2
Congo, Dem.
  Rep. of the ■ 56 E4
Conjeeveram =
  Kanchipuram 43 N11
Conlea 63 B3
Conn, L. 11 D2
Connacht □ ... 11 E2
Connecticut □ . 73 D9
Connecticut → 73 D9
Connemara ... 11 E2
Conoble 63 B3
Cononaco → . 90 D3
Conran, C. 63 C4
Conselheiro
  Lafaiete 93 G5
Constance =
  Konstanz ... 14 E5
Constance, L. =
  Bodensee .. 13 C8
Constanța 22 B7
Constantine .. 54 A6
Constitución .. 94 D2
Contai 40 G6
Contamana ... 91 E4
Contas → 93 E6
Conway, L. 62 A2
Coober Pedy . 62 A1
Cooch Behar =
  Koch Bihar . 41 D7
Cook, B. 95 H2
Cook, Aoraki Mt. 65 E4
Cook Inlet 71 C4

Cook Is. 65 L14
Cook Strait 65 D6
Cooktown ... 61 D8
Coolabah ... 63 B4
Cooladdi ... 63 A4
Coolah 63 B4
Coolamon ... 63 B4
Coolangatta ... 63 A5
Cooma 63 C4
Coonabarabran 63 B4
Coonamble .. 63 B4
Coondapoor .. 43 N9
Coongie 62 A3
Coongoola ... 63 A4
Cooninie, L. ... 62 A2
Cooper Cr. →,
  N. Terr.,
  Australia 60 C5
Cooper Cr. →,
  S. Austral.,
  Australia 62 A2
Cooroy 63 A5
Cootamundra . 63 B4
Cooyar 63 A5
Copenhagen =
  København .. 9 G10
Copiapó 94 B2
Copiapó → ... 94 B2
Copley 62 B2
Copper Center . 71 B5
Copper Cliff ... 69 D2
Coppermine =
  Kugluktuk ... 70 B8
Coppermine → 70 B8
Coquimbo ... 94 C2
Corabia 22 C5
Coracora 91 G4
Coral Harbour =
  Salliq 68 B2
Coral Sea ... 64 L10
Corato 21 D6
Corby 11 E6
Corcaigh = Cork 11 F2
Corcubión 18 A1
Córdoba,
  Argentina ... 94 C4
Córdoba, *Spain* 18 D3
Córdoba, Sierra
  de 94 C4
Cordon 38 A2
Cordova 71 B5
Corfu = Kérkira 23 E2
Coria 18 C2
Corigliano
  Cálabro ... 21 E6
Corinna 62 D4
Corinth =
  Kórinthos .. 23 F4
Corinth, G. of =
  Korinthiakós
  Kólpos 23 E4
Corinto 93 F5
Cork 11 F2
Çorlu 22 D6
Corner Brook .. 69 D5
Corneşti 17 E9
Cornwall 69 D3
Corny Pt. 62 B2
Coro 90 A5
Coroatá 92 C5
Corocoro 91 G5
Coroico 91 G5
Coromandel .. 64 B6
Corona 62 B3
Coronation Gulf 70 B8
Coronation I. .. 96 A4
Coronel 94 D2
Coronel Dorrego 94 D4
Coronel Suárez 94 D4

Corowa 63 C4
Corpus Christi . 78 F5
Corque 91 G5
Corrib, L. 11 E2
Corrientes 94 B5
Corrientes → . 90 D4
Corrientes, C.,
  Colombia ... 90 B3
Corrientes, C.,
  Mexico 84 C3
Corse 13 E8
Corse, C. 13 E8
Corsica = Corse 13 E8
Corsicana 79 C5
Corte 13 E8
Çorum 46 B3
Corumbá 91 G7
Corumbá de
  Goiás 93 F4
Corunna = La
  Coruña 18 A1
Corvallis 80 C2
Cosenza 21 E6
Costa Blanca . 19 C5
Costa Brava ... 19 B7
Costa del Sol . 18 D3
Costa Dorada . 19 C6
Costa Rica ■ .. 86 E3
Cotabato 38 C2
Cotagaita 91 H5
Côte d'Azur ... 13 E7
Côte-d'Ivoire ■
  = Ivory
  Coast ■ 55 G3
Cotentin 12 B3
Cotonou 55 G5
Cotopaxi 90 D3
Cotswold Hills . 11 F5
Cottbus 15 C8
Couedic, C. du . 62 C2
Coulman I. ... 96 B15
Council 71 B3
Council Bluffs . 77 E7
Courantyne → 90 B7
Courtrai =
  Kortrijk 14 C2
Coventry 11 E6
Covilhã 18 B2
Covington 72 E3
Cowal, L. 63 B4
Cowangie 62 C3
Cowarie 62 A2
Cowell 62 B2
Cowra 63 B4
Coxim 93 F3
Cox's Bazar .. 41 G8
Cozumel, I. de . 85 C7
Craboon 63 B4
Cracow =
  Kraków 16 C4
Cracow 63 A5
Cradock 59 E5
Craigavon ... 11 D5
Crailsheim 14 D6
Craiova 22 B4
Cranbrook,
  Australia 62 D4
Cranbrook,
  Canada 71 D8
Crateús 92 D5
Crato 92 D6
Crawley 11 F6
Crazy Mts. ... 81 B8
Crema 20 B2
Cremona 20 B3
Cres 20 B5
Cressy 62 C3
Crete = Kríti . 23 G5
Créteil 12 B5

Creus, C. de ... 19 A7
Creuse → 12 C4
Crewe 11 E5
Criciúma 94 B7
Crimean Pen. =
  Krymskyy
  Pivostriv 25 D3
Crişul Alb → . 16 E5
Crişul Negru → 16 E5
Crna Gora =
  Montenegro □ 22 C2
Crna Gora 22 C3
Crna Reka → . 22 D3
Croatia ■ 20 B6
Crocker,
  Banjaran 36 C5
Croker, C. 60 C5
Cromer 11 E7
Cromwell 65 F3
Cronulla 63 B5
Crookwoll 63 B4
Cross Sound .. 71 C6
Crotone 21 E6
Crows Nest ... 63 A5
Crowsnest Pass 71 D8
Cruz Alta 94 B6
Cruz del Eje .. 94 C4
Cruzeiro 93 G5
Cruzeiro do Sul 91 E4
Crystal Brook . 62 B2
Csongrád 16 E5
Cuamba 59 A7
Cuando → 58 B4
Cuarto → 94 C4
Cuba ■ 86 B4
Cubango → ... 58 B4
Cuchi 58 A3
Cúcuta 90 B4
Cuddalore 43 P11
Cuddapah ... 43 M11
Cudgewa 63 C4
Cuenca, Ecuador 90 D3
Cuenca, Spain . 19 B4
Cuenca,
  Serranía de . 19 C5
Cuernavaca ... 84 D5
Cuevas del
  Almanzora . 19 D5
Cuevo 91 H6
Cuiabá 93 F2
Cuiabá → 93 F2
Cuima 58 A3
Cuito → 58 B4
Cukai 36 D2
Culcairn 63 C4
Culgoa → 63 A4
Culiacán 84 C3
Culion 38 B2
Cullarin Ra. ... 63 B4
Cullera 19 C5
Culuene → 93 E3
Culverden 65 E5
Cumaná 90 A6
Cumberland,
  Canada 71 D7
Cumberland,
  U.S.A. 73 E6
Cumberland
  Pen. 68 B4
Cumberland
  Plateau 72 F3
Cumberland Sd. 68 B4
Cumborah 63 A4
Cumbum 43 M11
Cummins 62 B2
Cumnock 63 B4
Cunene → 58 B2
Cúneo 20 B1
Cunnamulla ... 63 A4

Cupica, G. de .. 90 B3
Curaçao 87 D6
Curaray → ... 90 D4
Curiapo 90 B6
Curicó 94 C2
Curitiba 94 B7
Currabubula .. 63 B5
Currais Novos . 92 D6
Curralinho 92 C4
Curraweena ... 63 B4
Currie 62 C3
Curtea de Argeş 17 F7
Curtis Group .. 62 C4
Curuápanema →
  .... 92 C2
Curuçá 92 C4
Curup 37 E2
Cururupu 92 C5
Curuzú Cuatiá . 94 B5
Cuttaburra → . 63 A3
Cuttack 40 G5
Cuvier I. 64 B6
Cuxhaven 14 B5
Cuyo 38 B2
Cuzco, Bolivia . 91 H5
Cuzco, Peru ... 91 F4
Cwmbran 11 F5
Cyclades =
  Kikládhes ... 23 F5
Cygnet 62 D4
Cyprus ■ 46 D3
Cyrenaica 52 C3
Cyrene =
  Shahḥat 52 B3
Czech Rep. ■ .. 16 D2
Częstochowa .. 16 C4

D

Da Hinggan Ling 35 B7
Da Lat 36 B3
Da Nang 36 A3
Da Qaidam ... 34 C4
Da Yunhe → . 35 C7
Daba Shan ... 35 C5
Dabakala 55 G4
Dabo 37 E2
Dabola 55 F2
Daboya 55 G4
Dacca = Dhaka 41 F8
Dacca =
  Dhaka □ ... 41 E8
Dachau 15 D6
Dadanawa 90 C7
Dadra and
  Nagar
  Haveli □ 43 J8
Dadu 42 F5
Daet 38 B2
Dagana 55 E1
Dagestan □ ... 25 E6
Daghestan
  Republic =
  Dagestan □ . 25 E6
Dagö = Hiiumaa 24 B1
Dagupan 38 A2
Dahlak Kebir .. 49 D3
Dahod 43 H9
Dahomey =
  Benin ■ 55 G5
Dahra 55 E1
Daiō-Misaki .. 32 B5
Dairût 52 C5
Dakar 55 F1
Dakhla 54 D1

Dakhla, El
  Wâhât el- ... 52 C4
Dakhovskaya .. 25 E5
Đakovica 22 C3
Dalaman → .. 23 F7
Dalandzadgad . 35 B5
Dālbandīn 42 E4
Dalby 63 A5
Dalhousie 69 D4
Dali 34 D5
Dalian 35 C7
Daliang Shan . 34 D5
Dallarnil 63 A5
Dallas 79 C5
Dalmacija 20 C6
Dalmatia =
  Dalmacija .. 20 C6
Daloa 55 G3
Dalton 74 B5
Dalton Iceberg
  Tongue 96 A13
Daly Waters ... 60 D5
Daman 43 J8
Damanhûr 52 B5
Damar 39 F3
Damaraland ... 58 C3
Damascus =
  Dimashq ... 46 D4
Damāvand 44 C3
Damāvand,
  Qolleh-ye ... 44 C3
Damba 56 F3
Dāmghān 44 B3
Damiel 18 C4
Damietta =
  Dumyât 52 B5
Dammam = Ad
  Dammām .. 47 F7
Damoh 43 H11
Dampier 60 E2
Dampier, Selat . 39 E4
Danbury 73 D9
Dandeldhura .. 40 C3
Dandeli 43 M9
Dandenong ... 63 C4
Dandong 35 B7
Danger Is. =
  Pukapuka .. 65 L14
Danger Pt. 58 E3
Dangora 55 F6
Danilov 24 B5
Dankhar Gompa 42 C11
Dannemora .. 9 F11
Dannevirke ... 64 D7
Dante 49 E5
Danube =
  Dunărea → . 17 F9
Danville 75 A8
Danzig =
  Gdańsk 16 A4
Dao 38 B2
Daoud = Aïn
  Beïda 54 A6
Dar el Beida =
  Casablanca .. 54 B3
Dar es Salaam . 57 F7
Dārāb 44 D3
Daraj 54 B7
Darband 42 B8
Darbhanga ... 40 D5
Dardanelles =
  Çanakkale
  Boğazı 23 D6
Dârfûr 53 F3
Dargai 42 B7
Dargan Ata ... 29 E7
Dargaville 64 A5
Danca 22 D7
Darién, G. del . 90 B3

Darjeeling =
  Darjiling 40 D7
Darjiling 40 D7
Darling → 62 B3
Darling Downs 63 A5
Darling Ra. ... 60 G2
Darlington 11 D6
Darłowo 16 A3
Darmstadt ... 14 D5
Darnah 52 B3
Darnley, C. ... 96 A10
Darnley B. 70 B7
Dart, C. 96 B18
Dartmoor 11 F5
Dartmouth ... 69 D4
Dartmouth, L. . 63 A4
Darvaza 29 E6
Darvel, Teluk . 38 D1
Darwha 43 J10
Darwin 60 C5
Daryoi Amu =
  Amudarya → 29 E6
Dās 44 E3
Dashhowuz ... 29 E6
Dasht → 42 G2
Dasht-e Kavīr .. 44 C3
Dasht-e Mārgow 42 D3
Datça 23 F6
Datia 43 G11
Datong 35 B6
Datu, Tanjung . 37 D3
Datu Piang ... 38 C2
Daugava → .. 24 B1
Daugavpils ... 24 B2
Daulpur 42 F10
Dauphin 71 C9
Dauphiné 13 D6
Davangere ... 43 M9
Davao 38 C3
Davao, G. of . 38 C3
Dāvar Panāh .. 45 E5
Davenport 77 E9
David 86 E3
David Gorodok
  = Davyd
  Haradok 17 B8
Davis Sea 96 A11
Davis Str. 68 B5
Davos 13 C8
Davyd Haradok 17 B8
Dawson 70 B6
Dawson, I. 95 G2
Dax 12 E3
Daxian 35 C5
Daxue Shan .. 34 C5
Daylesford ... 62 C3
Dayr az Zawr .. 46 D5
Dayton 72 E3
Daytona Beach 75 E7
Dead Sea 47 E3
Deakin 60 G4
Deal I. 62 C4
Deán Funes ... 94 C4
Death Valley .. 82 B4
Deba Habe 55 F7
Debar 22 D3
Dębica 16 C5
Debre Markos . 53 F6
Debre Tabor .. 53 F6
Debrecen 16 E5
Decatur, Ala.,
  U.S.A. 74 B4
Decatur, Ill.,
  U.S.A. 77 F10
Deccan 43 L11
Děčín 16 C2
Dedéagach =
  Alexandroúpolis
  .... 22 D5

Dédougou 55 F4
Dee → 10 C5
Deepwater 63 A5
Degeh Bur 49 F3
Deggendorf ... 15 D7
Deh Bīd 44 D3
Dehi Titan 42 C3
Dehibat 54 B7
Dehkareqan ... 46 C6
Dehra Dun 42 D11
Dej 17 E6
Dekese 56 E4
Delano 82 C3
Delaware □ ... 73 E8
Delaware → .. 73 E8
Delegate 63 C4
Delgado, C. ... 57 G8
Delgo 53 D5
Delhi 42 E10
Delice → 46 C3
Delicias 84 B3
Déline........ 70 B7
Delmenhorst .. 14 B5
Delmiro Gouveia 93 D6
Deloraine 62 D4
Delungra 63 A5
Delvinë 23 E3
Demanda, Sierra
  de la 18 A4
Demavand =
  Damāvand . 44 C3
Demba 56 F4
Dembecha .. 53 F6
Dembidolo ... 53 G5
Demini → 90 D6
Demirci 23 E7
Demirköy ... 22 D6
Dempo 37 E2
Den Haag = 's-
  Gravenhage . 14 B3
Den Helder ... 14 B3
Denau 29 F7
Dendang 37 E3
Denia 19 C6
Denial B. 62 B1
Deniliquin ... 63 C3
Denman Glacier 96 A11
Denmark ■ ... 9 G9
Denmark Str. .. 66 C17
Denpasar 37 F5
Denton 78 C5
D'Entrecasteaux
  Is. 61 B9
Denver 76 F2
Deoghar 40 E6
Deolali 43 K8
Deoria 40 D4
Deosai Mts. ... 42 B9
Dêqên 34 D4
Dera Ghazi Khan 42 D7
Dera Ismail
  Khan 42 D7
Derbent 25 E6
Derby, Australia 60 D3
Derby, U.K. ... 11 E6
Derg, L. 11 E2
Dergaon 41 D9
Derry =
  Londonderry 11 D3
Derudub 53 E6
Des Moines ... 77 E8
Des Moines → 77 E9
Desaguadero → 91 G5
Dese 49 E2
Desna → 17 C10
Desolación, I. .. 95 G2
Despeñaperros,
  Paso 18 C4
Dessau 15 C7

D'Estrees B. ... 62 C2
Detmold 14 C5
Detroit 72 C4
Deutsche Bucht 14 A5
Deva 17 F6
Devakottai 43 Q11
Deventer 14 B4
Devonport,
  Australia 62 D4
Devonport, N.Z. 64 B6
Dewas 43 H10
Deyhūk 44 C4
Deyyer 44 E2
Dezfūl 47 D7
Dezhneva, Mys 31 C16
Dhafra 44 F3
Dhahira 44 F4
Dhahran = Aẕ
  Ẕahrān 47 F7
Dhaka 41 F8
Dhaka □ 41 E8
Dhamar 49 E3
Dhamtari 40 G3
Dhanbad 40 F6
Dhangarhi 40 C3
Dhankuta 40 D6
Dhar 43 H9
Dharmapuri ... 43 N11
Dharwad 43 M9
Dhaulagiri ... 40 C4
Dhenkanal ... 40 G5
Dhíkti Óros ... 23 G5
Dhírfis 23 E4
Dhodhekánisos 23 F6
Dhrol 43 H7
Dhubaibah 44 F3
Dhuburi 41 D7
Dhule 43 J9
Dhut → 49 E5
Diafarabé 55 F4
Diamantina ... 93 F5
Diamantina → 62 A2
Diamantino .. 93 E2
Diamond
  Harbour 40 F7
Diapaga 55 F5
Dībā 44 E4
Dibaya 56 F4
Dibaya-Lubue . 56 E3
Dibbi 49 G3
Dibrugarh ... 41 D10
Dickson 28 B9
Didiéni 55 F3
Diébougou ... 55 F4
Diefenbaker L. . 71 C9
Dieppe 12 B4
Digby 69 D4
Digges Is. 68 B3
Dighinala 41 F9
Digne-les-Bains 13 D7
Digos 38 C3
Digul → 39 F5
Dihang → 41 D10
Dijlah, Nahr → 47 E6
Dijon 13 C6
Dikimdya 31 D10
Dikson =
  Dickson 28 B9
Dikwa 53 F1
Dili 39 F3
Dilling 53 F4
Dillingham ... 71 C4
Dilolo 56 G4
Dilston 62 D4
Dimashq 46 D4
Dimbokro ... 55 G4
Dimboola 62 C3
Dîmboviţa → . 22 B6
Dimitrovgrad,
  Bulgaria 22 C5

Dimitrovgrad,
  Russia 24 C6
Dimitrovo =
  Pernik 22 C4
Dinagat 38 B3
Dinajpur 41 E7
Dinan 12 B2
Dinant 14 C3
Dinar 46 C2
Dīnār, Kūh-e .. 44 D2
Dinara Planina . 20 B6
Dinard 12 B2
Dinaric Alps =
  Dinara Planina 20 B6
Dindigul 43 P11
Dingle 11 E1
Dinguiraye ... 55 F2
Dingwall 10 C4
Dinosaur
  National
  Monument .. 81 E9
Diourbel 55 F1
Dipolog 38 C2
Dir 42 B7
Diré 55 E4
Dire Dawa ... 49 F3
Dirico 58 B4
Dirranbandi ... 63 A4
Disa 43 G8
Disappointment,
  L. 60 E3
Disaster B. 63 C4
Discovery B. .. 62 C3
Disteghil Sar .. 42 A9
Distrito
  Federal □ ... 93 F4
Diu 43 J7
Divinópolis ... 93 G5
Divnoye 25 D5
Dīwāl Kol 42 B5
Diyarbakır ... 46 C5
Diz Chah 44 C3
Djado 52 D1
Djakarta =
  Jakarta 37 F3
Djambala 56 E2
Djanet 54 D6
Djawa = Jawa . 37 F3
Djelfa 54 B5
Djema 57 C5
Djenné 55 F4
Djerba, I. de .. 52 B1
Djerid, Chott .. 54 B6
Djibo 55 F4
Djibouti 49 E3
Djibouti ■ ... 49 E3
Djolu 56 D4
Djougou 55 G5
Djoum 56 D2
Djourab 53 E2
Djugu 57 D6
Dmitriya
  Lapteva, Proliv 31 B12
Dnepr → =
  Dnipro → .. 25 D3
Dneprodzerzhinsk
  =
Dniprodzerzhynsk
  .... 25 D3
Dnepropetrovsk
  =
Dnipropetrovsk
  .... 25 D4
Dnestr → =
  Dnister → .. 17 E10
Dnestrovski =
  Belgorod ... 24 C4
Dnieper =
  Dnipro → .. 25 D3

Dniester =
  Dnister → .. 17 E10
Dnipro → 25 D3
Dniprodzerzhynsk
  .... 25 D3
Dnipro
  petrovsk..... 25 D4
Dnister → 17 E10
Dnistrovskyy
  Lyman 17 E10
Dnyapro =
  Dnipro → .. 25 D3
Doba 53 G2
Doberai,
  Jazirah...... 39 E4
Doblas 94 D4
Dobo 39 F4
Doboj 20 B7
Dobrich 22 C6
Dobruja 22 B7
Dobrush 17 B10
Dodecanese =
  Dhodhekánisos
  .... 23 F6
Dodge City ... 78 A3
Dodoma 57 F7
Dogi 42 C3
Doha = Ad
  Dawhah 44 E2
Dohazari 41 F9
Doi 39 D3
Dois Irmãos, Sa. 93 D5
Dolbeau 69 D3
Dole 13 C6
Dolomites =
  Dolomiti 20 A3
Dolomiti 20 A3
Dolores 94 D5
Dolphin, C. ... 95 G5
Dolphin and
  Union Str. .. 70 B8
Dombarovskiy . 29 D6
Dominica ■ ... 87 C7
Dominican
  Rep. ■ 87 C5
Domo 49 F4
Domodóssola . 20 A2
Domville, Mt. .. 63 A5
Don →, Russia 25 D4
Don →, U.K. ... 10 C5
Don Benito ... 18 C3
Donald 62 C3
Donau =
  Dunărea → . 17 F9
Donauwörth .. 14 D6
Doncaster 11 E6
Dondo, Angola 56 F2
Dondo, Mozam. 59 B6
Dondo, Teluk .. 39 D2
Donegal 11 D2
Donets → 25 D5
Donetsk 25 D6
Donggala 39 E1
Dongola 53 E5
Dongou 56 D3
Dongting Hu .. 35 D6
Dongxing 35 D5
Donington, C. . 62 B2
Donnelly's
  Crossing 64 A5
Donostia = San
  Sebastián ... 19 A5
Dora Báltea → 20 B2
Dorchester, C. . 68 B3
Dordogne → . 12 D3
Dordrecht ... 14 C3
Dori 55 F4
Dornbirn 14 E5
Dorohoi 17 E8

Döröö Nuur ...	34	B4
Dorrigo ...	63	B5
Dortmund ...	14	C4
Doruma ...	57	D5
Dos Bahías, C. .	95	E3
Dos Hermanas	18	D3
Dosso ...	55	F5
Dothan ...	74	D5
Douai ...	13	A5
Douala ...	56	D1
Douarnenez ..	12	B1
Double Island Pt. ...	63	A5
Doubs → ..	13	C6
Doubtful Sd. ..	65	F2
Doubtless B. ..	64	A5
Douentza ...	55	F4
Douglas, U.K. .	11	D4
Douglas, U.S.A.	83	E8
Doumé ...	56	D2
Dourados ...	94	A6
Douro → ...	18	B1
Dover, Australia	62	D4
Dover, U.K. ...	11	F7
Dover, Str. of .	11	F7
Dovrefjell ...	8	F9
Dowlat Yār ...	45	C6
Dowlatābād ..	44	D4
Dowshī ...	45	C7
Draa, Oued →	54	C2
Drăgăşani ...	22	B5
Dragichyn ...	17	B7
Dragoman, Prokhod ...	22	C4
Draguignan ..	13	E7
Drake ...	63	A5
Drakensberg ..	59	E5
Dráma ...	22	D5
Drammen ...	9	G10
Drau = Drava → ...	20	B7
Drava → ...	20	B7
Dresden ...	15	C7
Dreux ...	12	B4
Drina → ...	20	B7
Drini → ...	22	C2
Drobeta-Turnu-Severin	22	B4
Drochia ...	17	D8
Drogheda ...	11	E3
Drogobych = Drohobych ..	17	D6
Drohobych ...	17	D6
Droichead Atha = Drogheda .	11	E3
Dromedary, C. .	63	C5
Drumheller ...	71	C8
Drummond Pt.	62	B2
Drut → ...	17	B10
Drygalski I. ...	96	A11
Dschang ...	55	G7
Ďubá ...	47	F3
Dubai = Dubayy	44	E3
Dubăsari ...	17	E9
Dubăsari Vdkhr.	17	E9
Dubawnt → ..	70	B9
Dubawnt, L. ...	70	B9
Dubayy ...	44	E3
Dubbo ...	63	B4
Dublin, Ireland	11	E3
Dublin, U.S.A. .	75	C6
Dubno ...	17	C7
Dubossary = Dubăsari ...	17	E9
Dubossary Vdkhr. = Dubăsari Vdkhr. ...	17	E9
Dubovka ...	24	D5

Dubréka ...	55	G2
Dubrovitsa = Dubrovytsya	17	C8
Dubrovnik ...	20	C7
Dubrovytsya ..	17	C8
Dudhi ...	40	E4
Dudinka ...	30	C6
Duero = Douro → ...	18	B1
Dugi Otok ...	20	B5
Duisburg ...	14	C4
Dukelský Průsmyk ...	16	D5
Dukhān ...	44	E2
Duki ...	42	D6
Duku ...	55	F7
Dulce → ...	94	C4
Dulit, Banjaran	37	D4
Duluth ...	77	B8
Dum Duma ..	41	D10
Dum Hadjer ...	53	F2
Dumaguete ...	38	C2
Dumai ...	37	D2
Dumaran ...	38	B1
Dumfries ...	11	D5
Dumyât ...	52	B5
Dún Dealgan = Dundalk ...	11	D3
Dun Laoghaire	11	E3
Duna = Dunărea → .	17	F9
Dunaj = Dunărea → .	17	F9
Dunakeszi ...	16	E4
Dunărea → ..	17	F9
Dunaújváros .	16	E4
Dunav = Dunărea → .	17	F9
Dunback ...	65	F4
Dunbar ...	10	D5
Duncan ...	78	B5
Dundalk ...	11	D3
Dundee, S. Africa ...	59	D6
Dundee, U.K. ..	10	C5
Dundoo ...	63	A3
Dunedin ...	65	F4
Dunfermline ..	10	C5
Dungarvan ...	11	E3
Dungog ...	63	B5
Dungu ...	57	D5
Dunhuang ...	34	B4
Dunkerque ...	12	A5
Dunkirk = Dunkerque ..	12	A5
Dunkwa ...	55	G4
Dúnleary = Dun Laoghaire ...	11	E3
Dunolly ...	62	C3
Dunqul ...	52	D5
Dunstan Mts. ..	65	F3
Durance → ..	13	E6
Durango, Mexico ...	84	C4
Durango, Spain	19	A4
Durazno ...	94	C5
Durazzo = Durrësi ...	22	D2
Durban ...	59	D6
Düren ...	14	C4
Durg ...	40	G3
Durgapur ...	40	F6
Durham, U.K. ..	11	D6
Durham, U.S.A.	75	B8
Durham Downs	63	A4
Durmitor ...	22	C2
Durrësi ...	22	D2
Dursunbey ...	23	E7

D'Urville, Tanjung ...	39	E5
D'Urville I. ...	65	D5
Dusa Mareb ...	49	F4
Dushak ...	29	F7
Dushanbe ...	29	F7
Dusky Sd. ...	65	F2
Düsseldorf ...	14	C4
Dutch Harbor ..	71	C3
Duwādimi ...	47	F6
Duyun ...	35	D5
Düzce ...	46	B2
Duzdab = Zāhedān ...	45	D5
Dvina, Severnaya →	28	C5
Dvinsk = Daugavpils ..	24	B2
Dwarka ...	43	H6
Dyatlovo = Dzyatlava ...	17	B7
Dyer, C. ...	68	B4
Dyer Plateau ..	96	D3
Dyersburg ...	79	A9
Dymer ...	17	C10
Dynevor Downs	63	A3
Dzamin Üüd ..	35	B6
Dzerzhinsk ...	24	B5
Dzhambul = Taraz ...	29	E8
Dzhankoy ...	25	D3
Dzhardzhan ...	30	C10
Dzhezkazgan = Zhezqazghan	29	E7
Dzhizak = Jizzakh ...	29	E7
Działdowa ...	16	B5
Dzierzoniów ...	16	C3
Dzungaria = Junggar Pendi	34	B3
Dzungarian Gate = Alataw Shankou ...	34	B3
Dzuumod ...	35	B5
Dzyarzhynsk ..	17	B8
Dzyatlava ...	17	B7

E

Earnslaw, Mt. .	65	F3
East Bengal ..	41	E7
East Beskids = Vychodné Beskydy ...	17	D5
East C. ...	64	B8
East China Sea	35	C7
East Falkland .	95	G5
East Kilbride ..	10	D4
East London ..	59	E5
East Orange ..	73	D8
East St. Louis .	77	F9
East Sea = Japan, Sea of	31	G11
East Timor ...	39	F3
East Toorale ..	63	B4
Eastbourne, N.Z.	65	D6
Eastbourne, U.K.	11	F7
Eastern Ghats .	43	N11
Eastmain ...	69	C3
Eastmain → ..	69	C3
Eau Claire ...	77	C9
Eberswalde-Finow ...	15	B7
Ebolowa ...	56	D2
Ebro → ...	19	B6
Eceabat ...	23	D6
Ech Cheliff ...	54	A5

Echo Bay ...	70	B8
Echuca ...	63	C3
Ecija ...	18	D3
Ecuador ■ ...	90	D3
Ed Dâmer ...	53	E5
Ed Debba ...	53	E5
Ed Dueim ...	53	F5
Edd ...	49	E3
Eddystone Pt. .	62	D4
Édea ...	56	D2
Eden ...	63	C4
Eder → ...	14	C5
Édhessa ...	23	D4
Edievale ...	65	F3
Edinburg ...	78	F4
Edinburgh ...	10	D5
Edinița ...	17	D8
Edirne ...	22	D6
Edithburgh ...	62	C2
Edmonton ...	71	C8
Edmundston ...	69	D4
Edremit ...	23	E6
Edremit Körfezi	23	E6
Edson ...	71	C8
Edward → ...	62	C3
Edward, L. ...	57	E5
Edward VII Land	96	C17
Edwards Plateau	78	D3
Égadi, Ísole ..	21	F4
Eger = Cheb ..	16	C1
Eger ...	16	E5
Egersund ...	9	G9
Egmont, C. ...	64	C5
Egmont, Mt. ..	64	C6
Eğridir ...	46	C2
Eğridir Gölü ..	46	C2
Egypt ■ ...	52	C5
Eibar ...	19	A4
Eidsvold ...	63	A5
Eifel ...	14	C4
Eigg ...	10	C3
Eil ...	49	F4
Eildon, L. ...	63	C4
Eindhoven ...	14	C3
Eire = Ireland ■	11	E3
Eirunepé ...	91	E5
Eisenach ...	14	C6
Eisenerz ...	15	E8
Eivissa = Ibiza .	19	C6
Eketahuna ...	64	D6
Ekibastuz ...	29	D8
El Aaiún ...	54	C2
El Alamein ...	52	B4
El Aricha ...	54	B4
El 'Arîsh ...	52	B5
El Asnam = Ech Cheliff ...	54	A5
El Bawiti ...	52	C4
El Bayadh ...	54	B5
El Callao ...	90	B6
El Centro ...	82	D5
El Cerro ...	91	G6
El Cuy ...	95	D3
El Cuyo ...	85	C7
El Dere ...	49	G4
El Diviso ...	90	C3
El Djouf ...	55	D3
El Dorado, Ark., U.S.A. ...	79	C7
El Dorado, Kans., U.S.A.	78	A5
El Dorado, Venezuela ...	90	B6
El Escorial ...	18	B3
El Faiyûm ...	52	C5
El Fâsher ...	53	F4
El Ferrol ...	18	A1
El Fuerte ...	84	B3
El Gal ...	49	E5

El Geneina

El Geneina = Al
Junaynah ... 53 F3
El Geteina 53 F5
El Gîza 52 C5
El Iskandarîya . 52 B4
El Jadida 54 B3
El Jebelein ... 53 F5
El Kab 53 E5
El Kala 54 A6
El Kamlin 53 E5
El Kef 54 A6
El Khandaq ... 53 E5
El Khârga 52 C5
El Khartûm ... 53 E5
El Khartûm
Bahrî 53 E5
El Laqâwa 53 F4
El Mafâza 53 F5
El Mahalla el
Kubra 52 B5
El Mansûra ... 52 B5
El Minyâ 52 C5
El Obeid 53 F5
El Odaiya 53 F4
El Oued 54 B6
El Paso 83 E9
El Prat de
Llobregat ... 19 B7
El Puerto de
Santa María . 18 D2
El Qâhira 52 B5
El Qantara 52 B5
El Qasr 52 C4
El Reno 78 B5
El Salvador ■ . 85 E7
El Shallal 52 D5
El Suweis 52 C5
El Tigre 90 B6
El Tocuyo 90 B5
El Turbio 95 G2
El Uqsur 52 C5
El Vigía 90 B4
El Wak 57 D8
El Wuz 53 E5
Elat 47 E3
Elâziğ 46 C4
Elba 20 C3
Elbasani 22 D3
Elbe ➤ 14 B5
Elbert, Mt. 83 A9
Elbeuf 12 B4
Elbidtan 46 C4
Elbing = Elbląg 16 A4
Elbląg 16 A4
Elbrus 25 E5
Elburz Mts. =
Alborz,
Reshteh-ye
Kūhhā-ye ... 44 B3
Elche 19 C5
Elda 19 C5
Elde ➤ 15 B6
Eldoret 57 D7
Elektrostal 24 B4
Elephant I. 96 A4
Eleuthera 86 A4
Elgin, U.K. 10 C5
Elgin, U.S.A. .. 72 C1
Elgon, Mt. 57 D6
Eliase 39 F4
Elisabethville =
Lubumbashi . 59 A5
Elista 25 D5
Elizabeth,
Australia 62 B2
Elizabeth, U.S.A. 73 D8
Elizabeth City . 75 A9
Elizabethton ... 75 A6
Ełk 16 B6

Elkhart 72 D3
Elkhovo 22 C6
Elko 80 E6
Ellery, Mt. 63 C4
Ellesmere, L. .. 65 G5
Ellice Is. =
Tuvalu ■ ... 64 K12
Elliston 62 B1
Ellore = Eluru . 40 J3
Ellsworth Land 96 B2
Ellsworth Mts. . 96 B2
Elmore 63 C3
Elmshorn 14 B5
Eltham 64 C6
Eluru 40 J3
Elvas 18 C2
Elx = Elche ... 19 C5
Ely 11 E7
Emāmrūd 44 B3
Emba = Embi . 29 E6
Emba ➤ =
Embi ➤ ... 29 E6
Embarcación .. 94 A4
Embi 29 E6
Embi ➤ 29 E6
Embrun 13 D7
Embu 57 E7
Emden 14 B4
Emerson 71 D10
Emet 23 E7
Emi Koussi ... 53 E2
Emine, Nos ... 22 C6
Emmen 14 B4
Empalme 84 B2
Empangeni ... 59 D6
Empedrado ... 94 B5
Empty Quarter
= Rub' al
Khali 48 D4
Ems ➤ 14 B4
En Nahud 53 F4
Enaratoli 39 E5
Enare =
Inarijärvi 8 E13
Encanto, C. ... 38 A2
Encarnación .. 94 B5
Encounter B. .. 62 C2
Ende 39 F2
Enderby Land . 96 A9
Enewetak Atoll 64 H11
Enez 23 D6
Engadin 13 C9
Engaño, C. 38 A2
Engels 24 C6
Enggano 37 F2
Engkilili 37 D4
England □ 11 E6
Englewood ... 76 F2
English Bazar =
Ingraj Bazar . 40 E7
English Channel 11 F5
Enid 78 A5
Enna 21 F5
Ennedi 53 E3
Enngonia 63 A4
Ennis 11 E2
Enniskillen 11 D3
Enns ➤ 15 D8
Enschede 14 B4
Ensenada 84 A1
Entebbe 57 D6
Entroncamento 18 C1
Enugu 55 G6
Enugu Ezike .. 55 G6
Eólie, Ís. 21 E5
Épernay 13 B5
Ephesus 23 F6
Épinal 13 B7
Epukiro 58 C3

Equatorial
Guinea ■ ... 56 D1
Er Rahad 53 F5
Er Rif 54 A4
Er Roseires ... 53 F5
Erāwadī Myit =
Irrawaddy ➤ 41 K10
Erbil = Arbīl .. 46 C6
Ercıyaş Dağı ... 46 C3
Érd 16 E4
Erdek 23 D6
Erebus, Mt. ... 96 B15
Erechim 94 B6
Ereğli, Konya,
Turkey 46 C3
Ereğli,
Zonguldak,
Turkey 46 B2
Eresma ➤ ... 18 B3
Erewadi
Myitwanya .. 41 K10
Erfurt 15 C6
Ergani 46 C4
Érice 21 E4
Erie 73 C5
Erie, L. 72 C5
Erigavo 49 E4
Erímanthos ... 23 F3
Erimo-misaki .. 32 F12
Eritrea ■ 49 E2
Erlangen 15 D6
Ermenak 46 C3
Ermoúpolis =
Síros 23 F5
Ernakulam =
Cochin 43 Q10
Erne, Lower L. . 11 D3
Erode 43 P10
Eromanga 63 A3
Erramala Hills . 43 M11
Ertis ➤ =
Irtysh ➤ ... 28 C7
Erzgebirge 15 C7
Erzincan 46 C4
Erzurum 46 C5
Es Sahrâ' Esh
Sharqîya ... 52 C5
Es Sînâ' 52 C5
Esbjerg 9 G9
Esch-sur-Alzette 13 B6
Escuinapa 84 C3
Eşfahān 44 C2
Esh Sham =
Dimashq 46 D4
Esil ➤ =
Ishim ➤ ... 29 D8
Eskilstuna 9 G11
Eskimo Pt. =
Arviat 70 B10
Eskişehir 46 C2
Esla ➤ 18 B2
Eslāmābād-e
Gharb 46 D6
Eşme 23 E7
Esmeraldas ... 90 C3
Esperance 60 G3
Esperanza 94 C4
Espichel, C. ... 18 C1
Espinal 90 C4
Espinazo, Sierra
del =
Espinhaço,
Serra do 93 F5
Espinhaço, Serra
do 93 F5
Espírito Santo □ 93 G5
Esquel 95 E2
Esquina 94 C5
Essaouira 54 B3

Essen 14 C4
Essequibo ➤ . 90 B7
Esslingen 14 D5
Estados, I. de
Los 95 G4
Estância 93 E6
Estevan 71 D9
Estonia ■ 24 B2
Estrêla, Serra da 18 B2
Estremoz 18 C2
Estrondo, Serra
do 92 D4
Esztergom ... 16 E4
Etadunna 62 A2
Étampes 12 B5
Etawah 42 F11
Ethiopia ■ 49 F2
Etna 21 F5
Etosha Pan ... 58 B3
Euboea =
Évvoia 23 E5
Eucumbene, L. 63 C4
Eufaula 74 D5
Eugene 80 C2
Eugowra 63 B4
Eulo 63 A4
Euphrates =
Furāt, Nahr
al ➤ 47 E6
Eureka 80 E1
Euroa 63 C4
Europa, I. 59 J8
Europa, Picos de 18 A3
Europa, Pta. de 18 D3
Europa Pt. =
Europa, Pta.
de 18 D3
Evans Head .. 63 A5
Evanston 72 C2
Evansville 72 F2
Everard, L. ... 62 B1
Everest, Mt. .. 40 C6
Everett 80 B2
Everglades
National Park 75 G7
Evinayong ... 56 D2
Évora 18 C2
Évreux 12 B4
Évros ➤ 22 D3
Evry 12 B5
Évvoia 23 E5
Ewo 56 E2
Exaltación ... 91 F5
Exeter 11 F5
Exmoor 11 F5
Exmouth 11 F5
Extremadura □ 18 C2
Eyasi, L. 57 E6
Eyre (North), L. 62 A2
Eyre (South), L. 62 A2
Eyre, L. 60 F6
Eyre Cr. ➤ ... 62 A2
Eyre Mts. 65 F3
Eyre Pen. 62 B2
Ezine 23 E6

F

F.Y.R.O.M. =
Macedonia ■ 22 D3
Fabriano 20 C4
Facatativá ... 90 C4
Fachi 55 E7
Fada 53 E3
Fada-n-Gourma 55 F5
Faddeyevskiy,
Ostrov 31 B12

Fāḏilī 47 F7
Faenza 20 B3
Færoe Is. =
  Føroyar 6 C4
Fāgăras 17 F7
Fagnano, L. ... 95 G3
Fahraj 45 D4
Fahūd 44 F4
Fair Isle 10 B6
Fairbanks 71 B5
Fairfield, *Ala.,*
  U.S.A. 74 C4
Fairfield, *Calif.,*
  U.S.A. 80 F2
Fairlie 65 F4
Fairweather, Mt. 71 C6
Faisalabad 42 D8
Faizabad 40 D4
Fakfak 39 E4
Falaise 12 B3
Falam 41 F9
Falconara
  Maríttima ... 20 C4
Falcone, C. 20 D2
Faleshty =
  Fălești 17 E8
Fălești 17 E8
Falkland Is. □ . 95 G5
Falkland Sd. ... 95 G5
Fall River 73 D10
Falmouth 11 F4
False B. 58 E3
Fălticeni 17 E8
Falun 9 F11
Famagusta 46 D3
Fandriana 59 J9
Fano 20 C4
Fao = Al Fāw . 47 E7
Faradje 57 D5
Farafangana .. 59 J9
Farāh 42 C3
Farāh □ 42 C3
Faranah 55 F2
Farasān, Jazā'ir 49 D3
Farasan Is. =
  Farasān,
  Jazā'ir ... 49 D3
Fareham 11 F6
Farewell, C. ... 64 D5
Farewell C. =
  Farvel, Kap . 68 C6
Farghona 29 E8
Fargo 76 B6
Farim 55 F1
Farīmān 45 C4
Farina 62 B2
Faro, *Brazil* .. 92 C2
Faro, *Portugal* . 18 D2
Farrāshband .. 44 D3
Farrell Flat ... 62 B2
Farrukhabad-
  cum-
  Fatehgarh ... 42 F11
Fārs □ 44 D3
Fársala 23 E4
Fartak, Râs ... 47 E3
Farvel, Kap ... 68 C6
Fāryāb □ 45 B6
Fasā 44 D3
Fasano 21 D6
Fastiv 17 C9
Fastov = Fastiv 17 C9
Fatagar, Tanjung 39 E4
Fatehgarh 42 F11
Fatehpur, *Raj.,*
  India 42 F9
Fatehpur, *Ut. P.,*
  India 40 E3
Favara 21 F4

Favignana 21 F4
Faya-Largeau .. 53 E2
Fayd 47 F5
Fayetteville,
  Ark., U.S.A. . 79 A6
Fayetteville,
  N.C., U.S.A. . 75 B8
Fazilka 42 D9
Fdérik 54 D2
Feather → ... 80 F3
Featherston ... 65 D6
Fécamp 12 B4
Fehmarn 15 A6
Feilding 64 D6
Feira de Santana 93 E6
Feldkirch 14 E5
Felipe Carrillo
  Puerto 85 D7
Felixstowe 11 F7
Fengjie 35 C5
Fenyang 35 C6
Feodosiya 25 D4
Ferdows 44 C4
Ferfer 49 F4
Fergana =
  Farghona ... 29 E8
Fermo 20 C4
Fernando de
  Noronha 92 C7
Fernando Póo =
  Bioko 56 D1
Ferozepore =
  Firozpur 42 D9
Ferrara 20 B3
Ferreñafe 91 E3
Ferret, C. 12 D3
Ferrol = El
  Ferrol 18 A1
Fès 54 B4
Feshi 56 F3
Fetești 22 B6
Fetlar 10 A6
Feuilles → ... 68 C3
Fezzan 52 C2
Fianarantsoa .. 59 J9
Fianga 53 G2
Ficksburg 59 D5
Fieri 23 D2
Figeac 12 D5
Figueira da Foz 18 B1
Figueras 19 A7
Figuig 54 B4
Fiji ■ 64 L12
Filiatrá 23 F3
Filyos → 46 B3
Fíngōe 59 A6
Finike 46 C2
Finisterre, C. .. 18 A1
Finke → 62 A2
Finland ■ 8 F13
Finland, G. of . 9 G13
Finlay → 70 C7
Finley 63 C4
Finniss, C. 62 B1
Fiora → 20 C3
Firat = Furāt,
  Nahr al → .. 47 E6
Firenze 20 C3
Firozabad 42 F11
Firozpur 42 D9
Firūzābād 44 D3
Firūzkūh 44 C3
Fish → 58 D3
Fishguard 11 E4
Fitri, L. 53 F2
Fitz Roy 95 F3
Fiume = Rijeka 20 B5
Fizi 57 E5
Flagstaff 83 C7

Flaming Gorge
  Reservoir ... 81 E9
Flamingo, Teluk 39 F5
Flandre 14 C2
Flathead L. 81 B6
Flattery, C. 80 A1
Flensburg 14 A5
Flers 12 B3
Flesko, Tanjung 39 D2
Flin Flon 71 C9
Flinders → ... 61 D7
Flinders I. 62 C4
Flinders Ras. .. 62 B2
Flint 72 C4
Flint I. 65 L15
Flinton 63 A4
Florence =
  Firenze 20 C3
Florence, *Ala.,*
  U.S.A. 74 B4
Florence, *S.C.,*
  U.S.A. 75 B8
Florence, L. ... 62 A2
Flores 39 F2
Flores Sea 39 F2
Florești 17 E9
Floriano 92 D5
Florianópolis .. 94 B7
Florida 94 C5
Florida □ 75 F6
Florida, Straits
  of 86 B3
Flórina 23 D3
Florø 8 F9
Fluk 39 E3
Flushing =
  Vlissingen .. 14 C2
Fly → 61 B7
Flying Fish, C. . 96 B1
Foça 23 E6
Focșani 17 F8
Fóggia 20 D5
Föhr 14 A5
Foix 12 E4
Foligno 20 C4
Folkestone ... 11 F7
Fond du Lac .. 77 D10
Fondi 20 D4
Fonsagrada ... 18 A2
Fonseca, G. de 85 E7
Fontainebleau . 13 B5
Fonte Boa 90 D5
Fontenay-le-
  Comte 12 C3
Foochow =
  Fuzhou 35 D6
Forbes 63 B4
Ford's Bridge . 63 A4
Forécariah ... 55 G2
Forestier Pen. . 62 D4
Forfar 10 C5
Forlì 20 B4
Formentera .. 19 C6
Formentor, C. de 19 C7
Former
  Yugoslav
  Republic of
  Macedonia =
  Macedonia ■ 22 D3
Fórmia 20 D4
Formosa =
  Taiwan ■ ... 35 D7
Formosa 94 B5
Formosa, Serra 93 E3
Formosa Bay . 57 E8
Føroyar =
  Føroyar 6 C4
Føroyar 6 C4
Forrest 62 C3

Forsayth 61 D7
Forst 15 C8
Forster 63 B5
Fort Albany .. 69 C2
Fort Collins .. 76 E2
Fort-de-France . 87 D7
Fort de Possel =
  Possel 56 C3
Fort Dodge ... 77 D7
Fort
  Good-Hope .. 70 B7
Fort Hertz =
  Putao 41 D11
Fort Lauderdale 75 F7
Fort Liard 70 B7
Fort Macleod .. 71 D8
Fort MacMahon 54 C5
Fort McPherson 70 B6
Fort Miribel ... 54 C5
Fort Myers ... 75 F7
Fort Peck L. ... 81 B10
Fort Pierce ... 75 F7
Fort Portal ... 57 D6
Fort Providence 70 B8
Fort Resolution 70 B8
Fort Rosebery =
  Mansa 57 G5
Fort Rupert =
  Waskaganish 69 C3
Fort Sandeman 42 D6
Fort Scott 79 A6
Fort Severn ... 69 C2
Fort
  Shevchenko .. 29 E6
Fort Simpson . 70 B7
Fort Smith,
  Canada 70 B8
Fort Smith,
  U.S.A. 79 B6
Fort Trinquet =
  Bir Mogrein . 54 C2
Fort Walton
  Beach 74 D4
Fort Wayne .. 72 D3
Fort William ... 10 C4
Fort Worth ... 78 C5
Fort Yukon ... 71 B5
Fortaleza 92 C6
Forūr 44 E3
Foshan 35 D6
Fossano 20 B1
Fouçamou ... 56 E2
Fougères 12 B3
Foula 10 A5
Foumban 55 G7
Foúrnoi 23 F6
Fouta Djalon .. 55 F2
Foveaux Str. .. 65 G3
Foxe Basin ... 68 B3
Foxe Chan. ... 68 B2
Foxe Pen. 68 B3
Foxton 64 D6
Foz do Gregório 91 E4
Foz do Iguaçu . 94 B6
Franca 93 G4
Francavilla
  Fontana 21 D6
France ■ 13 C5
Frances 62 C3
Franceville ... 56 E2
Franche-Comté 13 C6
Francistown ... 59 C5
Frankfurt,
  Brandenburg,
  Germany ... 15 B8
Frankfurt,
  Hessen,
  Germany ... 14 C5
Fränkische Alb 15 D6

Franklin B.

Franklin B. 70 B7
Franklin I. 96 B15
Franklin Mts. .. 70 B7
Franklin Str. ... 70 A10
Frankston 63 C4
Frantsa Iosifa,
  Zemlya 28 A6
Franz 69 D2
Franz Josef
  Land =
  Frantsa Iosifa,
  Zemlya 28 A6
Fraser → 71 D7
Fraser I. 63 A5
Fraserburgh ... 10 C5
Fray Bentos ... 94 C5
Fredericksburg 73 E7
Fredericton ... 69 D4
Fredrikstad 9 G10
Freeport,
  Bahamas ... 86 A4
Freeport, *U.S.A.* 77 D10
Freetown 55 G2
Fregenal de la
  Sierra 18 C2
Freibourg =
  Fribourg 13 C7
Freiburg 14 E4
Freire 95 D2
Freising 15 D6
Freistadt 15 D8
Fréjus 13 E7
Fremont 82 B2
French
  Guiana ■ ... 92 B3
French
  Polynesia ■ . 65 M16
Fresco → 92 D3
Freshfield, C. .. 96 A14
Fresnillo 84 C4
Fresno 82 B3
Freycinet Pen. . 62 D4
Fria, C. 58 B2
Frías 94 B3
Fribourg 13 C7
Friedrichshafen 14 E5
Friendly Is. =
  Tonga ■ 65 L13
Frobisher B. ... 68 B4
Frobisher Bay =
  Iqaluit 68 B4
Frome, L. 62 B2
Frome Downs . 62 B2
Front Range ... 81 E11
Frosinone 20 D4
Frunze =
  Bishkek 29 E8
Frutal 93 F4
Frýdek-Místek . 16 D4
Fuchou =
  Fuzhou 35 D6
Fuengirola 18 D3
Fuentes de
  Oñoro 18 B2
Fuerte → 84 B3
Fuerte Olimpo . 91 H7
Fuerteventura . 54 C2
Fuhai 34 B3
Fuji-San 32 B6
Fujian □ 35 D6
Fujinomiya ... 32 B6
Fujisawa 32 B6
Fukien =
  Fujian □ 35 D6
Fukuchiyama .. 32 B4
Fukui 32 A5
Fukuoka 32 C2
Fukushima ... 33 G12
Fukuyama 32 B3

Fulda 14 C5
Fulda → 14 C5
Fullerton 82 D4
Funabashi ... 32 B7
Funchal 54 B1
Fundación ... 90 A4
Fundão 18 B2
Fundy, B. of .. 69 D4
Funtua 55 F6
Furāt, Nahr
  al → 47 E6
Furneaux Group 62 D4
Fürstenwalde .. 15 B8
Fürth 14 D6
Fury and Hecla
  Str. 68 B2
Fusagasuga ... 90 C4
Fushun 35 B7
Futuna 64 L12
Fuxin 35 B7
Fuyuan 35 B8
Fuzhou 35 D6
Fyn 9 G10

G

Gabela 56 G2
Gabès 54 B7
Gabès, G. de . 52 B1
Gabon ■ 56 E2
Gaborone 59 C5
Gabrovo 22 C5
Gachsārān ... 44 D2
Gadag 43 M9
Gadarwara ... 43 H11
Gadhada 43 J7
Gadsden 74 B4
Gadwal 43 L10
Gafsa 54 B6
Gagnoa 55 G3
Gagnon 69 C4
Gaillimh =
  Galway 11 E2
Gainesville, *Fla.*,
  U.S.A. 75 E6
Gainesville, *Ga.*,
  U.S.A. 75 B6
Gainesville,
  Tex., U.S.A. . 78 C5
Gairdner, L. ... 62 B2
Galangue 58 A3
Galashiels 10 D5
Galaţi 17 F9
Galatina 21 D7
Galcaio 49 F4
Galdhøpiggen . 8 F9
Galela 39 D3
Galesburg ... 77 E9
Galich 24 B5
Galicia □ 18 A2
Galilee, Sea of
  = Yam
  Kinneret ... 46 D3
Gallabat 53 F6
Gállego → ... 19 B5
Gallegos → .. 95 G3
Gallinas, Pta. . 90 A4
Gallipoli =
  Gelibolu ... 23 D6
Gallípoli 21 D6
Gällivare 8 E12
Galloway, Mull
  of 11 D4
Galong 63 B4
Galveston 79 E6
Gálvez 94 C4

Galway 11 E2
Galway B. 11 E2
Gambaga 55 F4
Gambela 53 G5
Gambia ■ 55 F1
Gambia → ... 55 F1
Gambier Is. ... 62 C2
Gamboma ... 56 E3
Gan Jiang → . 35 D6
Ganāveh 44 D2
Gäncä 25 E6
Gand = Gent .. 14 C2
Ganda 58 A2
Gandak → ... 40 E5
Gandava 42 E5
Gander 69 D5
Gandhi Sagar . 43 G9
Gandi 55 F6
Gandía 19 C5
Ganedidalem =
  Gani 39 E3
Ganga → 41 F8
Ganganagar .. 42 E8
Gangara 55 F6
Gangaw 41 F10
Gangdisê Shan 40 B3
Ganges =
  Ganga → .. 41 F8
Gangtok 41 D7
Gani 39 E3
Gansu □ 34 C5
Ganta 55 G3
Gantheaume, C. 62 C2
Gantsevichi =
  Hantsavichy . 17 B8
Ganyem 39 E6
Ganzhou 35 D6
Gaoua 55 F4
Gaoual 55 F2
Gaoxiong 35 D7
Gap 13 D7
Gar 34 C2
Garabogazköl
  Aylagy 29 E6
Garanhuns ... 92 D6
Garawe 55 H3
Gard 49 F4
Garda, L. di ... 20 B3
Garden City ... 78 A3
Garden Grove . 82 D4
Gardēz 42 C6
Gargano, Mte. . 20 D5
Garigliano → . 20 D4
Garland 81 E7
Garm 29 F8
Garmisch-
  Partenkirchen 14 E6
Garmsār 44 C3
Garoe 49 F4
Garonne → .. 12 D3
Garoua 53 G1
Garrison Res. =
  Sakakawea, L. 76 B4
Garry, L. 70 B9
Garsen 57 E8
Garvie Mts. ... 65 F3
Garwa =
  Garoua 53 G1
Gary 72 D2
Garzê 34 C5
Garzón 90 C3
Gasan Kuli =
  Hasan Kuli .. 29 F6
Gascogne ... 12 E4
Gascogne, G. de 12 D2
Gascony =
  Gascogne ... 12 E4
Gashaka 55 G7
Gaspé 69 D4

Gaspé, C. de .. 69 D4
Gaspé, Pén. de 69 D4
Gasteiz = Vitoria 19 A4
Gastonia 75 B7
Gastre 95 E3
Gata, C. de ... 19 D4
Gata, Sierra de 18 B2
Gateshead ... 11 D6
Gauhati 41 D8
Gaväter 45 E5
Gávdhos 23 G5
Gävle 8 F11
Gawilgarh Hills 43 J10
Gawler 62 B2
Gaxun Nur 34 B5
Gaya, *India* ... 40 E5
Gaya, *Niger* ... 55 F5
Gayndah 63 A5
Gaysin =
  Haysyn 17 D9
Gayvoron =
  Hayvoron ... 17 D9
Gaza 47 E3
Gaziantep 46 C4
Gazli 29 E7
Gdańsk 16 A4
Gdańska, Zatoka 16 A4
Gdov 24 B2
Gdynia 16 A4
Gebe 39 D3
Gebeit Mine ... 52 D6
Gebze 22 D7
Gedaref 53 F6
Gede, Tanjung 37 F3
Gediz → 23 E6
Gedser 9 H10
Geelong 63 C3
Geesthacht ... 14 B6
Geidam 53 F1
Geili 53 E5
Geita 57 E6
Gejiu 34 D5
Gela 21 F5
Geladi 49 F4
Gelehun 55 G2
Gelibolu 23 D6
Gelsenkirchen . 14 C4
Gemas 37 D2
Gemena 56 D3
Gemerek 46 C4
Gemlik 23 D7
General Acha . 94 D4
General Alvear,
  *Buenos Aires,
  Argentina* ... 94 D5
General Alvear,
  *Mendoza,
  Argentina* ... 94 D3
General Artigas 94 B5
General
  Belgrano ... 94 D5
General Guido . 94 D5
General Juan
  Madariaga . 94 D5
General La
  Madrid 94 D4
General
  MacArthur .. 38 B3
General Martin
  Miguel de
  Güemes ... 94 A4
General Paz ... 94 B5
General Pico .. 94 D4
General Pinedo 94 B4
General Santos 38 C3
General Villegas 94 D4
Geneva =
  Genève 13 C7

Geneva, L. =
Léman, L. ... 13 C7
Genève 13 C7
Genil → 18 D3
Gennargentu,
Mti. del 21 D2
Genoa =
Génova 20 B2
Genoa 63 C4
Génova 20 B2
Génova, G. di . 20 C2
Gent 14 C2
Georga, Zemlya 28 A5
George 58 E4
George → 68 C4
George, L.,
N.S.W.,
Australia 63 C4
George, L.,
S. Austral.,
Australia 62 C3
George, L.,
Uganda 57 D6
George River =
Kangiqsualujjuaq
.... 68 C4
George Sound . 65 F2
George Town . 36 C2
George V Land 96 A14
George VI
Sound 96 B3
Georgetown,
Gambia 55 F2
Georgetown,
Guyana 90 B7
Georgia □ ... 75 C6
Georgia ■ ... 25 E5
Georgian B. ... 69 D2
Georgiu-Dezh =
Liski 24 C4
Georgiyevsk .. 25 E5
Gera 15 C7
Geral de Goiás,
Serra 93 E4
Geraldton 60 F1
Gerede 46 B3
Gereshk 42 D4
Gerlogubi 49 F4
Germany ■ ... 14 C6
Germiston 59 D5
Gerona 19 B7
Geser 39 E4
Getafe 18 B4
Gettysburg .. 73 E7
Getz Ice Shelf . 96 B18
Ghaghara → . 40 E5
Ghana ■ 55 G4
Ghanzi 58 C4
Ghardaïa 54 B5
Gharyän 52 B1
Ghat 54 D7
Ghawdex =
Gozo 21 F5
Ghayl 47 G6
Ghazal, Bahr
el →, Chad . 53 F2
Ghazâl, Bahr
el →, Sudan 57 C6
Ghazaouet ... 54 A4
Ghaziabad 42 E10
Ghazipur 40 E4
Ghazni 42 C6
Ghazni □ 42 C6
Ghèlinsor 49 F4
Ghent = Gent . 14 C2
Ghizao 42 C4
Ghowr □ 42 C4
Ghugus 43 K11
Ghūriān 42 B2

Gia Lai = Pleiku 36 B3
Gian 38 C3
Giarabub = Al
Jaghbūb 52 C3
Giarre 21 F5
Gibraltar ■ ... 18 D3
Gibraltar, Str. of 18 E3
Gibson Desert . 60 E4
Gidole 53 G6
Giessen 14 C5
Gifu 32 B5
Giglio 20 C3
Gijón 18 A3
Gila → 82 D5
Gīlān □ 46 C7
Gilbert Is. 64 J12
Gilgandra 63 B4
Gilgit 42 B9
Gilles, L. 62 B2
Gilmore 63 C4
Gimbi 53 G6
Gin Gin 63 A5
Ginir 49 F3
Giohar 49 G4
Gióna, Óros ... 23 E4
Girardot 90 C4
Giresun 46 B4
Girga 52 C5
Giridih 40 E6
Girilambone .. 63 B4
Girne = Kyrenia 46 D3
Girona =
Gerona 19 B7
Gironde → ... 12 D3
Girvan 10 D4
Gisborne 64 C8
Gisenyi 57 E5
Gitega 57 E5
Giuba → 49 G3
Giurgiu 22 C5
Giza = El Gîza . 52 C5
Giżycko 16 A5
Gjirokastra ... 23 D3
Gjoa Haven .. 70 B10
Glace Bay 69 D5
Gladstone,
Queens.,
Australia 61 E9
Gladstone,
S. Austral.,
Australia 62 B2
Glåma =
Glomma → . 9 G10
Glasgow 10 D4
Glazov 28 D6
Gleiwitz =
Gliwice 16 C4
Glen Canyon
National
Recreation
Area 83 B7
Glen Innes ... 63 A5
Glendale 82 C3
Glenelg 62 B2
Glenelg → ... 62 C3
Glenmorgan .. 63 A4
Glenorchy ... 62 D4
Glenreagh ... 63 B5
Glenrothes ... 10 C5
Glens Falls ... 73 C9
Gliwice 16 C4
Głogów 16 C3
Glomma → .. 9 G10
Glorieuses, Is. . 59 G9
Gloucester,
Australia 63 B5
Gloucester, U.K. 11 F5
Glusk 17 B9
Gmünd 15 D8

Gmunden 15 E7
Gniezno 16 B3
Go Cong 36 B3
Goa 43 M8
Goa □ 43 M8
Goalen Hd. ... 63 C5
Goalpara 41 D8
Goba, Ethiopia 49 F2
Goba, Mozam. . 59 D6
Gobabis 58 C3
Gobi 35 B6
Gochas 58 C3
Godavari → .. 40 J4
Godavari Point 40 J4
Godhra 43 H8
Gods → 71 C10
Gods L. 71 C10
Godthåb=Nuuk . 68 B5
Godwin Austen
= K2 ...... 42 B10
Goeie Hoop,
Kaap die =
Good Hope, C.
of 58 E3
Gogra =
Ghaghara → 40 E5
Goiânia 93 F4
Goiás 93 F3
Goiás □ 93 E4
Goio-Ere 94 A6
Gojra 42 D8
Gökçeada ... 23 D5
Gokteik 41 F11
Gold Coast ... 63 A5
Golden Gate . 80 G2
Goldsboro ... 75 B9
Goleniów 16 B2
Golfo Aranci . 20 D2
Golspie 10 C5
Goma 57 E5
Gomel =
Homyel 17 B10
Gomera 54 C1
Gómez Palacio 84 B4
Gomogomo ... 39 F4
Gomoh 40 F6
Gompa = Ganta 55 G3
Gonābād 44 C4
Gonaïves 87 C5
Gonbad-e Kāvūs 44 B3
Gonda 40 D3
Gonder 53 F6
Gönen 23 D6
Gonghe 34 C5
Gongolgon ... 63 B4
Goniri 53 F1
Good Hope, C.
of 58 E3
Goodooga 63 A4
Goolgowi 63 B4
Goombalie ... 63 A4
Goondiwindi .. 63 A5
Gooray 63 A5
Gop 43 H6
Göppingen ... 14 D5
Gorakhpur 40 D4
Goražde 20 C7
Gordon → ... 62 D4
Gore, Australia 63 A5
Goré, Chad .. 53 G2
Gore, Ethiopia 53 G6
Gore, N.Z. 65 G3
Gorgān 44 B3
Gorgona, I. ... 90 C3
Gorízia 20 B4
Gorki = Nizhniy
Novgorod .. 24 B5
Gorkiy =
Nizhniy
Novgorod ... 24 B5

Gorkovskoye
Vdkhr. 24 B5
Görlitz 15 C8
Gorlovka =
Horlivka 25 D4
Gorna
Dzhumayo =
Blagoevgrad 22 C4
Gorna
Oryakhovitsa 22 C5
Gorno-Altay □ . 29 D9
Gorno-Altaysk . 29 D9
Gorno Slinkino
=
Gornopravdinsk
.... 29 C8
Gornopravdinsk 29 C8
Gorodenka =
Horodenka .. 17 D7
Gorodok =
Horodok 17 D6
Gorokhov =
Horokhiv 17 C7
Gorontalo ... 39 D2
Gorzów
Wielkopolski 16 B2
Gosford 63 B5
Goslar 14 C6
Gospič 20 B5
Göta kanal ... 9 G11
Göteborg ... 9 G10
Gotha 14 C6
Gothenburg =
Göteborg ... 9 G10
Gotland 9 G11
Göttingen 14 C5
Gottwaldov =
Zlin 16 D3
Gouda 14 B3
Gouln, Rés. ... 69 D3
Goulburn 63 B4
Gounou-Gaya 53 G2
Gouri 53 E2
Gourma
Rharous 55 E4
Gourock Ra. ... 63 C4
Governador
Valadares ... 93 F5
Gowd-e Zirreh . 42 E3
Goya 94 B5
Goyder Lagoon 62 A2
Goyllarisquisga 91 F3
Goz Beïda ... 53 F3
Gozo 21 F5
Graaff-Reinet .. 58 E4
Gračac 20 B5
Gracias a Dios,
C. 86 D3
Grado 18 A2
Gradule 63 A4
Grafton 63 A5
Graham Bell,
Os. 28 A7
Graham Land . 96 A3
Grahamstown . 59 E5
Grajaú 92 D4
Grajaú → 92 C5
Grampian
Highlands =
Grampian
Mts. 10 C4
Grampian Mts. 10 C4
Gran Canaria . 54 C1
Gran Chaco ... 94 B4
Gran Paradiso . 20 B1
Gran Sasso
d'Italia 20 C4
Granada, Nic. . 85 E7
Granada, Spain 18 D4

Granby	69	D3
Grand Bahama	86	A4
Grand Bassam	55	G4
Grand Canyon .	83	B6
Grand Cayman	86	C3
Grand Coulee Dam	80	B4
Grand Forks, *Canada*	71	D8
Grand Forks, *U.S.A.*	76	B6
Grand Island . .	76	E5
Grand Lahou . .	55	G3
Grand Rapids, *Canada*	71	C10
Grand Rapids, *U.S.A.*	72	C3
Grand St.-Bernard, Col du	13	D7
Grand Teton . .	81	D8
Grande →, *Argentina*	94	A3
Grande →, *Bolivia*	91	G6
Grande →, *Bahia, Brazil*	93	E5
Grande →, *Minas Gerais, Brazil*	93	G3
Grande, B.	95	G3
Grande, Rio →	79	F5
Grande Baleine, R. de la → . .	69	C3
Grande de Santiago →	84	C3
Granite City . . .	77	F9
Granity	65	D4
Granja	92	C5
Granollers	19	B7
Grantham	11	E6
Granville	12	B3
Gras, L. de	70	B8
Grasse	13	E7
Grassmere	62	B3
Graulhet	12	E4
's-Gravenhage .	14	B3
Gravesend	63	A5
Graz	15	E8
Great Abaco I. .	86	A4
Great Australian Bight	60	G4
Great Barrier I.	64	B6
Great Barrier Reef	61	D8
Great Basin . .	80	F5
Great Bear → .	70	B7
Great Bear L. . .	70	B7
Great Belt = Store Bælt . .	9	G10
Great Dividing Ra.	61	E8
Great Falls	81	B8
Great Inagua I.	86	B5
Great Indian Desert = Thar Desert	42	F7
Great Karoo . .	58	E4
Great Lake . . .	62	D4
Great Ouse →	11	E7
Great Ruaha →	57	F7
Great Saint Bernard P. = Grand St.-Bernard, Col du	13	D7
Great Salt L. . .	81	E7
Great Salt Lake Desert	81	E7
Great Sandy Desert	60	E3
Great Sangi = Sangihe, P. . .	39	D3
Great Slave L. .	70	B8
Great Smoky Mts. Nat. Pk.	75	B6
Great Victoria Desert	60	F4
Great Wall	35	C5
Great Yarmouth	11	E7
Greater Antilles	86	C5
Greater Sunda Is.	37	F4
Gredos, Sierra de	18	B3
Greece ■	23	E4
Greeley	76	E2
Green →	83	A8
Green Bay	72	B2
Green C.	63	C5
Greenland ■ . .	66	C9
Greenock	10	D4
Greensboro	75	A8
Greenville, *Liberia*	55	G3
Greenville, *Ala., U.S.A.*	74	D4
Greenville, *Miss., U.S.A.*	79	C8
Greenville, *N.C., U.S.A.*	75	B9
Greenville, *S.C., U.S.A.*	75	B6
Greenwood, *Miss., U.S.A.*	79	C8
Greenwood, *S.C., U.S.A.*	75	B6
Gregory, L. . . .	62	A2
Greifswald . . .	15	A7
Greiz	15	C7
Gremikha	28	C4
Grenada ■	87	D7
Grenfell	63	B4
Grenoble	13	D6
Grey →	65	E4
Grey Ra.	63	A3
Greymouth	65	E4
Greytown, *N.Z.*	65	D6
Greytown, *S. Africa* . . .	59	D6
Griffin	75	C5
Griffith	63	B4
Grimari	56	C4
Grimaylov = Hrymayliv . .	17	D8
Grimsby	11	E6
Gris-Nez, C. . .	12	A4
Grodno = Hrodna	17	B6
Grodzyanka = Hrodzyanka .	17	B9
Grójec	16	C5
Groningen	14	B4
Grootfontein . .	58	B3
Gross Glockner	15	E7
Grosser Arber .	15	D7
Grosseto	20	C3
Groznyy	25	E6
Grudziądz	16	B4
Gryazi	24	C4
Gryazovets . . .	28	D5
Gua	40	F5
Guadalajara, *Mexico*	84	C4
Guadalajara, *Spain*	18	B4
Guadalcanal . .	64	K11
Guadalete → . .	18	D2
Guadalquivir →	18	D2
Guadalupe = Guadeloupe ■	87	C7
Guadalupe, Sierra de . . .	18	C3
Guadarrama, Sierra de . . .	18	B4
Guadeloupe ■ .	87	C7
Guadiana → . . .	18	D2
Guadix	18	D4
Guafo, Boca del	95	E2
Guaíra	94	A6
Guaitecas, Is. . .	95	E2
Guajará-Mirim .	91	F5
Guajira, Pen. de la	90	A4
Gualeguay . . .	94	C5
Gualeguaychú .	94	C5
Guam ■	64	H9
Guamúchil . . .	84	B3
Guan Xian . . .	34	C5
Guanahani = San Salvador	86	B5
Guanajuato . . .	84	C4
Guandacol . . .	94	B3
Guane	86	B3
Guangdong □ .	35	D6
Guanghua . . .	35	C6
Guangxi Zhuangzu Zizhiqu □ . . .	35	D5
Guangzhou . . .	35	D6
Guanipa → . . .	90	B6
Guantánamo . .	86	B4
Guaporé → . .	91	F5
Guaqui	91	G5
Guarapuava . . .	94	B6
Guarda	18	B2
Guardafui, C. = Asir, Ras . .	49	E5
Guasdualito . . .	90	B4
Guasipati	90	B6
Guatemala ■ . .	85	E6
Guatemala ■ . .	85	D6
Guatire	90	A5
Guaviare □ . . .	90	C4
Guaviare → . . .	90	C5
Guaxupé	93	G4
Guayama	87	C6
Guayaquil	90	D3
Guayaquil, G. de	90	D2
Guaymas	84	B2
Guddu Barrage	42	E6
Gudivada	40	J3
Gudur	43	M11
Guecho	19	A4
Guékédou . . .	55	G2
Guelma	54	A6
Guelph	69	D2
Guéréda	53	F3
Guéret	12	C4
Guernica	19	A4
Guernsey	11	G5
Guidónia-Montecélio .	20	C4
Guiglo	55	G3
Guildford	11	F6
Guilin	35	D6
Guimarães, *Brazil*	92	C5
Guimarães, *Portugal*	18	B1
Guimaras	38	B2
Guinea ■	55	F2
Guinea, Gulf of	51	F3
Guinea-Bissau ■	55	F1
Guingamp	12	B2
Guiping	35	D6
Güiria	90	A6
Guiuan	38	B3
Guiyang	35	D5
Guizhou □	35	D5
Gujarat □	43	H7
Gujranwala . . .	42	C9
Gujrat	42	C9
Gulbarga	43	L10
Gulf, The	44	E2
Gulgong	63	B4
Güllük	23	F6
Gulshad	29	E8
Gulu	57	D6
Gum Lake	62	B3
Gummi	55	F6
Gümüşhane . .	46	B4
Gumzai	39	F4
Guna	43	G10
Gundagai	63	C4
Gungu	56	F3
Gunnedah	63	B5
Gunningbar Cr. →	63	B4
Guntakal	43	M10
Guntur	40	J3
Gunungapi . . .	39	F3
Gunungsitoli . .	37	D1
Gunza	56	G2
Gupis	42	A8
Gürchän	46	D7
Gurdaspur	42	C9
Gurgaon	42	E10
Gurkha	40	C5
Gurley	63	A4
Gurupá	92	C3
Gurupá, I. Grande de	92	C3
Gurupi →	92	C4
Guryev = Atyraū . . .	29	E6
Gusau	55	F6
Güstrow	15	B7
Gütersloh	14	C5
Guthrie	78	B5
Guyana ■	90	B7
Guyane française ■ = French Guiana ■	92	B3
Guyenne	12	D4
Guyra	63	B5
Gwa	41	J10
Gwaai	59	B5
Gwabegar . . .	63	B4
Gwädar	42	G3
Gwalior	42	F11
Gwanda	59	C5
Gweru	59	B5
Gwydir →	63	A4
Gyandzha = Gäncä	25	E6
Gyaring Hu . . .	34	C4
Gydanskiy P-ov.	28	B8
Gympie	63	A5
Gyöngyös . . .	16	E4
Győr	16	E3
Gypsumville . .	71	C10
Gyula	16	E5
Gyumri	25	E5
Gyzylarbat . . .	29	F6

H

Ha 'Arava → .	47	E3
Haarlem	14	B3
Haast →	65	E3
Habaswein . . .	57	D7
Hachinohe . . .	33	F12
Hadarba, Ras . .	52	D6

Hadd, R'as al .. 45 F4
Hadejia 55 F7
Haden 63 A5
Hadera 46 D3
Hadhramaut =
　Hadramawt . 49 D4
Hadramawt ... 49 D4
Haeju 35 C7
Haerhpin =
　Harbin 35 B7
Hafar al Bāṭin . 47 E6
Hafizabad 42 C8
Haflong 41 E9
Haft Gel 47 E7
Hafun, Ras 49 E5
Hagen 14 C4
Hagerstown ... 73 E7
Hagi 32 B2
Hagondange-
　Briey 13 B7
Hague, C. de la 12 B3
Hague, The = 's-
　Gravenhage . 14 B3
Haguenau 13 B7
Hai'an 35 C7
Haifa = Ḥefa .. 46 D3
Haikou 35 D6
Ḥā'il 47 F5
Hailar 35 B6
Haileybury 69 D3
Hailun 35 B7
Hainan □ 35 E5
Haiphong 35 D5
Haiti ■ 87 C5
Haiya Junction 53 E6
Hajar Bangar .. 53 F3
Hajdúböszörmény
　.......... 16 E5
Hajnówka 17 B6
Hakken-Zan .. 32 B4
Hakodate 32 F12
Hala 42 G6
Ḥalab 46 C4
Halabjah 46 D6
Halaib 52 D6
Halberstadt ... 15 C6
Halcombe 64 D6
Halcon, Mt. .. 38 B2
Halden 9 G10
Haldia 40 F7
Haldwani 42 E11
Halifax, Canada 69 D4
Halifax, U.K. .. 11 E6
Halīl → 44 E4
Hall Beach =
　Sanirajak ... 68 B2
Halle 15 C6
Hallett 62 B2
Halmahera ... 39 D3
Halmstad 9 G10
Halq el Oued .. 52 A1
Hälsingborg =
　Helsingborg . 9 G10
Halul 44 E3
Hamada 32 B3
Hamadān 46 D7
Hamadān □ .. 46 D7
Hamāh 46 D4
Hamamatsu .. 32 B5
Hamar 8 F10
Hamburg 14 B5
Hameln 14 B5
Hamersley Ra. . 60 E2
Hamhung 35 C7
Hami 34 B4
Hamilton,
　Australia 62 C3
Hamilton,
　Canada 69 D3

Hamilton, N.Z. . 64 B6
Hamilton, U.K. . 10 D4
Hamley Bridge 62 B2
Hamlin =
　Hameln 14 B5
Hamm 14 C4
Hammerfest .. 8 D12
Hammond ... 72 D2
Hampden 65 F4
Hampton 73 F7
Hamrat esh
　Sheykh 53 F4
Han Pijesak ... 20 B7
Hanamaki 33 G12
Hanau 14 C5
Hancock 77 C7
Handa 49 E5
Handan 35 C6
Handeni 57 F7
Hangayn Nuruu 34 B4
Hangchou =
　Hangzhou ... 35 C7
Hangu 35 C6
Hangzhou 35 C7
Hangzhou Wan 35 C7
Ḥanīsh 49 E3
Hanle 42 C11
Hanmer Springs 65 E5
Hanna 71 C8
Hannibal 77 F9
Hannover 14 B5
Hanoi 35 D5
Hanover =
　Hannover ... 14 B5
Hanover, I. 95 G2
Hansi 42 E9
Hanson, L. 62 B2
Hantsavichy ... 17 B8
Hanzhong 35 C5
Haora 40 F7
Haparanda 8 E12
Happy Valley-
　Goose Bay .. 69 C4
Hapur 42 E10
Ḥaql 47 E3
Har 39 F4
Har Hu 34 C4
Har Us Nuur .. 34 B4
Haraḍ 47 F7
Haraisan Plateau
　= Huraysān . 47 G6
Harardera 49 G4
Harare 59 B6
Harazé 53 F2
Harbin 35 B7
Harbour Grace 69 D5
Hardangerfjorden
　.......... 8 F9
Hardap Dam .. 58 C3
Hardwar =
　Haridwar ... 42 E11
Hardy, Pen. .. 95 H3
Harer 49 F3
Hargeisa 49 F3
Hari → 37 E2
Haridwar 42 E11
Haringhata → 41 G7
Harīrūd 45 C5
Harīrūd → 42 A2
Harlingen 78 F5
Harlow 11 F7
Harney Basin .. 80 D4
Härnösand 8 F11
Ḥarrat al Kishb 47 G5
Harrat al
　'Uwairidh .. 47 F4
Harris 10 C3
Harris L. 62 B2
Harrisburg 73 D7

Harrison, C. ... 68 C5
Harrison Bay .. 71 A4
Harrogate 11 D6
Hart, L. 62 B2
Hartford 73 D9
Hartlepool ... 11 D6
Harvey 72 D2
Harwich 11 F7
Haryana □ ... 42 E10
Haryn → 17 B8
Harz 14 C6
Hasa 47 F7
Hasan Kuli ... 29 F6
Hassi Inifel 54 C5
Hassi Messaoud 54 B6
Hastings, N.Z. . 64 C7
Hastings, U.K. . 11 F7
Hastings, U.S.A. 76 E5
Hastings Ra. .. 63 B5
Hatay = Antalya 46 C2
Hatfield P.O. .. 62 B3
Hatgal 34 A5
Hathras 42 F11
Hatia 41 F8
Hattah 62 B3
Hatteras, C. ... 75 B10
Hattiesburg ... 79 D9
Hatvan 16 E4
Hau Bon = Cheo
　Reo 36 B3
Haugesund ... 9 G9
Hauraki G. 64 B6
Haut Atlas 54 B3
Hautah, Wahāt
　al 47 G6
Hauts Plateaux 54 B4
Havana = La
　Habana 86 B3
Havant 11 F6
Havel → 15 B7
Havelock 65 D5
Haverfordwest . 11 F4
Havlíčkův Brod 16 D2
Havre 81 A9
Havza 46 B3
Hawaii □ 82 J12
Hawaiian Is. ... 82 H12
Hawea, L. 65 F3
Hawera 64 C6
Hawick 10 D5
Hawke B. 64 C7
Hawker 62 B2
Hawkwood 63 A5
Hay 63 B3
Hay River 70 B8
Haya 39 E3
Hayes → 71 C10
Hayrabolu 22 D6
Haysyn 17 D9
Hayvoron 17 D9
Hazaribag 40 F5
Healesville ... 63 C4
Hearst 69 D2
Hebei □ 35 C6
Hebel 63 A4
Hebron = Al
　Khalīl 47 E3
Hebron 68 C4
Hechi 35 D5
Hechuan 35 C5
Heerlen 13 A6
Ḥefa 46 D3
Hefei 35 C6
Hegang 35 B8
Heidelberg ... 14 D5
Heilbron 59 D5
Heilbronn 14 D5
Heilongjiang □ 35 B7

Heilunkiang =
　Heilongjiang □
　.......... 35 B7
Heinze Is. 41 K11
Hejaz = Al Ḥijāz 47 F4
Hekimhan 46 C4
Hekou 34 D5
Helena, Ark.,
　U.S.A. 79 B8
Helena, Mont.,
　U.S.A. 81 B7
Helensville 64 B6
Helgoland 14 A4
Heligoland =
　Helgoland ... 14 A4
Heligoland B. =
　Deutsche
　Bucht 14 A5
Hellín 19 C5
Helmand □ ... 42 D3
Helmand → .. 42 D2
Helmand,
　Hamun 45 D5
Helmsdale 10 B5
Helsingborg ... 9 G10
Helsingfors =
　Helsinki 9 F13
Helsinki 9 F13
Helwân 52 C5
Hemel
　Hempstead .. 11 F6
Henan □ 35 C6
Henares → ... 18 B4
Henderson ... 75 A8
Hendon 63 A5
Hengyang 35 D6
Henrietta Maria,
　C. 69 C2
Hentiyn Nuruu 35 B5
Henty 63 C4
Henzada 41 J10
Herāt 42 B3
Herāt □ 42 B3
Hercegnovi ... 22 C2
Hereford 11 E5
Herford 14 B5
Hermidale 63 B4
Hermitage 65 E4
Hermite, I. 95 H3
Hermon, Mt. =
　Ash Shaykh,
　J. 46 D3
Hermosillo 84 B2
Hernád → 16 E5
Hernandarias .. 94 B6
Heroica Nogales
　= Nogales .. 84 A2
Heron Bay 69 D2
Herrick 62 D4
's-
　Hertogenbosch
　.......... 14 C3
Hesse =
　Hessen □ ... 14 C5
Hessen □ 14 C5
Hewett, C. ... 68 A4
Hexham 11 D5
Heyfield 63 C4
Heywood 62 C3
Hibbing 77 B8
Hibbs B. 62 D4
Hickory 75 B7
Hicks, Pt. 63 C4
Hida-Sammyaku 32 A5
Hidalgo del
　Parral 84 B3
Higashiōsaka .. 32 B4
High Atlas =
　Haut Atlas .. 54 B3

High Point 75 B8
High River 71 C8
High Tatra =
Tatry 16 D4
High Wycombe 11 F6
Hiiumaa 24 B1
Ḥijārah, Ṣaḥrā'
al 47 E6
Ḥijāz □ 48 C2
Hijo = Tagum . 38 C3
Hikone 32 B5
Hikurangi 64 A6
Hikurangi, Mt. . 64 C7
Hildesheim .. 14 B5
Hillston 63 B4
Hilo 82 J13
Hilversum 14 B3
Himachal
Pradesh □ .. 42 D10
Himalaya 40 C5
Himatnagar ... 43 H8
Himeji 32 B4
Himi 32 A5
Ḥimş 46 D4
Hindmarsh, L. . 62 C3
Hindu Kush ... 42 B7
Hindubagh ... 42 D5
Hindupur 43 N10
Hinganghat ... 43 J11
Hingoli 43 K10
Hinna = Imi ... 49 F3
Hinojosa del
Duque ... 18 C3
Hirakud Dam .. 40 G4
Hiratsuka ... 32 B6
Hirosaki 33 F12
Hiroshima ... 32 B3
Hisar 42 E9
Hispaniola .. 87 C5
Hita 32 C2
Hitachi 32 A7
Hjälmaren ... 9 G11
Hlyboka 17 D7
Ho 55 G5
Ho Chi Minh
City = Phanh
Bho Ho Chi
Minh 36 B3
Hoai Nhon ... 36 B3
Hoare B. 68 B4
Hobart 62 D4
Hobbs Coast . 96 B18
Hodgson ... 71 C10
Hódmezővásárhely
.... 16 E5
Hodna, Chott el 54 A5
Hodonín 16 D3
Hoek van
Holland 14 B3
Hof 15 C6
Hōfu 32 B2
Hogan Group . 62 C4
Hoggar =
Ahaggar 54 D6
Hoh Xil Shan . 34 C3
Hohe Rhön .. 14 C5
Hohhot 35 B6
Hoi An 36 A3
Hokianga
Harbour 64 A5
Hokitika 65 E4
Hokkaidō □ ... 32 F12
Holbrook 63 C4
Holguín 86 B4
Hollandia =
Jayapura ... 39 E6
Holman Island . 70 A8
Holy Cross ... 71 B4
Holyhead 11 E4

Homalin 41 E10
Hombori 55 E4
Home B. 68 B4
Homer 71 C4
Homs = Ḥimş . 46 D4
Homyel 17 B10
Hon Chong ... 36 B2
Honan =
Henan □ 35 C6
Honda 90 B4
Hondeklipbaai . 58 E3
Honduras ■ ... 85 E7
Honduras, G. de 85 D7
Honfleur ... 12 B4
Hong Kong ... 35 D6
Hongjiang ... 35 D5
Hongshui He ➤ 35 D5
Hongze Hu ... 35 C6
Honiara 64 K10
Honolulu 82 H12
Honshū 32 G11
Hood, Mt. 80 C3
Hooghly ➤ =
Hughli ➤ . 40 G7
Hook of Holland
= Hoek van
Holland 14 B3
Hoorn 14 B3
Hoover Dam . 82 B5
Hope, L. 62 A2
Hope, Pt. 71 B3
Hopedale 68 C4
Hopei =
Hebei □ 35 C6
Hopetoun ... 62 C3
Hopetown 58 D4
Hoquiam 80 B2
Horlick Mts. ... 96 C1
Horlivka 25 D4
Hormoz 44 E3
Hormoz, Jaz. ye 44 E4
Hormozgān □ . 44 E3
Hormuz, Str. of 44 E4
Horn 15 D8
Horn, Cape =
Hornos, C. de 95 H3
Hornavan 8 E11
Hornos, C. de . 95 H3
Hornsby 63 B5
Horodenka ... 17 D7
Horodok,
Khmelnytskyy,
Ukraine 17 D8
Horodok, Lviv,
Ukraine 17 D6
Horokhiv ... 17 C7
Horqin Youyi
Qianqi 35 B7
Horqueta ... 94 A5
Horsham 62 C3
Horton ➤ 70 B7
Hose, Gunung-
Gunung 37 D4
Hoshangabad . 43 H10
Hoshiarpur ... 42 D9
Hospet 43 M10
Hospitalet de
Llobregat ... 19 B7
Hoste, I. 95 H3
Hot Springs ... 79 B7
Hotan 34 C2
Houhora Heads 64 A5
Houlton 73 A12
Houma 79 E8
Houston 79 E6
Hovd 34 B4
Hövsgöl Nuur . 34 A5
Howard 63 A5
Howe, C. 63 C5

Howitt, L. 62 A2
Howrah = Haora 40 F7
Höxter 14 C5
Hoy 10 B5
Høyanger 8 F9
Hoyerswerda . 15 C8
Hpungan Pass . 41 D11
Hradec Králové 16 C2
Hrodna 17 B6
Hrodzyanka ... 17 B9
Hron ➤ 16 E4
Hrvatska =
Croatia ■ ... 20 B6
Hrymayliv ... 17 D8
Hsenwi 41 F11
Hsiamen =
Xiamen 35 D6
Hsian = Xi'an . 35 C5
Hsinhailien =
Lianyungang 35 C6
Hsisha Chuntao 36 A4
Hsüchou =
Xuzhou ... 35 C6
Hua Hin 36 B1
Huacho 91 F3
Huachón ... 91 F3
Huai He ➤ ... 35 C6
Huainan ... 35 C6
Huallaga ➤ .. 90 E3
Huambo ... 58 A3
Huancabamba . 91 E3
Huancane ... 91 G5
Huancapi 91 F4
Huancavelica . 91 F3
Huancayo 91 F3
Huang Hai =
Yellow Sea .. 35 C7
Huang He ➤ .. 35 C6
Huangliu ... 35 E5
Huangshi ... 35 C6
Huánuco ... 91 E3
Huaraz 91 E3
Huarmey 91 F3
Huascarán ... 91 E3
Huasco 94 B2
Huatabampo .. 84 B3
Huayllay 91 F3
Hubei □ 35 C6
Hubli-Dharwad
= Dharwad . 43 M9
Huddersfield .. 11 E6
Hudiksvall ... 8 F11
Hudson ➤ ... 73 D8
Hudson Bay ... 68 B2
Hudson Mts. ... 96 B2
Hudson Str. ... 68 B4
Hue 36 A3
Huelva 18 D2
Huesca 19 A5
Hughenden ... 61 E7
Hughli ➤ 40 G7
Huila, Nevado
del 90 C3
Huinca Renancó 94 C4
Huize 34 D5
Hukawng Valley 41 D11
Hulan 35 B7
Ḥulayfā' 47 F5
Huld 35 B5
Hull = Kingston
upon Hull ... 11 E6
Hull 69 D3
Hulun Nur 35 B6
Humahuaca ... 94 A3
Humaitá, Brazil 91 E6
Humaitá,
Paraguay ... 94 B5
Humber ➤ ... 11 E6
Humboldt 71 C9

Humboldt ➤ . 80 F4
Hume, L. 63 C4
Humenné 16 D5
Hūn 52 C2
Hunan □ 35 D6
Hunedoara ... 17 F6
Hungary ■ .. 16 E4
Hungerford ... 63 A3
Hŭngnam ... 35 C7
Hunsrück 14 D4
Hunter I. 62 D3
Hunter Ra. ... 63 B5
Hunterville ... 64 C6
Huntington ... 72 E4
Huntington
Beach 82 D3
Huntly, N.Z. ... 64 B6
Huntly, U.K. ... 10 C5
Huntsville ... 74 B4
Huonville ... 62 D4
Hupeh =
Hubei □ ... 35 C6
Huraysān 47 G6
Huron, L. 72 B4
Hurunui ➤ ... 65 E5
Huşi 17 E9
Hutchinson ... 78
Hutton, Mt. ... 63 A4
Hvar 20 C6
Hwang Ho =
Huang He ➤ 35 C6
Hwange 59 B5
Hyargas Nuur . 34 B2
Hyderabad,
India 43 L11
Hyderabad,
Pakistan 42 G6
Hyères 13 E7
Hyères, Is. d' .. 13 E7

I

I-n-Gall 55 E6
Iaco ➤ 91 E5
Ialomiţa ➤ .. 22 B6
Iaşi 17 E8
Iba 38 A2
Ibadan 55 G5
Ibagué 90 C3
Ibar ➤ 22 C3
Ibarra 90 C3
Ibi 55 G6
Ibiá 93 F4
Ibicuy 94 C5
Ibioapaba, Sa.
da 92 C5
Ibiza 19 C6
Ibonma 39 E4
Ibotirama ... 93 E5
Ibu 39 D3
Icá 91 F3
Iça ➤ 90 D5
Içana 90 C4
İçel = Mersin .. 46 C3
Iceland ■ 8 D4
Ich'ang =
Yichang 35 C6
Ichchapuram .. 40 H5
Ichihara 32 B7
Ichikawa 32 B6
Ichilo ➤ 91 G6
Ichinomiya .. 32 B5
Idaho □ 81 C6
Idaho Falls ... 81 D7
Idar-Oberstein . 14 D4
Idd el Ghanam 53 F3

Iddan 49 F4
Idehan 52 C1
Idehan Marzūq . 52 D1
Idelès 54 D6
Idfû 52 D5
Ídhi Óros 23 G5
Ídhra 23 F4
Idi 36 C1
Idiofa 56 E3
Idlip 46 D4
Ierápetra 23 G5
Iesi 20 C4
Ifanadiana 59 J9
Ife 55 G5
Ifni 54 C2
Iforas, Adrar des 54
Igarapava 93 G4
Igarapé Açu ... 92 C4
Igarka 28 C9
Igbetti 55 G5
Iglésias 21 E2
Igli 54 B4
Igloolik 68 B2
Igluligaarjuk ... 68 B1
Iğneada Burnu . 22 D7
Igoumenítsa .. 23 E3
Iguaçu → 94 B6
Iguaçu, Cat. del 94 B6
Iguaçu Falls =
   Iguaçu, Cat.
   del 94 B6
Iguala 84 D5
Igualada 19 B6
Iguassu =
   Iguaçu → .. 94 B6
Iguatu 92 D6
Iguéla 56 E1
Ihosy 59 J9
Iida 32 B5
Iisalmi 8 F13
Iizuka 32 C2
Ijebu-Ode 55 G5
IJsselmeer 14 B3
Ikaluktutiak .. 70 B9
Ikaría 23 F6
Ikela 56 E4
Iki 32 C1
Ilagan 38 A2
Ilâm 46 D6
Ilawa 16 B4
Île-de-France .. 12 B5
Ilebo 56 E4
Ilhéus 93 E6
Ili → 29 E8
Ilich 29 E7
Iligan 38 C2
Illampu =
   Ancohuma,
   Nevada 91 G5
Illana B. 38 C2
Illapel 94 C2
Iller → 14 D5
Illimani 91 G5
Illium = Troy .. 23 E6
Ilmen, Ozero . 24 B3
Ilo 91 G4
Iloilo 38 B2
Ilorin 55 G5
Ilwaki 39 F3
Imabari 32 B3
Imandra, Ozero 28 C4
Imari 32 C1
imeni 26
   Bakinskikh
   Komissarov =
   Neftçala 46 C7
Imeri, Serra ... 90 C5
Imi 49 F3
Imola 20 B3

Imperatriz 92 D4
Impéria 20 C2
Imperial Dam . 82 D5
Impfondo 56 D3
Imphal 41 E9
İmroz =
   Gökçeada ... 23 D5
Imuruan B. 38 B1
In Belbel 54 C5
In Salah 54 C5
Ina 32 B5
Inangahua
   Junction 65 D4
Inanwatan 39 E4
Iñapari 91 F5
Inarijärvi 8 E13
Inca 19 C7
İnce-Burnu 46 B3
Inchon 35 C7
İncirliova 23 F6
Incomáti → .. 59 D6
Indalsälven → 8 F11
Indaw 41 E11
Independence,
   Kans., U.S.A. 79 A6
Independence,
   Mo., U.S.A. . 77 F7
India ■ 43 J10
Indian → 75 F7
Indian Harbour 68 C5
Indian Head .. 71 C9
Indiana □ 72 D3
Indianapolis ... 72 E2
Indiga 28 C5
Indigirka → .. 31 B12
Indonesia ■ ... 37 E4
Indore 43 H9
Indravati → .. 40 H3
Indre → 12 C4
Indus → 43 G5
İnebolu 46 B3
Ingende 56 E3
Inglewood,
   Queens.,
   Australia 63 A5
Inglewood, Vic.,
   Australia 62 C3
Inglewood, N.Z. 64 C6
Ingolstadt 15 D6
Ingraj Bazar ... 40 E7
Ingrid
   Christensen
   Coast 96 A10
Ingulec =
   Inhulec 25 D3
Inhambane ... 59 C7
Inhaminga ... 59 B7
Inharrime 59 C7
Inhulec 25 D3
Ining = Yining . 34 B3
Inírida → 90 C5
Injune 63 A4
Inle L. 41 G11
Inn → 15 D7
Innamincka ... 62 A3
Inner Hebrides 10 C3
Inner Mongolia
   = Nei
   Monggol
   Zizhiqu □ ... 35 B6
Innisfail 71 C8
Innsbruck 15 E6
Inongo 56 E3
Inoucdjouac =
   Inukjuak 68 C3
Inowrocław ... 16 B4
Inquisivi 91 G5
Insein 41 J11
Interlaken 13 C7

International
   Falls 77 A8
Intiyaco 94 B4
Inukjuak 68 C3
Inútil, B. 95 G2
Inuvik 70 B6
Invercargill 65 G3
Inverell 63 A5
Invergordon ... 10 C4
Inverness 10 C4
Inverurie 10 C5
Investigator
   Group 62 B1
Investigator Str. 62 C2
Inya 29 D9
Inza 24 C6
Ioánnina 23 E3
Ionian Is. =
   Iónioi Nísoi . 23 E3
Ionian Sea ... 21 F6
Iónioi Nísoi ... 23 E3
Íos 23 F5
Iowa □ 77 D8
Iowa City 77 E9
Ipameri 93 F4
Ipatinga 93 F5
Ipiales 90 C3
Ipin − Yibin ... 35 D5
Ipixuna 91 E4
Ipoh 36 D2
Ippy 56 C4
İpsala 22 D6
Ipswich,
   Australia 63 A5
Ipswich, U.K. .. 11 E7
Ipu 92 C5
Iqaluit 68 B4
Iquique 91 H4
Iquitos 90 D4
Iracoubo 92 A3
Iráklion 23 G5
Iran ■ 44 C3
Iran, Gunung-
   Gunung 37 D4
Iran Ra. = Iran,
   Gunung-
   Gunung 37 D4
Īrānshahr 45 E5
Irapuato 84 C4
Iraq ■ 46 D5
Irbid 46 D3
Irebu 56 E3
Ireland ■ 11 E3
Irian Jaya □ .. 39 E5
Iringa 57 F7
Iriri → 92 C3
Irish Sea 11 E4
Irkineyeva 30 D7
Irkutsk 30 D8
Iron Baron ... 62 B2
Iron Gate =
   Portile de Fier 22 B4
Iron Knob 62 B2
Ironwood 77 B9
Irpin 17 C10
Irrara Cr. → .. 63 A4
Irrawaddy □ .. 41 J10
Irrawaddy → . 41 K10
Irtysh → 28 C7
Irumu 57 D5
Irún 19 A5
Irunea =
   Pamplona ... 19 A5
Irvine 10 D4
Irymple 62 B3
Isabella 38 C2
Isangi 56 D4
Isar → 15 D7
Íschia 21 D4

Ise 32 B5
Ise-Wan 32 B5
Isère → 13 D6
Isérnia 20 D5
Ishikari-Wan .. 32 F12
Ishim → 29 D8
Ishinomaki ... 33 G12
Ishkuman 42 A8
Isil Kul 29 D8
Isiolo 57 D7
Isiro 57 D5
İskenderun 46 C4
Iskŭr → 22 C5
Islamabad 42 C8
Island L. 71 C10
Island Lagoon . 62 B2
Islay 10 D3
Isle → 12 D3
Isle of Wight □ 11 F6
Ismail = Izmayil 17 F9
Ismâ'ilîya 47 E3
Isna 52 C5
Ísparta 46 C2
İspica 21 F5
Israel ■ 46 E3
Issoire 13 D5
Issyk-Kul, Ozero
   = Ysyk-Köl,
   Ozero 29 E8
İstanbul 22 D7
Istiaía 23 E4
Istra 20 B4
İstranca Dağları 22 D6
Istres 13 E6
Istria = Istra .. 20 B4
Itabaiana 92 D6
Itaberaba 93 E5
Itabira 93 F5
Itabuna 93 E6
Itaipú, Reprêsa
   de 94 B6
Itaituba 92 C2
Itajaí 94 B7
Italy ■ 20 C4
Itapecuru-Mirim 92 C5
Itaperuna 93 G5
Itapicuru →,
   Bahia, Brazil . 93 E6
Itapicuru →,
   Maranhão,
   Brazil 92 C5
Itapipoca 92 C6
Itaquatiara ... 90 D7
Itaquí 94 B5
Itatuba 91 E6
Ithaca = Itháki . 23 E3
Itháki 23 E3
Ito 32 B6
Itonamas → .. 91 F6
Ituaçu 93 E5
Ituiutaba 93 F4
Itumbiara 93 F4
Iturbe 94 A3
Itzehoe 14 B5
Ivanava 17 B7
Ivanhoe 63 B3
Ivano-Frankivsk 17 D7
Ivano-Frankovsk
   = Ivano-
   Frankivsk ... 17 D7
Ivanovo =
   Ivanava 17 B7
Ivanovo 24 B5
Ivatsevichy ... 17 B7
Ivory Coast ■ . 55 G3
Ivrea 20 B1
Ivujivik 68 B3
Iwahig 36 C5
Iwaki 33 G12

Iwakuni 32 B3
Iwata 33 H11
Iwate-San 33 G12
Iwo 55 G5
Ixiamas 91 F5
Izhevsk 28 D6
Izmayil 17 F9
İzmir 23 E6
İzmit 25 E2
İznik Gölü 23 D7
Izumi-sano 32 B4
Izumo 32 B3
Izyaslav 17 C8

J

Jabalpur 43 H11
Jablah 46 D4
Jablanica 22 D3
Jablonec 16 C2
Jaboatão 92 D6
Jaca 19 A5
Jacareí 94 A7
Jacarèzinho ... 94 A7
Jackson,
  Australia 63 A4
Jackson, Mich.,
  U.S.A. 72 C3
Jackson, Miss.,
  U.S.A. 79 C8
Jackson, Tenn.,
  U.S.A. 74 B3
Jackson B. 65 E3
Jacksons 65 E4
Jacksonville,
  Fla., U.S.A. .. 75 D7
Jacksonville, Ill.,
  U.S.A. 77 F9
Jacksonville,
  N.C., U.S.A. . 75 B9
Jacmel 87 C5
Jacobabad 42 E6
Jacobina 93 E5
Jacundá → ... 92 C3
Jadotville =
  Likasi 57 G5
Jādū 52 B1
Jaén, Peru 91 E3
Jaén, Spain .. 18 D4
Jaffa = Tel Aviv-
  Yafo 46 D3
Jaffa, C. 62 C2
Jaffna 43 Q12
Jagadhri 42 D10
Jagdalpur 40 H3
Jagraon 42 D9
Jagtial 43 K11
Jaguariaíva ... 94 A7
Jaguaribe → .. 92 C6
Jahrom 44 D3
Jailolo 39 D3
Jailolo, Selat .. 39 D3
Jaipur 42 F9
Jakarta 37 F3
Jalalabad 42 B7
Jalapa Enríquez 84 D5
Jalas, Jabal al . 47 F4
Jalgaon,
  Maharashtra,
  India 43 J10
Jalgaon,
  Maharashtra,
  India 43 J9
Jalna 43 K9
Jalón → 19 B5
Jalpaiguri 41 D7

Jalq 45 E5
Jaluit I. 64 J11
Jamaica ■ 86 C4
Jamalpur,
  Bangla. 41 E7
Jamalpur, India 40 E6
Jamanxim → . 92 C2
Jambe 39 E4
Jambi 37 E2
Jambi □ 37 E2
James → 76 D6
James B. 69 C2
James Ross I. . 96 A4
Jamestown,
  Australia 62 B2
Jamestown,
  N. Dak., U.S.A. 76 B5
Jamestown,
  N.Y., U.S.A. . 73 C6
Jamkhandi 43 L9
Jammu 42 C9
Jammu &
  Kashmir □ .. 42 B10
Jamnagar 43 H7
Jamrud 42 C7
Jamshedpur .. 40 F6
Jand 42 C8
Jandaq 44 C3
Jandowae 63 A5
Janesville 77 D10
Januária 93 F5
Jaora 43 H9
Japan ■ 33 G11
Japan, Sea of . 33 G11
Japen = Yapen 39 E5
Japurá → 90 D5
Jaque 90 B3
Jarama → ... 18 B4
Jargalant =
  Hovd 34 B4
Jarosław 17 C6
Jarso 53 G6
Jarvis I. 65 K15
Jarwa 40 D4
Jāsk 44 E4
Jasło 16 D5
Jasper 74 C4
Jászberény ... 16 E4
Jataí 93 F3
Játiva 19 C5
Jaú 93 G4
Jauja 91 F3
Jaunpur 40 E4
Java = Jawa .. 37 F3
Java Sea 37 E3
Javhlant =
  Ulyasutay ... 34 B4
Jawa 37 F3
Jaya, Puncak . 39 E5
Jayanti 41 D7
Jayapura 39 E6
Jayawijaya,
  Pegunungan 39 E5
Jaynagar 40 D6
Jean Marie
  River 70 B7
Jebba 55 G5
Jebel, Bahr
  el → 53 G5
Jedburgh 10 D5
Jedda = Jiddah 47 G4
Jędrzejów 16 C5
Jefferson City . 77 F8
Jega 55 F5
Jelenia Góra .. 16 C2
Jelgava 24 B1
Jemaja 37 D3
Jembongan ... 36 C5
Jena 15 C6

Jeparit 62 C3
Jequié 93 E5
Jequitinhonha . 93 F5
Jequitinhonha→ 93 F6
Jerada 54 B4
Jerantut 37 D2
Jérémie 86 C5
Jerez de la
  Frontera 18 D2
Jerez de los
  Caballeros .. 18 C2
Jerilderie 63 C4
Jersey 11 G5
Jersey City .. 73 D8
Jerusalem 47 E3
Jervis B. 63 C5
Jesselton =
  Kota Kinabalu 36 C5
Jessore 41 F7
Jeypore 40 H4
Jhal Jhao 42 F4
Jhalawar 43 G10
Jhang Maghiana 42 D8
Jhansi 43 G11
Jharkand □ 40 F5
Jharsaguda ... 40 G5
Jhelum 42 C8
Jhelum → ... 42 D8
Jhunjhunu 42 E9
Jiamusi 35 B8
Ji'an 35 D6
Jianchuan 34 D4
Jiangling 35 C6
Jiangmen 35 D6
Jiangsu □ 35 C6
Jiangxi □ 35 D6
Jian'ou 35 D6
Jianshui 34 D5
Jiao Xian 35 C7
Jiaozuo 35 C6
Jiaxing 35 C7
Jiayi 35 D7
Jibuti =
  Djibouti ■ .. 49 E3
Jiddah 47 G4
Jido 41 C10
Jihlava 16 D2
Jihlava → 16 D3
Jijel 54 A6
Jijiga 49 F3
Jilin 35 B7
Jilong 35 D7
Jima 53 G6
Jiménez 84 B4
Jinan 35 C6
Jindabyne 63 C4
Jindrichuv
  Hradeç 16 D2
Jingdezhen ... 35 D6
Jinggu 34 D5
Jingxi 35 D5
Jinhua 35 D6
Jining,
  Nei Mongol Zizhiqu,
  China 35 B6
Jining,
  Shandong,
  China 35 C6
Jinja 57 D6
Jinnah Barrage 42 C7
Jinotega 85 E7
Jinshi 35 D6
Jinzhou 35 B7
Jiparaná → .. 91 E6
Jipijapa 90 D2
Jisr ash
  Shughūr ... 46 D4
Jiu → 22 C4
Jiujiang 35 D6

Jiuquan 34 C4
Jixi 35 B8
Jizzakh 29 E7
Joaçaba 94 B6
João Pessoa .. 92 D7
Joaquín V.
  González ... 94 B4
Jodhpur 42 F8
Jofane 59 C6
Jogjakarta =
  Yogyakarta .. 37 F4
Johannesburg . 59 D5
Johnson City .. 75 A6
Johnston Falls
  = Mambilima
  Falls 57 G5
Johnstown 73 D6
Johor Baharu . 37 D2
Joinvile 94 B7
Joinville I. 96 A4
Joliet 72 D1
Joliette 69 D3
Jolo 38 C2
Jome 39 E3
Jonesboro 79 B8
Jönköping .. 9 G10
Jonquière 69 D3
Joplin 79 A6
Jordan ■ 47 E4
Jorhat 41 D10
Jorong 37 E4
Jos 55 G6
Jowzjān □ ... 45 B2
Juan de Fuca
  Str. 80 A1
Juan de Nova . 59 H8
Juan Fernández,
  Arch. de 89 G3
Juárez 94 D5
Juàzeiro 93 D5
Juàzeiro do
  Norte 92 D6
Jubbulpore =
  Jabalpur 43 H11
Juby, C. 54 C2
Júcar → 19 C5
Juchitán 85 D5
Jugoslavia =
  Yugoslavia ■ 22 B3
Juiz de Fora ... 93 G5
Juli 91 G5
Juliaca 91 G4
Jullundur 42 D9
Jumilla 19 C5
Jumla 40 C4
Jumna =
  Yamuna → . 40 E3
Junagadh 43 J7
Jundiaí 94 A7
Juneau 71 C6
Junee 63 B4
Jungfrau 13 C7
Junggar Pendi . 34 B3
Junín 94 C4
Junín de los
  Andes 95 D2
Jūniyah 46 D3
Jur, Nahr el → 53 G4
Jura = Jura,
  Mts. du 13 C7
Jura =
  Schwäbische
  Alb 14 D5
Jura 10 D4
Jura, Mts. du .. 13 C7
Jurado 90 B3
Juruá → 90 D5
Juruena → ... 91 E7
Juruti 92 C2

Justo Daract .. 94 C3
Jutland =
Jylland 9 G9
Juventud, I. de
la 86 B3
Juwain 42 D2
Jylland 9 G9
Jyväskylä 8 F13

K

K2 .... 42 B10
Kaapkruis 58 C2
Kaapstad =
Cape Town .. 58 E3
Kabaena 39 F2
Kabala 55 G2
Kabale 57 E6
Kabalo 57 F5
Kabambare ... 57 E5
Kabanjahe 37 D1
Kabara 55 E4
Kabardino-
Balkar
Republic =
Kabardino
Balkaria □ .. 25 E5
Kabardino
Balkaria □ .. 25 E5
Kabare 39 E4
Kabarega Falls 57 D6
Kabasalan 38 C2
Kabba 55 G6
Kabīr, Zab al → 46 C5
Kabīr Kūh 47 D6
Kabkabīyah ... 53 F3
Kabompo → .. 58 A4
Kabongo 57 F5
Kabūd Gonbad 44 B4
Kābul 42 B6
Kābul □ 42 B6
Kabul → 42 C8
Kaburuang 39 D3
Kabwe 59 A5
Kachchh, Gulf of 43 H6
Kachchh, Rann
of 43 G6
Kachin □ 41 D11
Kachiry 29 D8
Kaçkar 46 B5
Kadan Kyun .. 36 B1
Kadina 62 B2
Kadirli 46 C4
Kadiyevka =
Stakhanov .. 25 D4
Kadoma 59 B5
Kâdugli 53 F4
Kaduna 55 F6
Kaédi 55 E2
Kaélé 53 F1
Kaesŏng 35 C7
Kāf 47 E4
Kafakumba ... 56 F4
Kafan = Kapan 25 F6
Kafanchan 55 G6
Kaffrine 55 F1
Kafia Kingi ... 53 G3
Kafirévs, Ákra . 23 E5
Kafue → 59 B5
Kafulwe 57 F5
Kaga Bandoro . 56 C3
Kagan 29 F7
Kağizman 46 B5
Kagoshima ... 33 D2
Kagoshima-Wan 33 D2
Kagul = Cahul . 17 F9

Kahama 57 E6
Kahayan → . 37 E4
Kahemba 56 F3
Kahnūj 44 E4
Kahoolawe ... 82 H12
Kahramanmaraş 46 C4
Kai, Kepulauan 39 F4
Kai Besar 39 F4
Kai Is. = Kai,
Kepulauan .. 39 F4
Kai Kecil 39 F4
Kaiama 55 G5
Kaiapoi 65 E5
Kaieteur Falls . 90 B7
Kaifeng 35 C6
Kaikohe 64 A5
Kaikoura 65 E5
Kaikoura Ra. .. 65 D5
Kaimana 39 E4
Kaimanawa Mts. 64 C6
Kaingaroa
Forest 64 C7
Kainji Res. 55 F5
Kaipara Harbour 64 B6
Kaironi 39 E4
Kairouan 54 A7
Kaiserslautern . 14 D4
Kaitaia 64 A5
Kaitangata ... 65 G3
Kajaani 8 F13
Kajabbi 61 D6
Kajana =
Kajaani 8 F13
Kajo Kaji 53 H5
Kaka 53 F5
Kakamas 58 D4
Kakamega 57 D6
Kakanui Mts. .. 65 F4
Kakhovka 25 D3
Kakhovske
Vdskh. 25 D3
Kakinada 40 J4
Kalaallit Nunaat
=
Greenland ■ 66 C9
Kalabagh 42 C7
Kalabahi 39 F2
Kalabo 58 A4
Kalach 24 C5
Kaladan → ... 41 G9
Kalahari 58 C4
Kalakan 31 D9
Kalámai 23 F4
Kalamata =
Kalámai 23 F4
Kalamazoo ... 72 C3
Kalan 46 C4
Kalao 39 F2
Kalaotoa 39 F2
Kalat 42 E5
Kalce 20 B5
Kale 23 F7
Kalegauk Kyun 41 K11
Kalemie 57 F5
Kalewa 41 F10
Kalgan =
Zhangjiakou . 35 B6
Kalgoorlie-
Boulder 60 G3
Kaliakra, Nos .. 22 C7
Kalianda 37 F3
Kalibo 38 B2
Kalima 57 E5
Kalimantan ... 37 E4
Kalimantan
Barat □ 37 D4
Kalimantan
Selatan □ ... 37 E5

Kalimantan
Tengah □ ... 37 E4
Kalimantan
Timur □ 37 D5
Kálimnos 23 F6
Kalinin = Tver . 24 B4
Kaliningrad,
Kaliningd.,
Russia 24 C1
Kaliningrad,
Moskva,
Russia 24 B4
Kalinkavichy .. 17 B9
Kalinkovichi =
Kalinkavichy . 17 B9
Kalispell 81 A6
Kalisz 16 C4
Kaliua 57 F6
Kalkrand 58 C3
Kalmar 9 G11
Kalmyk Republic
= Kalmykia □ 25 D6
Kalmykia □ ... 25 D6
Kalocsa 16 E4
Kalomo 59 B5
Kaluga 24 C4
Kalush 17 D7
Kalutara 43 R11
Kama → 29 D6
Kamaishi 33 G12
Kamaran 49 D3
Kamchatka, P-
ov. 31 D13
Kamchatka Pen.
= Kamchatka,
P-ov. 31 D13
Kamchiya → . 22 C6
Kamen 29 D9
Kamenjak, Rt. . 20 B4
Kamenka
Bugskaya =
Kamyanka-
Buzka 17 C7
Kamensk
Uralskiy 29 D7
Kamin-
Kashyrskyy .. 17 C7
Kamina 57 F5
Kamloops 71 C7
Kampala 57 D6
Kampar → ... 37 D2
Kampen 14 B3
Kampot 36 B2
Kampuchea =
Cambodia ■ 36 B3
Kampung → .. 39 F5
Kampungbaru =
Tolitoli 39 D2
Kamrau, Teluk . 39 E4
Kamsack 71 C9
Kamyanets-
Podilskyy ... 17 D8
Kamyanka-Buzka 17 C7
Kamyshin 24 C6
Kanaaupscow . 69 C3
Kananga 56 F4
Kanash 24 B6
Kanastraíon,
Ákra =
Palioúrion,
Ákra 23 E4
Kanazawa ... 32 A5
Kanchanaburi . 36 B1
Kanchenjunga . 40 D7
Kanchipuram .. 43 N11
Kanda Kanda . 56 F4
Kandahar =
Qandahār ... 42 D4
Kandalaksha .. 28 C4

Kandalu 42 E3
Kandangan ... 37 E5
Kandi 55 F5
Kandla 43 H7
Kandos 63 B4
Kandy 43 R12
Kangaroo I. ... 62 C2
Kangâvar 46 D7
Kangean,
Kepulauan .. 37 F5
Kangean Is. =
Kangean,
Kepulauan .. 37 F5
Kangiqsualujjuaq
.... 68 C4
Kangiqsujuaq . 68 B3
Kangirsuk 68 C4
Kangnŭng 35 C7
Kango 56 D2
Kangto 41 D9
Kaniapiskau → 68 C4
Kaniapiskau L. . 69 C4
Kanin,
Poluostrov .. 28 C5
Kanin Nos, Mys 28 C5
Kanin Pen. =
Kanin,
Poluostrov .. 28 C5
Kaniva 62 C3
Kankakee 72 D2
Kankan 55 F3
Kankendy =
Xankändi ... 25 F6
Kanker 40 G3
Kannapolis 75 B7
Kannauj 42 F11
Kannod 43 H10
Kano 55 F6
Kanowit 37 D4
Kanoya 33 D2
Kanpetlet 41 G9
Kanpur 40 D3
Kansas □ 76 F5
Kansas City,
Kans., U.S.A. 77 F7
Kansas City,
Mo., U.S.A. . 77 F7
Kansk 30 D7
Kansu =
Gansu □ 34 C5
Kantang 36 C1
Kanuma 32 A6
Kanye 59 C5
Kaohsiung =
Gaoxiong ... 35 D7
Kaokoveld 58 B2
Kaolack 55 F1
Kapan 25 F6
Kapanga 56 F4
Kapchagai =
Qapshaghay . 29 E8
Kapfenberg ... 15 E8
Kapiri Mposhi . 59 A5
Kāpīsā □ 45 C7
Kapit 37 D4
Kapoeta 53 H5
Kaposvár 16 E3
Kapuas → 37 E3
Kapuas Hulu,
Pegunungan 37 D4
Kapuas Hulu Ra.
= Kapuas
Hulu,
Pegunungan 37 D4
Kapunda 62 B2
Kapuni 64 C6
Kaputar 63 B5
Kara 28 C7

Kara Bogaz Gol, Zaliv = Garabogazköl Aylagy 29 E6
Kara Kalpak Republic □ = Karakalpakstan □ 29 E6
Kara Kum 29 F6
Kara Sea 28 B8
Karabiğa 23 D6
Karabük 46 B3
Karaburun 23 E6
Karabutak = Qarabutaq .. 29 E7
Karacabey 23 D7
Karacasu 23 F7
Karachi 43 G5
Karad 43 L9
Karadeniz Boğazı 22 D7
Karaganda = Qaraghandy . 29 E8
Karagayly 29 E8
Karaikal 43 P11
Karaikkudi ... 43 P11
Karaj 44 C2
Karakalpakstan □ 29 E6
Karakas 29 E9
Karakelong .. 38 D3
Karakitang 39 D3
Karaklis = Vanadzor ... 25 E5
Karakoram Pass 42 B10
Karakoram Ra. 42 B10
Karalon 30 D9
Karaman 46 C3
Karamay 34 B3
Karambu 37 E5
Karamea Bight 65 D4
Karasburg ... 58 D3
Karasino 28 C9
Karasuk 29 D8
Karatau = Qarataū 29 E8
Karatau, Khrebet 29 E7
Karawanken ... 20 A5
Karazhal 29 E8
Karbalā 47 D6
Karcag 16 E5
Kardhítsa 23 E3
Karelia □ 28 C4
Karelian Republic □ = Karelia □ ... 28 C4
Kargänrüd 46 C7
Kargasok 29 D9
Kargat 29 D9
Kargil 42 B10
Kariba, L. 59 B5
Kariba Dam ... 59 B5
Kariba Gorge . 59 B5
Karibib 58 C3
Karimata, Kepulauan .. 37 E3
Karimata, Selat 37 E3
Karimata Is. = Karimata, Kepulauan .. 37 E3
Karimnagar ... 43 K11
Karimunjawa, Kepulauan .. 37 F4
Karin 49 E4
Karkaralinsk = Qarqaraly ... 29 E8
Karkinitska Zatoka 25 D3

Karkinitskiy Zaliv = Karkinitska Zatoka 25 D3
Karl-Marx-Stadt = Chemnitz . 15 C7
Karlovac 20 B5
Karlovo 22 C5
Karlovy Vary .. 16 C1
Karlsbad = Karlovy Vary 16 C1
Karlskrona 9 G11
Karlsruhe 14 D5
Karlstad 9 G10
Karnal 42 E10
Karnali ➝ 40 C3
Karnaphuli Res. 41 F9
Karnataka □ .. 43 N10
Karnische Alpen 20 A4
Kärnten □ 15 E7
Karonga 57 F6
Karoonda 62 C2
Karora 53 E6
Kárpathos 23 G6
Kars 46 B5
Karsakpay 29 E7
Karshi = Qarshi 29 F7
Karsun 24 C6
Karufa 39 E4
Karungu 57 E6
Karviná 16 D4
Karwar 43 M9
Kasai ➝ 56 E3
Kasama 57 G6
Kasanga 57 F6
Kasangulu ... 56 E3
Kasaragod ... 43 N9
Kasba L. 70 B9
Kasempa 59 A5
Kasenga 57 G5
Käshän 44 C2
Kashi 34 C2
Kashk-e Kohneh 42 B3
Kāshmar 44 C4
Kashun Noerh = Gaxun Nur .. 34 B5
Kasimov 24 C5
Kasiruta 39 E3
Kasongo 57 E5
Kasongo Lunda 56 F3
Kásos 23 G6
Kassalâ 53 E6
Kassel 14 C5
Kassue 39 F5
Kastamonu ... 46 B3
Kasulu 57 E6
Kasur 42 D9
Katako Kombe . 56 E4
Katamatite ... 63 C4
Katanga = Shaba □ 57 F4
Katangi 43 J11
Kateríni 23 D4
Katha 41 E11
Kathiawar 43 H7
Katihar 40 E6
Katima Mulilo . 58 B4
Katingan = Mendawai ➝ 37 E4
Katiola 55 G3
Katmandu 40 D5
Katoomba 63 B5
Katowice 16 C4
Katsina 55 F6
Kattegat 9 G10
Kauai 82 G11
Kaunas 24 C1
Kaura Namoda 55 F6
Kaválla 22 D5
Kaw 92 B3

Kawagoe 32 B6
Kawaguchi 32 B6
Kawambwa ... 57 F5
Kawardha 40 G3
Kawasaki 32 B6
Kawerau 64 C7
Kawhia Harbour 64 C6
Kawio, Kepulauan .. 38 D3
Kawnro 41 F12
Kawthoolei = Kawthule □ . 41 H11
Kawthule □ ... 41 H11
Kaya 55 F4
Kayah □ 41 H11
Kayan ➝ 37 D5
Kayeli 39 E3
Kayes 55 F2
Kayoa 39 D3
Kayrunnera ... 62 B3
Kayseri 46 C3
Kayuagung ... 37 E2
Kazachye 31 B11
Kazakstan ■ .. 29 E7
Kazan 24 B6
Kazanlŭk 22 C5
Kazatin = Kozyatyn ... 17 D9
Kāzerūn 44 D2
Kazumba 56 F4
Kazym ➝ 28 C7
Ké-Macina 55 F3
Kéa 23 F5
Kebnekaise ... 8 E11
Kebri Dehar .. 49 F3
Kecskemét ... 16 E4
Kediri 37 F4
Kédougou 55 F2
Keetmanshoop 58 D3
Kefallinía 23 E3
Kefamenanu . 39 F2
Keffi 55 G6
Keighley 11 E6
Keith 62 C3
Keith Arm 70 B7
Kekri 42 G9
Kël 30 C10
Kelang 37 D2
Kelibia 52 A1
Kells = Ceanannus Mor 11 E3
Kélo 53 G2
Kelowna 71 D8
Kelso 65 F3
Keluang 37 D2
Kem 28 C4
Kema 39 D3
Kemah 46 C4
Kemerovo 29 D9
Kemi 8 E12
Kemi älv = Kemijoki ➝ . 8 E12
Kemijoki ➝ .. 8 E12
Kemp Land ... 96 A9
Kempsey 63 B5
Kempten 14 E6
Kendal 37 F4
Kendall 63 B5
Kendari 39 E2
Kendawangan . 37 E4
Kende 55 F5
Kendrapara ... 40 G6
Kenema 55 G2
Keng Tawng .. 41 G12
Keng Tung ... 41 G12
Kenge 56 E3
Kenhardt 58 D4

Kenitra 54 B3
Kennedy Taungdeik .. 41 F9
Kennewick 80 B4
Kenogami ➝ . 69 C2
Kenosha 72 C2
Kent Group ... 62 C4
Kent Pen. 70 B9
Kentau 29 E7
Kentucky □ ... 72 F3
Kentville 69 D4
Kenya ■ 57 D7
Kenya, Mt. 57 E7
Kepi 39 F5
Kerala □ 43 P10
Kerang 62 C3
Kerch 25 D4
Kerchoual 55 E5
Keren 53 E6
Kericho 57 E7
Kerinci 37 E2
Kerki 29 F7
Kérkira 23 E2
Kermadec Is. .. 64 M13
Kermadec Trench 65 N13
Kermān 44 D4
Kermān □ 44 D4
Kermānshāh = Bākhtarān ... 46 D6
Kerme Körfezi . 23 F6
Kerrobert 71 C9
Kerulen ➝ ... 35 B6
Kerzaz 54 C4
Keşan 22 D6
Kestenga 28 C4
Ket ➝ 29 D9
Keta 55 G5
Ketapang 37 E4
Ketchikan 71 C6
Kętrzyn 16 A5
Keweenaw B. . 69 D2
Key West 86 B3
Khabarovo ... 28 C7
Khabarovsk ... 31 E11
Khābūr ➝ 46 D5
Khairpur 42 F6
Khakassia □ .. 30 D6
Khakhea 58 C4
Khalkhāl 46 C7
Khalkís 23 E4
Khalmer-Sede = Tazovskiy ... 28 C8
Khalmer Yu ... 28 C7
Khalturin 24 B6
Khalûf 48 C6
Khambat, G. of 43 J8
Khambhat 43 H8
Khamir 49 D3
Khānābād 45 B7
Khānaqin 46 D6
Khandwa 43 J10
Khanewal 42 D7
Khaniá 23 G5
Khaníon, Kólpos 23 G4
Khankendy = Xankändi 25 F6
Khanty-Mansiysk 29 C7
Khapcheranga . 30 E9
Kharagpur 40 F6
Kharan Kalat .. 42 E4
Kharānaq 44 C3
Kharda 43 K9
Khârga, El Wâhât el .. 52 C5
Khargon 43 J9
Khārk, Jazireh . 47 E7
Kharkiv 24 D4

Kharkov =
Kharkiv 24 D4
Kharovsk 24 B5
Kharsānīya 47 F7
Kharta 22 D7
Khartoum = El
Khartûm 53 E5
Khāsh 42 E2
Khashm el Girba 53 F6
Khaskovo 22 D5
Khatanga 30 B8
Khatanga → .. 30 B8
Khaybar, Harrat 47 F5
Khed Brahma . 43 G8
Khemmarat ... 36 A3
Khenchela 54 A4
Khenifra 54 B3
Kherson 25 D3
Kheta → 30 B8
Khilok 30 D9
Khíos 23 E6
Khiuma =
Hiiumaa 24 B1
Khiva 29 E7
Khīyāv 46 C6
Khmelnik 17 D8
Khmelnitskiy =
Khmelnytskyy 17 D8
Khmelnytskyy . 17 D8
Khmer Rep. =
Cambodia ■ 36 B3
Khodoriv 17 D7
Khodzent =
Khudzhand .. 29 E7
Khojak P. 42 D5
Kholm, Afghan. 45 B6
Kholm, Russia . 24 B3
Khomeyn 44 C2
Khon Kaen ... 36 A2
Khoper → 29 E5
Khóra Sfakíon . 23 G5
Khorat =
Nakhon
Ratchasima . 36 B2
Khorramābād . 46 D7
Khorrāmshahr . 47 E7
Khotyn 17 D8
Khouribga 54 B3
Khowai 41 E8
Khoyniki 17 C9
Khu Khan 36 B2
Khudzhand ... 29 E7
Khūgiānī 42 D4
Khulna 41 F7
Khulna □ 41 F7
Khûr 44 C4
Khurayş 47 F7
Khūriyā Mūriyā,
Jazā 'ir 48 D6
Khush 42 C3
Khushab 42 C8
Khust 17 D6
Khuzdar 42 F5
Khvor 44 C3
Khvormūj 44 D2
Khvoy 46 C6
Khyber Pass .. 42 B7
Kiama 63 B5
Kiamba 38 C2
Kiangsi =
Jiangxi □ .. 35 D6
Kiangsu =
Jiangsu □ .. 35 C6
Kibangou 56 E2
Kibombo 57 E5
Kibondo 57 E6
Kibwesa 57 F5
Kibwezi 57 E7
Kicking Horse
Pass 71 C8

Kidal 55 E5
Kidnappers, C. . 64 C7
Kiel 14 A6
Kiel Canal =
Nord-Ostsee-
Kanal → ... 14 A5
Kielce 16 C5
Kieler Bucht ... 14 A6
Kiev = Kyyiv .. 17 C10
Kiffa 55 E2
Kifrī 46 D6
Kigali 57 E6
Kigoma-Ujiji . 57 E5
Kihee 62 A3
Kii-Suidō 32 C4
Kikinda 22 B3
Kikládhes 23 F5
Kikwit 56 E3
Kilcoy 63 A5
Kilimanjaro .. 57 E7
Kilindini 57 E7
Kilis 46 C4
Kiliya 17 F9
Kilkenny 11 E3
Kilkis 23 D4
Killarney,
Australia 63 A5
Killarney, Ireland 11 E2
Killeen 78 D5
Killíni 23 F4
Kilmarnock ... 10 D4
Kilmore 63 C3
Kilosa 57 F7
Kilrush 11 E2
Kilwa Kivinje .. 57 F7
Kimaam 39 F5
Kimba 62 B2
Kimberley 58 D4
Kimberley
Plateau 60 D4
Kimry 24 B4
Kinabalu,
Gunong ... 36 C5
Kindia 55 G2
Kindu 57 E5
Kineshma ... 24 B5
King George B. 95 G4
King George I. . 96 A4
King George Is. 69 C2
King I. = Kadan
Kyun 36 B1
King I. 62 C3
King William I. 70 B10
King William's
Town 59 E5
Kingaroy 63 A5
Kingoonya 62 B2
Kings Canyon
National Park 82 B3
King's Lynn .. 11 E7
Kingscote ... 62 C2
Kingsport 75 A6
Kingston,
Canada 69 D3
Kingston,
Jamaica 86 C4
Kingston, N.Z. . 65 F3
Kingston South
East 62 C2
Kingston upon
Hull 11 E6
Kingstown 87 D7
Kingsville 78 F5
Kınık 23 E6
Kinkala 56 E2
Kinleith 64 C6
Kinsale 11 F2
Kinshasa 56 E3
Kinston 75 B9

Kintampo 55 G4
Kintap 37 E5
Kiparissía 23 F3
Kiparissiakós
Kólpos ... 23 F3
Kipembawe ... 57 F6
Kipili 57 F6
Kipushi 59 A5
Kirghizia ■ =
Kyrgyzstan ■ 29 E8
Kirghizstan =
Kyrgyzstan ■ 29 E8
Kiri 56 E3
Kiribati ■ ... 64 K12
Kırıkkale 46 C3
Kirillov 24 B4
Kirin = Jilin ... 35 B7
Kiritimati ... 65 J15
Kirkcaldy 10 C5
Kirkcudbright . 11 D4
Kirkee 43 K8
Kirkenes 8 E14
Kirkland Lake . 69 D2
Kırklareli ... 22 D6
Kirkūk 46 D6
Kirkwall 10 B5
Kirov 28 D5
Kirovabad =
Gäncä 25 E6
Kirovakan =
Vanadzor ... 25 E5
Kirovograd =
Kirovohrad .. 25 D3
Kirovohrad ... 25 D3
Kirovsk =
Babadayhan . 29 F7
Kirovsk 28 C4
Kirsanov 24 C5
Kırşehir 46 C3
Kirteh 45 C5
Kirthar Range . 42 F6
Kiruna 8 E12
Kirundu 57 E5
Kiryū 32 A6
Kisangani ... 57 D5
Kisar 39 F3
Kiselevsk 29 D9
Kishanganj 40 D7
Kishangarh ... 42 F7
Kishinev =
Chişinău 17 E9
Kishiwada ... 32 B4
Kishtwar 42 C9
Kisii 57 E6
Kisiju 57 F7
Kiska I. 71 C1
Kiskörös 16 E4
Kiskunfélegyháza
.... 16 E4
Kiskunhalas ... 16 E4
Kislovodsk 25 E5
Kiso-Sammyaku 32 B5
Kissidougou .. 55 G2
Kisumu ... 57 E6
Kita 55 F3
Kitab 29 F7
Kitakami-
Gawa → .. 33 G12
Kitakyūshū ... 32 C2
Kitale 57 D7
Kitchener ... 69 D2
Kitega = Gitega 57 E5
Kitgum 57 D6
Kíthira 23 F4
Kíthnos 23 F5
Kittakittaooloo,
L. 62 A2
Kitui 57 E7
Kitwe 59 A5

Kivertsi 17 C7
Kivu, L. 57 E5
Kiyev = Kyyiv . 17 C10
Kiyevskoye
Vdkhr. =
Kyyivske
Vdskh. 17 C10
Kızıl Irmak → . 25 E4
Kizlyar 25 E6
Kizyl-Arvat =
Gyzylarbat .. 29 F6
Kladno 16 C2
Klagenfurt ... 15 E8
Klaipeda 24 B1
Klamath Falls . 80 D3
Klamath Mts. .. 80 E2
Klarälven → . 9 G10
Klatovy 16 D1
Klawer 58 E3
Klerksdorp ... 59 D5
Kletsk = Klyetsk 17 B8
Klin 28 D4
Kłodzko 16 C3
Klondike 70 B6
Klouto 55 G5
Kluane L. 70 B6
Kluczbork ... 16 C4
Klyetsk 17 B8
Knossós 23 G5
Knox Coast .. 96 A12
Knoxville 75 B6
Koartac =
Quaqtaq ... 68 B4
Koba, Aru,
Indonesia ... 39 F4
Koba, Bangka,
Indonesia ... 37 E3
Kobarid 20 A4
Kobdo = Hovd 34 B4
Kōbe 32 B4
København ... 9 G10
Koblenz 14 C4
Kobroor,
Kepulauan . 39 F4
Kobryn 17 B7
Kocaeli = İzmit 25 E2
Kočani 22 D4
Koch Bihar ... 41 D7
Kōchi 32 C3
Kochiu = Gejiu 34 D5
Kodiak 71 C4
Kodiak I. 71 C4
Koes 58 D3
Kofiau 39 E3
Koforidua ... 55 G4
Kōfu 32 B6
Kogan 63 A5
Koh-i-Bābā ... 42 B5
Kohat 42 C7
Kohima 41 E10
Kohkīlūyeh va
Būyer
Aḥmadi □ .. 44 D2
Kohler Ra. 96 B1
Kokand =
Qŭqon 29 E8
Kokas 39 E4
Kokchetav =
Kökshetaū .. 29 D7
Koko Kyunzu . 41 K9
Kokomo 72 D2
Kokonau 39 E5
Kökshetaū ... 29 D7
Koksoak → .. 68 C4
Kokstad 59 E5
Kola, Indonesia 39 F4
Kola, Russia .. 28 C4
Kola Pen. =
Kolskiy
Poluostrov .. 28 C4

Kolaka

Kolaka	39	E2	Kopaonik	22	C3	Koumra	53	G2
Kolar	43	N11	Koper	20	B4	Kounradskiy	29	E8
Kolar Gold Fields	43	N11	Kopeysk	29	D7	Kouroussa	55	F3
Kolayat	42	F8	Kopi	62	B2	Kousseri	53	F1
Kolchugino =			Koprivnica	20	A6	Koutiala	55	F3
Leninsk-			Kopychyntsi	17	D7	Kovel	17	C7
Kuznetskiy	29	D9	Korab	22	D3	Kovrov	24	B5
Kolda	55	F2	Korça	23	D3	Kowloon	35	D6
Kole	56	E4	Korce = Korça	23	D3	Köyceğiz	23	F7
Kolepom = Yos			Korčula	20	C6	Koyuk	71	B3
Sudarso,			Kordestan	46	D5	Koyukuk ─►	71	B4
Pulau	39	F5	Kordestān □	46	D6	Kozan	46	C3
Kolguyev,			Kordofân	53	F4	Kozáni	23	D3
Ostrov	28	C5	Korea, North ■	35	C7	Kozhikode =		
Kolhapur	43	L9	Korea, South ■	35	C7	Calicut	43	P9
Kolín	16	C2	Korea Bay	35	C7	Kozyatyn	17	D9
Kolkata	41	F7	Korea Strait	35	C7	Kpalimé	55	G5
Köln	14	C4	Korets	17	C8	Kra, Isthmus of		
Koło	16	B4	Korhogo	55	G3	= Kra, Kho		
Kołobrzeg	16	A2	Korim	39	E5	Khot	36	B1
Kolokani	55	F3	Korinthiakós			Kra, Kho Khot	36	B1
Kolomna	24	B4	Kólpos	23	E4	Kragujevac	22	B3
Kolomyya	17	D7	Kórinthos	23	F4	Krajina	20	B6
Kolonodale	39	E2	Kōriyama	33	G12	Krakatau =		
Kolosib	41	E9	Korneshty =			Rakata, Pulau	37	F3
Kolpashevo	29	D9	Corneşti	17	E9	Kraków	16	C4
Kolpino	24	B3	Koro, Ivory C.	55	G3	Kraljevo	22	C3
Kolskiy			Koro, Mali	55	F4	Kramatorsk	25	D4
Poluostrov	28	C4	Korogwe	57	F7	Kranj	20	A5
Kolwezi	57	G5	Koroit	62	C3	Kraśnik	16	C6
Kolyma ─►	31	C13	Koror	38	C4	Krasnoarmeysk	29	D5
Komárno	16	E4	Körös ─►	16	E5	Krasnodar	25	D4
Komatsu	32	A5	Korosten	17	C9	Krasnoperekopsk		
Komi □	28	C6	Korostyshev	17	C9		25	D3
Kommunarsk =			Korti	53	E5	Krasnoselkupsk	28	C9
Alchevsk	25	D4	Kortrijk	14	C2	Krasnoturinsk	28	D7
Kommunizma,			Kos	23	F6	Krasnoufimsk	29	D6
Pik	29	F8	Kościan	16	B3	Krasnouralsk	29	D7
Komodo	39	F1	Kosciuszko, Mt.	63	C4	Krasnovodsk =		
Komono	56	E2	Kosha	52	D5	Krasnowodsk	29	E6
Komoran, Pulau	39	F5	K'oshih = Kashi	34	C2	Krasnowodsk	29	E6
Komotini	22	D5	Košice	16	D5	Krasnoyarsk	30	D7
Kompong Cham	36	B3	Kosovo □	22	C3	Krasnyy Luch	25	D4
Kompong			Kosovska-			Krasnyy Yar	25	D6
Chhnang	36	B2	Mitrovica	22	C3	Kratie	36	B3
Kompong Som	36	B2	Kôstî	53	F5	Krau	39	E6
Komrat =			Kostopil	17	C8	Krefeld	14	C4
Comrat	17	E9	Kostroma	24	B5	Kremen	20	B5
Komsomolets,			Kostrzyn	16	B2	Kremenchug =		
Ostrov	30	A7	Koszalin	16	A3	Kremenchuk	24	D3
Konarhá □	42	B7	Kota	43	G9	Kremenchuk	24	D3
Konch	42	G11	Kota Baharu	36	C2	Kremenchuksk		
Kondoa	57	E7	Kota Belud	36	C5	Vdskh.	24	D3
Konduga	53	F1	Kota Kinabalu	36	C5	Kremenets	17	C7
Köneürgench	29	E6	Kota Tinggi	37	D2	Krems	15	D8
Kong	55	G4	Kotaagung	37	F2	Kribi	56	D1
Kong, Koh	36	B2	Kotabaru	37	E5	Krichev =		
Konglu	41	D11	Kotabumi	37	E2	Krychaw	17	B10
Kongolo	57	F5	Kotamobagu	39	D2	Krishna ─►	40	K3
Kongor	53	G5	Kotawaringin	37	E4	Krishnanagar	41	F7
Königsberg =			Kotelnich	24	B6	Kristiansand	9	G9
Kaliningrad	24	C1	Kotelnyy, Ostrov	31	B11	Kristiansund	8	F9
Konin	16	B4	Kotka	9	F13	Kríti	23	G5
Konjic	20	C6	Kotlas	28	C5	Krivoy Rog =		
Konosha	28	C5	Kotli	42	C8	Kryvyy Rih	25	D3
Konotop	24	C3	Kotor	22	C2	Krk	20	B5
Konqi He ─►	34	B4	Kotovsk	17	E9	Kronprins Olav		
Końskie	16	C5	Kotri	42	G6	Kyst	96	A9
Konstanz	14	E5	Kottayam	43	Q10	Kronshtadt	24	B2
Kontagora	55	F6	Kotturu	43	M10	Kroonstad	59	D5
Kontum	36	B3	Kotuy ─►	30	B8	Kropotkin,		
Konya	46	C3	Kotzebue	71	B3	Irkutsk, Russia	30	D9
Konya Ovası	46	C3	Kouango	56	D4	Kropotkin,		
Konza	57	E7	Koudougou	55	F4	Krasnodar,		
Kooloonong	62	B3	Kouilou ─►	56	E2	Russia	25	D5
Koondrook	63	C3	Kouki	56	C3	Krosno	16	D5
Koonibba	62	B1	Koula Moutou	56	E2	Krotoszyn	16	C3
Koorawatha	63	B4	Koulen	36	B2	Krugersdorp	59	D5
Kootenay L.	71	D8	Koulikoro	55	F3			

Krung Thep =		
Bangkok	36	B2
Krupki	17	A9
Kruševac	22	C3
Krychaw	17	B10
Krymskiy		
Poluostrov =		
Krymskyy		
Pivostriv	25	D3
Krymskyy		
Pivostriv	25	D3
Kryvyy Rih	25	D3
Ksar el Boukhari	54	A5
Ksar el Kebir	54	B3
Ksar es Souk =		
Ar Rachidiya	54	B4
Kuala	37	D3
Kuala Kubu		
Baharu	37	D2
Kuala Lipis	37	D2
Kuala Lumpur	37	D2
Kuala		
Terengganu	36	C2
Kualajelai	37	E4
Kualakapuas	37	E4
Kualakurun	37	E4
Kualapembuang	37	E4
Kualasimpang	37	D1
Kuandang	39	D2
Kuangchou =		
Guangzhou	35	D6
Kuantan	37	D2
Kuba = Quba	25	E6
Kuban ─►	25	D4
Kucing	37	D4
Kuda	43	H7
Kudat	36	C5
Kudymkar	28	D6
Kueiyang =		
Guiyang	35	D5
Kufra Oasis = Al		
Kufrah	52	D3
Kufstein	15	E7
Kugluktuk	70	B8
Kūh-e 'Alījūq	44	D2
Kūh-e-Hazārām	44	D4
Kūh-e Sorkh	44	C3
Kūh-e Taftān	45	D5
Kūhak	42	F3
Kūhhā-ye-		
Bashākerd	45	E4
Kūhpāyeh	44	C3
Kuito	58	A3
Kujū-San	32	C2
Kukawa	53	F1
Kukësi	22	C3
Kula	23	E7
Kulasekarappattinam		
	43	Q11
Kuldja = Yining	34	B3
Kŭlob	29	F7
Kulsary	29	E6
Kulunda	29	D8
Kulwin	62	C3
Kulyab = Kŭlob	29	F7
Kum Tekei	29	E8
Kuma ─►	25	E6
Kumagaya	32	A6
Kumai	37	E4
Kumamba,		
Kepulauan	39	E5
Kumamoto	32	C2
Kumanovo	22	C3
Kumara	65	E4
Kumasi	55	G4
Kumayri =		
Gyumri	25	E5
Kumba	56	D1
Kumbakonam	43	P11

Kumbarilla 63 A5
Kumo 55 F7
Kumon Bum .. 41 D11
Kunama 63 C4
Kungala 63 A5
Kungrad =
   Qŭnghirot ... 29 E6
Kungur 29 D6
Kunlong 41 F12
Kunlun Shan .. 34 C3
Kunming 34 D5
Kunsan 35 C7
Kunya-Urgench
   =
   Köneürgench 29 E6
Kuopio 8 F13
Kupa → 20 B6
Kupyansk 28 E4
Kuqa 34 B3
Kür → 25 E6
Kura = Kür → 25 E6
Kurashiki 32 B3
Kurayoshi 32 B3
Kürdzhali 22 D5
Kure 32 B3
Kurgaldzhinskiy 29 D8
Kurgan 29 D7
Kuria Maria Is.
   = Khūrīyā
   Mūrīyā, Jazā
   'ir 48 D6
Kurigram 41 E7
Kuril Is. =
   Kurilskiye
   Ostrova 31 E12
Kurilskiye
   Ostrova 31 E12
Kurmuk 53 F5
Kurnool 43 L11
Kurow 65 F4
Kurrajong 63 B5
Kurri Kurri 63 B5
Kursk 24 C4
Kuruktag 34 B3
Kuruman 58 D4
Kurume 32 C2
Kus Gölü 23 D6
Kuşadası 23 F6
Kushiro 32 F12
Kushtia 41 F7
Kuskokwim → 71 B3
Kuskokwim B. . 71 C3
Kustanay =
   Qostanay .. 29 D7
Kütahya 46 C2
Kutaisi 25 E5
Kutaraja =
   Banda Aceh . 36 C1
Kutch, Gulf of =
   Kachchh, Gulf
   of 43 H6
Kutch, Rann of
   = Kachchh,
   Rann of 43 G6
Kutno 16 B4
Kutu 56 E3
Kutum 53 F3
Kuujjuaq 68 C4
Kuwait = Al
   Kuwayt ... 47 E7
Kuwait ■ 47 E6
Kuwana 32 B5
Kuybyshev =
   Samara 24 C7
Kuybyshev ... 29 D8
Kuybyshevskoye
   Vdkhr. ... 24 B6
Kūysanjaq 46 C6
Kuyumba 30 C7

Kuzey Anadolu
   Dağları 46 B3
Kuznetsk 24 C6
Kvarner 20 B5
Kvarnerič 20 B5
Kwakoegron .. 92 A2
Kwamouth 56 E3
Kwando → ... 58 B4
Kwangju 35 C7
Kwangsi-Chuang
   = Guangxi
   Zhuangzu
   Zizhiqu □ ... 35 D5
Kwangtung –
   Guangdong □ 35 D6
Kwatisore 39 E4
Kweichow =
   Guizhou □ .. 35 D5
Kwekwe 59 B5
Kwidzyn 16 B4
Kwoka 39 E4
Kyabé 53 G2
Kyabra Cr. → . 63 A3
Kyabram 63 C4
Kyancutta 62 B2
Kyangin 41 H10
Kyaukpadaung 41 G10
Kyaukpyu 41 H9
Kyaukse 41 G11
Kyle Dam 59 C6
Kyneton 63 C3
Kyō-ga-Saki ... 32 B4
Kyoga, L. =
   Kyoga, L. .. 57 D6
Kyogle 63 A5
Kyongpyaw .. 41 J10
Kyōto 32 B4
Kyrenia 46 D3
Kyrgyzstan ■ .. 29 E8
Kystatyam 30 C10
Kytal Ktakh ... 31 C10
Kyunhla 41 F10
Kyūshū 32 C2
Kyūshū-Sanchi 32 C2
Kyustendil ... 22 C4
Kyusyur 30 B10
Kywong 63 B4
Kyyiv 17 C10
Kyyivske Vdskh. 17 C10
Kyzyl Kum ... 29 E7
Kyzyl-Kyya ... 29 E8
Kzyl-Orda =
   Qyzylorda ... 29 E7

L

La Albufera ... 19 C5
La Alcarria ... 19 B4
La Asunción .. 90 A6
La Banda 94 B4
La Calera 94 C2
La Carlota 94 C4
La Ceiba 85 D7
La Chaux de
   Fonds 13 C7
La Cocha 94 B3
La Coruña ... 18 A1
La Crosse 77 D9
La Dorada 90 B4
La Estrada ... 18 A1
La Grange 74 C5
La Guaira 90 A5
La Güera 54 D1
La Habana ... 86 B3
La Línea de la
   Concepción . 18 D3
La Mancha 19 C4

La Palma,
   Canary Is. ... 54 C1
La Palma,
   Panama 86 E4
La Palma del
   Condado 18 D2
La Paragua ... 90 B6
La Paz,
   Entre Ríos,
   Argentina ... 94 C5
La Paz, San Luis,
   Argentina ... 94 C3
La Paz, Bolivia . 91 G5
La Paz, Mexico . 84 C2
La Pedrera 90 D5
La Plata 94 D5
La Quiaca 94 A3
La Rioja 94 B3
La Rioja □ 19 A4
La Robla 18 A3
La Roche-sur-
   Yon 12 C3
La Rochelle ... 12 C3
La Roda 19 C4
La Romana 87 C6
La Serena 94 B2
La Seyne-sur-
   Mer 13 E6
La Spézia 20 B2
La Tortuga 87 D6
La Tuque 69 D3
La Unión 95 E2
La Urbana 90 B5
La Vega 87 C5
Labe = Elbe → 14 B5
Labé 55 F2
Labis 37 D2
Laboulaye 94 C4
Labrador
   □ 69 C4
Lábrea 91 E6
Labuan 36 C5
Labuha 39 E3
Labuhanbajo .. 39 F2
Labuk, Telok .. 36 C5
Labyrinth, L. .. 62 B2
Labytnangi 28 C7
Lac La Biche .. 71 C8
Lac la Martre .. 70 B8
Lacanau 12 D3
Laccadive Is. =
   Lakshadweep
   Is. 26 H11
Lacepede B. ... 62 C2
Lachine 69 D3
Lachlan → 63 B3
Lackawanna .. 73 C6
Lacombe 71 C8
Ladakh Ra. 42 B10
Lādīz 45 D5
Ladoga, L. =
   Ladozhskoye
   Ozero 28 C4
Ladozhskoye
   Ozero 28 C4
Ladysmith,
   Canada 71 D7
Ladysmith,
   S. Africa ... 59 D5
Lae 61 B8
Lafayette 79 D7
Lafia 55 G6
Laghmān □ ... 45 C7
Laghouat 54 B5
Lagonoy Gulf . 38 B2
Lagos, Nigeria . 55 G5
Lagos, Portugal 18 D1
Laguna 94 B7
Lagunas, Chile 91 H5

Lagunas, Peru . 90 E3
Lahad Datu ... 38 C1
Lahat 37 E2
Lahewa 37 D1
Lāhījān 46 C7
Lahn → 14 C4
Lahore 42 D9
Lahti 8 F13
Lahtis = Lahti . 8 F13
Laï 53 G2
Laibin 35 D5
Laidley 63 A5
Laila = Laylá .. 47 G6
Lairg 10 B4
Lajere 55 F7
Lajes 94 B6
Lake Cargelligo 63 B4
Lake Charles .. 79 D7
Lake City 75 D6
Lake Worth ... 75 F7
Lakeland 75 E7
Lakes Entrance 63 C4
Lakewood 72 D5
Lakonikós
   Kólpos 23 F4
Lakor 39 F3
Lakota 55 G3
Lakshadweep
   Is. 26 H11
Lala Ghat 41 E9
Lalibela 53 F6
Lalín 18 A1
Lalitapur =
   Patan 40 D5
Lamaing 41 K11
Lamas 91 E3
Lambaréné ... 56 E2
Lambert Glacier 96 B10
Lame 55 F6
Lamego 18 B2
Lameroo 62 C3
Lamía 23 E4
Lamon Bay ... 38 B2
Lampa 91 G4
Lampedusa ... 21 G4
Lampione 21 G4
Lampung □ ... 37 F2
Lamu 57 E8
Lanai I. 82 H12
Lanak La 42 B11
Lanak'o
   Shank'ou =
   Lanak La 42 B11
Lanao, L. 38 C2
Lancaster, U.K. 11 D5
Lancaster,
   U.S.A. 73 D7
Lancaster Sd. . 68 A2
Lanchow =
   Lanzhou ... 35 C5
Lanciano 20 C5
Landeck 14 E6
Landes 12 D3
Landi Kotal ... 42 B7
Land's End 11 F4
Landshut 15 D7
La'nga Co 40 B3
Langkawi, P. .. 36 C1
Langkon 36 C5
Langres 13 C6
Langres, Plateau
   de 13 C6
Langsa 36 D1
Languedoc 13 E5
Langzhong ... 35 C5
Lannion 12 B2
Lansdowne ... 63 B5
Lansing 72 C3
Lanusei 21 E2

Lanzarote

Lanzarote 54 C2
Lanzhou 35 C5
Laoag 38 A2
Laoang 38 B3
Laon 13 B5
Laos ■ 36 A3
Lapa 94 B7
Laparan 38 C1
Lapland =
  Lappland ... 8 E12
Lappland 8 E12
Lapseki 23 D6
Laptev Sea ... 30 B10
L'Áquila 20 C4
Lär 44 E3
Larache 54 A3
Laramie 76 E2
Larantuka 39 F2
Larap 38 B2
Larat 39 F4
Laredo 78 F4
Lariang 39 E1
Lárisa 23 E4
Larnaca 46 D3
Larne 11 D4
Larrimah 60 D5
Larsen Ice Shelf 96 A3
Larvik 9 G9
Laryak 29 C8
Las Anod 49 F4
Las Cruces ... 83 D9
Las Flores 94 D5
Las Khoreh ... 49 E4
Las Lajas 94 D2
Las Lomitas ... 94 A4
Las Palmas ... 54 C1
Las Pipinas ... 94 D5
Las Plumas ... 95 E3
Las Rosas 94 C4
Las Varillas ... 94 C4
Las Vegas 82 B5
Lashio 41 F11
Lassen Pk. ... 80 E3
Lastoursville . 56 E2
Lastovo 20 C6
Latacunga 90 D3
Latakia = Al
  Ládhiqīyah .. 46 D3
Latina 20 D4
Latium =
  Lazio □ 20 C4
Latrobe 62 D4
Latvia ■ 24 B1
Lauchhammer . 15 C7
Launceston ... 62 D4
Laurel 79 D9
Lauria 21 D5
Laurium 69 D2
Lausanne 13 C7
Laut 36 D3
Laut Kecil,
  Kepulauan .. 37 E5
Laval 12 B3
Lávrion 23 F5
Lawas 36 D5
Lawele 39 F2
Lawng Pit 41 E11
Lawrence, N.Z. 65 F3
Lawrence,
  U.S.A. 77 F7
Lawton 78 B4
Laylá 47 G6
Lazio □ 20 C4
Le Creusot 13 C6
Le Havre 12 B4
Le Mans 12 C4
Le Mont-St.-
  Michel 12 B3
Le Moule 87 C7

Le Puy-en-Velay 13 D5
Le Touquet-
  Paris-Plage .. 12 A4
Le Tréport 12 A4
Le Verdon-sur-
  Mer 12 D3
Leamington Spa
  = Royal
  Leamington
  Spa 11 E6
Leandro Norte
  Alem 94 B5
Leavenworth .. 77 F7
Lebak 38 C2
Lebanon ■ 46 D3
Lębork 16 A3
Lebrija 18 D2
Lebu 94 D2
Lecce 23 D2
Lecco 20 B2
Lech → 14 D6
Łęczyca 16 B4
Leduc 71 C8
Leeds 11 E6
Leer 14 B4
Leeton 63 B4
Leeuwarden ... 14 B3
Leeuwin, C. ... 60 G2
Leeward Is. ... 87 C7
Leganés 18 B4
Legazpi 38 B2
Leghorn =
  Livorno 20 C3
Legionowo 16 B5
Legnago 20 B3
Legnica 16 C3
Legume 63 A5
Leh 42 B10
Leicester 11 E6
Leiden 14 B3
Leie → 14 C2
Leine → 14 B5
Leinster □ 11 E3
Leipzig 15 C7
Leiria 18 C1
Leitrim 11 D2
Leizhou Bandao 35 D6
Leksula 39 E3
Lékva Ori 23 G5
Leleque 95 E2
Léman, L. 13 C7
Lemhi Ra. 81 C7
Lena → 30 B10
Leninabad =
  Khudzhand .. 29 E7
Leninakan =
  Gyumri 25 E5
Leningrad =
  Sankt-
  Peterburg .. 24 B3
Leninogorsk =
  Ridder 29 D9
Leninsk 25 D6
Leninsk-
  Kuznetskiy .. 29 D9
Lenmalu 39 E4
Lens 13 A5
Lentini 21 F5
Leoben 15 E8
Leodhas =
  Lewis 10 B3
León, Mexico .. 84 C4
León, Nic. 85 E7
León, Spain .. 18 A3
León, Montañas
  de 18 A2
Leongatha 63 C4
Léopold II, Lac
  = Mai-
  Ndombe, L. . 56 E3

Léopoldville =
  Kinshasa 56 E3
Leova 17 E9
Lepel = Lyepyel 24 C2
Lepikha 31 C10
Léré 53 G1
Lérida 19 B6
Lerwick 10 A6
Les Cayes 86 C5
Les Sables-
  d'Olonne ... 12 C3
Lesbos =
  Lésvos 23 E6
Leskovac 22 C3
Lesotho ■ 59 D5
Lesser Antilles . 87 D7
Lesser Sunda Is. 39 F2
Lésvos 23 E6
Leszno 16 C3
Lethbridge ... 71 D8
Leti, Kepulauan 39 F3
Leti Is. = Leti,
  Kepulauan .. 39 F3
Leticia 90 D4
Letpadan 41 J10
Letpan 41 H10
Letterkenny ... 11 D3
Leuser, G. 37 D1
Leuven 14 C3
Levádhia 23 E4
Levice 16 D4
Levin 64 D6
Lévis 69 D3
Levkás 23 E3
Levkôsia =
  Nicosia 46 D3
Levskigrad =
  Karlovo 22 C5
Lewis 10 B3
Lewisporte ... 69 D5
Lewiston, Idaho,
  U.S.A. 80 B5
Lewiston,
  Maine, U.S.A. 73 B10
Lexington, Ky.,
  U.S.A. 72 E3
Lexington, N.C.,
  U.S.A. 75 B7
Leyte 38 B2
Lezha 22 D2
Lhasa 34 D4
Lhazê 34 D3
Lhokkruet 36 D1
Lhokseumawe . 36 C1
Lhuntsi Dzong . 41 D8
Lianga 38 C3
Lianyungang .. 35 C6
Liaoning □ 35 B7
Liaoyuan 35 B7
Liard → 70 B7
Libau = Liepāja 24 B1
Libenge 56 D3
Liberal 78 A3
Liberec 16 C2
Liberia ■ 55 G3
Lîbîya, Sahrâ' . 52 C4
Libobo, Tanjung 39 E3
Libonda 58 A4
Libourne 12 D3
Libreville 56 D1
Libya ■ 52 C2
Libyan Desert =
  Lîbîya, Sahrâ' 52 C4
Licantén 94 D2
Licata 21 F4
Lichinga 59 A7
Lichtenburg ... 59 D5
Lida 17 B7
Liechtenstein ■ 14 E5

Liège 14 C3
Liegnitz =
  Legnica 16 C3
Lienyünchiangshih
  =
  Lianyungang 35 C6
Lienz 15 E7
Liepāja 24 B1
Liffey → 11 E3
Lifford 11 D3
Lightning Ridge 63 A4
Liguria □ 20 B2
Ligurian Sea .. 20 C2
Lijiang 34 D5
Likasi 57 G5
Lille 13 A5
Lillehammer .. 8 F10
Lilongwe 59 A6
Liloy 38 C2
Lim → 20 C7
Lima, Indonesia 39 E3
Lima, Peru 91 F3
Lima, U.S.A. .. 72 D3
Lima → 18 B1
Limassol 46 D3
Limay Mahuida 94 D3
Limbang 36 D5
Limbe 56 D1
Limbri 63 B5
Limburg 14 C5
Limeira 94 A7
Limerick 11 E2
Limfjorden 9 G9
Limia =
  Lima → 18 B1
Límnos 23 E5
Limoeiro do
  Norte 92 D6
Limoges 12 D4
Limón 86 E3
Limousin 12 D4
Limoux 12 E5
Limpopo → .. 59 D6
Limuru 57 E7
Linares, Chile . 94 D2
Linares, Mexico 84 C5
Linares, Spain . 18 C4
Linchuan 35 D6
Lincoln,
  Argentina ... 94 C4
Lincoln, N.Z. .. 65 E5
Lincoln, U.K. .. 11 E6
Lincoln, U.S.A. 77 E6
Linden 90 B7
Líndhos 23 F7
Lindi 57 F7
Lingayen 38 A2
Lingayen G. ... 38 A2
Lingen 14 B4
Lingga 37 E2
Lingga,
  Kepulauan .. 37 E2
Lingga Arch. =
  Lingga,
  Kepulauan .. 37 E2
Linguéré 55 E1
Lingyun 35 D5
Linhai 35 D7
Linhares 93 F5
Linköping 9 G11
Linosa, I. 21 G4
Lins 94 A7
Linville 63 A5
Linxia 34 C5
Linz 15 D8
Lion, G. du ... 13 E6
Lions, G. of =
  Lion, G. du .. 13 E6
Lipa 38 B2

Lípari 21 E5
Lípari, Is. =
 Eólie, Ís. 21 E5
Lipcani 17 D8
Lipetsk 24 C4
Lipkany =
 Lipcani 17 D8
Lipovets 17 D9
Lippe → 14 C4
Liptrap C. 63 C4
Lira 57 D6
Liria 19 C5
Lisala 56 D4
Lisboa 18 C1
Lisbon = Lisboa 18 C1
Lisburn 11 D3
Lisburne, C. .. 71 B3
Lishui 35 D6
Lisichansk =
 Lysychansk . 25 D4
Lisieux 12 B4
Liski 24 C4
Lismore 63 A5
Lister, Mt. 96 B15
Liston 63 A5
Listowel 11 E2
Litang 38 C1
Litani → 46 D3
Lithgow 63 B5
Líthinon, Ákra . 23 G5
Lithuania ■ .. 24 B1
Litoměřice 16 C2
Little Barrier I. . 64 B6
Little Laut Is. =
 Laut Kecil,
 Kepulauan .. 37 E5
Little
 Missouri → . 76 B3
Little River ... 65 E5
Little Rock 79 B7
Liukang
 Tenggaja ... 39 F1
Liuwa Plain ... 58 A4
Liuzhou 35 D5
Liverpool,
 Australia 63 B5
Liverpool,
 Canada 69 D4
Liverpool, U.K. 11 E5
Liverpool Plains 63 B5
Liverpool Ra. .. 63 B5
Livingstone ... 59 B5
Livingstonia .. 57 G6
Livny 24 C4
Livorno 20 C3
Livramento ... 94 C5
Liwale 57 F7
Ljubljana 20 A5
Ljungan → .. 8 F11
Ljusnan → .. 8 F11
Llancanelo,
 Salina 94 D3
Llanelli 11 F4
Llanes 18 A3
Llano Estacado 78 C2
Llanos 90 C4
Lleida = Lérida 19 B6
Llobregat → . 19 B7
Lloret de Mar . 19 B7
Lluchmayor ... 19 C7
Llullaillaco,
 Volcán 94 A3
Loa → 94 A2
Lobatse 59 D5
Lobería 94 D5
Lobito 58 A2
Locarno 13 C8
Loch Garman =
 Wexford 11 E3

Loches 12 C4
Lock 62 B2
Lodhran 42 E7
Lodi, Italy 20 B2
Lodi, U.S.A. ... 80 F3
Lodja 56 E4
Lodwar 57 D7
Łódź 16 C4
Lofoten 8 E10
Logan 81 E8
Logan, Mt. =
 Pierre Elliott
 Trudeau, Mt... 70 B5
Logone → ... 53 F2
Logroño 19 A4
Lohardaga ... 40 F5
Loi-kaw 41 H11
Loir → 12 C3
Loire → 12 C2
Loja, Ecuador . 90 D3
Loja, Spain ... 18 D3
Loji 39 E3
Lokandu 57 E5
Lokitaung 57 D7
Lokoja 55 G6
Lokolama 56 E3
Loliondo 57 E7
Lom 22 C4
Lomami → ... 56 D4
Lombardy =
 Lombárdia □ 20 B2
Lomblen 39 F2
Lombok 37 F5
Lomé 55 G5
Lomela 56 E4
Lomela → 56 E4
Lomié 56 D2
Lomond, L. ... 10 C4
Lompobatang . 39 F1
Łomza 16 B6
Loncoche 95 D2
Londa 43 M9
London 11 F6
Londonderry . 11 D3
Londonderry, C. 60 C4
Londonderry, I. 95 H2
Londrina 94 A6
Long Beach ... 82 D3
Long I.,
 Bahamas ... 86 B4
Long I., U.S.A. . 73 D9
Long Xuyen ... 36 B3
Longford,
 Australia 62 D4
Longford,
 Ireland 11 E3
Longiram 37 E5
Longlac 69 D2
Longnawan ... 37 D4
Longreach 61 E7
Longview, Tex.,
 U.S.A. 79 C6
Longview,
 Wash., U.S.A. 80 B2
Lons-le-Saunier 13 C6
Lop Nor = Lop
 Nur 34 B4
Lopez, C. 56 E1
Lora → 42 D4
Lora, Hamun-i- 42 E4
Lora Cr. → ... 62 A2
Lora del Río ... 18 D3
Lorain 72 D4
Loralai 42 D6
Lorca 19 D5
Lorestān □ ... 46 D6
Loreto 92 D4
Lorient 12 C2
Lorne 62 C3

Lorraine 13 B7
Los Alamos ... 83 C9
Los Andes 94 C2
Los Angeles,
 Chile 94 D2
Los Angeles,
 U.S.A. 82 C3
Los Blancos .. 94 A4
Los Hermanos . 90 A6
Los Mochis ... 84 B3
Los Roques .. 90 A5
Los Testigos .. 90 A6
Los Vilos 94 C2
Lošinj 20 B5
Lot → 12 D4
Lota 94 D2
Loubomo 56 E2
Louga 55 E1
Louis Trichardt 59 C5
Louis XIV, Pte. . 69 C3
Louisiade Arch. 61 C9
Louisiana □ ... 79 D0
Louisville 72 E3
Loulé 18 D1
Lourdes 12 E3
Louth, Australia 63 B4
Louth, U.K. ... 11 E6
Louvain =
 Leuven 14 C3
Lovech 22 C5
Low Tatra =
 Nízké Tatry .. 16 D4
Lowell 73 C10
Lower California
 – Baja
 California ... 84 A1
Lower Hutt ... 65 D6
Lower Saxony =
 Niedersachsen □
 .... 14 B5
Lower Tunguska
 = Tunguska,
 Nizhnyaya → 30 C6
Lowestoft 11 E7
Łowicz 16 B4
Lowyar □ 45 C7
Loxton 62 B3
Loyalty Is. =
 Loyauté, Is. . 64 M11
Loyang =
 Luoyang ... 35 C6
Loyauté, Is. .. 64 M11
Loyev = Loyew 17 C10
Loyew 17 C10
Luachimo 56 F4
Luacono 56 G4
Lualaba → ... 57 D5
Luanda 56 F2
Luangwa 59 B6
Luangwa → .. 59 A6
Luanshya 59 A5
Luapula → ... 57 F5
Luarca 18 A2
Luashi 56 G4
Luau 56 G4
Lubalo 56 F3
Lubang Is. 38 B2
Lubbock 78 C3
Lübeck 15 B6
Lubefu 56 E4
Lubero = Luofu 57 E5
Lubin 16 C3
Lublin 17 C6
Lubuagan 38 A2
Lubuk Antu ... 37 D4
Lubuklinggau . 37 E2
Lubuksikaping . 37 D2
Lubumbashi .. 59 A5
Lubutu 57 E5

Lucca 20 C3
Lucena, Phil. .. 38 B2
Lucena, Spain . 18 D3
Lučenec 16 D4
Lucerne =
 Luzern 13 C8
Lucira 58 A2
Luckenwalde . 15 B7
Lucknow 40 D3
Lüda = Dalian . 35 C7
Lüderitz 58 D3
Ludhiana 42 D9
Ludwigsburg . 14 D5
Ludwigshafen . 14 D5
Luebo 56 F4
Lufira → 57 F5
Lufkin 79 D6
Luga 24 B2
Lugano 13 C8
Lugansk =
 Luhansk 25 D4
Lugh Ganana . 49 G3
Lugo, Italy ... 20 B3
Lugo, Spain .. 18 A2
Lugoj 17 F5
Lugovoy 29 E8
Luhansk 25 D4
Luiana 58 B4
Luimneach =
 Limerick 11 E2
Luís Correia .. 92 C5
Luitpold Coast . 96 B5
Luiza 56 F4
Luján 94 C5
Lukanga Swamp 59 A5
Lukenie → ... 56 E3
Lukolela 56 E3
Łuków 17 C6
Lule älv → ... 8 E12
Luleå 8 E12
Lüleburgaz ... 22 D6
Lulonga → ... 56 D3
Lulua → 56 E4
Luluabourg =
 Kananga 56 F4
Lumai 58 A4
Lumbala
 N'guimbo ... 58 A4
Lumsden 65 F3
Lumut, Tg. ... 37 E3
Lundazi 59 A6
Lundu 37 D3
Lüneburg 14 B6
Lüneburg Heath
 = Lüneburger
 Heide 14 B6
Lüneburger
 Heide 14 B6
Lunéville 13 B7
Lunglei 41 F9
Luni 42 G8
Luni → 43 G7
Luninets =
 Luninyets ... 17 B8
Luninyets 17 B8
Luofu 57 E5
Luoyang 35 C6
Luozi 56 E2
Luremo 56 F3
Lurgan 11 D3
Lusaka 59 B5
Lusambo 56 E4
Lushnja 23 D2
Lushoto 57 E7
Luta = Dalian . 35 C7
Luton 11 F6
Lutong 36 D4
Lutsk 17 C7

Lützow
  Holmbukta .. 96 A8
Luwuk 39 E2
Luxembourg .. 13 B7
Luxembourg ■ 14 D4
Luxor = El
  Uqsur 52 C5
Luza 24 A6
Luzern 13 C8
Luzhou 35 D5
Luziânia 93 F4
Luzon 38 A2
Lviv 17 D7
Lvov = Lviv .. 17 D7
Lyakhavichy ... 17 B8
Lyakhovskiye,
  Ostrova 31 B12
Lyallpur =
  Faisalabad .. 42 D8
Lydenburg 59 D6
Lydia 23 E7
Lyell 65 D5
Lyepyel 24 C2
Łyna → 16 A5
Lynchburg 73 F6
Lynd Ra. 63 A4
Lyndhurst 62 B2
Lynn Lake ... 71 C9
Lyon 13 D6
Lyonnais 13 D6
Lyons = Lyon . 13 D6
Lys = Leie → . 14 C2
Lysychansk ... 25 D4
Lyttelton 65 E5
Lyubertsy 24 B4
Lyuboml 17 C7

M

Ma'alah 47 F6
Ma'ān 47 E3
Ma'anshan 35 C6
Ma'arrat an
  Nu'mān 46 D4
Maas → 14 C3
Maastricht ... 13 A6
Mabrouk 55 E4
Macaé 93 G5
McAllen 78 F4
Macao =
  Macau ■ ... 35 D6
Macapá 92 B3
Macau 92 D6
Macau ■ 35 D6
M'Clintock Chan. 70 A9
McComb 79 D8
MacDonnell Ras. 60 E5
McDouall Peak 62 A1
Macdougall L. . 70 B10
Macedonia =
  Makedhonía □ 23 D4
Macedonia ■ .. 22 D3
Maceió 93 D6
Macenta 55 G3
Macerata 20 C4
Macfarlane, L. . 62 B2
Macgillycuddy's
  Reeks 11 F2
McGregor Ra. . 62 A3
Mach 42 E5
Machado =
  Jiparaná → . 91 E6
Machakos 57 E7
Machala 90 D3
Machilipatnam 40 J3
Machiques 90 A4

Machupicchu .. 91 F4
Macintyre → . 63 A5
Mackay 61 E8
Mackay, L. 60 E4
Mackenzie → . 70 B6
Mackenzie City
  = Linden .. 90 B7
Mackenzie Mts. 70 B6
McKinley, Mt. . 71 B4
McKinney 79 C5
Macksville 63 B5
Maclean 63 A5
Maclear 59 E5
Macleay → .. 63 B5
McMurdo Sd. . 96 B15
Mâcon, France 13 C6
Macon, U.S.A. . 75 C6
Macondo 58 A4
McPherson Ra. 63 A5
Macquarie
  Harbour 62 D4
MacRobertson
  Land 96 B10
Madagali 53 F1
Madagascar ■ . 59 J9
Madā'in Sālih . 47 F4
Madama 52 D1
Madang 61 B8
Madaoua 55 F6
Madaripur 41 F8
Madauk 41 J11
Madaya 41 F11
Maddalena ... 20 D2
Madeira 54 B1
Madeira → .. 90 D7
Madha 43 L9
Madhya
  Pradesh □ .. 43 H10
Madikeri 43 N9
Madimba 56 E3
Madīnat ash
  Sha'b 49 E3
Madingou 56 E2
Madison 77 D10
Madiun 37 F4
Madras = Tamil
  Nadu □ 43 P10
Madras 43 N12
Madre, Laguna 78 F5
Madre, Sierra . 38 A2
Madre de
  Dios → 91 F5
Madre de Dios,
  I. 95 G1
Madre
  Occidental,
  Sierra 84 B3
Madrid 18 B4
Madurai 43 Q11
Madurantakam 43 N11
Mae Sot 36 A1
Maebashi 32 A6
Maestrazgo,
  Mts. del ... 19 B5
Maevatanana .. 59 H9
Mafeking =
  Mafikeng ... 59 D5
Maffra 63 C4
Mafia I. 57 F7
Mafikeng 59 D5
Mafra, Brazil . 94 B7
Mafra, Portugal 18 C1
Magadan 31 D13
Magadi 57 E7
Magallanes,
  Estrecho de . 95 G2
Magangué 90 B4
Magburaka ... 55 G2
Magdalena,
  Argentina .. 94 D5

Magdalena,
  Bolivia 91 F6
Magdalena,
  Malaysia 36 D5
Magdalena → . 90 A4
Magdeburg ... 15 B6
Magelang 37 F4
Magellan's Str.
  = Magallanes,
  Estrecho de . 95 G2
Maggiore, L. .. 20 B2
Magnetic Pole
  (South) =
  South
  Magnetic Pole 96 A13
Magnitogorsk . 29 D6
Magosa =
  Famagusta .. 46 D3
Maguarinho, C. 92 C4
Magusa =
  Famagusta .. 46 D3
Magwe 41 G10
Mahābād 46 C6
Mahabo 59 J8
Mahagi 57 D6
Mahajanga ... 59 H9
Mahakam → . 37 E5
Mahalapye ... 59 C5
Mahallāt 44 C2
Mahanadi → . 40 G6
Mahanoro 59 H9
Maharashtra □ 43 J9
Mahbubnagar . 43 L10
Mahdia 52 A1
Mahenge 57 F7
Maheno 65 F4
Mahesana ... 43 H8
Mahia Pen. ... 64 C7
Mahilyow 17 B10
Mahón 19 C8
Mai-Ndombe, L. 56 E3
Maicurú → ... 92 C3
Maidstone ... 11 F7
Maiduguri ... 53 F1
Maijdi 41 F8
Maikala Ra. .. 40 G3
Main → 14 D5
Maine 12 C3
Maingkwan ... 41 D11
Mainit, L. 38 C3
Mainland,
  Orkney, U.K. 10 B5
Mainland, Shet.,
  U.K. 10 A6
Maintirano 59 H8
Mainz 14 C5
Maipú 94 D5
Maiquetía 90 A5
Mairabari 41 D9
Maitland,
  N.S.W.,
  Australia 63 B5
Maitland,
  S. Austral.,
  Australia 62 B2
Maizuru 32 B4
Majene 39 E1
Maji 53 G6
Majorca =
  Mallorca 19 C7
Maka 55 F2
Makale 39 E1
Makari 56 B2
Makarikari =
  Makgadikgadi
  Salt Pans .. 59 C5
Makasar =
  Ujung
  Pandang 39 F1

Makasar, Selat 39 E1
Makasar, Str. of
  = Makasar,
  Selat 39 E1
Makat 29 E6
Makedhonía □ 23 D4
Makedonija =
  Macedonia ■ 22 D3
Makeni 55 G2
Makeyevka =
  Makiyivka .. 25 D4
Makgadikgadi
  Salt Pans .. 59 C5
Makhachkala . 25 E6
Makian 39 D3
Makindu 57 E7
Makinsk 29 D8
Makiyivka ... 25 D4
Makkah 47 G4
Makó 16 E5
Makokou 56 D2
Makoua 56 E3
Makrai 43 H10
Makran 45 E5
Makran Coast
  Range 42 G4
Maksimkin Yar 29 D9
Mākū 46 C6
Makumbi 56 F4
Makurazaki ... 33 D2
Makurdi 55 G6
Malabang 38 C2
Malabar Coast . 43 P9
Malabo = Rey
  Malabo 56 D1
Malacca, Str. of 36 D1
Maladzyechna . 17 A8
Málaga 18 D3
Malakâl 53 G5
Malakand ... 42 B7
Malang 37 F4
Malanje 56 F3
Mälaren 9 G11
Malargüe 94 D3
Malaryta 17 C7
Malatya 46 C4
Malawi ■ 59 A6
Malawi, L. 59 A6
Malaybalay ... 38 C3
Malāyer 46 D7
Malaysia ■ ... 36 D4
Malazgirt 46 C5
Malbooma ... 62 B1
Malbork 16 A4
Malden I. 65 K15
Maldives ■ ... 26 J11
Maldonado ... 94 C6
Malé Karpaty . 16 D3
Maléa, Ákra .. 23 F4
Malegaon 43 J9
Malema 59 A7
Malha 53 E4
Mali ■ 55 E4
Mali → 41 E11
Malik 39 E2
Malili 39 E2
Malin Hd. 10 D3
Malindi 57 E8
Malines =
  Mechelen ... 14 C3
Malino 39 D2
Malita 38 C3
Malkara 22 D6
Mallacoota ... 63 C4
Mallacoota Inlet 63 C4
Mallaig 10 C4
Mallawi 52 C5
Mallorca 19 C7
Mallow 11 E2

Malmö	9	G10
Malolos	38	B2
Malpelo	90	C2
Malta ■	21	G5
Maltahöhe	58	C3
Maluku	39	E3
Maluku □	39	E3
Maluku Sea = Molucca Sea	39	E2
Malvan	43	L8
Malvinas, Is. = Falkland Is. □	95	G5
Malyn	17	C9
Malyy Lyakhovskiy, Ostrov	31	B12
Mamahatun	46	C5
Mamanguape	92	D6
Mamasa	39	E1
Mamberamo →	39	E5
Mambilima Falls	57	G5
Mamburao	38	B2
Mamfe	55	G6
Mamoré →	91	F5
Mamou	55	F2
Mamuju	39	E1
Man	55	G3
Man, I. of	11	D4
Man Na	41	F11
Mana	92	A3
Manaar, G. of = Mannar, G. of	43	Q11
Manacapuru	90	D6
Manacor	19	C7
Manado	39	D2
Managua	85	E7
Manakara	59	J9
Manama = Al Manāmah	44	E2
Mananara	59	H9
Mananjary	59	J9
Manaos = Manaus	90	D7
Manapouri	65	F2
Manapouri, L.	65	F2
Manas	34	B3
Manas →	41	D8
Manasir	44	E2
Manaung	41	H9
Manaus	90	D7
Manay	38	C3
Manchester, U.K.	11	E5
Manchester, U.S.A.	73	C10
Mand →	44	D3
Manda	57	G6
Mandal	9	G9
Mandalay	41	F11
Mandale = Mandalay	41	F11
Mandalī	46	D6
Mandar, Teluk	39	E1
Mandaue	38	B2
Mandi	42	D10
Mandimba	59	A7
Mandioli	39	E3
Mandla	40	F3
Mandritsara	59	H9
Mandsaur	43	G9
Mandvi	43	H6
Mandya	43	N10
Manfalût	52	C5
Manfred	63	B3
Manfredónia	20	D5
Mangalia	22	C7
Mangalore	43	N9
Mangaweka	64	C6
Manggar	37	E3
Manggawitu	39	E4
Mangkalihat, Tanjung	39	D1
Mangla Dam	42	C8
Mangnai	34	C4
Mango	55	F5
Mangoche	59	A7
Mangole	39	E3
Mangonui	64	A5
Mangueigne	53	F3
Mangueira, L. da	94	C6
Mangyshlak Poluostrov	29	E6
Manhuaçu	93	G5
Manica	59	B6
Manicoré	91	E6
Manicouagan →	69	D4
Manīfah	47	F7
Manihiki	65	L14
Manila	38	B2
Manila B.	38	B2
Manilla	63	B5
Manipur □	41	E9
Manipur →	41	F10
Manisa	23	E6
Manitoba □	71	C10
Manitoba, L.	71	C10
Manitowoc	72	B2
Manizales	90	B3
Manja	59	J8
Manjacaze	59	C6
Manjhand	42	G6
Manjil	46	C7
Manjra →	43	K10
Mankono	55	G3
Manly	63	B5
Manmad	43	J9
Manna	37	E2
Mannahill	62	B3
Mannar	43	Q11
Mannar, G. of	43	Q11
Mannar I.	43	Q11
Mannheim	14	D5
Mannum	62	B2
Mano	55	G2
Manokwari	39	E4
Manombo	59	J8
Manono	57	F5
Manosque	13	E6
Manresa	19	B6
Mansa	57	G5
Mansel I.	68	B2
Mansfield, Australia	63	C4
Mansfield, U.K.	11	E6
Mansfield, U.S.A.	72	D4
Manta	90	D2
Mantalingajan, Mt.	36	C5
Mantes-la-Jolie	12	B4
Manthani	43	K11
Mantiqueira, Serra da	93	G5
Mántova	20	B3
Mantua = Mántova	20	B3
Manu	91	F4
Manuae	65	L15
Manuel Alves →	93	E4
Manui	39	E2
Manyara, L.	57	E7
Manych-Gudilo, Ozero	25	D5
Manyoni	57	F6
Manzai	42	C7
Manzanares	18	C4
Manzanillo, Cuba	86	B4
Manzanillo, Mexico	84	D4
Manzhouli	35	B6
Mao	53	F2
Maoke, Pegunungan	39	E5
Maoming	35	D6
Mapam Yumco	40	B3
Mapia, Kepulauan	39	D4
Mapuera →	90	D7
Maputo	59	D6
Maqnā	47	E3
Maquela do Zombo	56	F3
Maquinchao	95	E3
Mar, Serra do	94	B7
Mar Chiquita, L.	94	C4
Mar del Plata	94	D5
Mar Menor	19	D5
Maraã	90	D5
Marabá	92	D4
Maracá, I. de	92	B3
Maracaibo	90	A4
Maracaibo, L. de	90	B4
Maracay	90	A5
Marādah	52	C2
Maradi	55	F6
Marāgheh	46	C6
Marāh	47	F6
Marajó, I. de	92	C4
Maralal	57	D7
Marama	62	C3
Marampa	55	G2
Marand	46	C6
Maranguape	92	C6
Maranhão = São Luís	92	C5
Maranhão □	92	D4
Maranoa →	63	A4
Marañón →	90	D4
Marão	59	C6
Maraş = Kahramanmaraş	46	C4
Maratua	39	D1
Marbella	18	D3
Marburg	14	C5
Marche	12	C4
Marchena	18	D3
Mardan	42	B8
Mardin	46	C5
Marek = Stanke Dimitrov	22	C4
Marek	39	E2
Margarita, I. de	90	A6
Margate	11	F7
Margelan = Marghilon	29	E8
Marghilon	29	E8
Mari El □	24	B6
Mari Republic □ = Mari El □	24	B6
Maria I.	62	D4
Maria van Diemen, C.	64	A5
Mariana Trench	64	H9
Marianao	86	B3
Ma'rib	49	D4
Maribor	20	A5
Marīdī	53	H4
Marie Byrd Land	96	B18
Marie-Galante	87	C7
Mariecourt = Kangiqsujuaq	68	B3
Mariental	58	C3
Mariinsk	29	D9
Marília	93	G3
Marín	18	A1
Marinduque	38	B2
Maringá	94	A6
Marion	79	A9
Mariscal Estigarribia	91	H6
Maritime Alps = Maritimes, Alpes	13	D7
Maritimes, Alpes	13	D7
Maritsa = Évros →	22	D6
Mariupol	25	D4
Marīvān	46	D6
Markazī □	44	C2
Markham, Mt.	96	C15
Marks	24	C6
Marla	62	A1
Marmagao	43	M8
Marmara	23	D6
Marmara, Sea of = Marmara Denizi	22	D7
Marmara Denizi	22	D7
Marmaris	23	F7
Marmolada, Mte.	20	A3
Marne →	12	B5
Maroantsetra	59	H9
Marondera	59	B6
Maroni →	92	A3
Maroochydore	63	A5
Maroona	62	C3
Maroua	53	F1
Marovoay	59	H9
Marquesas Is. = Marquises, Is.	65	K17
Marquette	69	D2
Marquises, Is.	65	K17
Marrakech	54	B3
Marrawah	62	D3
Marree	62	A2
Marromeu	59	B7
Marrowie Cr. →	63	B4
Marrupa	59	A7
Marsá Matrûh	52	B4
Marsá Susah	52	B3
Marsabit	57	D7
Marsala	21	F4
Marsden	63	B4
Marseille	13	E6
Marseilles = Marseille	13	E6
Marshall, Liberia	55	G2
Marshall, U.S.A.	81	H7
Marshall Is. ■	64	J12
Marshalltown	77	D8
Martaban	41	J11
Martaban, G. of	41	J11
Martapura, Kalimantan, Indonesia	37	E4
Martapura, Sumatera, Indonesia	37	E2
Marte	53	F1
Martigny	13	C7
Martigues	13	E6
Martin	16	D4
Martina Franca	21	D6
Martinborough	65	D6
Martinique ■	87	D7
Martinique Passage	87	C7
Martinsville	75	A8
Marton	64	D6
Martos	18	D4
Marudi	37	D4

Ma'ruf 42 D5
Marugame 32 B3
Marulan 63 B5
Marwar 42 G8
Mary 29 F7
Maryborough =
Port Laoise .. 11 E3
Maryborough,
Queens.,
Australia 63 A5
Maryborough,
Vic., Australia 62 C3
Maryland □ .. 73 E7
Maryvale 63 A5
Marzūq 52 C1
Masaka 57 E6
Masalembo,
Kepulauan .. 37 F4
Masalima,
Kepulauan .. 37 F5
Masamba 39 E2
Masan 35 C7
Masandam, Ras 44 E4
Masasi 57 G7
Masaya 85 E7
Masbate 38 B2
Mascara 54 A5
Masela 39 F3
Maseru 59 D5
Mashābih 47 F4
Mashhad 44 B4
Mashike 32 F12
Mashkel,
Hamun-i- ... 42 E3
Mashki Chāh .. 42 E3
Masi Manimba 56 E3
Masindi 57 D6
Masisea 91 E4
Masjed
Soleyman ... 47 E7
Mask, L. 11 E2
Masohi 39 E3
Mason City .. 77 D8
Masqat 45 F4
Massa 20 B3
Massachusetts □
.... 73 C9
Massaguet 53 F2
Massakory 53 F2
Massangena .. 59 C6
Massawa =
Mitsiwa 53 E6
Massena 73 B8
Massénya 53 F2
Massif Central . 13 D5
Massinga 59 C7
Masson I. 96 A11
Mastanli =
Momchilgrad 22 D5
Masterton 65 D6
Mastuj 42 A8
Mastung 42 E5
Masty 17 B7
Masuda 32 B2
Masvingo 59 C6
Mataboor 39 E5
Matad 35 B6
Matadi 56 F2
Matagalpa 85 E7
Matagami, L. .. 69 D3
Matak, P. 37 D3
Matakana 63 B4
Matam 55 E2
Matamoros,
Coahuila,
Mexico 84 B4
Matamoros,
Tamaulipas,
Mexico 84 B5

Ma'ṭan as Sarra 52 D3
Matane 69 D4
Matanzas 86 B3
Matapan, C. =
Taínaron, Ákra 23 F4
Mataram 37 F5
Matarani 91 G4
Mataró 19 B7
Mataura 65 G3
Matehuala 84 C4
Matera 21 D6
Mathura 42 F10
Mati 38 C3
Matiri Ra. 65 D5
Matmata 54 B6
Mato Grosso □ 93 E3
Mato Grosso,
Planalto do .. 93 F3
Mato Grosso do
Sul □ 93 F3
Matochkin Shar 28 B6
Matosinhos ... 18 B1
Matrah 45 F4
Matsue 32 B3
Matsumoto ... 32 A6
Matsusaka 32 B5
Matsuyama ... 32 C3
Mattagami → . 69 C2
Mattancheri ... 43 Q10
Matterhorn ... 13 D7
Matthew's Ridge 90 B6
Matucana 91 F3
Matun 42 C6
Maturín 90 B6
Mau Ranipur .. 43 G11
Maubeuge 13 A5
Maude 63 B3
Maudin Sun ... 41 K10
Maués 90 D7
Mauganj 40 E3
Maui 82 H12
Maulamyaing =
Moulmein ... 41 J11
Maumere 39 F2
Maun 58 B4
Maungmagan
Kyunzu 41 K11
Mauritania ■ .. 55 D2
Mauritius ■ ... 51 H9
Mavinga 58 B4
Mawk Mai 41 G11
Mawlaik 41 F10
Mawson Coast . 96 A10
Maxixe 59 C7
Mayaguana ... 87 B5
Mayagüez 87 C6
Maydena 62 D4
Mayenne → . 12 C3
Maykop 25 E5
Mayo 70 B6
Mayo L. 70 B6
Mayon Volcano 38 B2
Mayor I. 64 B7
Mayu 39 D3
Mazabuka 59 B5
Mazagán = El
Jadida 54 B3
Mazagão 92 C3
Mazán 90 D4
Māzandarān □ 44 B3
Mazar-e Sharīf . 45 B6
Mazara del Vallo 21 F4
Mazarredo 95 F3
Mazarrón 19 D5
Mazaruni → .. 90 B7
Mazatlán 84 C3
Māzhān 44 C4
Mazīnān 44 B4
Mazoe → 59 B6

Mazurian Lakes
= Mazurski,
Pojezierze ... 16 B5
Mazurski,
Pojezierze ... 16 B5
Mazyr 17 C9
Mbabane 59 D6
Mbaïki 56 D3
Mbala 57 F6
Mbale 57 D6
Mbalmayo 56 D2
Mbamba Bay .. 57 G6
Mbandaka 56 D3
Mbanza Congo 56 F2
Mbanza Ngungu 56 F2
Mbarara 57 E6
Mbeya 57 F6
Mbini □ 56 D2
Mbour 55 F1
Mbout 55 E2
Mbuji-Mayi ... 56 F4
Mbulu 57 E7
Mchinji 59 A6
Mead, L. 82 B5
Mearim → ... 92 C5
Meaux 13 B5
Mecca =
Makkah 47 G4
Mechelen 14 C3
Mecheria 54 B4
Mecklenburg .. 15 B6
Mecklenburger
Bucht 15 A6
Meconta 59 A7
Medan 37 D1
Medanosa, Pta. 95 F3
Medéa 54 A5
Medellín 90 B3
Mederdra 55 E1
Medford 80 D2
Medgidia 22 B7
Mediaş 17 E7
Medicine Bow
Ra. 81 E10
Medicine Hat . 71 C8
Medina = Al
Madīnah 47 F4
Medina del
Campo 18 B3
Medina-Sidonia 18 D3
Medinipur 40 F6
Mediterranean
Sea 50 C5
Médoc 12 D3
Medveditsa → 24 D5
Medvezhyegorsk 28 C4
Meekatharra . 60 F2
Meerut 42 E10
Mega 53 H6
Mégara 23 F4
Meghalaya □ .. 41 E8
Mei Xian 35 D6
Meiganga 56 C2
Meiktila 41 G10
Meissen 15 C7
Mejillones 94 A2
Mékambo 56 D2
Mekdela 53 F6
Mekhtar 42 D6
Meknès 54 B3
Mekong → ... 36 C3
Mekongga 39 E2
Mekvari =
Kür → 25 E6
Melagiri Hills .. 43 N10
Melaka 37 D2
Melalap 36 C5
Melanesia 64 K10
Melbourne,
Australia 63 C3

Melbourne,
U.S.A. 75 E7
Mélèzes → .. 68 C3
Melfi 53 F2
Melfort 71 C9
Melilla 19 E4
Melitopol 25 D4
Melk 15 D8
Melo 94 C6
Melolo 39 F2
Melrose 63 B4
Melun 13 B5
Melut 53 F5
Melville 71 C9
Melville I. 60 C5
Melville Pen. .. 68 B2
Memba 59 G8
Memboro 39 F5
Memel =
Klaipėda 24 B1
Memmingen .. 14 E6
Mempawah ... 37 D3
Memphis, Tenn.,
U.S.A. 74 B3
Memphis, Tex.,
U.S.A. 78 B3
Ménaka 55 E5
Menan = Chao
Phraya → .. 36 B2
Menate 37 E4
Mendawai → . 37 E4
Mende 13 D5
Mendocino, C. . 80 E1
Mendoza 94 C3
Mene Grande . 90 B4
Menemen 23 E6
Menggala 37 E3
Mengzi 34 D5
Menindee 62 B3
Menindee L. .. 62 B3
Meningie 62 C2
Menominee ... 72 B2
Menongue 58 A3
Menorca 19 C7
Mentawai,
Kepulauan .. 37 E1
Menton 13 E7
Meppel 14 B4
Merabéllou,
Kólpos 23 G5
Meran =
Merano 20 A3
Merano 20 A3
Merauke 39 F6
Merbein 62 B3
Merca 49 G3
Merced 82 B2
Mercedes,
Buenos Aires,
Argentina ... 94 C5
Mercedes,
Corrientes,
Argentina ... 94 B5
Mercedes,
San Luis,
Argentina ... 94 C3
Mercedes,
Uruguay 94 C5
Merceditas ... 94 B2
Mercer 64 B6
Mercy C. 68 B4
Meredith, C. ... 95 G4
Merga =
Nukheila 53 E4
Mergui Arch. =
Myeik Kyunzu 36 B1
Mérida, Mexico 85 C7
Mérida, Spain . 18 C2

Mérida,
  Venezuela ... 90 B4
Mérida, Cord. de 87 E5
Meridian 74 C3
Meriruma 92 B3
Merowe 53 E5
Merriwa 63 B5
Merriwagga .. 63 B4
Merrygoen ... 63 B4
Mersa Fatma . 49 E3
Merseburg ... 15 C6
Mersin 46 C3
Mersing 37 D2
Merthyr Tydfil . 11 F5
Mértola 18 D2
Meru 57 D7
Mesa 83 D7
Meshed =
  Mashhad ... 44 B4
Meshra er Req 53 G4
Mesolóngion .. 23 E3
Mesopotamia =
  Al Jazirah ... 46 D5
Messina, *Italy* . 21 E5
Messina,
  S. Africa 59 C6
Messina, Str. di 21 E5
Messíni 23 F4
Messiniakós
  Kólpos 23 F4
Mesta → 22 D5
Meta → 90 B5
Metairie 79 E8
Metán 94 B4
Metangula ... 59 A6
Metema 53 F6
Methven 65 E4
Metil 59 B7
Metlakatla 71 C6
Mettur Dam .. 43 P10
Metz 13 B7
Meulaboh 37 D1
Meureudu 36 C1
Meuse → 13 A6
Mexiana, I. 92 C4
Mexicali 84 A1
México 84 D5
México □ 84 D5
Mexico ■ 84 C4
Mexico, G. of .. 85 B7
Meymaneh ... 42 B4
Mezen 28 C5
Mezen → 28 C5
Mézene 13 D6
Mezökövesd .. 16 E5
Mezötúr 16 E5
Mhow 43 H9
Miami 75 G7
Miami Beach .. 75 G7
Mīāndowāb .. 46 C6
Miandrivazo ... 59 H9
Mīāneh 46 C6
Mianwali 42 C7
Miaoli 35 D7
Miarinarivo .. 59 H9
Miass 29 D7
Michalovce ... 17 D5
Michigan □ ... 72 C3
Michigan, L. ... 72 C2
Michipicoten .. 69 D2
Michurin 22 C6
Michurinsk 24 C5
Micronesia,
  Federated
  States of ■ .. 64 J10
Middelburg .. 58 E5
Middlesbrough 11 D6
Midi, Canal
  du → 12 E4

Midland 78 D3
Midyat 46 C5
Midzŏr 22 C4
Międzychód ... 16 B2
Międzyrzec
  Podlaski 17 C6
Mielec 16 C5
Miercurea Ciuc 17 E7
Mieres 18 A3
Miguel Alves .. 92 C5
Mihara 32 B3
Mikhaylovgrad 22 C4
Míkonos 23 F5
Mikura-Jima .. 32 C6
Milagro 90 D3
Milan = Milano 20 B2
Milang 62 B2
Milano 20 B2
Milâs 23 F6
Milazzo 21 E5
Mildura 62 B3
Miles 63 A5
Miletus 23 F6
Milford Haven . 11 F4
Milford Sd. ... 65 F2
Milḥ, Baḥr al .. 47 D5
Miliana 54 C5
Mill I. 96 A12
Millau 13 D5
Millicent 62 C3
Millinocket 73 B11
Millmerran ... 63 A5
Milne Inlet ... 68 A2
Mílos 23 F5
Milparinka P.O. 62 A3
Milton 65 G3
Milton Keynes . 11 E6
Miltou 53 F2
Milwaukee 72 C2
Min Chiang → 35 D6
Min Jiang → .. 35 D5
Mina Pirquitas . 94 A3
Mina Su'ud .. 47 E7
Mīnā'al Aḥmadī 47 E7
Mināb 44 E4
Minamata 32 C2
Minas 94 C5
Minas Gerais □ 93 F4
Minbu 41 G10
Mindanao 38 C2
Mindanao Sea =
  Bohol Sea .. 38 C2
Mindanao
  Trench 38 B3
Minden 14 B5
Mindiptana ... 39 F6
Mindoro 38 B2
Mindoro Str. .. 38 B2
Mindouli 56 E2
Mingäçevir Su
  Anban 25 E6
Mingan 69 C4
Mingechaurskoye
  Vdkhr. =
  Mingäçevir Su
  Anban 25 E6
Mingin 41 F10
Mingt'iehkaitafan
  = Mintaka
  Pass 42 A9
Minho =
  Miño → 18 B1
Minho 18 B1
Minna 55 G6
Minneapolis .. 77 C8
Minnedosa .. 71 C10
Minnesota □ .. 77 B7
Minnipa 62 B2
Miño → 18 B1

Minorca =
  Menorca 19 C7
Minore 63 B4
Minot 76 A4
Minsk 24 C2
Mińsk
  Mazowiecki . 16 B5
Mintaka Pass .. 42 A9
Minto 71 B5
Minutang 41 C11
Minvoul 56 D2
Mir 53 F1
Mira 20 B4
Miraj 43 L9
Miram Shah .. 42 C7
Miranda 93 G2
Miranda de Ebro 19 A4
Miranda do
  Douro 18 B2
Miri 36 D4
Mirim, L. 94 C6
Mirpur Khas .. 42 G6
Mirzapur 40 E4
Mirzapur-cum-
  Vindhyachal =
  Mirzapur 40 E4
Mish'āb, Ra'as
  al 47 E7
Mishan 35 B8
Miskin 44 F4
Miskolc 16 D5
Misool 39 E4
Misrātah 52 B2
Misriç 46 C5
Missinaibi → . 69 C2
Mississippi □ . 79 C9
Mississippi → 79 E9
Mississippi River
  Delta 79 E9
Missoula 81 B6
Missouri □ ... 77 F8
Missouri → .. 77 F9
Mistassini L. .. 69 C3
Misurata =
  Misrātah 52 B2
Mitchell,
  Australia 63 A4
Mitchell, *U.S.A.* 76 D5
Mitchell → ... 61 D7
Mitilíni 23 E6
Mito 32 A7
Mitrovica =
  Titova-
  Mitrovica ... 22 C3
Mitsinjo 59 H9
Mitsiwa 53 E6
Mittagong ... 63 B5
Mitú 90 C4
Mitumba,
  Chaîne des .. 57 F5
Mitumba Mts. =
  Mitumba,
  Chaîne des .. 57 F5
Mitwaba 57 F5
Mitzic 56 D2
Miyake-Jima .. 32 B6
Miyako 33 G12
Miyakonojō .. 32 D2
Miyazaki 32 D2
Miyet, Bahr el =
  Dead Sea ... 47 E3
Mizal 47 G6
Mizdah 52 B1
Mizoram □ ... 41 F9
Mjøsa 8 F10
Mladá Boleslav 16 C2
Mława 16 B5
Mljet 20 C6
Mmabatho ... 59 D5

Moa 39 F3
Moabi 56 E2
Moalie Park .. 62 A3
Moba 57 F5
Mobaye 56 D4
Mobayi 56 D4
Mobile 74 D3
Mobutu Sese
  Seko, L. =
  Albert L. 57 D6
Moçambique .. 59 H8
Moçâmedes =
  Namibe 58 B2
Mochudi 59 C5
Mocimboa da
  Praia 57 G8
Mocoa 90 C3
Mocuba 59 B7
Modane 13 D7
Módena 20 B3
Modesto 82 B2
Módica 21 F5
Moe 63 C4
Moengo 92 A3
Mogadishu =
  Muqdisho ... 49 G4
Mogador =
  Essaouira ... 54 B3
Mogami → .. 33 G12
Mogaung 41 E11
Mogi das Cruzes 94 A7
Mogi-Mirim ... 94 A7
Mogilev =
  Mahilyow ... 17 B10
Mogilev-
  Podolskiy =
  Mohyliv-
  Podilskyy ... 17 D8
Mogoi 39 E4
Mogok 41 F11
Mohács 16 F4
Moḥammadābād
  .... 44 B4
Mohoro 57 F7
Mohyliv-
  Podilskyy ... 17 D8
Mointy 29 E8
Moisie 69 C4
Moisie → 69 C4
Moïssala 53 G2
Mojave Desert . 82 C4
Mokai 64 C6
Mokokchung .. 41 D10
Mokra Gora .. 22 C3
Molchanovo .. 29 D9
Moldavia ■ =
  Moldova ■ .. 17 E9
Molde 8 F9
Moldova ■ ... 17 E9
Moldoveanu, Vf. 17 F7
Molepolole ... 59 C5
Molfetta 20 D6
Moline 77 E9
Moliro 57 F6
Mollendo 91 G4
Molodechno =
  Maladzyechna 17 A8
Molokai 82 H12
Molong 63 B4
Molopo → ... 58 D4
Molotov = Perm 29 D6
Moloundou .. 56 D3
Molu 39 F4
Molucca Sea .. 39 E2
Moluccas =
  Maluku 39 E3
Moma 59 B7
Mombasa 57 E7
Momchilgrad .. 22 D5

Mompós

Mompós 90 B4
Mon → 41 G10
Mona, Canal de
la 87 C6
Monaco ■ 13 E7
Monahans ... 78 D2
Monastir =
Bitola 22 D3
Monastir 52 A1
Moncayo, Sierra
del 19 B5
Mönchengladbach
.... 14 C4
Monchique ... 18 D1
Monclova 84 B4
Mondego → .. 18 B1
Mondeodo ... 39 E2
Mondovì 20 B1
Monforte de
Lemos 18 A2
Mong Hsu 41 G12
Mong Kung ... 41 G11
Mong Nai 41 G11
Mong Pawk ... 41 F12
Mong Ton 41 G12
Mong Wa 41 G13
Mong Yai 41 F12
Mongalla 53 G5
Monghyr =
Munger 40 E6
Mongibello =
Etna 21 F5
Mongo 53 F2
Mongolia ■ ... 35 B5
Mongororo ... 53 F3
Mongu 58 B4
Monkoto 56 E4
Monópoli 21 D6
Monqoumba .. 56 D3
Monroe, La.,
U.S.A. 79 C7
Monroe, N.C.,
U.S.A. 75 B7
Monrovia 55 G2
Mons 14 C2
Monse 39 E2
Mont-de-Marsan 12 E3
Mont-St.-Michel,
Le = Le Mont-
St.-Michel ... 12 B3
Montalbán 19 B5
Montana □ ... 81 B9
Montargis 13 C5
Montauban .. 12 D4
Montbéliard . 13 C7
Montceau-les-
Mines 13 C6
Monte Alegre . 92 C3
Monte Azul ... 93 F5
Monte-Carlo .. 20 C1
Monte Caseros 94 C5
Monte Comán . 94 C3
Monte Santu, C.
di 21 D2
Montecristi ... 90 D2
Montecristo ... 20 C3
Montego Bay .. 86 C4
Montélimar ... 13 D6
Montemorelos . 84 B5
Montenegro □ 22 C2
Montepuez 59 A7
Monterey 82 B2
Montería 90 B3
Monterrey 84 B4
Montes Claros . 93 F5
Montesilvano
Marina 20 C5
Montevideo ... 94 C5
Montgomery =
Sahiwal 42 D8

Montgomery .. 74 C4
Montijo 18 C2
Montilla 18 D3
Montluçon ... 13 C5
Montmorillon . 12 C4
Montoro 18 C3
Montpellier .. 13 E5
Montréal 69 D3
Montreux 13 C7
Montrose, U.K. 10 C5
Montrose,
U.S.A. 83 A9
Montserrat ■.. 87 C7
Monveda 56 D4
Monywa 41 F10
Monza 20 B2
Monze 59 B5
Monze, C. 43 G5
Monzón 19 B6
Moolawatana . 62 A2
Moomin Cr. → 63 A4
Moonie 63 A5
Moonie → ... 63 A4
Moonta 62 B2
Mooroopna ... 63 C4
Moose Jaw ... 71 C9
Moosomin 71 C9
Moosonee 69 C2
Mopeia Velha . 59 B7
Mopti 55 F4
Moquegua 91 G4
Mora 8 F10
Moradabad ... 42 E11
Morafenobe ... 59 H8
Moramanga .. 59 H9
Moratuwa 43 R11
Morava →,
Serbia, Yug. . 22 B3
Morava →,
Slovak Rep. . 16 D3
Moravian Hts. =
Ceskomoravská
Vrchovina .. 16 D2
Morawhanna .. 90 B7
Moray Firth ... 10 C5
Morden 71 D10
Mordovian
Republic □ =
Mordvinia □ 24 C5
Mordvinia □ .. 24 C5
Morea 62 C3
Moree 63 A4
Morelia 84 D4
Morella 19 B5
Morena, Sierra 18 C3
Moreton I. 63 A5
Morgan 62 B2
Morgan City .. 79 E8
Morioka 33 G12
Morlaix 12 B2
Mornington .. 63 C4
Mornington, I. . 95 F1
Moro G. 38 C2
Morocco ■ ... 54 B3
Morococha .. 91 F3
Morogoro 57 F7
Morombe 59 J8
Morón 86 B4
Mörön → 35 B6
Morón de la
Frontera 18 D3
Morondava .. 59 J8
Morotai 39 D3
Moroto 57 D6
Morphou 46 D3
Morrinhos ... 93 F4
Morrinsville .. 64 B6
Morristown ... 75 A6
Morrumbene .. 59 C7

Morshansk 24 C5
Morteros 94 C4
Mortes, R.
das → 93 E3
Mortlake 62 C3
Morundah 63 B4
Moruya 63 C5
Morvan 13 C6
Morven 63 A4
Morwell 63 C4
Moscos Is. 41 L11
Moscow =
Moskva 24 B4
Moscow 80 B5
Mosel → 13 A7
Moselle =
Mosel → ... 13 A7
Mosgiel 65 F4
Moshi 57 E7
Moskva 24 B4
Moskva → ... 24 B4
Moson-
magyaróvar . 16 E3
Mosquera ... 90 C3
Moss Vale ... 63 B5
Mossaka 56 E3
Mossburn ... 65 F3
Mosselbaai ... 58 E4
Mossendjo ... 56 E2
Mossgiel 63 B3
Mossoró 92 D6
Mossuril 59 G8
Most 16 C1
Mostaganem .. 54 A5
Mostar 20 C6
Mostardas ... 94 C6
Mostiska =
Mostyska ... 17 D6
Mosty = Masty 17 B7
Mostyska 17 D6
Mosul = Al
Mawşil 46 C5
Motihari 40 D5
Motril 18 D4
Motueka 65 D5
Motueka → ... 65 D5
Mouanda 56 E2
Moúdhros 23 E5
Moudjeria ... 55 E2
Mouila 56 E2
Moulamein .. 63 C3
Moulins 13 C5
Moulmein ... 41 J11
Moundou 53 G2
Mount Barker . 62 C2
Mount Darwin . 59 B6
Mount Eba ... 62 B2
Mount Gambier 62 C3
Mount Hope,
N.S.W.,
Australia 63 B4
Mount Hope,
S. Austral.,
Australia 62 B2
Mount Howitt . 62 A3
Mount Isa ... 61 E6
Mount Lofty Ra. 62 B2
Mount McKinley
National Park 71 B4
Mount Margaret 63 A3
Mount
Maunganui .. 64 B7
Mount Olympus
= Uludağ .. 23 D7
Mount Perry . 63 A5
Mount Vernon . 73 D9
Mountain View 82 B1
Moura, Brazil .. 90 D6
Moura, Portugal 18 C2

Mourdi,
Dépression du 53 E3
Mourdiah 55 F3
Moussoro 53 F2
Moutohara 64 C7
Moutong 39 D2
Moyale 57 D7
Moyamba 55 G2
Moyen Atlas .. 54 B3
Moyo 37 F5
Moyyero → .. 30 C8
Mozambique =
Moçambique 59 H8
Mozambique ■ 59 B7
Mozambique
Chan. 59 H8
Mozdok 25 E5
Mozyr = Mazyr 17 C9
Mpanda 57 F6
Mpika 59 A6
Mpwapwa ... 57 F7
Msaken 52 A1
Msoro 59 A6
Mu Us Shamo . 35 C5
Muaná 92 C4
Muar 37 D2
Muarabungo . 37 E2
Muaraenim .. 37 E2
Muarajuloi ... 37 E4
Muarakaman . 37 E5
Muaratebo ... 37 E2
Muaratembesi . 37 E2
Muaratewe .. 37 E4
Mubarraz = Al
Mubarraz ... 47 F7
Mubende 57 D6
Mubi 53 F1
Muckadilla ... 63 A4
Muconda 56 G4
Mucuri 93 F6
Mudanjiang .. 35 B7
Mudanya 23 D7
Mudgee 63 B4
Mufulira 59 A5
Muğla 23 F7
Mugu 40 C4
Muhammad Qol 52 D6
Mühlhausen .. 14 C6
Mühlig Hofmann
fjell 96 B7
Mukacheve ... 17 D6
Mukachevo =
Mukacheve .. 17 D6
Mukah 37 D4
Mukden =
Shenyang ... 35 B7
Mukomuko ... 37 E2
Muktsar 42 D9
Mukur 42 C5
Mula 19 C5
Mulchén 94 D2
Mulde → 15 C7
Mulgathing .. 62 B1
Mulgrave 69 D4
Mulhacén ... 18 D4
Mulhouse ... 13 C7
Mull 10 C4
Mullengudgery 63 B4
Muller,
Pegunungan 37 D4
Mullingar 11 E3
Mullumbimby . 63 A5
Multan 42 D7
Mulwala 63 C4
Mumbaī =
Bombay 43 K8
Mumbwa 59 A5
Muna 39 F2
München 15 D6

Munchen-
Gladbach =
Mönchengladbach
.... 14 C4
Muncie 72 D3
Mundala 39 E6
Münden 14 C5
Mundo Novo .. 93 E5
Mungallala 63 A4
Mungallala
Cr. → 63 A4
Mungbere 57 D5
Munger 40 E6
Mungindi 63 A4
Munhango 58 A3
Munich =
München ... 15 D6
Muñoz Gamero,
Pen......... 95 G2
Münster 14 C4
Munster □ ... 11 E2
Muntok 37 E3
Mupa 58 B3
Muqdisho ... 49 G4
Murallón,
Cuerro 95 F2
Murang'a 57 E7
Murashi 24 B6
Muratlı 22 D6
Murchison → . 60 F1
Murchison, Mt. 96 B15
Murchison Falls
= Kabarega
Falls 57 D6
Murcia 19 C5
Murcia □ 19 D5
Mureş → 16 E5
Mureşul =
Mureş → .. 16 E5
Murfreesboro . 74 B4
Murgab =
Murghob .. 29 F8
Murghob 29 F8
Murgon 63 A5
Müritz-see ... 15 B7
Murmansk 28 C4
Murom 24 B5
Muroran 32 F12
Muroto-Misaki . 32 C4
Murray → ... 62 C2
Murray Bridge . 62 C2
Murree 42 C8
Murrumbidgee →
.... 62 B3
Murrumburrah 63 B4
Murrurundi ... 63 B5
Murtoa 62 C3
Murwara 40 F3
Murwillumbah . 63 A5
Mürzzuschlag . 15 E8
Muş 46 C5
Mûsa, G. 47 E3
Musa Khel .. 42 D6
Müsá Qal'eh .. 42 C4
Musaffargarh .. 42 D7
Musala, Bulgaria 22 C4
Musala,
Indonesia ... 37 D1
Musay'īd 44 E2
Muscat =
Masqat 45 F4
Muscat & Oman
= Oman ■ .. 48 C6
Muscatine 77 E9
Musgrave Ras. 60 F5
Mushie 56 E3
Musi → 37 E2
Muskogee 79 B6
Musmar 53 E6

Musoma 57 E6
Mussoorie 42 D11
Mustafakemalpaşa
.... 23 D7
Mustang 40 C4
Musters, L. ... 95 F3
Muswellbrook . 63 B5
Mût, Egypt ... 52 C4
Mut, Turkey ... 46 C3
Mutare 59 B6
Muting 39 F6
Mutoray 30 C8
Muxima 56 F2
Muynak 29 E6
Muzaffarabad . 42 B8
Muzaffarnagar . 42 E10
Muzaffarpur ... 40 D5
Muzhi 28 C7
Muztag 34 C3
Mvuma 59 B6
Mwanza,
Tanzania 57 E6
Mwanza,
Dem. Rep. of the Congo
.... 57 F5
Mweka 56 E4
Mwenezi 59 C6
Mwenga 57 E5
Mweru, L. 57 F5
Mwinilunga ... 58 A4
My Tho 36 B3
Myanaung ... 41 H10
Myanmar =
Burma ■ ... 41 G11
Myaungmya .. 41 J10
Mycenæ 23 F4
Myeik Kyunzu . 36 B1
Myingyan 41 G10
Myitkyina 41 E11
Mykolayiv ... 25 D3
Mymensingh .. 41 E8
Mysia 23 E6
Mysore =
Karnataka □ . 43 N10
Mysore 43 N10
Myszków 16 C4
Mytishchi 24 B4

N

Na Hearadh =
Harris 10 C3
Naab → 15 D7
Naberezhnyye
Chelny 29 D6
Nabeul 52 A1
Nabire 39 E5
Nablus =
Nābulus 46 D3
Nābulus 46 D3
Nachingwea .. 57 G7
Nackara 62 B2
Nacogdoches . 79 D6
Nacozari 84 A3
Nadiad 43 H8
Nadūshan 44 C3
Nadvirna 17 D7
Nadvornaya =
Nadvirna ... 17 D7
Nadym 28 C8
Nadym → ... 28 C8
Nafada 55 F7
Nafūd ad Dahy 47 G6
Nafud Desert =
An Nafūd ... 47 E5
Naga 38 B2

Nagaland □ ... 41 E10
Nagano 32 A6
Nagaoka 33 G11
Nagappattinam 43 P11
Nagar Parkar .. 43 G7
Nagasaki 32 C1
Nagaur 42 F8
Nagercoil 43 Q10
Nagīneh 44 C4
Nagoya 32 B5
Nagpur 43 J11
Nagykanizsa .. 16 E3
Nagykörös ... 16 E4
Nahanni Butte . 70 B7
Nahāvand ... 46 D7
Nā'ifah 48 D5
Nain, Canada .. 68 C4
Nā'īn, Iran ... 44 C3
Nairn 10 C5
Nairobi 57 E7
Naivasha 57 E7
Najafābad 44 C2
Najd 47 F5
Najibabad 42 E11
Nakamura ... 32 C3
Nakfa 53 E6
Nakhichevan =
Naxçıvan ... 25 F6
Nakhichevan
Republic □ =
Naxçıvan □ . 25 F6
Nakhodka 31 E11
Nakhon Phanom 36 A2
Nakhon
Ratchasima . 36 B2
Nakhon Sawan 36 A2
Nakhon Si
Thammarat . 36 C2
Nakina 69 C2
Nakuru 57 E7
Nal → 42 G4
Nalchik 25 E5
Nalgonda 43 L11
Nallamalai Hills 43 M11
Nālūt 52 B1
Nam Co 34 C4
Nam-Phan ... 36 B3
Namacurra 59 B7
Namak,
Daryācheh-ye 44 C3
Namak, Kavir-e 44 C4
Namaland ... 58 C3
Namangan ... 29 E8
Namapa 59 A7
Namber 39 E4
Nambour 63 A5
Nambucca
Heads 63 B5
Nameh 37 D5
Namib Desert =
Namibwoestyn
.... 58 C2
Namibe 58 B2
Namibia ■ 58 C3
Namibwoestyn 58 C2
Namlea 39 E3
Namoi → 63 B4
Nampa 80 D5
Nampula 59 B7
Namrole 39 E3
Namse Shankou 40 C4
Namtu 41 F11
Namur 14 C3
Namutoni 58 B3
Namwala 59 B5
Nanaimo 71 D7
Nanango 63 A5
Nanao 32 A5
Nanchang ... 35 D6

Nanching =
Nanjing 35 C6
Nanchong ... 35 C5
Nancy 13 B7
Nanda Devi ... 42 D11
Nanded 43 K10
Nandewar Ra. . 63 B5
Nandurbar ... 43 J9
Nandyal 43 M11
Nanga-Eboko .. 56 D2
Nanga Parbat . 42 B9
Nangapinoh ... 37 E4
Nangarhár □ .. 42 B7
Nangatayap ... 37 E4
Nanjing 35 C6
Nanking =
Nanjing 35 C6
Nanning 35 D5
Nanping 35 D6
Nansei-Shotō =
Ryūkyū-rettō 35 D7
Nantes 12 C3
Nanuque 93 F5
Nanusa,
Kepulauan .. 38 D3
Nanyang 35 C6
Nanyuki 57 D7
Nao, C. de la .. 19 C6
Naoetsu 32 A6
Napa 80 F2
Napier 64 C7
Naples = Nápoli 21 D5
Naples 75 F7
Napo → 90 D4
Nápoli 21 D5
Nappa Merrie . 62 A3
Nara, Japan ... 32 B4
Nara, Mali ... 55 E3
Naracoorte ... 62 C3
Naradhan ... 63 B4
Narasapur ... 40 J3
Narathiwat ... 36 C2
Narayanganj .. 41 F8
Narayanpet ... 43 L10
Narbonne ... 13 E5
Nardò 23 D2
Narew → 16 B5
Narin 42 A6
Narmada → .. 43 J8
Narooma 63 C5
Narrabri 63 B4
Narran → 63 A4
Narrandera ... 63 B4
Narromine ... 63 B4
Narsimhapur .. 43 H11
Narva 24 B2
Narvik 8 E11
Naryan-Mar ... 28 C6
Naryilco 62 A3
Narym 29 D9
Narymskoye .. 29 E9
Naryn 29 E8
Nasarawa ... 55 G6
Naseby 65 F4
Naser, Buheirat
en 52 D5
Nashville 74 A4
Nasik 43 K8
Nasirabad ... 42 F9
Nassau 86 A4
Nassau, B. .. 95 H3
Nasser, L. =
Naser,
Buheirat en . 52 D5
Nat Kyizin 41 K11
Nata 59 C5
Natagaima 90 C3
Natal, Brazil ... 92 D6
Natal, Indonesia 37 D1

Naţanz 44 C2
Natashquan ... 69 C4
Natashquan - ► 69 C4
Natchez 79 D8
Nathalia 63 C4
Nathdwara 43 G8
Natitingou 55 F5
Natron, L. 57 E7
Natuna Besar,
　Kepulauan .. 37 D3
Natuna Is. =
　Natuna Besar,
　Kepulauan .. 37 D3
Natuna Selatan,
　Kepulauan .. 37 D3
Naturaliste, C. . 62 D4
Naumburg 15 C6
Nauru ■ 64 K11
Naushahra =
　Nowshera ... 42 B8
Nauta 90 D4
Nautanwa 40 D4
Navahrudak ... 17 B7
Navalmoral de
　la Mata 18 C3
Navarino, I. ... 95 H3
Navarra □ 19 A5
Năvodari 22 B7
Navoi = Nawoiy 29 E7
Navojoa 84 B3
Návpaktos 23 E3
Návplion 23 F4
Navsari 43 J8
Nawabshah ... 42 F6
Nawakot 40 D5
Nawalgarh 42 F9
Nawāsif, Harrat 47 G5
Nawoiy 29 E7
Naxçivan 25 F6
Naxçivan □ ... 25 F6
Náxos 23 F5
Năy Band 44 E3
Nazas - ► 84 B4
Nazilli 23 F7
Nazir Hat 41 F8
Ncheu 59 A6
Ndalatando ... 56 F2
Ndélé 56 C4
Ndendé 56 E2
Ndjamena 53 F1
Ndjolé 56 E2
Ndola 59 A5
Neagh, Lough . 11 D3
Near Is. 71 C1
Neath 11 F5
Nebine Cr. - ► . 63 A4
Nebitdag 29 F6
Nebraska □ ... 76 E5
Néckar - ► 14 D5
Necochea 94 D5
Neemuch =
　Nimach 43 G9
Neepawa 71 C10
Nefta 54 B6
Neftçala 46 C7
Negapatam =
　Nagappattinam
　.......... 43 P11
Negele 49 F2
Negombo 43 R11
Negotin 22 B4
Negra Pt. 38 A2
Negrais, C. =
　Maudin Sun . 41 K10
Negro - ►,
　Argentina ... 95 E4
Negro - ►, Brazil 90 D6

Negro - ►,
　Uruguay 94 C5
Negros 38 C2
Nehbandān ... 45 D5
Nei Monggol
　Zizhiqu □ ... 35 B6
Neijiang 35 D5
Neiva 90 C3
Nejd = Najd . 47 F5
Nekemte 53 G6
Nellore 43 M11
Nelson, Canada 71 D8
Nelson, N.Z. .. 65 D5
Nelson - ► 71 C10
Nelson, C. 62 C3
Nelson, Estrecho 95 G2
Nelspruit 59 D6
Néma 55 E3
Neman - ► 24 B1
Nemunas =
　Neman - ► .. 24 B1
Nemuro 32 F13
Nemuro-Kaikyō 32 F13
Nenagh 11 E2
Nenana 71 B5
Nenjiang 35 B7
Nepal ■ 40 D5
Nepalganj 40 C3
Neretva - ► ... 20 C6
Ness, L. 10 C4
Nesterov 17 C6
Nesvizh =
　Nyasvizh ... 17 B8
Netherlands ■ . 14 B3
Netherlands
　Antilles ■ ... 87 D6
Nettilling L. ... 68 B3
Neubrandenburg
　.......... 15 B7
Neuchâtel 13 C7
Neuchâtel, Lac
　de 13 C7
Neumünster .. 14 A5
Neunkirchen .. 14 D4
Neuquén 94 D3
Neuruppin 15 B7
Neustrelitz 15 B7
Neva - ► 24 B3
Nevada □ 80 F5
Nevada, Sierra,
　Spain 18 D4
Nevada, Sierra,
　U.S.A. 80 F3
Nevers 13 C5
Nevertire 63 B4
Nevinnomyssk 25 E5
Nevis 87 C7
Nevşehir 46 C3
New Amsterdam 90 B7
New Angledool 63 A4
New Bedford .. 73 D10
New Bern 75 B9
New Brighton . 65 E5
New Britain,
　Papua N. G. . 64 K10
New Britain,
　U.S.A. 73 D9
New
　Brunswick □ 69 D4
New
　Caledonia ■ . 64 M11
New Delhi 42 E10
New England
　Ra. 63 B5
New Glasgow . 69 D4
New Guinea .. 64
New
　Hampshire □ 73 C10
New Haven ... 73 D9

New Hebrides =
　Vanuatu ■ .. 64 L11
New Ireland ... 64 K10
New Jersey □ . 73 E9
New London .. 73 D9
New Mexico □ 83 C9
New Norfolk .. 62 D4
New Orleans .. 79 E8
New Plymouth 64 C6
New Providence 86 A4
New Siberian Is.
　=
　Novosibirskiye
　Ostrova 31 B12
New South
　Wales □ 63 B4
New
　Westminster 71 D7
New York □ ... 73 C8
New York City . 73 D9
New Zealand ■ 64 D7
Newala 57 G7
Newark 73 D8
Newburgh 73 D8
Newbury 11 F6
Newcastle,
　Australia 63 B5
Newcastle,
　S. Africa 59 D5
Newcastle-upon-
　Tyne 11 D6
Newfoundland □
　.......... 69 C5
Newman 60 E2
Newport,
　I. of W., U.K. 11 F6
Newport, Newp.,
　U.K. 11 F5
Newport, U.S.A. 73 D10
Newport News 73 F7
Newquay 11 F4
Newry 11 D3
Newton Boyd . 63 A5
Neya 24 B5
Neyrīz 44 D3
Neyshābūr ... 44 B4
Nezhin = Nizhyn 24 C3
Ngabang 37 D3
Ngabordamlu,
　Tanjung ... 39 F4
Ngami
　Depression .. 58 C4
Nganglong
　Kangri 40 A3
Ngaoundéré .. 56 C2
Ngapara 65 F4
Ngoring Hu ... 34 C4
Ngudu 57 E6
Nguigmi 53 F1
Nguru 55 F7
Nha Trang ... 36 B3
Nhill 62 C3
Niafounké 55 E4
Niagara Falls,
　Canada 69 D3
Niagara Falls,
　U.S.A. 73 C6
Niah 37 D4
Niamey 55 F5
Niangara 57 D5
Nias 37 D1
Nicaragua ■ .. 85 E7
Nicaragua, L. de 85 E7
Nicastro 21 E6
Nice 13 E7
Nichinan 33 D2
Nicobar Is. 27 J13
Nicosia 46 D3
Nicoya, Pen. de 85 F7

Niedersachsen □
　.......... 14 B5
Niemen =
　Neman - ► .. 24 B1
Nienburg 14 B5
Nieuw
　Amsterdam . 92 A2
Nieuw Nickerie 92 A2
Niğde ■ 46 C3
Niger ■ 55 E6
Niger - ► 55 G6
Nigeria ■ 55 G6
Nightcaps 65 F3
Nii-Jima 32 B6
Niigata 33 G11
Niihama 32 C3
Niihau 82
Nijmegen 14 C3
Nikiniki 39 F2
Nikki 55 G5
Nikolayev =
　Mykolayiv ... 25 D3
Nikolayevsk ... 24 C6
Nikopol 25 D3
Nīkshahr 45 E5
Nikšić 22 C2
Nîl, Nahr en - ► 52 B5
Nîl el Abyad - ► 53 E5
Nîl el Azraq - ► 53 E5
Nile = Nîl, Nahr
　en - ► 52 B5
Nimach 43 G9
Nîmes 13 E6
Nimfaíon, Ákra
　= Pínnes,
　Ákra 23 D5
Nimmitabel ... 63 C4
Nīmrūz □ 45 D5
Nimule 57 E6
Nīnawá 46 C5
Nindigully 63 A4
Nineveh =
　Nīnawá 46 C5
Ningbo 35 D7
Ningde 35 D6
Ningpo =
　Ningbo 35 D7
Ningsia Hui A.R.
　= Ningxia
　Huizu
　Zizhiqu □ ... 35 C5
Ningxia Huizu
　Zizhiqu □ ... 35 C5
Niobrara - ► .. 76 D5
Nioro du Sahel 55 E3
Niort 12 C3
Nipawin 71 C9
Nipigon, L. ... 69 D2
Niquelândia ... 93 E4
Nirmal 43 K11
Nirmali 40 D6
Niš 22 C3
Nişāb, Si. Arabia 47 E6
Nişāb, Yemen . 49 E4
Nishinomiya .. 32 B4
Nistru =
　Dnister - ► .. 17 E10
Niţă' 47 F7
Niterói 93 G5
Nitra 16 D4
Nitra - ► 16 E4
Niue 65 L14
Niut 37 D4
Nivernais 13 C5
Nizamabad ... 43 K11
Nizamghat ... 41 C10
Nizhne-Vartovsk 29 C8
Nizhneyansk .. 31 B11
Nizhniy
　Novgorod ... 24 B5

Nizhniy Tagil . . 29 D6
Nizhyn 24 C3
Nizip 46 C4
Nízké Tatry . . . 16 D4
Njombe 57 F6
Nkambe 55 G7
Nkawkaw 55 G4
Nkhata Bay . . 57 G6
Nkhota Kota . . 59 A6
Nkongsamba . . 56 D1
Nmai ⇢ 41 E11
Noakhali =
  Maijdi 41 F8
Noatak 71 B3
Nobeoka 32 C2
Nocera Inferiore 21 D5
Nockatunga . . . 62 A3
Nogales, *Mexico* 84 A2
Nogales, *U.S.A.* 83 E7
Nōgata 32 C2
Noginsk 30 C7
Noire, Mts. 12 B2
Noirmoutier, I.
  de 12 C2
Nok Kundi . . 42 E3
Nokhtuysk 30 C9
Nokomis 71 C9
Nola 56 D3
Nome 71 B3
Nong Khai 36 A2
Noondoo 63 A4
Nóqui 56 F2
Noranda 69 D3
Nord-Ostsee-
  Kanal ⇢ . . . 14 A5
Nordegg 71 C8
Norderney . . . 14 B4
Norderstedt . . . 14 B5
Nordfriesische
  Inseln 14 A5
Nordhausen . . 14 C6
Nordkapp 8 D13
Nordrhein-
  Westfalen □ . 14 C4
Nordvik 30 B9
Norfolk 73 F7
Norfolk I. 64 M11
Norilsk 30 C6
Norley 63 A3
Norman 78 B5
Norman Wells . 70 B7
Normandie . . . 12 B4
Normandy =
  Normandie . . 12 B4
Normanton . . . 61 D7
Norquinco 95 E2
Norrköping . . . 9 G11
Norrland 8 F11
Norseman 60 G3
North Battleford 71 C9
North Bay 69 D3
North Bend . . . 80 D1
North C. 64 A5
North Cape =
  Nordkapp . . . 8 D13
North
  Carolina □ . . 75 B7
North Channel,
  Canada 69 D2
North Channel,
  U.K. 11 D4
North Dakota □ 76 B4
North Frisian Is.
  =
  Nordfriesische
  Inseln 14 A5
North I. 64 B5
North Korea ■ 35 C7

North
  Lakhimpur . . 41 D10
North Minch . . 10 B4
North Ossetia □ 25 E5
North Pagai, I. =
  Pagai Utara . 37 E2
North Platte . . 76 E4
North Platte ⇢ 76 E4
North Rhine
  Westphalia □
  = Nordrhein-
  Westfalen □ . 14 C4
North
  Saskatchewan ⇢
  . . . . 71 C8
North Sea 10 D8
North Sporades
  = Voríai
  Sporádhes . . 23 E4
North Taranaki
  Bight 64 C6
North
  Thompson ⇢ 71 C7
North Uist . . . 10 C3
North West C. . 60 E1
North West
  Frontier □ . . 42 B8
North West
  Highlands . . . 10 C4
North West
  River 69 C4
North West
  Territories □ 70 B7
Northampton . . 11 E6
Northern Circars 40 J4
Northern
  Ireland □ . . . 11 D3
Northern
  Marianas ■ . 64 H9
Northern
  Territory □ . . 60 D5
Northland □ . . 64 A5
Northumberland,
  C. 62 C3
Northumberland
  Str. 69 D4
Norton Sd. . . . 71 B3
Norway ■ 8 F10
Norway House 71 C10
Norwegian Sea 6 B5
Norwich 11 E7
Nosok 28 B9
Noṣratābād . . . 45 D4
Nossob ⇢ . . . 58 D4
Nosy Bé 59 G9
Nosy Boraha . . 59 H9
Nosy Mitsio . . 59 G9
Nosy Varika . . 59 J9
Noteć ⇢ 16 B2
Noto-Hanto . . . 33 G11
Notre Dame B. 69 D5
Notre Dame de
  Koartac =
  Quaqtaq 68 B4
Notre Dame
  d'Ivugivic =
  Ivujivik 68 B3
Nottaway ⇢ . . 69 C3
Nottingham . . . 11 E6
Nouâdhibou . . 54 D1
Nouâdhibou,
  Ras 54 D1
Nouakchott . . . 55 E1
Nouméa 64 M11
Noupoort 58 E4
Nouveau
  Comptoir =
  Wemindji . . . 69 C3

Nouvelle-
  Calédonie =
  New
  Caledonia ■ . 64 M11
Nova Casa Nova 93 D5
Nova Cruz 92 D6
Nova Friburgo . 93 G5
Nova Gaia =
  Cambundi-
  Catembo 56 G3
Nova Iguaçu . . 93 G5
Nova Iorque . . 92 D5
Nova Lima 93 F5
Nova Mambone 59 C7
Nova Scotia □ . 69 D4
Nova Sofala . . . 59 C6
Nova Venécia . 93 F5
Nova Zagora . . 22 C5
Novara 20 B2
Novaya Ladoga 24 A3
Novaya Lyalya 29 D7
Novaya Zemlya 28 B6
Nové Zámky . . 16 D4
Novgorod 24 B3
Novgorod-
  Severskiy =
  Novhorod-
  Siverskyy . . . 24 C3
Novhorod-
  Siverskyy . . . 24 C3
Novi Lígure . . . 20 B2
Novi Pazar 22 C3
Novi Sad 22 B2
Novo Mesto . . . 20 B5
Novo Remanso 93 D5
Novoataysk . . . 29 D9
Novocherkassk 25 D5
Novogrudok =
  Navahrudak . 17 B7
Novohrad-
  Volynskyy . . . 17 C8
Novokazalinsk =
  Zhangaqazaly 29 E7
Novokuybyshevsk
  . . . . 24 C6
Novokuznetsk . 29 D9
Novomoskovsk 24 C4
Novorossiysk . . 25 E4
Novorybnoye . 30 B8
Novoselytsya . 17 D8
Novoshakhtinsk 25 D4
Novosibirsk . . . 29 D9
Novosibirskiye
  Ostrova 31 B12
Novotroitsk . . . 29 D6
Novouzensk . . . 24 C6
Novovolynsk . . 17 C7
Novska 20 B6
Novyy Port . . . 28 C8
Now Shahr 44 B2
Nowa Sól 16 C2
Nowgong 41 D9
Nowra 63 B5
Nowshera 42 B8
Nowy Sącz 16 D5
Nowy Targ 16 D5
Nowy Tomyśl . . 16 B3
Noyon 13 B5
Nsanje 59 B7
Nsawam 55 G4
Nsukka 55 G6
Nubian Desert =
  Nûbîya, Es
  Sahrâ En . . . 52 D5
Nûbîya, Es
  Sahrâ En . . . 52 D5
Nuboai 39 E5
Nueltin L. 70 B10
Nueva Imperial 94 D2

Nueva Rosita . . 84 B4
Nuéve de Julio 94 D4
Nuevitas 86 B4
Nuevo, G. 95 E4
Nuevo Laredo . 84 B5
Nugget Pt. 65 G3
Nuhaka 64 C7
Nukey Bluff . . 62 B2
Nukheila 53 E4
Nukus 29 E6
Nulato 71 B4
Nullarbor Plain 60 G4
Numalla, L. . . . 63 A3
Numan 53 G1
Numazu 32 B6
Numfoor 39 E4
Numurkah 63 C4
Nunavut □ . . . 66 C10
Nuneaton 11 E6
Nunivak I. 71 B3
Nunkun 42 C10
Núoro 21 D2
Nuremberg =
  Nürnberg . . . 15 D6
Nuriootpa 62 B2
Nürnberg 15 D6
Nurran, L. =
  Terewah, L. . 63 A4
Nusa Tenggara
  Barat □ 37 F5
Nusa Tenggara
  Timur □ 39 F2
Nushki 42 E5
Nutak 68 C4
Nuuk 68 B5
Nuwakot 40 C4
Nuweveldberge 58 E4
Nuyts Arch. . . . 62 B1
Nyah West . . . 62 C3
Nyahanga 57 E6
Nyahururu 57 D7
Nyainqentanglha
  Shan 34 C4
Nyâlâ 53 F3
Nyasa, L. =
  Malawi, L. . . 59 A6
Nyasvizh 17 B8
Nyda 28 C8
Nyeri 57 E7
Nyíregyháza . . 17 E5
Nylstroom 59 C5
Nymagee 63 B4
Nyngan 63 B4
Nyoman =
  Neman ⇢ . . . 24 B1
Nysa 16 C3
Nysa ⇢ 16 B2
Nyurbe 30 C9
Nzega 57 E6
N'Zérékoré . . . 55 G3
Nzeto 56 F2

O

Ō-Shima 32 B6
Oahe, L. 76 C4
Oahu 82 H12
Oak Ridge . . . 75 A5
Oakbank 62 B3
Oakey 63 A5
Oakland 82 B1
Oamaru 65 F4
Oates Land . . . 96 A15
Oaxaca 84 D5
Ob ⇢ 28 C7

Oba	69	D2	Okavango			Omul, Vf.	17	F7	Orense	18	A2
Oban	10	C4	Swamps	58	B4	Ōmura	32	C1	Orepuki	65	G2
Obbia	49	F4	Okaya	32	A6	Omuramba			Øresund	9	G10
Oberhausen	14	C4	Okayama	32	B3	Omatako →	58	B4	Orgaz	18	C4
Oberon	63	B4	Okazaki	32	B5	Ōmuta	32	C2	Orgeyev =		
Obi, Kepulauan	39	E3	Okeechobee, L.	75	F7	Onang	39	E1	Orhei	17	E9
Obi Is. = Obi,			Okefenokee			Oncócua	58	B2	Orgün	45	C7
Kepulauan	39	E3	Swamp	75	D6	Onda	19	C5	Orhaneli	23	E7
Óbidos	92	C2	Okhotsk, Sea of	31	D12	Ondangua	58	B3	Orhangazi	23	D7
Obihiro	32	F12	Oki-Shotō	32	A3	Ondo	55	G5	Orhei	17	E9
Obilatu	39	E3	Okiep	58	D3	Öndörhaan	35	B6	Orhon Gol →	35	A5
Obo	57	C5	Okinawa-Jima	35	D7	Onega →	28	C4	Orient	62	A3
Obozerskaya =			Oklahoma □	78	B5	Onega →	8	F15	Oriental,		
Obozerskiy	28	C5	Oklahoma City	78	B5	Onega, G. of =			Cordillera	90	B4
Obozerskiy	28	C5	Okmulgee	79	B6	Onezhskaya			Orihuela	19	C5
Obskaya Guba	28	C8	Oknitsa =			Guba	28	C4	Orinoco →	90	B6
Obuasi	55	G4	Ocniţa	17	D8	Onega, L. =			Orissa □	40	G5
Ocala	75	E6	Okrika	55	H6	Onezhskoye			Oristano	21	E2
Ocaña	18	C4	Oktabrsk =			Ozero	28	C4	Oristano, G. di	21	E2
Occidental,			Oktyabrsk	29	E6	Onehunga	64	B6	Orizaba	84	D5
Cordillera	90	C3	Oktyabrsk	29	E6	Oneşti	17	E8	Orkney Is.	10	B5
Ocean I. =			Oktyabrskiy =			Onezhskaya			Orlando	75	E7
Banaba	64	K11	Aktsyabrski	17	B9	Guba	28	C4	Orléanais	12	C5
Oceanside	82	D4	Oktyabrskoy			Onezhskoye			Orléans	12	C4
Ocniţa	17	D8	Revolyutsii,			Ozero	28	C4	Ormara	42	G4
Ocumare del			Os.	30	B7	Ongarue	64	C6	Ormoc	38	B2
Tuy	90	A5	Oktyabrskoye	28	C7	Onilahy →	59	J8	Ormond	64	C7
Odate	33	F12	Okuru	65	E3	Onitsha	55	G6	Örnsköldsvik	8	F11
Odawara	32	B6	Okushiri-Tō	32	F11	Onoda	32	B2	Orocué	90	C4
Oddur	49	G3	Öland	9	G11	Ontario □	69	D2	Orol Dengizi =		
Ödemiş	23	E7	Olary	62	B3	Ontario, L.	73	C7	Aral Sea	29	E6
Odense	9	G10	Olavarría	94	D4	Oodnadatta	62	A2	Oroquieta	38	C2
Oder →	15	B8	Oława	16	C3	Oostende	14	C2	Orós	92	D6
Odesa	25	D3	Ólbia	20	D2	Ootacamund	43	P10	Orosháza	16	E5
Odessa = Odesa	25	D3	Old Crow	70	B6	Opala	56	E4	Orroroo	62	B2
Odessa	78	D2	Oldenburg	14	B5	Opava	16	D3	Orsha	24	C3
Odienné	55	G3	Oldham	11	E5	Opole	16	C3	Orsk	29	D6
Odintsovo	24	B4	Olekma →	31	C10	Oporto = Porto	18	B1	Orşova	22	B4
Odorheiu			Olekminsk	31	C10	Opotiki	64	C7	Ortaca	23	F7
Secuiesc	17	E7	Oleksandriya	17	C8	Opua	64	A6	Ortegal, C.	18	A2
Odra = Oder →	15	B8	Olenek	30	C9	Opunake	64	C5	Orthez	12	E3
Odra →	16	B2	Olenek →	30	B10	Oradea	17	E5	Ortigueira	18	A2
Oeiras	92	D5	Oléron, I. d'	12	D3	Orai	42	G11	Ortles	20	A3
Ofanto →	20	D6	Oleśnica	16	C3	Oral =			Ortón →	91	F5
Offa	55	G5	Olevsk	17	C8	Zhayyq →	29	E6	Orümīyeh	46	C6
Offenbach	14	C5	Olhão	18	D2	Oral	24	C7	Orümīyeh,		
Offenburg	14	D4	Olifants →	59	C6	Oran, Algeria	54	A4	Daryācheh-ye	46	C6
Oga-Hantō	33	G11	Ólimbos, Óros	23	D4	Oran, Argentina	94	A4	Oruro	91	G5
Ōgaki	32	B5	Olinda	92	D7	Orange =			Oruzgān □	42	C5
Ogbomosho	55	G5	Oliveira	93	G5	Oranje →	58	D3	Orvieto	20	C4
Ogden	81	E8	Olivenza	18	C2	Orange,			Oryakhovo	22	C4
Ogdensburg	73	B8	Ollagüe	91	H5	Australia	63	B4	Ōsaka	32	B4
Oglio →	20	B3	Olomouc	16	D3	Orange, France	13	D6	Ösel =		
Ogooué →	56	E1	Olongapo	38	B2	Orange, U.S.A.	79	D7	Saaremaa	24	B1
Ogowe =			Olot	19	A7	Orange, C.	92	B3	Osh	29	E8
Ogooué →	56	E1	Olsztyn	16	B5	Orangeburg	75	C7	Oshawa	69	D3
Ohai	65	F2	Olt →	22	C5	Oranienburg	15	B7	Oshkosh	76	E3
Ohakune	64	C6	Olteniţa	22	B6	Oranje →	58	D3	Oshmyany =		
Ohanet	54	C6	Oltu	46	B5	Oranjemund	58	D3	Ashmyany	17	A7
Ohau, L.	65	F3	Olympia, Greece	23	F3	Oras	38	B3	Oshogbo	55	G5
Ohio □	72	D4	Olympia, U.S.A.	80	B2	Oraşul Stalin =			Oshwe	56	E3
Ohio →	72	F1	Olympic Mts. =			Braşov	17	F7	Osijek	20	B7
Ohre →	16	C2	Olympus, Mt. =			Orbetello	20	C3	Osipenko =		
Ohrid	22	D3	Ólimbos, Óros	23	D4	Orbost	63	C4	Berdyansk	25	D4
Ohridsko Jezero	23	D3	Om →	29	D8	Orchila, I.	90	A5	Osipovichi =		
Oise →	12	B5	Omagh	11	D3	Ordos = Mu Us			Asipovichy	17	B9
Ōita	32	C2	Omaha	77	E7	Shamo	35	C5	Oskarshamn	9	G11
Oiticica	92	D5	Oman ■	48	C6	Ordu	46	B4	Öskemen	29	E9
Ojos del Salado,			Oman, G. of	45	E4	Ordzhonikidze =			Oslo	9	G10
Cerro	94	B3	Omaruru	58	C3	Vladikavkaz	25	E5	Oslob	38	C2
Oka →	28	D5	Omate	91	G4	Ore Mts. =			Oslofjorden	9	G10
Okaba	39	F5	Ombai, Selat	39	F2	Erzgebirge	15	C7	Osmanabad	43	K10
Okahandja	58	C3	Omboué	56	E1	Örebro	9	G11	Osmaniye	46	C4
Okahukura	64	C6	Ombrone →	20	C3	Oregon □	80	C3	Osnabrück	14	B5
Okandja	56	E2	Omdurmân	53	E5	Orekhovo-			Osorio	94	B6
Okanogan →	80	A4	Ometepec	84	D5	Zuyevo	24	B4	Osorno	95	E2
Okara	42	D8	Ōmiya	32	B6	Orel	24	C4	Ossa, Mt.	62	D4
Okarito	65	E4	Omo →	53	G6	Ören	23	F6	Óssa, Oros	23	E4
Okaukuejo	58	B3	Omsk	29	D8	Orenburg	29	D6	Ostend =		
									Oostende	14	C2

Oster 17 C10
Österdalälven . 8 F10
Östersund 8 F10
Ostfriesische
  Inseln 14 B4
Ostrava 16 D4
Ostróda 16 B4
Ostroh 17 C8
Ostrołęka 16 B5
Ostrów
  Mazowiecka . 16 B5
Ostrów
  Wielkopolski 16 C3
Ostrowiec-
  Świętokrzyski 16 C5
Ostuni 21 D6
Ôsumi-Kaikyō . 33 D2
Osuna 18 D3
Oswego 73 C7
Oświęcim 16 C4
Otago □ 65 F3
Otago Harbour 65 F4
Ōtake 32 B3
Otaki 64 D6
Otaru 32 F12
Otaru-Wan =
  Ishikari-Wan . 32 F12
Otavalo 90 C3
Otavi 58 B3
Otira Gorge ... 65 E4
Otjiwarongo . 58 C3
Otorohanga ... 64 C6
Otranto 23 D2
Otranto, C. d' . 23 D2
Otranto, Str. of 23 D2
Ōtsu 32 B4
Ottawa 69 D3
Ottawa Is. 68 C2
Ottumwa 77 E8
Oturkpo 55 G6
Otway, B. 95 G2
Otway, C. 62 C3
Otwock 16 B5
Ouachita Mts. . 79 B6
Ouadâne 54 D2
Ouadda 56 C4
Ouagadougou . 55 F4
Ouahran = Oran 54 A4
Ouallene 54 D5
Ouanda Djallé . 56 C4
Ouango 56 D4
Ouargla 54 B6
Ouarzazate ... 54 B3
Oubangi → ... 56 E3
Oudtshoorn ... 58 E4
Ouessant, I. d' . 12 B1
Ouesso 56 D3
Ouezzane 54 B3
Ouidah 55 G5
Oujda 54 B4
Oujeft 55 D2
Ouled Djellal . 54 B6
Oulu 8 E13
Oulujärvi 8 F13
Oulujoki → ... 8 E13
Oum Chalouba 53 E3
Ounianga-Kébir 53 E3
Ounianga Sérir 53 E3
Ourense =
  Orense 18 A2
Ouricuri 92 D5
Ouro Prêto ... 93 G5
Ouse 62 D4
Outer Hebrides 10 C3
Outjo 58 C2
Ouyen 62 C3
Ovalle 94 C2
Ovamboland . 58 B3
Oviedo 18 A3

Ovruch 17 C9
Owaka 65 G3
Owambo =
  Ovamboland 58 B3
Owase 32 B5
Owbeh 42 B3
Owen Sound . 69 D2
Owen Stanley
  Ra. 61 B8
Owendo 56 D1
Owo 55 G6
Owyhee → ... 80 D5
Oxford, N.Z. ... 65 E5
Oxford, U.K. .. 11 F6
Oxley 63 B3
Oxnard 82 C3
Oxus =
  Amudarya → 29 E6
Oya 37 D4
Oyama 32 A6
Oyem 56 D2
Uyo 55 G5
Ozamiz 38 C2
Ozark Plateau . 79 A8
Ózd 16 D5

P

Paamiut 68 B6
Pa-an 41 J11
Paarl 58 E3
Pab Hills 42 F5
Pabianice 16 C4
Pabna 41 E7
Pacaja → 92 C3
Pacaraima,
  Sierra 90 C6
Pacasmayo ... 91 E3
Pachpadra ... 42 G8
Pachuca 84 C5
Padaido,
  Kepulauan .. 39 E5
Padang 37 E2
Padangpanjang 37 E2
Padangsidempuan
  .... 37 D1
Paderborn ... 14 C5
Pádova 20 B3
Padua = Pádova 20 B3
Paducah 72 F1
Paeroa 64 B6
Pafúri 59 C6
Pag 20 B5
Pagadian 38 C2
Pagai Selatan, P. 37 E2
Pagai Utara ... 37 E2
Pagalu =
  Annobón ... 51 G4
Pagastikós
  Kólpos 23 E4
Pagatan 37 E5
Pahiatua 64 D6
Painan 37 E2
Paint Hills =
  Wemindji ... 69 C3
Painted Desert . 83 C7
País Vasco □ .. 19 A4
Paisley 10 D4
Paita 90 E2
Pajares, Puerto
  de 18 A3
Pakaraima Mts. 90 B6
Pakistan ■ ... 42 E7
Pakokku 41 G10
Pakse 36 A3
Paktīā □ 42 C6

Pala 53 G2
Palagruža 20 C6
Palam 43 K10
Palampur 42 C10
Palana 62 C4
Palanan 38 A2
Palanan Pt. ... 38 A2
Palangkaraya . 37 E4
Palani Hills 43 P10
Palanpur 43 G8
Palanro 39 E1
Palapye 59 C5
Palau ■ 38 C4
Palawan 36 C5
Palayankottai .. 43 Q10
Paleleh 39 D2
Palembang ... 37 E2
Palencia 18 A3
Palermo 21 E4
Palestine 79 D6
Paletwa 41 G9
Palghat 43 P10
Pali 42 G8
Palioúrion, Ákra 23 E4
Palitana 43 J7
Palk Bay 43 Q11
Palk Strait 43 Q11
Pallanza =
  Verbánia 20 B2
Palm Springs .. 82 D4
Palma 57 G8
Palma → 93 E4
Palma, B. de .. 19 C7
Palma de
  Mallorca 19 C7
Palmares 92 D6
Palmas, C. ... 55 H3
Pálmas, G. di . 21 E2
Palmeira dos
  Índios 93 D6
Palmeirinhas,
  Pta. das 56 F2
Palmer 71 B5
Palmer Arch. .. 96 A3
Palmer Land . 96 B3
Palmerston ... 65 F4
Palmerston
  North 64 D6
Palmi 21 E5
Palmira 90 C3
Palmyra =
  Tudmur ... 46 D4
Palopo 39 E2
Palos, C. de ... 19 D5
Palu, Indonesia 39 E1
Palu, Turkey .. 46 C5
Paluan 38 B2
Pama 55 F5
Pamiers 12 E4
Pamirs 29 F8
Pamlico Sd. ... 75 B10
Pampa 78 B3
Pampa de las
  Salinas 94 C3
Pampanua ... 39 E2
Pampas,
  Argentina ... 94 D4
Pampas, Peru . 91 F4
Pamplona,
  Colombia ... 90 B4
Pamplona,
  Spain 19 A5
Panaji 43 M8
Panamá 85 F9
Panamá ■ ... 86 E4
Panamá, G. de 86 E4
Panama City . 74 D5
Panão 91 E3
Panay 38 B2

Panay, G. 38 B2
Pančevo 22 B3
Pandan 38 B2
Pandharpur ... 43 L9
Pando 94 C5
Pando, L. =
  Hope, L. 62 A2
Panevežys ... 24 B1
Panfilov 29 E8
Pang-Long ... 41 F12
Pang-Yang ... 41 F12
Pangani 57 F7
Pangfou =
  Bengbu 35 C6
Pangkajene ... 39 E1
Pangkalanbrandan
  .... 37 D1
Pangkalanbuun 37 E4
Pangkalansusu 37 D1
Pangkalpinang 37 E3
Pangkoh 37 E4
Pangnirtung ... 68 B4
Panqutaran
  Group 38 C2
Panjgur 42 F4
Panjim = Panaji 43 M8
Panjinad
  Barrage 42 E7
Panorama 94 A6
Pantar 39 F2
Pante Macassar 39 F2
Pantelleria ... 21 F3
Pánuco 84 C5
Panyam 55 G6
Paoting =
  Baoding 35 C6
Paot'ou =
  Baotou 35 B6
Paoua 56 C3
Pápa 16 E3
Papakura 64 B6
Papantla 84 C5
Papar 36 C5
Papua New
  Guinea ■ ... 61 B8
Papudo 94 C2
Papun 41 H11
Pará = Belém . 92 C4
Pará □ 92 C3
Paracatu 93 F4
Paracel Is. =
  Hsisha
  Chuntao 36 A4
Parachilna 62 B2
Parachinar ... 42 C7
Paradip 40 G6
Parado 39 F1
Paragua → .. 90 B6
Paraguaçu → . 93 E6
Paraguaná, Pen.
  de 90 A4
Paraguarí 94 B5
Paraguay ■ .. 94 A5
Paraguay → .. 94 B5
Paraíba = João
  Pessoa 92 D7
Paraíba □ 92 D6
Paraíba do
  Sul → 93 G5
Parakou 55 G5
Paramaribo .. 92 A2
Paraná,
  Argentina ... 94 C4
Paraná, Brazil . 93 E4
Paraná □ 94 A6
Paraná → 94 C5
Paranaguá ... 94 B7
Paranaíba → . 93 G3

Paranapanema

Paranapanema → 94 A6
Paranapiacaba, Serra do 94 A7
Parang, Jolo, Phil. 38 C2
Parang, Mindanao, Phil. 38 C2
Paratinga 93 E5
Paratoo 62 B2
Parattah 62 D4
Parbhani 43 K10
Parchim 15 B6
Pardo →, Bahia, Brazil . 93 F6
Pardo →, Mato Grosso, Brazil 93 G3
Pardo →, São Paulo, Brazil 93 G4
Pardubice 16 C2
Parecis, Serra dos 91 F7
Parepare 39 E1
Párga 23 E3
Pariaguán 90 B6
Pariaman 37 E2
Parigi 39 E2
Parika 90 B7
Parima, Serra . 90 C6
Parinari 90 D4
Parîngul Mare . 17 F6
Parintins 92 C2
Pariparit Kyun . 41 K9
Paris, France .. 12 B5
Paris, U.S.A. .. 79 C6
Park Range ... 81 F10
Parkersburg .. 72 E5
Parkes 63 B4
Parla 18 B4
Parma 20 B3
Parnaguá 93 E5
Parnaíba, Piauí, Brazil 92 C5
Parnaíba, São Paulo, Brazil 93 F3
Parnaíba → .. 92 C5
Parnassós 23 E4
Parnu 24 B1
Paroo → 63 B3
Páros 23 F5
Parral 94 D2
Parramatta 63 B5
Parry Sound .. 69 D3
Partinico 21 E4
Paru → 92 C3
Paruro 91 F4
Parvãn □ 42 B6
Parvatipuram .. 40 H4
Pasadena, Calif., U.S.A. 82 C3
Pasadena, Tex., U.S.A. 79 E6
Pasaje 90 D3
Pascagoula .. 79 D9
Paşcani 17 E8
Pasco 80 B4
Pasco, Cerro de 91 F3
Pashmakli = Smolyan 22 D5
Pašman 20 C5
Pasni 42 G3
Paso de Indios 95 E3
Passau 15 D7
Passero, C. .. 21 F5
Passo Fundo .. 94 B6

Passos 93 G4
Pastaza → ... 90 D3
Pasto 90 C3
Patagonia 95 F3
Patan, India ... 43 H8
Patan, Nepal .. 40 D5
Patani 39 D3
Patchewollock . 62 C3
Patea 64 C6
Pategi 55 G6
Paternò 21 F5
Paterson 73 D8
Pathankot 42 C9
Patiala 42 D10
Patkai Bum ... 41 D10
Pátmos 23 F6
Patna 40 E5
Patos, L. dos .. 94 C6
Patos de Minas 93 F4
Patquía 94 C3
Pátrai 23 E3
Pátraikós Kólpos 23 E3
Patras = Pátrai 23 E3
Patrocínio 93 F4
Pattani 36 C2
Patuakhali 41 F8
Pau 12 E3
Pauini → 90 D6
Pauk 41 G10
Paulis = Isiro . 57 D5
Paulistana 92 D5
Paulo Afonso . 93 D6
Pavia 20 B2
Pavlodar 29 D8
Pavlograd = Pavlohrad ... 25 D4
Pavlohrad ... 25 D4
Pavlovo 24 B5
Pavlovsk 24 C5
Pawtucket ... 73 D10
Paxoí 23 E3
Payakumbuh .. 37 E2
Payne Bay = Kangirsuk .. 68 C4
Paysandú 94 C5
Paz, B. la 84 C2
Pazar 46 B5
Pazardzhik 22 C5
Peace → 70 C8
Peak Hill 63 B4
Peake 62 C2
'Peake Cr. → .. 62 A2
Pebane 59 B7
Pebas 90 D4
Peć 22 C3
Pechenga 28 C4
Pechenizhyn .. 17 D7
Pechora → ... 28 C6
Pechorskaya Guba 28 C6
Pecos → 78 E3
Pécs 16 E4
Pedder, L. 62 D4
Pedirka 62 A2
Pedra Azul ... 93 F5
Pedreiras 92 C5
Pedro Afonso . 93 D4
Pedro Juan Caballero ... 94 A5
Peebinga 62 B3
Peel →, Australia 63 B5
Peel →, Canada 70 B6
Peera Peera Poolanna L. . 62 A2
Pegasus Bay .. 65 E5
Pegu 41 J11
Pegu Yoma ... 41 H10
Pehuajó 94 D4

Peine 14 B6
Peip'ing = Beijing 35 C6
Peipus, L. = Chudskoye, Oz. 24 B2
Peixe 93 E4
Pekalongan ... 37 F3
Pekanbaru 37 D2
Pekin 77 E10
Peking = Beijing 35 C6
Pelagie, Is. 21 G4
Pelaihari 37 E4
Peleaga, Vf. ... 17 F6
Peleng 39 E2
Pelješac 20 C6
Pelly → 70 B6
Pelly Bay 68 B2
Pelly L. 70 B9
Peloponnese = Pelopónnisos □ 23 F4
Pelopónnisos □ 23 F4
Peloro, C. 21 E5
Pelorus Sd. ... 65 D5
Pelotas 94 C6
Pelvoux, Massif du 13 D7
Pematangsiantar 37 D1
Pemba I. 57 F7
Pembroke, Canada 69 D3
Pembroke, U.K. 11 F4
Penang = Pinang 36 C2
Penápolis 94 A6
Peñarroya-Pueblonuevo 18 C3
Peñas, C. de .. 18 A3
Penas, G. de .. 95 F2
Pench'i = Benxi 35 B7
Pend Oreille L. 80 A5
Pendembu 55 G2
Pendleton 80 C4
Penedo 93 E6
Penguin 62 D4
Peniche 18 C1
Penida 37 F5
Peninsular Malaysia □ .. 37 D2
Penmarch, Pte. de 12 C1
Pennines 11 D5
Pennsylvania □ 73 D7
Penola 62 C3
Penong 60 G5
Penrith 63 B5
Pensacola 74 D4
Pensacola Mts. 96 C4
Penshurst 62 C3
Penticton 71 D8
Pentland Firth . 10 B5
Penza 24 C6
Penzance 11 F4
Peoria 77 E10
Perabumulih .. 37 E2
Perche, Collines du 12 B4
Perdido, Mte. . 19 A6
Perdu, Mt. = Perdido, Mte. 19 A6
Pereira 90 C3
Perekerten 62 B3
Pereyaslav-Khmelnytskyy 24 C3
Pergamino 94 C4
Péribonca → . 69 D3
Perico 94 A3
Périgueux 12 D4

Perijá, Sierra de.... 90 B4
Perlas, Arch. de las 86 E4
Perm 29 D6
Pernambuco = Recife 92 D7
Pernatty Lagoon 62 B2
Pernik 22 C4
Perpendicular Pt. 63 B5
Perpignan 13 E5
Persepolis 44 D3
Pershotravensk 17 C8
Persian Gulf = Gulf, The ... 44 E2
Perth, Australia 60 G2
Perth, U.K. 10 C5
Perth Amboy . 73 D8
Peru ■ 90 C3
Perúgia 20 C4
Pervomaysk .. 25 D3
Pervouralsk ... 29 D6
Pésaro 20 C4
Pescara 20 C5
Peshawar 42 B7
Peshkopi 22 D3
Pesqueira 92 D6
Petah Tiqwa . 46 D3
Petauke 59 A6
Peter I.s Øy ... 96 A2
Peterborough, Australia 62 B2
Peterborough, Canada 69 D3
Peterborough, U.K. 11 E6
Peterhead 10 C6
Petersburg, Alaska, U.S.A. 71 C6
Petersburg, Va., U.S.A. 73 F7
Petitsikapau, L. 69 C4
Petlad 43 H8
Peto 85 C7
Petone 65 D6
Petrich 22 D4
Petrikov = Pyetrikaw ... 17 B9
Petrograd = Sankt-Peterburg ... 24 B3
Petrolândia ... 93 D6
Petrolina 93 D5
Petropavl 29 D7
Petropavlovsk = Petropavl ... 29 D7
Petropavlovsk-Kamchatskiy 31 D13
Petrópolis 93 G5
Petrosani 17 F6
Petrovaradin .. 22 B2
Petrovsk 24 C6
Petrozavodsk .. 28 C4
Peureulak 36 D1
Pforzheim 14 D5
Phagwara 42 D9
Phalodi 42 F8
Phan Rang ... 36 B3
Phangan, Ko .. 36 C2
Phangnga 36 C2
Phatthalung .. 36 C2
Phetchabun .. 36 A2
Philadelphia .. 73 E9
Philippines ■ .. 38 B2
Philippopolis = Plovdiv 22 C5
Phillip I. 63 C4

Phillott 63 A4
Phitsanulok ... 36 A2
Phnom Dangrek 36 B2
Phnom Penh .. 36 B2
Phoenix 83 D6
Phra Nakhon Si
  Ayutthaya ... 36 B2
Phuket 36 C1
Phumiphon,
  Khuan 36 A1
Piacenza 20 B2
Pialba 63 A5
Pian Cr. → .. 63 B4
Pianosa 20 C3
Piatra Neamţ .. 17 E8
Piauí □ 92 D5
Piave → 20 B4
Pibor Post 53 G5
Pica 91 H5
Picardie 13 B5
Picardy =
  Picardie 13 B5
Pichilemu 94 C2
Pico Truncado . 95 F3
Picton, Australia 63 B5
Picton, N.Z. .. 65 D6
Pictou 69 D4
Picún Leufú ... 95 D3
Piedmont =
  Piemonte □ . 20 B1
Piedras, R. de
  las → 91 F5
Piedras Negras 84 B4
Piemonte □ ... 20 B1
Pierre Elliott
  Trudeau, Mt. . 70 B5
Piet Retief 59 D6
Pietermaritzburg 59 D6
Pietersburg ... 59 C5
Pietroşul,
  Romania 17 E7
Pigüe 94 D4
Piketberg 58 E3
Piła 16 B3
Pilar, Brazil ... 93 D6
Pilar, Paraguay 94 B5
Pilas Group ... 38 C2
Pilcomayo → . 94 B5
Pilibhit 42 E11
Pilica → 16 C5
Pílos 23 F3
Pilsen = Plzeň . 16 D1
Pimba 62 B2
Pimenta Bueno 91 F6
Pimentel 91 E3
Pinang 36 C2
Pinar del Río .. 86 B3
Pınarhisar ... 22 D6
Pińczów 16 C5
Pindiga 55 G7
Pindos Óros ... 23 E3
Pindus Mts. =
  Pindos Óros . 23 E3
Pine Bluff 79 B7
Pine Point 70 B8
Pinega → ... 28 C5
Pinerolo 20 B1
Pinetown 59 D6
Ping → 36 A2
Pingdong 35 D7
Pingliang 35 C5
Pingwu 35 C5
Pingxiang 35 D5
Pinhel 18 B2
Pini 37 D1
Piniós → 23 E4
Pinnaroo 62 C3
Pínnes, Ákra .. 23 D5
Pinrang 39 E1

Pinsk 17 B8
Pintados 91 H5
Pinyug 24 A6
Piombino 20 C3
Pioner, Os. 30 B7
Piorini, L. 90 D6
Piotrków
  Trybunalski . 16 C4
Pīp 45 E5
Piquiri → 94 A6
Piracicaba 94 A7
Piracuruca ... 92 C5
Piræus =
  Piraiévs 23 F4
Piraiévs 23 F4
Pirané 94 B5
Pirapora 93 F5
Pírgos 23 F3
Pirin Planina .. 22 D4
Piripiri 92 C5
Pirmasens ... 14 D4
Pirot 22 C4
Piru 39 E3
Pisa 20 C3
Pisagua 91 G4
Pisciotta 21 D5
Pisco 91 F3
Písek 16 D2
Pishan 34 C2
Pising 39 F2
Pistóia 20 C3
Pisuerga → ... 18 B3
Pitarpunga, L. . 62 B3
Pitcairn I. 65 M17
Piteå 8 E12
Piteşti 22 B5
Pithapuram ... 40 J4
Pittsburg 79 A6
Pittsburgh ... 73 D5
Pittsworth ... 63 A5
Piura 90 E2
Placentia 69 D5
Placentia B. ... 69 D5
Plainview 78 B3
Pláka, Ákra ... 23 G6
Plakhino 28 C9
Plasencia 18 B2
Plata, Río de la 94 C5
Platani → 21 F4
Plato 90 B4
Platte → 77 F7
Plauen 15 C7
Pleiku 36 B3
Plenty, B. of ... 64 B7
Pleven 22 C5
Plevlja 22 C2
Płock 16 B4
Plöckenstein .. 15 D7
Ploieşti 22 B6
Plovdiv 22 C5
Plumtree 59 C5
Plymouth 11 F4
Plzeň 16 D1
Po → 20 B4
Po Hai = Bo Hai 35 C6
Pobedy Pik ... 29 E8
Pocatello 81 D7
Poços de Caldas 93 G4
Podgorica 22 C2
Podilska
  Vysochyna .. 17 D8
Podkamennaya
  Tunguska → 30 C7
Podolsk 24 B4
Podor 55 E1
Pofadder 58 D3
Poh 39 E2
Pohnpei 64 J10

Poinsett, C. ... 96 A12
Pointe-à-Pitre .. 87 C7
Pointe Noire .. 56 E2
Poitiers 12 C4
Poitou 12 C3
Pokaran 42 F7
Pokataroo 63 A4
Pokrovsk =
  Engels 24 C6
Pola = Pula ... 20 B4
Polan 45 E5
Poland ■ 16 B5
Polatsk 24 B2
Polcura 94 D2
Polesye = Pripet
  Marshes ... 17 B9
Poli 56 C2
Police 16 B2
Polillo Is. 38 B2
Políyiros 23 D4
Pollachi 43 P10
Polnovat 28 C7
Polonne 17 C8
Polonnoye =
  Polonne 17 C8
Poltava 24 D3
Polunochnoye . 28 C7
Polynesia 65 L15
Polynésie
  française =
  French
  Polynesia ■ . 65 M16
Pombal, Brazil . 92 D6
Pombal,
  Portugal ... 18 C1
Pomézia 20 D4
Pomorski,
  Pojezierze ... 16 B3
Ponape =
  Pohnpei 64 J10
Ponca City 78 A5
Ponce 87 C6
Pond Inlet 68 A3
Pondicherry .. 43 P11
Ponferrada ... 18 A2
Ponnani 43 P9
Ponnyadaung . 41 F10
Ponoy → 28 C5
Ponta Grossa .. 94 B6
Ponta Pora ... 94 A5
Pontarlier 13 C7
Pontchartrain L. 79 D8
Ponte Nova .. 93 G5
Pontevedra ... 18 A1
Pontiac 72 C4
Pontianak 37 E3
Pontine =
  Ponziane,
  Ísole 21 D4
Pontine Mts. =
  Kuzey
  Anadolu
  Dağları 46 B3
Pontivy 12 B2
Pontoise 12 B5
Ponziane, Ísole 21 D4
Poochera 62 B1
Poole 11 F6
Poona = Pune . 43 K8
Pooncarie 62 B3
Poopelloe L. .. 63 B3
Poopó, L. de . 91 G5
Popayán 90 C3
Popigay 30 B9
Popilta, L. 62 B3
Popio L. 62 B3
Poplar Bluff .. 79 A8
Popocatépetl,
  Volcán 84 D5

Popokabaka ... 56 F3
Poprád 16 D5
Porbandar 43 J6
Porcupine → . 71 B5
Pordenone 20 B4
Pori 8 F12
Porkkala 9 G12
Porlamar 90 A6
Poroshiri-Dake . 32 F12
Porpoise B. ... 96 A13
Porretta, Passo
  di 20 B3
Port Adelaide . 62 B2
Port Alberni ... 71 D7
Port Alfred ... 59 E5
Port Angeles .. 80 A2
Port Antonio .. 86 C4
Port Arthur,
  Australia ... 62 D4
Port Arthur,
  U.S.A. 79 E7
Port-au-Prince . 87 C5
Port Augusta .. 62 B2
Port Augusta
  West 62 B2
Port Bergé
  Vaovao 59 H9
Port Bou 19 A7
Port Broughton 62 B2
Port-Cartier ... 69 C4
Port Chalmers . 65 F4
Port Darwin ... 95 G5
Port Davey ... 62 D4
Port Dickson .. 37 D2
Port Elizabeth . 59 E5
Port Fairy 62 C3
Port-Gentil 56 E1
Port Harcourt .. 55 H6
Port Harrison =
  Inukjuak 68 C3
Port
  Hawkesbury . 69 D4
Port Hedland .. 60 E2
Port Huron 72 C4
Port Kembla .. 63 B5
Port Kenny ... 62 B1
Port Lairge =
  Waterford ... 11 E3
Port Laoise ... 11 E3
Port Lincoln .. 62 B2
Port Loko 55 G2
Port MacDonnell 62 C3
Port Macquarie 63 B5
Port Moresby . 61 B8
Port Nelson ... 71 C10
Port Nolloth ... 58 D3
Port Nouveau-
  Québec =
  Kangiqsualujjuaq
  .... 68 C4
Port of Spain .. 87 D7
Port Pegasus . 65 G2
Port Phillip B. . 63 C3
Port Pirie 62 B2
Port Safaga =
  Bûr Safâga .. 52 C5
Port Said = Bûr
  Sa'îd 52 B5
Port Shepstone 59 E6
Port Stanley =
  Stanley 95 G5
Port Sudan =
  Bûr Sûdân .. 53 E6
Port Talbot ... 11 F5
Port-Vendres .. 13 E5
Port Wakefield 62 B2
Port Weld 36 D2
Porta Orientalis 22 B4

Portachuelo

Portachuelo ... 91 G6
Portadown 11 D3
Portage La
  Prairie 71 D10
Portalegre 18 C2
Portile de Fier . 22 B4
Portimão 18 D1
Portland,
  N.S.W.,
  Australia 63 B4
Portland, *Vic.,*
  Australia 62 C3
Portland, *Maine,*
  U.S.A. 73 C10
Portland, *Oreg.,*
  U.S.A. 80 C2
Portland B. 62 C3
Portland Prom. 68 C3
Porto 18 B1
Pôrto Alegre .. 94 C6
Porto Amboim
  = Gunza 56 G2
Pôrto de Móz .. 92 C3
Porto
  Empédocle .. 21 F4
Pôrto Esperança 91 G7
Pôrto Franco .. 92 D4
Porto Mendes . 94 A6
Pôrto Murtinho 91 H7
Pôrto Nacional 93 E4
Porto Novo ... 55 G5
Porto Santo .. 54 B1
Pôrto Seguro .. 93 F6
Porto Tórres .. 20 D2
Pôrto União .. 94 B6
Pôrto Válter ... 91 E4
Porto-Vecchio . 13 F8
Pôrto Velho ... 91 E6
Portoferráio ... 20 C3
Portoscuso 21 E2
Portoviejo 90 D2
Portree 10 C3
Portsmouth,
  U.K. 11 F6
Portsmouth,
  U.S.A. 73 F7
Porttipahtan
  tekojärvi 8 E13
Portugal ■ 18 C1
Porvenir 95 G2
Posadas 94 B5
Poshan =
  Boshan 35 C6
Poso 39 E2
Posse 93 E4
Possel 56 C3
Possession I. .. 96 B15
Poste Maurice
  Cortier 54 D5
Postojna 20 B5
Potchefstroom . 59 D5
Potenza 21 D5
Poteriteri, L. ... 65 G2
Potgietersrus . 59 C5
Poti 25 E5
Potiskum 55 F7
Potomac → .. 73 E7
Potosí 91 G5
Pototan 38 B2
Potrerillos 94 B3
Potsdam 15 B7
Poughkeepsie . 73 D9
Pouso Alegre .. 93 E2
Považská
  Bystrica 16 D4
Povenets 28 C4
Poverty B. 64 C8
Póvoa de Varzim 18 B1

Powder → ... 76 B2
Powell L. 83 B7
Poyang Hu 35 D6
Požarevac 22 B3
Poznań 16 B3
Pozo Almonte . 91 H5
Pozoblanco ... 18 C3
Pozzuoli 21 D5
Prachuap Khiri
  Khan 36 B1
Prado 93 F6
Prague = Praha 16 C2
Praha 16 C2
Prainha,
  Amazonas,
  Brazil 91 E6
Prainha, *Pará,*
  Brazil 92 C3
Prairies 71 C9
Prapat 37 D1
Prata 93 F4
Prato 20 C3
Pravia 18 A2
Praya 37 F5
Preparis North
  Channel 41 K9
Preparis South
  Channel 41 K9
Přerov 16 D3
Preservation
  Inlet 65 G2
Presidencia
  Roque Saenz
  Peña 94 B4
Presidente
  Epitácio 93 G3
Presidente
  Hermes 91 F6
Presidente
  Prudente ... 93 G3
Prešov 16 D5
Prespa, L. =
  Prespansko
  Jezero 23 D3
Prespansko
  Jezero 23 D3
Presque Isle ... 73 A11
Preston 11 E5
Pretoria 59 D5
Préveza 23 E3
Příbram 16 D2
Prichard 74 D3
Prieska 58 D4
Prievidza 16 D4
Prilep 22 D3
Priluki = Pryluky 24 C3
Prime Seal I. .. 62 D4
Prince Albert . 71 C9
Prince Albert
  Mts. 96 B15
Prince Albert
  Pen. 70 A8
Prince Albert Sd. 70 A8
Prince Charles I. 68 B3
Prince Charles
  Mts. 96 B10
Prince Edward
  I. □ 69 D4
Prince of Wales
  I., *Canada* .. 70 A10
Prince of Wales
  I., *U.S.A.* 71 C6
Principe da
  Beira 91 F6
Prins Harald
  Kyst 96 B8
Prinsesse Astrid
  Kyst 96 B7

Prinsesse
  Ragnhild Kyst 96 B8
Pripet → =
  Prypyat → .. 17 C10
Pripet Marshes 17 B9
Pripyat Marshes
  = Pripet
  Marshes 17 B9
Pripyats =
  Prypyat → .. 17 C10
Priština 22 C3
Privas 13 D6
Privolzhskaya
  Vozvyshennost
  .... 24 C6
Prizren 22 C3
Proddatur 43 M11
Progreso 85 C7
Prokopyevsk .. 29 D9
Prokuplje 22 C3
Prome = Pyè .. 41 H10
Propriá 93 E6
Prostějov 16 D3
Proston 63 A5
Provence 13 E6
Providence 73 D10
Providencia, I.
  de 86 D3
Provins 13 B5
Provo 81 E8
Prozna → ... 16 B3
Pruszków 16 B5
Prut → 17 F9
Pruzhany 17 B7
Prydz B. 96 A10
Pryluky 24 C3
Prypyat → ... 17 C10
Przemyśl 17 D6
Przhevalsk 29 E8
Psará 23 E5
Pskov 24 B2
Ptich =
  Ptsich → ... 17 B9
Ptsich → 17 B9
Puán 94 D4
Pucallpa 91 E4
Pudukkottai ... 43 P11
Puebla 84 D5
Pueblo 76 F2
Pueblo Hundido 94 B2
Puelches 94 D3
Puente Alto .. 94 C2
Puente-Genil . 18 D3
Puerto Aisén .. 95 F2
Puerto
  Ayacucho ... 90 B5
Puerto Barrios . 85 D7
Puerto Bermejo 94 B5
Puerto
  Bermúdez ... 91 F4
Puerto Bolívar . 90 D3
Puerto Cabello 90 A5
Puerto Cabezas 86 D3
Puerto Carreño 90 B5
Puerto Chicama 91 E3
Puerto Coig ... 95 G3
Puerto Cortés . 85 D7
Puerto
  Cumarebo .. 90 A5
Puerto del
  Rosario 54 C2
Puerto Deseado 95 F3
Puerto Heath . 91 F5
Puerto La Cruz 90 A6
Puerto
  Leguízamo .. 90 D4
Puerto Lobos . 95 E3
Puerto Madryn 95 E3

Puerto
  Maldonado .. 91 F5
Puerto Montt .. 95 E2
Puerto Morelos 85 C7
Puerto Natales 95 G2
Puerto Páez ... 90 B5
Puerto Pinasco 94 A5
Puerto
  Pirámides ... 95 E4
Puerto Plata .. 87 C5
Puerto Princesa 38 C1
Puerto Quellón 95 E2
Puerto Rico ■ . 87 C6
Puerto Sastre . 91 H7
Puerto Suárez . 91 G7
Puerto Wilches 90 B4
Puertollano ... 18 C3
Pueyrredón, L. . 95 F2
Pugachev 24 C6
Puget Sound .. 80 B2
Puigcerdá 19 A6
Pukaki L. 65 F4
Pukapuka 65 L14
Pukekohe 64 B6
Pula 20 B4
Puławy 16 C5
Pullman 80 B5
Pulog 38 A2
Pułtusk 16 B5
Puna 91 G5
Puná, I. 90 D2
Punakha 41 D7
Punata 91 G5
Punch 42 C9
Pune □ 43 K8
Punjab □, *India* 42 D9
Punjab □,
  Pakistan 42 D8
Puno 91 G4
Punta Alta 94 D4
Punta Arenas .. 95 G2
Punta de Díaz . 94 B2
Puntabie 62 B1
Puntarenas ... 86 E3
Punto Fijo 90 A4
Puquio 91 F4
Pur → 28 C8
Purace, Vol. ... 90 C3
Puralia =
  Puruliya 40 F6
Puri 40 H5
Purnia 40 E6
Purukcahu ... 37 E4
Puruliya 40 F6
Purus → 90 D6
Pusan 35 C7
Pushkino 24 C6
Putao 41 D11
Putaruru 64 C6
Puthein Myit → 41 K10
Putignano ... 21 D6
Puting, Tanjung 37 E4
Putorana, Gory 30 C7
Puttalam 43 Q11
Puttgarden ... 15 A6
Putumayo → . 90 D5
Putussibau ... 37 D4
Puy-de-Dôme . 13 D5
Pweto 57 F5
Pwllheli 11 E4
Pyapon 41 J10
Pyasina → ... 30 B6
Pyatigorsk ... 25 E5
Pyè 41 H10
Pyetrikaw ... 17 B9
Pyinmana ... 41 H11
P'yŏngyang ... 35 C7
Pyrénées 19 A6
Pyu 41 H11

142

Q

Qādib 49 E5
Qā'emshahr ... 44 B3
Qahremānshahr
= Bākhtarān . 46 D6
Qaidam Pendi . 34 C4
Qalāt 45 C6
Qal'at al Akhḍar 47 E4
Qal'eh Shaharak 42 B4
Qal'eh-ye Now 45 C5
Qamar, Ghubbat
al 49 D5
Qamruddīn
Karez 42 D6
Qandahār 42 D4
Qandahār □ ... 42 D4
Qapshaghay .. 29 E8
Qâra 52 C4
Qarabutaq 29 E7
Qarachuk 46 C5
Qaraghandy ... 29 E8
Qārah 47 E5
Qarataū 29 E8
Qarqan 34 C3
Qarqan He → . 34 C3
Qarqaraly 29 E8
Qarshi 29 F7
Qaṣr-e Qand .. 45 E5
Qasr Farâfra .. 52 C4
Qatar ■ 44 E2
Qattâra,
Munkhafed el 52 C4
Qattâra
Depression =
Qattâra,
Munkhafed el 52 C4
Qāyen 44 C4
Qazaqstan =
Kazakstan ■ . 29 E7
Qazvin 46 C7
Qena 52 C5
Qeshm 44 E4
Qila Safed 42 E2
Qila Saifullāh .. 42 D6
Qilian Shan ... 34 C4
Qingdao 35 C7
Qinghai □ 34 C4
Qinghai Hu ... 34 C5
Qinhuangdao . 35 C6
Qinzhou 35 D5
Qiqihar 35 B7
Qitai 34 B3
Qom 44 C2
Qomsheh 44 C2
Qondūz 45 B7
Qondūz □ 45 B7
Qostanay 29 D7
Qu Xian,
Sichuan,
China 35 C5
Qu Xian,
Zhejiang,
China 35 D6
Quambatook . 62 C3
Quambone 63 B4
Quan Long ... 36 C3
Quandialla ... 63 B4
Quang Ngai .. 36 A3
Quanzhou ... 35 D6
Quaqtaq 68 B4
Quaraí 94 C5
Quartu
Sant'Elena . 21 E2
Quatsino 71 C7
Quba 25 E6
Qūchān 44 B4
Queanbeyan .. 63 C4
Québec 69 D3

Québec □ 69 D3
Queen
Alexandra Ra. 96 C15
Queen Charlotte
Is. 70 C6
Queen Charlotte
Str. 71 C7
Queen Elizabeth
Is. 66 B9
Queen Mary
Land 96 B11
Queen Maud G. 70 B9
Queen Maud
Land 96 B7
Queen Maud
Mts. 96 C16
Queenscliff .. 63 C3
Queensland □ . 61 E7
Queenstown,
Australia 62 D4
Queenstown,
N.Z. 65 F3
Queenstown,
S. Africa ... 59 E5
Queimadas ... 93 E6
Quela 56 F3
Quelimane ... 59 B7
Quelpart =
Cheju Do ... 35 C7
Quequén 94 D5
Querétaro 84 C4
Quetta 42 D5
Quezon City .. 38 B2
Qui Nhon 36 B3
Quibaxe 56 F2
Quibdo 90 B3
Quiberon 12 C2
Quilán, C. 95 E2
Quilengues ... 58 A2
Quillabamba .. 91 F4
Quillagua ... 91 H5
Quillota 94 C2
Quilon 43 Q10
Quilpie 63 A3
Quimilí 94 B4
Quimper 12 B1
Quimperlé ... 12 C2
Quincy 77 F9
Quines 94 C3
Quinga 59 H8
Quintanar de la
Orden 18 C4
Quintero 94 C2
Quinyambie ... 62 B3
Quipungo ... 58 A2
Quirindi 63 B5
Quissanga ... 59 G8
Quitilipi 94 B4
Quito 90 D3
Quixadá 92 C6
Qŭnghirot ... 29 E6
Quondong ... 62 B3
Quorn 62 B2
Qŭqon 29 E8
Qûs 52 C5
Quseir 52 C5
Qyzylorda ... 29 E7

R

Raahe 8 F12
Raba 39 F1
Rába → 16 E3
Rabat, Malta .. 21 G5
Rabat, Morocco 54 B3
Rabaul 64 K10

Rābigh 47 G4
Race, C. 69 D5
Rach Gia 36 B3
Racibórz 16 C4
Racine 72 C2
Rădăuți 17 E7
Radekhiv 17 C7
Radekhov =
Radekhiv ... 17 C7
Radhwa, Jabal 47 F4
Radom 16 C5
Radomsko ... 16 C4
Radomyshl .. 17 C9
Radstock, C. .. 62 B1
Rae 70 B8
Rae Bareli ... 40 D3
Rae Isthmus .. 68 B2
Raetihi 64 C6
Rafaela 94 C4
Rafai 56 D4
Rafḥā 47 E5
Rafsanjān ... 44 D4
Ragachow ... 17 B10
Ragama 43 R11
Raglan 64 B6
Ragusa 21 F5
Raha 39 E2
Rahad al Bardī 53 F3
Rahaeng = Tak 36 A1
Rahimyar Khan 42 E7
Raichur 43 L10
Raigarh 40 G4
Railton 62 D4
Rainier, Mt. ... 80 B3
Raipur 40 G3
Ra'is 47 G4
Raj Nandgaon . 40 G3
Raja, Ujung .. 37 D1
Raja Ampat,
Kepulauan . 39 E3
Rajahmundry .. 40 J3
Rajang → ... 37 D4
Rajapalaiyam . 43 Q10
Rajasthan □ .. 42 F8
Rajasthan Canal 42 F8
Rajgarh 43 G10
Rajkot 43 H7
Rajpipla 43 J8
Rajshahi 41 E7
Rakaia 65 E5
Rakaia → ... 65 E5
Rakan, Ra's ... 44 E2
Rakaposhi .. 42 A9
Rakata, Pulau . 37 F3
Rakhiv 17 D7
Raleigh 75 B8
Ram Hd. 63 C4
Ramanathapuram
.... 43 Q11
Ramechhap .. 40 D6
Ramelau 39 F3
Ramgarh, Bihar,
India 40 F5
Ramgarh, Raj.,
India 42 F7
Rāmhormoz ... 47 E7
Ramnad =
Ramanathapuram
.... 43 Q11
Rampur 42 E11
Rampur Hat .. 40 E6
Ramree I. =
Ramree Kyun 41 H9
Ramree Kyun . 41 H9
Ramtek 43 J11
Ranaghat ... 41 F7
Ranau 36 C5
Rancagua ... 94 C2
Ranchi 40 F5

Randers 9 G10
Rangaunu B. .. 64 A5
Rangia 41 D8
Rangiora 65 E5
Rangitaiki → . 64 B7
Rangitata → .. 65 E4
Rangon → ... 41 J11
Rangoon → .. 41 J11
Rangpur 41 E7
Ranibennur ... 43 M9
Raniganj 40 F6
Raniwara 43 G8
Rankin Inlet ... 70 B10
Rankins Springs 63 B4
Ranong 36 C1
Ransiki 39 E4
Rantau 37 E5
Rantauprapat .. 37 D1
Rantemario ... 39 E1
Rapa 65 M16
Rapallo 20 B2
Rāpch 45 E4
Rapid City ... 76 C3
Rarotonga ... 65 M14
Ra's al Khaymah 44 E4
Ra's al-Unuf .. 52 B2
Ras Bânâs ... 52 D6
Ras Dashen ... 57 B7
Râs Timirist ... 55 E1
Rasa, Punta ... 95 E4
Rashad 53 F5
Rashîd 52 B5
Rasht 46 C7
Rat Islands 71 C1
Ratangarh ... 42 E9
Rathenow 15 B7
Ratibor =
Racibórz ... 16 C4
Ratlam 43 H9
Ratnagiri ... 43 L8
Raukumara Ra. 64 C7
Raurkela 40 F5
Rava-Ruska .. 17 C6
Rava Russkaya
= Rava-Ruska 17 C6
Rāvar 44 D4
Ravenna ... 20 B4
Ravensburg .. 14 E5
Ravi → ... 42 D7
Rawalpindi ... 42 C8
Rawāndūz .. 46 C6
Rawene 64 A5
Rawlins 81 E10
Rawson ... 95 E3
Ray, C. 69 D5
Rayadurg ... 43 M10
Rayagada ... 40 H4
Raymond 71 D8
Raz, Pte. du .. 12 B1
Razdel'naya =
Rozdilna ... 17 E10
Razelm, Lacul . 22 B7
Razgrad 22 C6
Ré, I. de 12 C3
Reading, U.K. . 11 F6
Reading, U.S.A. 73 D8
Realicó 94 D4
Rebi 39 F4
Rebiana ... 52 D3
Rebun-Tō ... 32 E12
Rechytsa 17 B10
Recife 92 D7
Reconquista .. 94 B5
Recreo 94 B3
Red →, La.,
U.S.A. 79 D8
Red →, N. Dak.,
U.S.A. 76 A6
Red Cliffs 62 B3

Red Deer 71 C8
Red Sea 48 C2
Red Tower Pass
= Turnu Roşu,
P. 17 F7
Redcar 11 D6
Redcliffe 63 A5
Redding 80 E2
Redditch 11 E6
Redon 12 C2
Redondela 18 A1
Redwood City . 82 B1
Ree, L. 11 E3
Reefton 65 E4
Regensburg ... 15 D7
Réggio di
Calábria 21 E5
Réggio
nell'Emília .. 20 B3
Reghin 17 E7
Regina 71 C9
Rehoboth 58 C3
Rehovot 46 E3
Rei-Bouba 53 G1
Reichenbach .. 15 C7
Reidsville 75 A8
Reigate 11 F6
Reims 13 B6
Reina Adelaida,
Arch. 95 G2
Reindeer L. ... 71 C9
Reinga, C. 64 A5
Reinosa 18 A3
Reliance 70 B9
Remarkable, Mt. 62 B2
Remeshk 45 E4
Rendsburg 14 A5
Rengat 37 E2
Reni 17 F9
Renk 53 F5
Renmark 62 B3
Rennes 12 B3
Reno 80 F4
Reno → 20 B4
Rentería 19 A5
Republican → 76 F6
Repulse Bay .. 68 B2
Requena, Peru . 90 E4
Requena, Spain 19 C5
Resadiye =
Datça 23 F6
Resht = Rasht . 46 C7
Resistencia ... 94 B5
Reşiţa 17 F5
Resolution I.,
Canada 68 B4
Resolution I.,
N.Z. 65 F2
Réthímnon 23 G5
Réunion ■ 51 J9
Reus 19 B6
Reutlingen 14 D5
Reval = Tallinn 24 B1
Revelstoke 71 C8
Rewa 40 E3
Rewari 42 E10
Rey Malabo ... 56 D1
Reykjavík 8 B2
Reynosa 84 B5
Rhein → ... 14 C4
Rhein-Main-
Donau-
Kanal → ... 15 D6
Rheine 14 B4
Rheinland-
Pfalz □ 14 C4
Rhin =
Rhein → ... 14 C4
Rhine =
Rhein → ... 14 C4

Rhineland-
Palatinate □ =
Rheinland-
Pfalz □ 14 C4
Rhode Island □ 73 D10
Rhodes =
Ródhos 23 F7
Rhodope Mts. =
Rhodopi
Planina 22 D5
Rhodopi Planina 22 D5
Rhön = Hohe
Rhön 14 C5
Rhondda 11 F5
Rhône → 13 E6
Rhum 10 C3
Riachão 92 D4
Riasi 42 C9
Riau □ 37 E2
Riau, Kepulauan 37 D2
Riau Arch. =
Riau,
Kepulauan .. 37 D2
Ribadeo 18 A2
Ribeirão Prêto . 93 G4
Riberalta 91 F5
Rîbniţa 17 E9
Riccarton 65 E5
Richland 80 B4
Richmond,
Australia 63 B5
Richmond, N.Z. 65 D5
Richmond,
Calif., U.S.A. 80 G2
Richmond, Va.,
U.S.A. 73 F7
Richmond Ra. . 63 A5
Ridder 29 D9
Ried 15 D7
Riesa 15 C7
Rieti 20 C4
Rig Rig 53 F1
Riga 24 B1
Riga, G. of .. 24 B1
Rīgas Jūras Līcis
= Riga, G. of 24 B1
Rīgestān □ ... 42 D4
Rigolet 68 C5
Riiser-Larsen-
halvøya 96 A8
Rijeka 20 B5
Rimah, Wadi
ar → 47 F5
Rímini 20 B4
Rîmnicu Sărat . 17 F8
Rîmnicu Vîlcea 17 F7
Rimouski 69 D4
Rinca 39 F1
Rinconada 94 A3
Rinjani 37 F5
Rio Branco,
Brazil 91 E5
Río Branco,
Uruguay 94 C6
Río Cuarto 94 C4
Rio de Janeiro . 93 G5
Rio de
Janeiro □ ... 93 G5
Rio do Sul 94 B7
Río Gallegos .. 95 G3
Río Grande,
Argentina ... 95 G3
Rio Grande,
Brazil 94 C6
Rio Grande → 78
Rio Grande do
Norte □ 92 D6
Rio Grande do
Sul □ 94 B6

Rio Largo 93 D6
Río Mulatos ... 91 G5
Río Muni =
Mbini □ 56 D2
Rio Negro 94 B7
Rio Verde 93 F3
Ríobamba 90 D3
Ríohacha 90 A4
Ríosucio,
Caldas,
Colombia ... 90 B3
Ríosucio, Choco,
Colombia ... 90 B3
Rishiri-Tō 32 E12
Riva del Garda . 20 B3
Rivadavia 94 B2
Rivera 94 C5
Riversdale 58 E4
Riverside 82 D4
Riverton,
Australia 62 B2
Riverton,
Canada 71 C10
Riverton, N.Z. . 65 G2
Riviera di
Levante 20 B2
Riviera di
Ponente 20 B2
Rivière-du-Loup 69 D4
Rivne 17 C8
Rívoli 20 B1
Rivoli B. 62 C3
Riyadh = Ar
Riyāḍ 47 F6
Rize 46 B5
Rizzuto, C. ... 21 E6
Roanne 13 C6
Roanoke 73 F6
Robbins I. 62 D4
Robertson 58 E3
Robertson I. ... 96 A4
Robertsport ... 55 G2
Robertstown .. 62 B2
Robinvale 62 B3
Roboré 91 G7
Robson, Mt. .. 71 C8
Roca, C. da ... 18 C1
Rocas, I. 92 C7
Rocha 94 C6
Rochefort 12 D3
Rochester,
Minn., U.S.A. 77 C8
Rochester, N.Y.,
U.S.A. 73 C7
Rock Hill 75 B7
Rock Island ... 77 E9
Rock Springs .. 81 E9
Rockefeller
Plateau 96 C18
Rockford 77 D10
Rockhampton . 61 E9
Rocky Mount .. 75 B9
Rocky Mts. 70 C7
Rod 42 E3
Rodez 13 D5
Ródhos 23 F7
Rodney, C. 64 B6
Roes Welcome
Sd. 68 B2
Rogachev =
Ragachow .. 17 B10
Rogagua, L. .. 91 F5
Rogatyn 17 D7
Rogoaguado, L. 91 F5
Rohri 42 F6
Rohtak 42 E10
Roi Et 36 A2
Rojas 94 C4
Rojo, C. 84 C5

Rokan → 37 D2
Rolândia 94 A6
Roma, Australia 63 A4
Roma, Italy ... 20 D4
Roman 17 E8
Romang 39 F3
Romania ■ .. 22 B5
Romanovka =
Basarabeasca 17 E9
Romans-sur-
Isère 13 D6
Romblon 38 B2
Rome = Roma 20 D4
Rome 74 B5
Romorantin-
Lanthenay .. 12 C4
Roncador, Serra
do 93 E3
Ronda 18 D3
Rondônia □ ... 91 F6
Rondonópolis . 93 F3
Ronge, L. la ... 71 C9
Ronne Ice Shelf 96 B3
Roodepoort ... 59 D5
Roorkee 42 E10
Roosevelt → .. 91 E6
Roosevelt I. ... 96 B16
Roquetas de
Mar 19 D4
Roraima □ ... 90 C6
Roraima, Mt. .. 90 B6
Rosa 57 F6
Rosa, Monte .. 13 D7
Rosario,
Argentina ... 94 C4
Rosário, Brazil . 92 C5
Rosario, Mexico 84 C3
Rosario,
Paraguay ... 94 A5
Rosario de la
Frontera 94 B3
Rosário do Sul 94 C6
Rosas, G. de .. 19 A7
Roscommon .. 11 E2
Roseau, Domin. 87 C7
Roseau, U.S.A. 77 A7
Rosebery 62 D4
Roseburg 80 D2
Rosenheim ... 15 E7
Rosetown 71 C9
Rosetta =
Rashîd 52 B5
Roseville 80 F3
Rosewood 63 A5
Rosignano
Maríttimo .. 20 C3
Rosignol 90 B7
Roşiori-de-Vede 22 B5
Roslavl 24 C3
Roslyn 63 B4
Ross, Australia 62 D4
Ross, N.Z. 65 E4
Ross I. 96 B15
Ross Ice Shelf . 96 C16
Ross Sea 96 B15
Rossano Cálabro 21 E6
Rossland 71 D8
Rosslare 11 E3
Rosso 55 F1
Rossosh 24 C4
Rosthern 71 C9
Rostock 15 A7
Rostov, Don,
Russia 25 D4
Rostov, Yarosl.,
Russia 24 B4
Roswell 78 C1
Rotherham ... 11 E6
Roto 63 B4

Rotondo Mte. .	13	E8
Rotorua	64	C7
Rotorua, L.	64	C7
Rotterdam	14	C3
Rottweil	14	D5
Rotuma	64	L12
Roubaix	13	A5
Rouen	12	B4
Round Mt.	63	B5
Roussillon	13	E5
Rouyn	69	D3
Rovaniemi	8	E13
Rovereto	20	B3
Rovigo	20	B3
Rovinj	20	B4
Rovno = Rivne	17	C8
Rovuma ⟶	57	G8
Rowena	63	A4
Roxas	38	B2
Roxburgh	65	F3
Royal Leamington Spa	11	E6
Royan	12	D3
Rozdilna	17	E10
Rozhyshche	17	C7
Rtishchevo	24	C5
Ruahine Ra.	64	C7
Ruapehu	64	C6
Ruapuke I.	65	G3
Rub' al Khali	48	D4
Rubio	90	B4
Rubtsovsk	29	D9
Rudall	62	B2
Rudolf, Ostrov .	28	A6
Rufa'a	53	F5
Rufiji ⟶	57	F7
Rufino	94	C4
Rufisque	55	F1
Rugby	11	E6
Rügen	15	A7
Ruhr ⟶	14	C4
Rukwa L.	57	F6
Rum = Rhum	10	C3
Rumāḥ	47	F6
Rumania = Romania ■ . .	22	B5
Rumbêk	53	G4
Rumia	16	A4
Rumoi	32	F12
Runanga	65	E4
Runaway, C. . .	64	B7
Rungwa	57	F6
Ruoqiang	34	C3
Rupa	41	D9
Rupat	37	D2
Rupert ⟶	69	C3
Rupert House = Waskaganish	69	C3
Rurrenabaque .	91	F5
Rusape	59	B6
Ruschuk = Ruse	22	C5
Ruse	22	C5
Rushworth	63	C4
Russas	92	C6
Russellkonda . .	40	H5
Russkaya Polyana	29	D8
Rustavi	25	E6
Rustenburg	59	D5
Ruteng	39	F2
Rutshuru	57	E5
Ruwenzori	57	D5
Ružomberok	16	D4
Rwanda ■	57	E6
Ryazan	24	C4
Ryazhsk	24	C5
Rybache = Rybachye	29	E9
Rybachye	29	E9
Rybinsk	24	B4
Rybinskoye Vdkhr.	24	B4
Rybnitsa = Rîbniţa	17	E9
Rylstone	63	B4
Rypin	16	B4
Ryūkyū Is. = Ryūkyū-rettō	35	D7
Ryūkyū-rettō .	35	D7
Rzeszów	16	C5
Rzhev	24	B3

S

Sa Dec	36	B3
Sa'ādatābād . .	44	D3
Saalo ►	16	C6
Saalfeld	15	C6
Saar ⟶	13	B7
Saarbrücken . .	14	D4
Saaremaa	24	B1
Šabac	22	B2
Sabadell	19	B7
Sabah □	36	C5
Şabāḥ, Wadi ⟶	47	G7
Sabalān, Kūhhā-ye	46	C6
Sábanalarga . .	90	A4
Sabang	36	C1
Sabará	93	F5
Saberania	39	E5
Sabhah	52	C1
Sabinas	84	B4
Sabinas Hidalgo	84	B4
Sablayan	38	B2
Sable, C., Canada	69	D4
Sable, C., U.S.A.	86	A3
Sable I.	69	D5
Sabrina Coast .	96	A12
Sabulubek	37	E1
Sabzevār	44	B4
Sabzvārān	44	D4
Săcele	17	F7
Sachsen □	15	C7
Sachsen-Anhalt □	15	C7
Sacramento	80	F3
Sacramento ⟶	80	F3
Sacramento Mts.	83	D10
Sadani	57	F7
Sadd el Aali . . .	52	D5
Sado	33	G11
Sadon	41	E11
Safi	54	B3
Safid Kūh	42	B3
Saga, Indonesia	39	E4
Saga, Japan . .	32	C2
Sagala	55	F3
Sagar	43	M9
Sagil	34	A4
Saginaw	72	C4
Şagīr, Zāb aş ⟶	46	D5
Saglouc = Salluit	68	B3
Sagua la Grande	86	B3
Saguenay ⟶	69	D3
Sagunto	19	C5
Sahagún	18	A3
Sahand, Kūh-e	46	C6
Sahara	54	D6
Saharan Atlas = Saharien, Atlas	54	B5

Saharanpur	42	E10
Saharien, Atlas	54	B5
Sahiwal	42	D8
Sa'id Bundas . .	53	G3
Saïda	54	B5
Sa'īdābād	44	D3
Sa'īdīyeh	46	C7
Saidpur	41	E7
Saidu	42	B8
Saigon = Phanh Bho Ho Chi Minh	36	B3
Saijō	32	C3
Saikhoa Ghat . .	41	D10
Saiki	32	C2
Sailolof	39	E4
St. Andrews	10	C5
St. Arnaud	62	C3
St. Augustine	75	E7
St. Austell	11	F4
St. Boniface	71	D10
St.-Brieuc	12	B2
St. Catharines	69	D3
St.-Chamond	13	D6
St. Christopher-Nevis ■ = St. Kitts & Nevis	87	C7
St. Cloud	77	C7
St. Croix	87	C7
St.-Denis	12	B5
St.-Dizier	13	B6
St. Elias, Mt. . .	70	B5
St.-Étienne	13	D6
St.-Flour	13	D5
St. Francis, C. .	58	E4
St. Gallen = Sankt Gallen	13	C8
St.-Gaudens	12	E4
St. George	63	A4
St.-Georges, Fr. Guiana	92	B3
St. George's, Grenada	87	D7
St. George's Channel	11	F3
St. Georges Hd.	63	C5
St. Gotthard P. = San Gottardo, P. del	13	C8
St. Helena ■	51	H3
St. Helena B. . .	58	E3
St. Helens	62	D4
St. Helier	11	G5
St-Hyacinthe	69	D3
St. John	69	D4
St. John's, Antigua	87	C7
St. John's, Canada	69	D5
St. Johns ⟶	75	D7
St. Joseph	77	F7
St. Joseph, L. .	69	C1
St. Kilda, N.Z. .	65	F4
St. Kilda, U.K. .	10	C2
St. Kitts & Nevis ■	87	C7
St.-Laurent	92	A3
St. Lawrence ⟶	69	D4
St. Lawrence, Gulf of	69	D4
St. Lawrence I.	71	B2
St. Leonard	69	D4
St.-Lô	12	B3
St-Louis	55	E1
St. Louis	77	F9
St. Lucia ■	87	D7
St. Lucia, L. . . .	59	D6

St. Maarten	87	C7
St.-Malo	12	B2
St-Marc	87	C5
St. Mary Pk. . .	62	B2
St. Marys	62	D4
St.-Mathieu, Pte.	12	B1
St. Matthews, I. = Zadetkyi Kyun	36	C1
St.-Nazaire	12	C2
St.-Omer	12	A5
St. Paul	77	C8
St. Peter Port . .	11	G5
St. Petersburg = Sankt-Peterburg . . .	24	B3
St. Petersburg .	75	F6
St.-Pierre et Miquelon □ .	69	D5
St.-Quentin	13	B5
St. Thomas I. . .	87	C7
St.-Tropez	13	E7
St. Vincent, G. .	62	C2
St. Vincent & the Grenadines ■	87	D7
Saintes	12	D3
Saintonge	12	D3
Saipan	64	H9
Sairang	41	F9
Sairecábur, Cerro	94	A3
Sajama	91	G5
Sajó	16	D5
Sakai	32	B4
Sakākah	47	E5
Sakakawea, L. .	76	B4
Sakarya = Adapazarı	46	B2
Sakarya ⟶	25	E3
Sakata	33	G11
Sakhalin	31	D12
Sakon Nakhon .	36	A2
Sala	9	G11
Sala Consilina .	21	D5
Saladillo	94	D5
Salado ⟶, Buenos Aires, Argentina . . .	94	D5
Salado ⟶, La Pampa, Argentina . . .	94	D3
Salado ⟶, Santa Fe, Argentina . . .	94	C4
Salaga	55	G4
Salālah	49	D5
Salamanca, Chile	94	C2
Salamanca, Spain	18	B3
Salamís	23	F4
Salar de Atacama	94	A3
Salar de Uyuni	91	H5
Salaverry	91	E3
Salawati	39	E4
Salayar	39	F2
Saldanha	58	E3
Sale, Australia .	63	C4
Salé, Morocco .	54	B3
Salekhard	28	C7
Salem, India . .	43	P11
Salem, U.S.A. .	80	C2
Salerno	21	D5
Salgótarján	16	D4
Salihli	23	E7
Salihorsk	17	B8
Salima	59	A6

Salina, *Italy* . . . 21 E5
Salina, *U.S.A.* . . 76 F6
Salina Cruz . . . 85 D5
Salinas, *Brazil* . 93 F5
Salinas, *Ecuador* 90 D2
Salinas, *U.S.A.* 82 B2
Salinas Grandes 94 C3
Salinópolis 92 C4
Salisbury,
  Australia 62 B2
Salisbury, *U.K.* 11 F6
Salisbury, *U.S.A.* 75 B7
Salliq 68 B2
Salluit 68 B3
Salmãs 46 C6
Salmon → . . . 80 C5
Salmon River
  Mts. 81 C6
Salon-de-
  Provence . . . 13 E6
Salonica =
  Thessaloníki . 23 D4
Salonta 16 E5
Salsk 25 D5
Salso → 21 F4
Salt Creek 62 C2
Salt Lake City . 81 E8
Salta 94 A3
Saltillo 84 B4
Salto 94 C5
Salto → 20 C4
Salton Sea . . . 82 D5
Saltpond 55 G4
Salûm 52 B4
Salûm, Khâlig el 52 B4
Salur 40 H4
Salvador 93 E6
Salwa 44 E2
Salween → . . . 41 J11
Salyan 25 F6
Salzach → . . . 15 D7
Salzburg 15 E7
Salzgitter 14 B6
Salzwedel 15 B6
Sama 28 C7
Sama de
  Langreo 18 A3
Samales Group 38 C2
Samangán □ . . 45 B7
Samar 38 B3
Samara 24 C7
Samarinda 37 E5
Samarkand =
  Samarqand . 29 F7
Samarqand . . 29 F7
Sãmarrã 46 D5
Sambalpur 40 G5
Sambar,
  Tanjung 37 E4
Sambas 37 D3
Sambava 59 G10
Sambhal 42 E11
Sambhar 42 F9
Sambiase 21 E6
Sambir 17 D6
Samoa ■ 65 L13
Samokov 22 C4
Sámos 23 F6
Samothráki,
  Évros, Greece 23 D5
Samothráki,
  Kérkira,
  Greece 23 E2
Sampacho 94 C4
Sampit 37 E4
Sampit, Teluk . 37 E4
Samra 47 F5
Samsun 46 B4
Samui, Ko 36 C2

Samut Prakan . 36 B2
Samut
  Songkhram →
  . . . . 36 B2
San 55 F4
San → 16 C5
San Agustin, C. 38 C3
San Andrés, I.
  de 86 D3
San Andrés
  Tuxtla 85 D5
San Angelo . . . 78 D3
San Antonio,
  Chile 94 C2
San Antonio,
  Spain 19 C6
San Antonio,
  U.S.A. 78 E4
San Antonio, C.,
  Argentina . . . 94 D5
San Antonio, C.,
  Cuba 85 C8
San Antonio
  Oeste 95 E4
San Benedetto
  del Tronto . . 20 C4
San Bernardino 82 C4
San Bernardino
  Str. 38 B2
San Bernardo . 94 C2
San Bernardo, I.
  de 90 B3
San Borja 91 F5
San Carlos,
  Argentina . . . 94 C3
San Carlos,
  Chile 94 D2
San Carlos, *Phil.* 38 B2
San Carlos,
  Amazonas,
  Venezuela . . . 90 C5
San Carlos,
  Cojedes,
  Venezuela . . . 90 B5
San Carlos de
  Bariloche . . . 95 E2
San Carlos del
  Zulia 90 B4
San Cristóbal,
  Argentina . . . 94 C4
San Cristóbal,
  Mexico 85 D6
San Cristóbal,
  Venezuela . . 90 B4
San Diego 82 D4
San Diego, C. . 95 G3
San Felipe, *Chile* 94 C2
San Felipe,
  Venezuela . . . 90 A5
San Felíu de
  Guíxols 19 B7
San Fernando,
  Chile 94 C2
San Fernando,
  La Union, Phil. 38 A2
San Fernando,
  Pampanga,
  Phil. 38 A2
San Fernando,
  Spain 18 D2
San Fernando,
  Trin. & Tob. . 87 D7
San Fernando,
  U.S.A. 82 C3
San Fernando
  de Apure . . . 90 B5
San Fernando
  de Atabapo . 90 C5
San Francisco,
  Argentina . . . 94 C4

San Francisco,
  U.S.A. 82 B1
San Francisco
  de Macorîs . . 87 C5
San Francisco
  del Monte de
  Oro 94 C3
San Gil 90 B4
San Gottardo, P.
  del 13 C8
San Ignacio,
  Bolivia 91 G6
San Ignacio,
  Paraguay . . . 94 B5
San Ildefonso,
  C. 38 A2
San Javier,
  Argentina . . . 94 C5
San Javier,
  Bolivia 91 G6
San Joaquin → 82 A2
San Jorge, B. de 84 A2
San Jorge, G. . 95 F3
San Jorge, G. de 19 B6
San José,
  Bolivia 91 G6
San José,
  Costa Rica . . 86 E3
San José,
  Guatemala . . 85 E6
San Jose, *Phil.* 38 A2
San Jose, *U.S.A.* 82 B2
San Jose de
  Buenovista . . 38 B2
San José de
  Jáchal 94 C3
San José de
  Mayo 94 C5
San José de
  Ocune 90 C4
San José del
  Guaviare 90 C4
San Juan,
  Argentina . . . 94 C3
San Juan, *Phil.* 38 C3
San Juan,
  Puerto Rico . 87 C6
San Juan → . . 86 D3
San Juan, C. . . 56 D1
San Juan de los
  Morros 90 B5
San Juan Mts. . 83 B9
San Julián 95 F3
San Justo 94 C4
San Leandro . . 82 B1
San Lorenzo . . 90 C3
San Lorenzo, I. 91 F3
San Lorenzo,
  Mt. 95 F2
San Lucas 91 H5
San Lucas, C. . 84 C2
San Luis 94 C3
San Luis Obispo 82 C2
San Luis Potosí 84 C4
San Marino . . . 20 C4
San Marino ■ . . 20 C4
San Martín, L. . 95 F2
San Matías . . . 91 G7
San Matías, G. 95 E4
San Miguel . . . 85 E7
San Miguel → . 91 F6
San Miguel de
  Tucumán . . . 94 B3
San Narciso . . 38 A2
San Nicolás de
  los Arroyas . 94 C4
San-Pédro 55 H3
San Pedro de
  las Colonias . 84 B4

San Pedro de
  Lloc 91 E3
San Pedro de
  Macorís . . . 87 C6
San Pedro del
  Paraná 94 B5
San Pedro Sula 85 D7
San Pieto 21 E2
San Rafael,
  Argentina . . . 94 C3
San Rafael,
  U.S.A. 80 G2
San Ramón de
  la Nueva Orán 94 A4
San Remo 20 C1
San Roque,
  Argentina . . . 94 B5
San Roque,
  Spain 18 D3
San Rosendo . 94 D2
San Salvador,
  Bahamas . . . 86 B5
San Salvador,
  El Salv. 85 E7
San Salvador de
  Jujuy 94 A4
San Sebastián,
  Argentina . . . 95 G3
San Sebastián,
  Spain 19 A5
San Severo . . . 20 D5
San Valentin,
  Mte. 95 F2
San Vicente de
  la Barquera . 18 A3
Sana' 49 D3
Sana → 20 B6
Sanaga → . . . 56 D1
Sanana 39 E3
Sanandaj 46 D6
Sanco Pt. 38 C3
Sancti-Spíritus . 86 B4
Sancy, Puy de . 13 D5
Sandakan 36 C5
Sandanski 22 D4
Sanday 10 B5
Sandgate 63 A5
Sandía 91 F5
Sandıklı 46 C2
Sandoa 56 F4
Sandomierz . . . 16 C5
Sandoway 41 H10
Sandusky 72 E3
Sandwip Chan. 41 F8
Sandy C. 62 D3
Sandy L. 71 C10
Sanford, *Fla.,*
  U.S.A. 75 E7
Sanford, *N.C.,*
  U.S.A. 75 B8
Sanford, Mt. . . 71 B5
Sanga → 56 E3
Sangamner . . . 43 K9
Sangar 31 C10
Sangasangadalam
  . . . . 37 E5
Sangeang 39 F1
Sangerhausen . 15 C6
Sanggau 37 D3
Sangihe, P. . . . 39 D3
Sangkapura . . . 37 F4
Sangli 43 L9
Sangmélina . . . 56 D2
Sangre de Cristo
  Mts. 78 A1
Sanirajak 68 B2
Sankt Gallen . 13 C8
Sankt Moritz . . 13 C8
Sankt-Peterburg 24 B3

Sankt Pölten .. 15 D8
Sankuru → ... 56 E4
Sanliurfa 46 C4
Sanlúcar de
  Barrameda .. 18 D2
Sannicandro
  Gargánico .. 20 D5
Sanok 17 D6
Sanshui 35 D6
Santa Ana,
  Bolivia 91 F5
Santa Ana,
  Ecuador 90 D2
Santa Ana,
  El Salv. 85 E7
Santa Ana,
  U.S.A. 82 D4
Santa Barbara . 82 C3
Santa Catalina I. 82 D3
Santa
  Catarina □ .. 94 B7
Santa Clara ... 86 B4
Santa Clotilde . 90 D4
Santa Coloma
  de Gramanet 19 B7
Santa Cruz,
  Argentina ... 95 G3
Santa Cruz,
  Bolivia 91 G6
Santa Cruz, Phil. 38 B2
Santa Cruz,
  U.S.A. 82 B1
Santa Cruz → . 95 G3
Santa Cruz de
  Tenerife 54 C1
Santa Cruz do
  Sul 94 B6
Santa Cruz I. .. 64 L11
Santa Elena .. 90 D2
Santa Eugenia,
  Pta. 84 B1
Santa Fe,
  Argentina ... 94 C4
Santa Fe, U.S.A. 83 C10
Santa Filomena 93 D4
Santa Inés, I. .. 95 G2
Santa Isabel =
  Rey Malabo . 56 D1
Santa Isabel,
  Argentina ... 94 D3
Santa Isabel,
  Brazil 93 E3
Santa Lucia
  Range 82 C2
Santa Maria,
  Brazil 94 B6
Santa Maria,
  U.S.A. 82 C2
Santa María → 84 A3
Santa Maria da
  Vitória 93 E5
Santa Maria di
  Leuca, C. ... 23 E2
Santa Marta ... 90 A4
Santa Marta,
  Sierra Nevada
  de 90 A4
Santa Maura =
  Levkás 23 E3
Santa Rosa,
  La Pampa,
  Argentina ... 94 D4
Santa Rosa,
  San Luis,
  Argentina ... 94 C3
Santa Rosa,
  Bolivia 91 F5
Santa Rosa,
  Brazil 94 B6

Santa Rosa,
  U.S.A. 80 F2
Santa Rosa de
  Copán 85 E7
Santa Vitória do
  Palmar 94 C6
Santai 35 C5
Santana, Coxilha
  de 94 C5
Santana do
  Livramento .. 94 C5
Santander 18 A4
Sant'Antíoco .. 21 E2
Santarém, Brazil 92 C3
Santarém,
  Portugal 18 C1
Santiago, Brazil 94 B6
Santiago, Chile 94 C2
Santiago → .. 90 D3
Santiago de
  Compostela . 18 A1
Santiago de
  Cuba 86 C4
Santiago de los
  Cabelleros .. 87 C5
Santiago del
  Estero 94 B4
Santo Amaro . 93 E6
Santo Ângelo . 94 B6
Santo Antonio . 93 F2
Santo Corazón 91 G7
Santo Domingo 87 C6
Santo Tomás .. 91 F4
Santo Tomé ... 94 B5
Santo Tomé de
  Guayana =
  Ciudad
  Guayana 90 B6
Santoña 18 A4
Santoríni =
  Thira 23 F5
Santos 94 A7
Santos Dumont 94 A8
Sanza Pombo . 56 F3
São Anastácio . 94 A6
São Bernado de
  Campo 93 G4
São Borja 94 B5
São Carlos ... 94 A7
São Cristóvão . 93 E6
São Domingos 93 E4
São Francisco . 93 F5
São
  Francisco → 93 E6
São Francisco
  do Sul 94 B7
São Gabriel ... 94 C6
São João da
  Madeira 18 B1
São João del
  Rei 93 G5
São João do
  Araguaia .. 92 D4
São João do
  Piauí 92 D5
São José do Rio
  Prêto 94 A7
São Leopoldo . 94 B6
São Lourenço . 93 G4
São
  Lourenço → 93 F2
São Luís 92 C5
São Marcos .. 93 F4
São Marcos, B.
  de 92 C5
São Mateus ... 93 F6
São Paulo 94 A7
São Paulo □ .. 94 A7
São Roque, C.
  de 92 D6

São Sebastião, I.
  de 94 A7
São Tomé &
  Principe ■ .. 51 F4
São Vicente, C.
  de 18 D1
Saône → 13 D6
Saonek 39 E4
Saparua 39 E3
Sapele 55 G6
Saposoa 91 E3
Sapporo 32 F12
Sapulpa 79 B5
Saqqez 46 C6
Sar-e Pol 45 B6
Sar-e Pol □ ... 45 B6
Sar Planina ... 22 C3
Saráb 46 C6
Sarada → 40 D3
Saragossa =
  Zaragoza ... 19 B5
Saraguro 90 D3
Sarajevo 20 C7
Saran, G. 37 E4
Sarandí del Yi . 94 C5
Sarangani B. .. 38 C3
Sarangani Is. .. 38 C3
Sarangarh 40 G4
Saransk 24 C6
Sarapul 29 D6
Sarasota 75 F6
Saratov 24 C6
Saravane 36 A3
Sarawak □ ... 37 D4
Saray 22 D6
Sarayköy 23 F7
Sarbāz 45 E5
Sarbīsheh 45 C4
Sarda →
  Sarada → .. 40 D3
Sardalas 54 C7
Sardarshahr ... 42 E9
Sardegna □ .. 21 D2
Sardinia =
  Sardegna □ . 21 D2
Sardis 23 E7
Sargodha 42 C8
Sarh 53 G2
Sārī 44 B3
Sangöl 23 E7
Sarikamiş 46 B5
Sarikei 37 D4
Sark 11 G5
Şarköy 23 D6
Sarlat-la-Canéda 12 D4
Sarmi 39 E5
Sarmiento 95 F3
Sarnia 69 D2
Sarny 24 C2
Sarolangun ... 37 E2
Saronikós
  Kólpos 23 F4
Sarre = Saar → 13 B7
Sarreguemines 13 B7
Sarro 55 F3
Sarthe → 12 C3
Sartynya 28 C7
Sarvestān 44 D3
Sary-Tash 29 F8
Saryshagan ... 29 E8
Sasabeneh 49 F3
Sasaram 40 E5
Sasebo 32 C1
Saser 42 B10
Saskatchewan □ 71 C9
Saskatchewan →
  .... 71 C9
Saskatoon ... 71 C9
Saskylakh 30 B9

Sasovo 24 C5
Sassandra ... 55 H3
Sassandra → . 55 H3
Sássari 21 D2
Sassnitz 15 A7
Sassuolo 20 B3
Sasyk, Ozero .. 17 F9
Sata-Misaki ... 33 D2
Satadougou ... 55 F2
Satara 43 L8
Satmala Hills .. 43 J9
Satna 40 E3
Sátoraljaújhely 16 D5
Satpura Ra. ... 43 J10
Satu Mare 17 E6
Satui 37 E5
Saturnina → . 91 F7
Saudi Arabia ■ 47 F6
Sauerland 14 C4
Sault Ste. Marie,
  Canada 69 D2
Sault Ste. Marie,
  U.S.A. 72 A3
Saumlaki 39 F4
Saumur 12 C3
Saunders C. .. 65 F4
Sauri 55 F6
Saurimo 56 F4
Sava → 22 B3
Savage I. =
  Niue 65 L14
Savalou 55 G5
Savanna la Mar 86 C4
Savannah 75 C7
Savannah → . 75 C7
Savannakhet .. 36 A2
Savanur 43 M9
Savé 55 G5
Save → 59 C6
Sāveh 46 D7
Savelugu 55 G4
Savoie □ 13 D7
Savona 20 B2
Sawahlunto ... 37 E2
Sawai 39 E3
Sawai
  Madhopur .. 42 F10
Sawara 32 B7
Sawatch Mts. . 83 A9
Sawmills 59 B5
Sawu 39 F2
Sawu Sea ... 39 F2
Saxony, Lower
  =
  Niedersachsen □
  .... 14 B5
Say 55 F5
Sayán 91 F3
Sayan,
  Zapadnyy ... 30 D7
Saydā 46 D3
Sayghān 45 C6
Sayḥut 49 D5
Saynshand 35 B6
Sazanit 23 D2
Săzava → 16 D2
Sazin 42 B8
Scandicci 20 C3
Scandinavia .. 8 F10
Scarborough .. 11 D6
Scebeli,
  Wabi → 49 G3
Schaffhausen . 13 C8
Schefferville .. 69 C4
Schelde → ... 14 C3
Schenectady .. 73 C9
Schiermonnikoog
  .... 14 B4
Schio 20 B3

Schleswig 14 A5
Schleswig-
Holstein □ .. 14 A5
Schouten I. ... 62 D4
Schouten Is. =
Supiori 39 E5
Schwäbische
Alb 14 D5
Schwaner,
Pegunungan 37 E4
Schwarzwald .. 14 D5
Schwedt 15 B8
Schweinfurt .. 14 C6
Schwenningen
= Villingen-
Schwenningen 14 D5
Schwerin 15 B6
Schwyz 13 C8
Sciacca 21 F4
Scilla 21 E5
Scilly, Isles of . 11 G3
Scone 63 B5
Scotland □ ... 10 C4
Scott Glacier .. 96 A12
Scott Inlet 68 A3
Scottsbluff 76 E3
Scottsdale 62 D4
Scranton 73 D8
Scunthorpe ... 11 E6
Scusciuban ... 49 E5
Scutari =
Üsküdar 25 E2
Seaspray 63 C4
Seattle 80 B2
Sebastopol =
Sevastopol .. 25 E3
Sebha =
Sabhah 52 C1
Şebinkarahisar 46 B4
Sebta = Ceuta . 18 E3
Sebuku 37 E5
Sebuku, Teluk . 37 D5
Secretary I. ... 65 F2
Secunderabad . 43 L11
Sedalia 77 F8
Sedan, Australia 62 B2
Sedan, France . 13 B6
Seddon 65 D6
Seddonville ... 65 D5
Sedhiou 55 F1
Sedova, Pik ... 28 B6
Seeheim 58 D3
Seferihisar 23 E6
Segamat 37 D2
Segesta 21 F4
Seget 39 E4
Ségou 55 F3
Segovia =
Coco → 86 D3
Segovia 18 B3
Segre → 19 B6
Séguéla 55 G3
Segura → 19 C5
Sehitwa 58 C4
Sehore 43 H10
Seine → 12 B4
Seistan 45 D5
Seistan,
Daryācheh-ye 45 D5
Sekayu 37 E2
Sekondi-
Takoradi 55 H4
Selaru 39 F4
Selçuk 23 F6
Sele → 21 D5
Selenga =
Selenge
Mörön → .. 35 A5
Selenge
Mörön → .. 35 A5

Seletan, Tg. ... 37 E4
Sélibabi 55 E2
Selîma, El
Wâhât el ... 52 D4
Selkirk 71 C10
Selkirk Mts. ... 71 C8
Selma 75 B8
Selpele 39 E4
Selu 39 F4
Selva 94 B4
Selvas 91 E5
Semani → ... 23 D2
Semarang 37 F4
Semey 29 D9
Semiozernoye . 29 D7
Semipalatinsk =
Semey 29 D9
Semirara Is. ... 38 B2
Semisopochnoi
I. 71 C1
Semitau 37 D4
Semiyarka 29 D8
Semiyarskoye =
Semiyarka ... 29 D8
Semmering P. . 15 E8
Semnān 44 C3
Semnān □ ... 44 C3
Semporna 38 D1
Semuda 37 E4
Sena Madureira 91 E5
Senador
Pompeu ... 92 D6
Senaja 36 C5
Senanga 58 B4
Sendai,
Kagoshima,
Japan 32 D2
Sendai, Miyagi,
Japan 33 G12
Senegal ■ 55 F2
Senegal → ... 55 E1
Senge Khambab
= Indus → . 43 G5
Sengkang 39 E2
Senhor-do-
Bonfim 93 E5
Senigállia 20 C4
Senj 20 B5
Senja 8 E11
Senlis 13 B5
Senmonorom . 36 B3
Sennâr 53 F5
Senneterre 69 D3
Sens 13 B5
Senta 22 B3
Sentani 39 E6
Seo de Urgel .. 19 A6
Seoul = Sŏul .. 35 C7
Sepīdān 44 D3
Sept-Îles 69 C4
Sequoia
National Park 82 B3
Seram 39 E3
Seram Laut,
Kepulauan .. 39 E4
Seram Sea 39 E3
Serasan 37 D3
Serbia □ 22 C3
Serdobsk 24 C5
Seremban 37 D2
Serenje 59 A6
Sereth =
Siret → 17 F9
Sergino 28 C7
Sergipe □ 93 E6
Sergiyev Posad 24 B4
Seria 36 D4
Serian 37 D4
Seribu,
Kepulauan .. 37 F3

Sérifos 23 F5
Sermata 39 F3
Serny Zavod .. 29 F6
Serov 28 D7
Serowe 59 C5
Serpukhov 24 C4
Sérrai 22 D4
Serrezuela 94 C3
Serrinha 93 E6
Sertânia 92 D6
Serua 39 F4
Serui 39 E5
Serule 59 C5
Sesepe 39 E3
Sesfontein 58 B2
Sesheke 58 B4
Sète 13 E5
Sete Lagôas .. 93 F5
Sétif 54 A6
Seto 32 B5
Settat 54 B3
Setté-Cama ... 56 E1
Setúbal 18 C1
Setúbal, B. de . 18 C1
Seulimeum ... 36 C1
Sevan, Ozero =
Sevana Lich . 25 E6
Sevana Lich ... 25 E6
Sevastopol 25 E3
Severn →,
Canada 69 C2
Severn →, U.K. 11 F5
Severnaya
Zemlya 30 B7
Severnyye Uvaly 24 B6
Severo-
Yeniseyskiy . 30 C7
Severodvinsk .. 28 C4
Sevilla 18 D2
Seville = Sevilla 18 D2
Sevlievo 22 C5
Seward 71 B5
Seward Pen. .. 71 B3
Sewer 39 F4
Seychelles ■ .. 26 K9
Seymour 63 C4
Sfax 52 B1
Sfîntu Gheorghe 17 F7
Shaanxi □ ... 35 C5
Shaba □ 57 F4
Shabunda 57 E5
Shache 34 C2
Shackleton Ice
Shelf 96 A11
Shackleton Inlet 96 C15
Shadrinsk 29 D7
Shāhābād 44 B4
Shahdād 44 D4
Shahdād,
Namakzār-e . 44 D4
Shahdadkot ... 42 F5
Shahgarh 42 F6
Shaḥḥāt 52 B3
Shahjahanpur . 42 F11
Shahr Kord ... 44 C2
Shahrig 42 D5
Shaikhabad ... 42 B6
Shajapur 43 H10
Shakhty 25 D5
Shakhunya ... 24 B6
Shaki 55 G5
Shala, L. 53 G6
Shalqar 29 E6
Sham, J. ash . 44 F4
Shamīl 44 E4
Shammar, Jabal 47 F5
Shamo = Gobi 35 B6
Shamo, L. 53 G6
Shamva 59 B6

Shan □ 41 G12
Shandong □ .. 35 C6
Shanghai 35 C7
Shangqiu 35 C6
Shangrao 35 D6
Shangshui 35 C6
Shannon 64 D6
Shannon → .. 11 E2
Shansi =
Shanxi □ ... 35 C6
Shantou 35 D6
Shantung =
Shandong □ 35 C6
Shanxi □ 35 C6
Shaoguan 35 D6
Shaowu 35 D6
Shaoxing 35 C7
Shaoyang 35 D6
Shaqra',
Si. Arabia ... 47 F6
Shaqrā', Yemen 49 E4
Sharjah = Ash
Shāriqah ... 44 E3
Sharon 72 D5
Sharya 24 B6
Shashi,
Botswana ... 59 C5
Shashi, China . 35 C6
Shasta, Mt. ... 80 E2
Shatt al'Arab → 47 E7
Shaunavon ... 71 C8
Shawan 34 B3
Shawinigan ... 69 D3
Shcherbakov =
Rybinsk 24 B4
Shchuchinsk .. 29 D8
Shebele =
Scebeli,
Wabi → 49 G3
Sheboygan ... 72 C2
Sheffield 11 E6
Shekhupura .. 42 D8
Shelburne 69 D4
Shelby 75 B7
Shelbyville 74 B4
Shellharbour .. 63 B5
Shenandoah → 73 E7
Shendam 55 G6
Shendî 53 E5
Shensi =
Shaanxi □ .. 35 C5
Shenyang 35 B7
Sheopur Kalan 42 G10
Shepetivka ... 17 C8
Shepetovka =
Shepetivka .. 17 C8
Shepparton ... 63 C4
Sherbro I. 55 G2
Sherbrooke ... 69 D3
Sheridan 81 C10
Sherman 79 C5
Sherridon 71 C9
Shetland Is. ... 10 A6
Shibām 49 D4
Shigaib 53 E3
Shihchiachuangi
=
Shijiazhuang 35 C6
Shijiazhuang .. 35 C6
Shikarpur 42 F6
Shikoku 32 C3
Shikoku □ ... 33 H10
Shikoku-Sanchi 32 C3
Shilabo 49 F3
Shiliguri 40 D7
Shillong 41 E8
Shilong 35 D6
Shimada 32 B6
Shimizu 32 B6

Shimoga 43 N9
Shimonoseki .. 32 C2
Shinano → ... 32 A6
Shindand 42 C3
Shingū 32 C4
Shinyanga 57 E6
Shipehenski
  Prokhod 22 C5
Shipki La 42 D11
Shīr Kūh 44 D3
Shirane-San ... 32 A6
Shīrāz 44 D3
Shire → 59 B7
Shiretoko-Misaki 32 F13
Shiriya-Zaki ... 32 F12
Shīrvān 44 B4
Shirwa, L. =
  Chilwa, L. .. 59 B7
Shivpuri 43 G10
Shizuoka 32 B6
Shklov –
  Shklow 17 A10
Shklow 17 A10
Shkoder =
  Shkodra 22 C2
Shkodra 22 C2
Shkumbini → .. 23 D2
Shmidta, O. ... 30 A7
Sholapur =
  Solapur 43 L9
Shoshone Mts. 80 F5
Shoshong 59 C5
Shreveport 79 C7
Shrewsbury ... 11 E5
Shrirampur ... 40 F7
Shu 29 E8
Shuangyashan 35 B8
Shule 34 C2
Shumagin Is. .. 71 C4
Shungnak 71 B4
Shūr → 44 D3
Shurugwi 59 B5
Shūsf 45 D5
Shūshtar 47 D7
Shwebo 41 F10
Shwegu 41 E11
Shweli → 41 F11
Shymkent 29 E7
Shyok 42 B11
Shyok → 42 B9
Si Kiang = Xi
  Jiang → ... 35 D6
Si-ngan = Xi'an 35 C5
Si Racha 36 B2
Siah 47 G6
Siahan Range . 42 F4
Siaksriindrapura 37 D2
Sialkot 42 C9
Siantan, P. 37 D3
Siārem 45 D5
Siargao 38 C3
Siasi 38 C2
Siau 39 D3
Šiauliai 24 B1
Šibenik 20 C5
Siberut 37 E1
Sibi 42 E5
Sibil 39 E6
Sibiti 56 E2
Sibiu 17 F7
Sibolga 37 D1
Sibsagar 41 D10
Sibu 37 D4
Sibuco 38 C2
Sibuguey B. ... 38 C2
Sibut 56 C3
Sibutu 38 D1
Sibutu Passage 38 D1
Sibuyan 38 B2

Sibuyan Sea .. 38 B2
Sichuan □ 34 C5
Sicilia 21 F5
Sicily = Sicilia . 21 F5
Sicuani 91 F4
Siddipet 43 K11
Sidéradougou . 55 F4
Sîdi Barrâni ... 52 B4
Sidi-bel-Abbès . 54 A4
Sidley, Mt. 96 B18
Sidon = Saydā 46 D3
Sidra, G. of =
  Surt, Khalīj .. 52 B2
Siedlce 17 B6
Sieg → 14 C4
Siegen 14 C5
Siem Reap 36 B2
Siena 20 C3
Sieradz 16 C4
Sierra Colorada 95 E3
Sierra Gorda .. 94 A3
Sierra Leone ■ 55 G2
Sífnos 23 F5
Sighetu-
  Marmatiei ... 17 E6
Sighişoara 17 E7
Sigli 36 C1
Sigsig 90 D3
Sigüenza 19 B4
Siguiri 55 F3
Sihanoukville =
  Kompong
  Som 36 B2
Siirt 46 C5
Sikar 42 F9
Sikasso 55 F3
Sikhote Alin,
  Khrebet 31 E11
Sikhote Alin Ra.
  – Sikhote
  Alin, Khrebet 31 E11
Síkinos 23 F5
Sikkim □ 40 D7
Sil → 18 A2
Silchar 41 E9
Silesia = Śląsk 16 C3
Silgarhi Doti .. 40 C3
Silghat 41 D9
Silifke 46 C3
Siliguri =
  Shiliguri 40 D7
Siling Co 34 C3
Silistra 22 B6
Silivri 22 D7
Sillajhuay,
  Cordillera ... 91 G5
Silva Porto =
  Kuito 58 A3
Simanggang .. 37 D4
Simav 23 E7
Simbirsk 24 C6
Simeria 17 F6
Simeulue 37 D1
Simferopol ... 25 E3
Sími 23 F6
Simikot 40 C3
Simla 42 D10
Simplon P. 13 C8
Simpson Desert 60 F6
Simunjan 37 D4
Sinabang 37 D1
Sinadogo 49 F4
Sinai = Es Sînâ' 52 C5
Sinai, Mt. =
  Mûsa, G. 47 E3
Sinaloa de
  Leyva 84 B3
Sīnāwan 54 B7
Sincelejo 90 B3

Sincorá, Serra
  do 93 E5
Sind □ 42 F6
Sind Sagar
  Doab 42 D7
Sindangan 38 C2
Sines 18 D1
Sines, C. de ... 18 D1
Singa 53 F5
Singapore ■ .. 37 D2
Singaraja 37 F5
Singida 57 E6
Singitikós
  Kólpos 23 D5
Singkaling
  Hkamti 41 E10
Singkawang ... 37 D3
Singleton 63 B5
Singora =
  Songkhla ... 36 C2
Sinjai 39 F2
Sinjär 46 C5
Sinkat 53 E6
Sinkiang Uighur
  = Xinjiang
  Uygur
  Zizhiqu □ ... 34 B3
Sinni → 21 D6
Sinnuris 52 C5
Sinop 46 B3
Sintang 37 D4
Sintra 18 C1
Sinŭiju 35 B7
Siocon 38 C2
Siófok 16 E4
Sioma 58 B4
Sion 13 C7
Sioux City 77 D6
Sioux Falls 76 D6
Sioux Lookout . 71 C10
Siping 35 B7
Sipura 37 E1
Siquijor 38 C2
Siracusa 21 F5
Sirajganj 41 E7
Sirdaryo =
  Syrdarya → .. 29 E7
Siret → 17 F9
Sirohi 43 G8
Sironj 43 G10
Síros 23 F5
Sirsa 42 E9
Sisak 20 B6
Sisaket 36 A2
Sisophon 36 B2
Sīstān va
  Balūchestān □ 45 E5
Sitapur 40 D3
Sitges 19 B6
Sitía 23 G6
Sitka 71 C6
Sittang Myit → 41 J11
Sittwe 41 G9
Siuri 40 F6
Sīvand 44 D3
Sivas 46 C4
Siverek 46 C4
Sivrihisar 46 C2
Sîwa 52 C4
Siwalik Range . 40 D4
Siwan 40 D5
Sjælland 9 G10
Sjumen =
  Šumen 22 C6
Skadarsko
  Jezero 22 C2
Skagerrak 9 G9
Skagway 71 C6
Skala-Podilska . 17 D8

Skala
  Podolskaya =
  Skala-Podilska 17 D8
Skalat 17 D7
Skardu 42 B9
Skarzysko-
  Kamienna ... 16 C5
Skeena → 70 C6
Skegness 11 E7
Skeldon 90 B7
Skellefte älv → 8 F12
Skellefteå 8 F12
Skíathos 23 E4
Skien 9 G9
Skierniewice .. 16 C5
Skikda 54 A6
Skipton 62 C3
Skíros 23 E5
Skole 17 D6
Skópelos 23 E4
Skopje 22 C3
Skvyra 17 D9
Skye 10 C3
Skyros = Skíros 23 E5
Slamet 37 F3
Śląsk 16 C3
Slatina 22 B5
Slave → 70 B8
Slavgorod 29 D8
Slavonski Brod 20 B7
Slavuta 17 C8
Slavyansk =
  Slovyansk ... 25 D4
Slawharad ... 17 B10
Sleaford B. 62 B2
Sleeper Is. 68 C2
Sligeach = Sligo 11 D2
Sligo 11 D2
Sliven 22 C6
Slobodskoy ... 24 B7
Slobozia 22 B6
Slonim 17 B7
Slough 11 F6
Slovak Rep. ■ . 16 D5
Slovakia =
  Slovak Rep. ■ 16 D5
Slovakian Ore
  Mts. =
  Slovenské
  Rudohorie .. 16 D4
Slovenia ■ ... 20 B5
Slovenija =
  Slovenia ■ .. 20 B5
Slovenská
  Republika =
  Slovak Rep. ■ 16 D5
Slovenské
  Rudohorie .. 16 D4
Slovyansk ... 25 D4
Sluch → 17 C8
Słupsk 16 A3
Slutsk 17 B8
Smara 54 B3
Smarhon 17 A8
Smederevo ... 22 B3
Smith Arm 70 B7
Smithton 62 D4
Smithtown 63 B5
Smoky Bay 62 B1
Smolensk 24 C3
Smolikas, Óros 23 D3
Smolyan 22 D5
Smorgon =
  Smarhon ... 17 A8
Smyrna = İzmir 23 E6
Snake → 80 B4
Snake I. 63 C4
Snake River
  Plain 81 D7

Sneek 14 B3
Sněžka 16 C2
Snøhetta 8 F9
Snowdon 11 E4
Snowdrift 70 B8
Snowtown 62 B2
Snowy . . . 63 C4
Snowy Mts. . . . 63 C4
Snyatyn 17 D7
Snyder 78 C3
Soalala 59 H9
Sobat, Nahr . . 53 G5
Sobral 92 C5
Soc Trang 36 C3
Soch'e =
  Shache 34 C2
Sochi 25 E4
Société, Is. de la 65 L15
Society Is. =
  Société, Is. de
  la 65 L15
Socompa,
  Portezuelo de 94 A3
Socorro 90 B4
Socotra 49 E5
Soda Plains . . . 42 B11
Söderhamn . . . 8 F11
Sodiri 53 F4
Sodo 53 G6
Sofia = Sofiya . 22 C4
Sofia . . 59 H9
Sofiya 22 C4
Sogamoso 90 B4
Sognefjorden . . 8 F9
Sohâg 52 C5
Soissons 13 B5
Sokal 17 C7
Söke 23 F6
Sokhumi 25 E5
Sokodé 55 G5
Sokol 24 B5
Sokółka 17 B6
Sokolo 55 F3
Sokolów
  Podlaski 17 B6
Sokoto 55 F6
Solano 38 A2
Solapur 43 L9
Soledad 90 B6
Soligalich 24 B5
Soligorsk =
  Salihorsk . . . 17 B8
Solikamsk . . . 28 D6
Solimões =
  Amazonas . . 92 C3
Solingen 14 C4
Sóller 19 C7
Sologne 12 C4
Solok 37 E2
Solomon Is. ■ . 64 K10
Solomon Sea . 61 B9
Solon 35 B7
Solor 39 F2
Solothurn 13 C7
Šolta 20 C6
Solţānābād . . . 44 B4
Solunska Glava 22 D3
Solwezi 59 A5
Soma 23 E6
Somali Rep. ■ . 49 F4
Somalia =
  Somali Rep. ■ 49 F4
Sombor 22 B2
Sombrerete . . . 84 C4
Sombrero . . . 87 C7
Somerset East . 59 E5
Somerset I. . . . 70 A10
Someş . . 17 E6
Sommariva . . . 63 A4

Somme . . 12 A4
Somosierra,
  Puerto de . . . 18 B4
Somport, Puerto
  de 12 E3
Sóndrio 20 A2
Sonepur 40 G4
Song Cau . . . 36 B3
Songea 57 G7
Songhua
  Jiang . . . 35 B8
Songkhla 36 C2
Songpan 34 C5
Sonipat 42 E10
Sonmiani 42 G5
Sono . . 93 D4
Sonora . . 84 B2
Sonsonate 85 E7
Soochow =
  Suzhou 35 C7
Sopi 39 D3
Sopot 16 A4
Sopron 16 E3
Sør-Rondane . . 96 B8
Sorata 91 G5
Sorel 69 D3
Sorgono 21 D2
Soria 19 B4
Sorkh, Kuh-e . . 44 C4
Soroca 17 D9
Sorocaba 94 A7
Soroki =
  Soroca 17 D9
Sorong 39 E4
Soroti 57 D6
Sørøya 8 D12
Sorrento 63 C3
Sorsogon 38 B2
Sosnowiec 16 C4
Souanké 56 D2
Soúdhas, Kólpos 23 G5
Sŏul 35 C7
Sound, The =
  Øresund 9 G10
Sources,
  Mt. aux 59 D5
Soure 92 C4
Souris 71 D9
Souris . . 71 D10
Sousa 92 D6
Sousel 92 C3
Sousse 52 A1
South Africa ■ . 58 E4
South
  Australia □ . . 62 B2
South Bend . . . 72 D2
South
  Carolina □ . . 75 C7
South China Sea 36 C4
South Dakota □ 76 C4
South East C. . 62 D4
South Horr . . . 57 D7
South I. 65 E3
South
  Invercargill . . 65 G3
South Korea ■ . 35 C7
South Magnetic
  Pole 96 A13
South
  Nahanni . . 70 B7
South Natuna Is.
  = Natuna
  Selatan,
  Kepulauan . . 37 D3
South Orkney Is. 96 A4
South Pagai, I.
  = Pagai
  Selatan, P. . . 37 E2
South Platte . . 76 E4

South Pole . . . . 96 C
South
  Ronaldsay . . 10 B5
South
  Saskatchewan 71 C9
South Shetland
  Is. 96 A4
South Shields . 11 D6
South Taranaki
  Bight 64 C6
South Uist 10 C3
South West C. . 62 D4
Southampton . . 11 F6
Southampton I. 68 B2
Southbridge . . 65 E5
Southend-on-
  Sea 11 F7
Southern Alps . 65 E4
Southern Indian
  L. 71 C10
Southern
  Ocean 96 A9
Southern
  Uplands 10 D5
Southport 63 A5
Southwest C. . . 65 G2
Soutpansberg . 59 C5
Sovetsk,
  Kaliningd.,
  Russia 24 B1
Sovetsk, Kirov,
  Russia 24 B6
Sōya-Misaki . . . 32 E12
Soyo 56 F2
Sozh . . 17 C10
Spain ■ 18 C4
Spalding 62 B2
Spanish Town . 86 C4
Sparta = Spárti 23 F4
Spartanburg . . 75 B7
Spárti 23 F4
Spartivento, C.,
  Calabria, Italy 21 F6
Spartivento, C.,
  Sard., Italy . . 21 E2
Spátha, Ákra . . 23 G4
Spencer, C. . . . 62 C2
Spencer G. . . . 62 B2
Spenser Mts. . . 65 E5
Spey . . 10 C5
Speyer 14 D5
Split 20 C6
Spokane 80 B5
Spoleto 20 C4
Sporyy Navolok,
  Mys 28 B7
Spratly I. 36 C4
Spree . . 15 B7
Springbok 58 D3
Springfield, N.Z. 65 E4
Springfield, Ill.,
  U.S.A. 77 F10
Springfield,
  Mass., U.S.A. 73 C9
Springfield, Mo.,
  U.S.A. 79 A7
Springfield,
  Ohio, U.S.A. . 72 E4
Springfield,
  Oreg., U.S.A. 80 C2
Springfontein . 59 E5
Springhill 69 D4
Springhurst . . . 63 C4
Springs 59 D5
Squamish 71 D7
Srbija =
  Serbia □ 22 C3
Sre Umbell . . . 36 B2

Srebrnica 20 B7
Sredinny Ra. =
  Sredinnyy
  Khrebet 31 D14
Sredinnyy
  Khrebet 31 D14
Srednevilyuysk 31 C10
Śrem 16 B3
Sremska
  Mitrovica . . . 22 B2
Sri Lanka ■ . . . 43 R12
Srikakulam 40 H4
Srinagar 42 B9
Stade 14 B5
Stadlandet 8 F9
Stafford 11 E5
Stakhanov . . . 25 D4
Stalingrad =
  Volgograd . . 25 D5
Staliniri =
  Tskhinvali . . . 25 E5
Stalino =
  Donetsk . . . 25 D4
Stalinogorsk =
  Novomoskovsk
  . . . . 24 C4
Stalowa Wola . 17 C6
Stamford 73 D9
Stanislav =
  Ivano-
  Frankivsk . . . 17 D7
Stanke Dimitrov 22 C4
Stanley,
  Australia 62 D4
Stanley, Canada 71 C9
Stanley, Falk. Is. 95 G5
Stanovoy
  Khrebet 31 D10
Stanovoy Ra. =
  Stanovoy
  Khrebet 31 D10
Stanthorpe 63 A5
Stara Planina . . 22 C4
Stara Zagora . . 22 C5
Starachowice . . 16 C5
Staraya Russa . 24 B3
Starbuck I. 65 K15
Stargard
  Szczeciński . . 16 B2
Staritsa 24 B3
Starogard
  Gdański 16 B4
Starokonstantinov
  =
  Starokonstyantyniv
  . . . . 17 D8
Starokonstyantyniv
  . . . . 17 D8
Staryy
  Chartoriysk . . 17 C7
Staryy Oskol . . 24 C4
State College . . 73 D7
Staten, I. =
  Estados, I. de
  Los 95 G4
Statesville 75 B7
Stavanger 9 G9
Staveley 65 E4
Stavropol 25 D5
Stawell 62 C3
Steenkool =
  Bintuni 39 E4
Stefanie L. =
  Chew Bahir . . 53 H6
Stefansson Bay 96 A9
Steiermark □ . . 15 E8
Steinkjer 8 F10
Stellenbosch . . 58 E3
Stendal 15 B6

Steornabhaigh
  = Stornoway   10   B3
Stepanakert =
  Xankändi   ...   25   F6
Stephens Creek   62   B3
Stepnoi = Elista   25   D5
Stepnyak   ...   29   D8
Sterlitamak   ...   29   D6
Stettin =
  Szczecin   ...   16   B2
Stettiner Haff   ..   15   B8
Stettler   71   C8
Steubenville   ..   72   D5
Stevenage   ...   11   F6
Stewart   70   B6
Stewart, I.   95   G2
Stewart I.   65   G2
Steyr   15   D8
Stillwater, N.Z.   65   E4
Stillwater,
  U.S.A.   78   A5
Štip   22   D4
Stirling   10   C5
Stockerau   ...   15   D9
Stockholm   9   G11
Stockport   11   E5
Stockton   82   B2
Stockton-on-
  Tees   11   D6
Stoke on Trent   11   E5
Stokes Pt.   62   D3
Stolac   20   C6
Stolbovoy,
  Ostrov   ...   30   B11
Stolbtsy =
  Stowbtsy   ...   17   B8
Stolin   17   C8
Stonehaven   ...   10   C5
Stonewall   71   C10
Stony Tunguska
  =
  Podkamennaya
  Tunguska   →   30   C7
Stora Lulevatten   8   E11
Storavan   8   E11
Store Bælt   9   G10
Store Creek   ..   63   B4
Storm B.   62   D4
Stormberge   ..   59   E5
Stornoway   ...   10   B3
Storozhinets =
  Storozhynets   17   D7
Storozhynets   ..   17   D7
Storsjön   8   F10
Storuman   8   E11
Stowbtsy   17   B8
Strahan   62   D4
Stralsund   15   A7
Strand   58   E3
Stranraer   11   D4
Strasbourg   13   B7
Stratford,
  Canada   69   D2
Stratford, N.Z.   .   64   C6
Strathalbyn   ...   62   C2
Straubing   15   D7
Streaky B.   62   B1
Streaky Bay   ...   62   B1
Strelka   30   D7
Strezhevoy   ...   29   C8
Strimón   →   ..   23   D4
Strimonikós
  Kólpos   23   D5
Strómboli   21   E5
Stronsay   10   B5
Stroud Road   ..   63   B5
Strumica   22   D4
Stryy   17   D6
Strzelecki Cr.   →   62   A2

Stuart Ra.   62   A1
Stung Treng   ..   36   B3
Stutterheim   ...   59   E5
Stuttgart   14   D5
Styria =
  Steiermark □   15   E8
Suakin   53   E6
Subansiri   →   ..   41   D9
Subi   37   D3
Subotica   16   E4
Suceava   17   E8
Suchou =
  Suzhou   35   C7
Süchow =
  Xuzhou   35   C6
Sucre   91   G5
Sudair   47   F6
Sudan ■   53   E4
Sudbury   69   D2
Sûdd   53   G4
Sudeten Mts =
  Sudety   16   C3
Sudety   16   C3
Sudirman,
  Pegunungan   39   E5
Sueca   19   C5
Suez = El
  Suweis   52   C5
Suez, G. of =
  Suweis, Khalîg
  el   52   C5
Sugluk = Salluit   68   B3
Suhār   44   E4
Suhbaatar   ...   35   A5
Suhl   14   C6
Suihua   35   B7
Sukadana,
  Kalimantan,
  Indonesia   ...   37   E3
Sukadana,
  Sumatera,
  Indonesia   ...   37   F3
Sukaraja   37   E4
Sukarnapura =
  Jayapura   ...   39   E6
Sukhona   →   ..   28   C5
Sukhumi =
  Sokhumi   25   E5
Sukkur   42   F6
Sukkur Barrage   42   F6
Sula, Kepulauan   39   E3
Sulaiman Range   42   D6
Sulawesi □   ..   39   E2
Sulawesi Sea =
  Celebes Sea   .   39   D2
Sulima   55   G2
Sulina   17   F9
Sulitjelma   8   E11
Sullana   90   D2
Sultanpur   40   D4
Sulu Arch.   38   C2
Sulu Sea   38   C2
Suluq   52   B3
Sulzberger Ice
  Shelf   96   B17
Sumalata   39   D2
Sumatera □   ...   37   D2
Sumatra =
  Sumatera □   .   37   D2
Sumba   39   F1
Sumba, Selat   ..   39   F1
Sumbawa   37   F5
Sumbawa Besar   37   F5
Sumbe   56   G2
Sümen   22   C6
Sumgait =
  Sumqayıt   ...   25   E6
Summerside   ..   69   D4
Sumperk   16   D3

Sumqayıt   25   E6
Sumter   75   C7
Sumy   24   C3
Sunbury   63   C3
Sunda, Selat   ..   37   F3
Sunda Str. =
  Sunda, Selat   37   F3
Sundarbans,
  The   41   G7
Sundargarh   ...   40   F5
Sunderland   ...   11   D6
Sundsvall   8   F11
Sungaigerong   .   37   E2
Sungailiat   ...   37   E3
Sungaipakning   37   D2
Sungaipenuh   ..   37   E2
Sungaitiram   ...   37   E5
Sungari =
  Songhua
  Jiang   →   ...   35   B8
Sungguminasa   39   F1
Sunghua Chiang
  = Songhua
  Jiang   →   ...   35   B8
Sungurlu   46   B3
Sunnyvale   ...   82   B1
Suntar   30   C9
Supaul   40   D6
Superior   77   B8
Superior, L.   ..   69   D2
Suphan Dağı   ..   46   C5
Supiori   39   E5
Sūr, Lebanon   ..   46   D3
Sūr, Oman   ...   45   F4
Sura   →   24   B6
Surabaja –
  Surabaya   →   37   F4
Surabaya   37   F4
Surakarta   37   F4
Surat, Australia   63   A4
Surat, India   ..   43   J8
Surat Thani   ...   36   C1
Suratgarh   42   E8
Surgut   29   C8
Suriapet   43   L11
Surigao   38   C3
Surinam ■   ...   92   B2
Suriname ■ =
  Surinam ■   ..   92   B2
Suriname   →   ..   92   A2
Surt   52   B2
Surt, Khalīj   52   B2
Suruga-Wan   ..   32   B6
Süsangerd   ...   47   E7
Susanville   80   E3
Susquehanna   →
    73   E7
Susques   94   A3
Susunu   39   E4
Susurluk   23   E7
Sutherland Falls   65   F2
Sutlej   →   42   E7
Suva   64   L12
Suva Planina   ..   22   C4
Suvorov Is. =
  Suwarrow Is.   65   L14
Suwałki   17   A6
Suwarrow Is.   ..   65   L14
Suweis, Khalîg
  el   52   C5
Suzdal   24   B5
Suzhou   35   C7
Suzu-Misaki   ..   32   A5
Svealand □   ...   9   G10
Sverdlovsk =
  Yekaterinburg   29   D7
Svetlogorsk =
  Svyetlahorsk   17   B9
Svetozarevo   ..   22   B3

Svishtov   22   C5
Svislach   17   B7
Svyetlahorsk   ..   17   B9
Swabian Alps =
  Schwäbische
  Alb   14   D5
Swakopmund   .   58   C2
Swan Hill   ...   62   C3
Swansea,
  Australia   63   B5
Swansea, U.K.   .   11   F5
Swatow =
  Shantou   35   D6
Swaziland ■   ..   59   D6
Sweden ■   9   G10
Sweetwater   ...   78   C3
Swellendam   ..   58   E4
Świdnica   16   C3
Świdnik   17   C6
Świebodzin   ...   16   B2
Świecie   16   B4
Swift Current   ..   71   C9
Swindon   11   F6
Swinemünde =
  Świnoujście   .   16   B2
Świnoujście   ..   16   B2
Switzerland ■   .   13   C8
Sydney,
  Australia   63   B5
Sydney, Canada   69   D4
Sydra, G. of =
  Surt, Khalīj   ..   52   B2
Syktyvkar   28   C6
Sylhet   41   E8
Sylt   14   A5
Sym   29   C9
Syracuse   73   C7
Syrdarya   →   ..   29   E7
Syria ■   46   D4
Syrian Desert =
  Ash Shām,
  Bādiyat   47   D4
Syzran   24   C6
Szczecin   16   B2
Szczecinek   16   B3
Szczytno   16   B5
Szechwan =
  Sichuan □   ..   34   C5
Szeged   16   E5
Székesfehérvár   16   E4
Szekszárd   ...   16   E4
Szentes   16   E5
Szolnok   16   E5
Szombathely   .   16   E3

T

Tabacal   94   A4
Tabaco   38   B2
Ṭābah   47   F5
Tabarka   54   A6
Ṭabas,
  Khorāsān, Iran   44   C4
Ṭabas,
  Khorāsān, Iran   45   C5
Tabatinga, Serra
  da   93   E5
Tablas   38   B2
Table B. =
  Tafelbaai   ...   58   E3
Table Mt.   58   E3
Tábor   16   D2
Tabora   57   F6
Tabou   55   H3
Tabrīz   46   C6
Tabūk   47   E4

Tacheng

Tacheng 34 B3
Tacloban 38 B2
Tacna 91 G4
Tacoma 80 B2
Tacuarembó .. 94 C5
Tademaït,
Plateau du .. 54 C5
Tadjoura 49 E3
Tadmor 65 D5
Tadoussac 69 D4
Tadzhikistan =
Tajikistan ■ . 29 F8
Taegu 35 C7
Taejŏn 35 C7
Tafalla 19 A5
Tafelbaai 58 E3
Tafermaar 39 F4
Taft 38 B3
Taga Dzong ... 41 D7
Taganrog 25 D4
Tagbilaran ... 38 C2
Tagish 70 B6
Tagish L. 70 B6
Tagliamento → 20 B4
Taguatinga ... 93 E5
Tagum 38 C3
Tagus =
Tejo → 18 C1
Tahakopa 65 G3
Tahan, Gunong 36 D2
Tahat 54 D6
Tāherī 44 E3
Tahiti 65 L16
Tahoe, L. 80 F3
Tahoua 55 F6
Tahta 52 C5
Tahulandang .. 39 D3
Tahuna 39 D3
Taï 55 G3
Tai Hu 35 C7
Taibei 35 D7
T'aichung =
Taizhong ... 35 D7
Taidong 35 D7
Taieri → 65 G4
Taihape 64 C6
Tailem Bend .. 62 C2
Taimyr
Peninsula =
Taymyr,
Poluostrov .. 30 B7
Tain 10 C4
Tainan 35 D7
Taínaron, Ákra 23 F4
T'aipei = Taibei 35 D7
Taiping 36 D2
Taitao, Pen. de 95 F1
Taiwan ■ 35 D7
Taïyetos Óros . 23 F4
Taiyuan 35 C6
Taizhong 35 D7
Ta'izz 49 E3
Tajikistan ■ .. 29 F8
Tajo = Tejo → 18 C1
Tājūrā 52 B1
Tak 36 A1
Takada 32 A6
Takaka 65 D5
Takamatsu 32 B4
Takaoka 32 A5
Takapuna 64 B6
Takasaki 32 A6
Takatsuki 32 B4
Takaungu 57 E7
Takayama 32 A5
Takefu 32 B5
Takengon 36 D1
Takeo 36 B2
Tākestān 46 D7

Takhār □ 45 B7
Takum 55 G6
Talara 90 D2
Talas 29 E8
Talaud,
Kepulauan .. 38 D3
Talaud Is. =
Talaud,
Kepulauan .. 38 D3
Talavera de la
Reina 18 C3
Talayan 38 C2
Talbragar → . 63 B4
Talca 94 D2
Talcahuano ... 94 D2
Talcher 40 G5
Taldy Kurgan =
Taldyqorghan 29 E8
Taldyqorghan . 29 E8
Ţalesh, Kūhhā-
ye 46 C7
Tali Post 53 G5
Talibon 38 B2
Taliwang 37 F5
Tall 'Afar 46 C5
Talladega 74 C4
Tallahassee .. 75 D5
Tallangatta 63 C4
Tallarook 63 C4
Tallinn 24 B1
Talodi 53 F5
Taltal 94 B2
Talwood 63 A4
Talyawalka
Cr. → 62 B3
Tamale 55 G4
Tamanrasset .. 54 D6
Tamarang 63 B5
Tamaské 55 F6
Tambacounda . 55 F2
Tambelan,
Kepulauan .. 37 D3
Tambo de Mora 91 F3
Tambora 37 F5
Tambov 24 C5
Tamburâ 53 G4
Tâmchekket .. 55 E2
Tamega → ... 18 B1
Tamenglong .. 41 E9
Tamgak, Mts. . 55 E6
Tamil Nadu □ . 43 P10
Tammerfors =
Tampere ... 8 F12
Tamo Abu,
Pegunungan 37 D5
Tampa 75 F6
Tampere 8 F12
Tampico 84 C5
Tamrida =
Qādib 49 E5
Tamsagbulag . 35 B6
Tamu 41 E10
Tamworth 63 B5
Tana →, Kenya 57 E8
Tana →,
Norway 8 D13
Tana, L. 53 F6
Tanahbala ... 37 E1
Tanahgrogot .. 37 E5
Tanahjampea . 39 F2
Tanahmasa ... 37 E1
Tanahmerah .. 39 F6
Tanami Desert . 60 D5
Tanana 71 B4
Tanana → ... 71 B4
Tananarive =
Antananarivo 59 H9
Tánaro → 20 B2
Tandag 38 C3

Tandil 94 D5
Tandil, Sa. del . 94 D5
Tando Adam .. 42 G6
Tandou L. 62 B3
Tane-ga-Shima 33 D2
Taneatua 64 C7
Tanen Tong Dan 41 J12
Tanezrouft 54 D5
Tanga 57 F7
Tanganyika, L. . 57 F5
Tanger =
Tangier 54 A3
Tanggula Shan 34 C4
Tangier 54 A3
Tangshan 35 C6
Tanimbar,
Kepulauan .. 39 F4
Tanimbar Is. =
Tanimbar,
Kepulauan .. 39 F4
Tanjay 38 C2
Tanjore =
Thanjavur ... 43 P11
Tanjung 37 E5
Tanjungbalai .. 37 D1
Tanjungbatu .. 37 D5
Tanjungkarang
Telukbetung . 37 F3
Tanjungpandan 37 E3
Tanjungpinang 37 D2
Tanjungredeb . 37 D5
Tanjungselor .. 37 D5
Tanout 55 F6
Tanta 52 B5
Tantung =
Dandong ... 35 B7
Tanunda 62 B2
Tanzania ■ ... 57 F6
Taolanaro 59 K9
Taoudenni 54 D4
Taourirt 54 B4
Tapa Shan =
Daba Shan .. 35 C5
Tapah 37 D2
Tapajós → ... 92 C3
Tapaktuan ... 37 D1
Tapanui 65 F3
Tapauá → 91 E6
Tapeta 55 G3
Tapi → 43 J8
Tapirapecó,
Serra 90 C6
Tapuaenuku, Mt. 65 D5
Tapul Group .. 38 C2
Taquari → ... 91 G7
Tara, Australia 63 A5
Tara, Russia ... 29 D8
Tara →,
Montenegro, Yug. 22 C2
Tara →, Russia 29 D8
Tarabagatay,
Khrebet 29 E9
Ţarābulus,
Lebanon 46 D3
Ţarābulus, Libya 52 B1
Tarakan 37 D5
Taralga 63 B4
Taranaki □ ... 64 C6
Tarancón 19 B4
Taranga Hill .. 43 H8
Táranto 21 D6
Táranto, G. di . 21 D6
Tarapacá 90 D5
Tararua Ra. ... 64 D6
Tarashcha 17 D10
Tarauacá 91 E4
Tarauacá → .. 91 E5
Tarawera 64 C7

Tarawera L. ... 64 C7
Taraz 29 E8
Tarbela Dam .. 42 B8
Tarbes 12 E4
Tarcoola 62 B1
Tarcoon 63 B4
Taree 63 B5
Tarfaya 54 C2
Tarifa 18 D3
Tarija 94 A4
Tariku → 39 E5
Tarim Basin =
Tarim Pendi . 34 C3
Tarim He → .. 34 C3
Tarim Pendi ... 34 C3
Taritatu → ... 39 E5
Tarkhankut, Mys 25 D3
Tarko Sale ... 28 C8
Tarkwa 55 G4
Tarlac 38 A2
Tarma 91 F3
Tarn → 12 D4
Tarnobrzeg ... 16 C5
Tarnów 16 C5
Tarnowskie
Góry 16 C4
Taroom 63 A4
Taroudannt ... 54 B3
Tarragona ... 19 B6
Tarrasa 19 B7
Tarso Emissi .. 52 D2
Tarsus 46 C3
Tartagal 94 A4
Tartu 24 B2
Tartūs 46 D3
Tarutung 37 D1
Tasāwah 52 C1
Taschereau ... 69 D3
Tash-Kömür .. 29 E8
Tash-Kumyr =
Tash-Kömür . 29 E8
Tashauz =
Dashhowuz . 29 E6
Tashi Chho
Dzong =
Thimphu 41 D7
Tashkent =
Toshkent ... 29 E7
Tashtagol 29 D9
Tasman B. ... 65 D5
Tasman Mts. .. 65 D5
Tasman Pen. .. 62 D4
Tasmania □ .. 62 D4
Tatabánya 16 E4
Tatar Republic □
= Tatarstan □ 29 D6
Tatarbunary .. 17 F9
Tatarsk 29 D8
Tatarstan □ ... 29 D6
Tateyama 32 B6
Tathra 63 C4
Tatra = Tatry . 16 D4
Tatry 16 D4
Tatta 43 G5
Tatuī 94 A7
Tat'ung =
Datong 35 B6
Tatvan 46 C5
Taubaté 94 A7
Tauern 15 E7
Taumarunui .. 64 C6
Taumaturgo .. 91 E4
Taungdwingyi . 41 G10
Taunggyi 41 G11
Taungup 41 H10
Taungup Pass . 41 H10
Taungya 41 H9
Taunton 11 F5

152

Taunus 14 C5
Taupo 64 C7
Taupo, L. 64 C6
Tauranga 64 B7
Tauranga Harb. 64 B7
Taurianova ... 21 E6
Taurus Mts. =
  Toros Dağları 46 C3
Tavda 29 D7
Tavda → 29 D7
Taveta 57 E7
Tavira 18 D2
Tavoy 36 B1
Tawau 36 D5
Tawitawi 38 C2
Tay → 10 C5
Tayabamba .. 91 E3
Taylakova ... 29 D8
Taylakovy =
  Taylakova ... 29 D8
Tayma 47 F4
Taymyr, Oz. ... 30 B8
Taymyr,
  Poluostrov .. 30 B7
Taytay 38 B1
Taz → 28 C8
Taza 54 B4
Tazovskiy 28 C8
Tbilisi 25 E5
Tchad = Chad ■ 53 E2
Tchad, L. 53 F1
Tch'eng-tou =
  Chengdu 35 C5
Tchibanga ... 56 E2
Tch'ong-k'ing =
  Chongqing .. 35 D5
Tczew 16 A4
Te Anau, L. ... 65 F2
Te Aroha 64 B6
Te Awamutu .. 64 C6
Te Kuiti 64 C6
Te Puke 64 B7
Te Waewae B. . 65 G2
Tebakang 37 D4
Tébessa 54 A6
Tebicuary → .. 94 B5
Tebingtinggi .. 37 D1
Tecuci 22 B6
Tedzhen =
  Tejen 29 F7
Tefé 90 D6
Tegal 37 F3
Tegina 55 F6
Tegucigalpa .. 85 E7
Tehachapi ... 82 C3
Tehrān 44 C2
Tehuantepec .. 85 D5
Tehuantepec, G.
  de 85 D5
Tehuantepec,
  Istmo de 85 D6
Tejen 29 F7
Tejo → 18 C1
Tekapo, L. 65 E4
Tekeli 29 E8
Tekirdağ 22 D6
Tekkali 40 H5
Tel Aviv-Yafo .. 46 D3
Tela 85 D7
Telanaipura =
  Jambi 37 E2
Telavi 25 E6
Telekhany =
  Tsyelyakhany 17 B7
Teles Pires → . 91 E7
Telford 11 E5
Télimélé 55 F2
Tellicherry ... 43 P9
Telsen 95 E3

Teluk Anson .. 37 D2
Teluk Betung =
  Tanjungkarang
  Telukbetung . 37 F3
Teluk Intan =
  Teluk Anson . 37 D2
Telukbutun ... 37 D3
Telukdalem ... 37 D1
Tema 55 G4
Temax 85 C7
Temerloh 37 D2
Temir 29 E6
Temirtau,
  Kazakstan ... 29 D8
Temirtau, Russia 29 D9
Temma 62 D3
Temora 63 B4
Tempe 83 D7
Temple 78 D5
Temuco 94 D2
Temuka 65 F4
Tenali 40 J3
Tenasserim ... 36 B1
Tenda, Col di .. 20 B1
Tendaho 49 E3
Tenerife 54 C1
Teng Xian 35 C6
Tengah □ 39 E2
Tengah
  Kepulauan .. 37 F5
Tengchong ... 34 D4
Tenggara □ .. 39 E2
Tenggarong .. 37 E5
Tengiz, Ozero . 29 D7
Tenkasi 43 Q10
Tenke 57 G5
Tenkodogo ... 55 F4
Tennessee □ .. 74 B4
Tennessee → .. 72 F1
Tenom 36 C5
Tenryū-
  Gawa → 32 B5
Tenterfield ... 63 A5
Teófilo Otoni .. 93 F5
Tepa 39 F3
Tepic 84 C4
Teplice 16 C1
Ter → 19 A7
Téra 55 F5
Téramo 20 C4
Terang 62 C3
Terebovlya ... 17 D7
Terek → 25 E6
Teresina 92 D5
Terewah, L. ... 63 A4
Terhazza 54 D3
Teridgerie
  Cr. → 63 B4
Termez =
  Termiz 29 F7
Términi Imerese 21 F4
Termiz 29 F7
Térmoli 20 C5
Ternate 39 D3
Terni 20 C4
Ternopil 17 D7
Ternopol =
  Ternopil 17 D7
Terowie, N.S.W.,
  Australia ... 63 B4
Terowie,
  S. Austral.,
  Australia 62 B2
Terracina 20 D4
Terralba 21 E2
Terranova =
  Ólbia 20 D2
Terrassa =
  Tarrasa 19 B7

Terre Haute ... 72 E2
Terschelling ... 14 B3
Teruel 19 B5
Teryaweyna L. . 62 B3
Teshio-
  Gawa 32 F12
Tesiyn
  Gol 34 A4
Teslin 70 B6
Tessalit 54 D5
Tessaoua 55 F6
Tetas, Pta. 94 A2
Tete 59 B6
Teterev → 17 C10
Teteven 22 C5
Tetiyev 17 D9
Tétouan 54 A3
Tetovo 22 C3
Teuco → 94 B4
Teun 39 F3
Teutoburger
  Wald 14 B5
Tévere → 20 D4
Tewantin 63 A5
Texarkana ... 79 C6
Texas 63 A5
Texas □ 78 D4
Texas City ... 79 E6
Texel 14 B3
Teyvareh 45 C6
Tezpur 41 D9
Thabana
  Ntlenyana ... 59 D5
Thabazimbi ... 59 C5
Thailand ■ 36 A2
Thailand, G. of 36 B2
Thakhek 36 A2
Thal 42 C7
Thala La 41 C11
Thallon 63 A4
Thames 64 B6
Thames → ... 11 F7
Thane 43 K8
Thanh Pho Ho
  Chi Minh ... 36 B3
Thanjavur 43 P11
Thar Desert .. 42 F7
Tharad 43 G7
Thargomindah 63 A3
Tharrawaddy .. 41 J10
Thásos 23 D5
Thaton 41 J11
Thaungdut ... 41 E10
Thayetmyo ... 41 H10
Thazi 41 G11
The Alberga → 62 A2
The Coorong . 62 C2
The Frome → . 62 A2
The Grampians 62 C3
The Great Divide
  = Great
  Dividing Ra. . 61 E8
The Hague = 's-
  Gravenhage . 14 B3
The
  Hamilton → 62 A2
The
  Macumba → 62 A2
The Neales → 62 A2
The Pas 71 C9
The Rock 63 C4
The Salt L. 62 B3
The
  Stevenson → 62 A2
The
  Warburton → 62 A2
Thebes = Thívai 23 E4
Theebine 63 A5

Thermaïkós
  Kólpos 23 D4
Thermopylae P. 23 E4
Thessaloníki .. 23 D4
Thessaloníki,
  Gulf of =
  Thermaïkós
  Kólpos 23 D4
Thetford 11 E7
Thetford Mines 69 D3
Thevenard ... 62 B1
Thiel Mts. 96 C2
Thiers 13 D5
Thies 55 F1
Thika 57 E7
Thimphu 41 D7
Thionville 13 B7
Thíra 23 F5
Thistle I. 62 C2
Thívai 23 E4
Thomas, L. ... 62 A2
Thomasville,
  Ga., U.S.A. .. 75 D6
Thomasville,
  N.C., U.S.A. . 75 B7
Thompson ... 71 C10
Thomson's Falls
  = Nyahururu 57 D7
Thrace 22 D6
Three Hummock
  I. 62 D3
Three Points, C. 55 H4
Thun 13 C7
Thunder Bay .. 69 D2
Thung Song .. 36 C1
Thunkar 41 D8
Thüringer Wald 14 C6
Thurles 11 E3
Thurloo Downs 63 A3
Thurso 10 B5
Thurston I. 96 B2
Thylungra 63 A3
Tia 63 B5
Tian Shan 34 B3
Tianjin 35 C6
Tianshui 35 C5
Tiaret 54 A5
Tiassalé 55 G4
Tibati 53 G1
Tiber =
  Tévere → .. 20 D4
Tiberias, L. =
  Yam Kinneret 46 D3
Tibesti 52 D2
Tibet =
  Xizang □ ... 34 C3
Tibooburra 62 A3
Tiburón 84 B2
Tichît 55 E3
Ticino → 20 B2
Tiddim 41 F9
Tidjikja 55 E2
Tidore 39 D3
Tiel 55 F1
Tierra de
  Campos .. 18 A3
Tierra del
  Fuego, I. Gr.
  de 95 G3
Tiétar → 18 C2
Tieyon 62 A1
Tiflis = Tbilisi . 25 E5
Tifu 39 E3
Tighina 17 E9
Tignish 69 D4
Tigre → 90 D4
Tigris = Dijlah,
  Nahr → 47 E6
Tigyaing 41 F11

Name	Map	Grid
Tīh, Gebel el	52	C5
Tijuana	84	A1
Tikamgarh	43	G11
Tikhoretsk	25	D5
Tikrīt	46	D5
Tiksi	30	B10
Tilamuta	39	D2
Tilburg	14	C3
Tillabéri	55	F5
Tílos	23	F6
Tilpa	63	B3
Tilsit = Sovetsk	24	B1
Timaru	65	F4
Timbedgha	55	E3
Timboon	62	C3
Timbuktu = Tombouctou	55	E4
Timimoun	54	C5
Timişoara	16	F5
Timmins	69	D2
Timok →	22	B4
Timon	92	D5
Timor	39	F2
Tinaca Pt.	38	C3
Tindouf	54	C3
Tingo Maria	91	E3
Tinjoub	54	C3
Tinnevelly = Tirunelveli	43	Q10
Tinogasta	94	B3
Tínos	23	F5
Tintinara	62	C3
Tioman, Pulau	37	D2
Tipongpani	41	D10
Tipperary	11	E2
Tirán	44	C2
Tirana	22	D2
Tiranë = Tirana	22	D2
Tiraspol	17	E9
Tire	23	E6
Tirebolu	46	B4
Tiree	10	C3
Tîrgovişte	22	B5
Tîrgu-Jiu	17	F6
Tîrgu Mureş	17	E7
Tirich Mir	42	A7
Tîrnăveni	17	E7
Tîrnavos	23	E4
Tirodi	43	J11
Tirol □	14	E6
Tirso →	21	E2
Tiruchchirappalli	43	P11
Tirunelveli	43	Q10
Tirupati	43	N11
Tiruppur	43	P10
Tiruvannamalai	43	N11
Tisa →	22	B3
Tisdale	71	C9
Tisza = Tisa →	22	B3
Tit-Ary	30	B10
Titicaca, L.	91	G5
Titograd = Podgorica	22	C2
Titov Veles	22	D3
Titova-Mitrovica = Kosovska-Mitrovica	22	C3
Titovo Užice	22	C2
Titule	57	D5
Tivaouane	55	F1
Tívoli	20	D4
Tiwī	45	F4
Tizi-Ouzou	54	A5
Tiznit	54	C3
Tjirebon = Cirebon	37	F3
Tlaxcala	84	D5
Tlaxiaco	84	D5
Tlemcen	54	B4
Tmassah	52	C2
Toamasina	59	H9
Toay	94	D4
Toba	32	B5
Toba Kakar	42	D6
Tobago	87	D7
Tobelo	39	D3
Tobermory	10	C3
Toboali	37	E3
Tobol →	29	D7
Toboli	39	E2
Tobolsk	29	D7
Tobruk = Tubruq	52	B3
Tobyl = Tobol →	29	D7
Tocantinópolis	92	D4
Tocantins □	93	E4
Tocantins →	92	C4
Tochigi	32	A6
Tocopilla	94	A2
Tocumwal	63	C4
Tocuyo →	90	A5
Todeli	39	E2
Todenyang	57	D7
Todos os Santos, B. de	93	E6
Togba	55	E2
Togian, Kepulauan	39	E2
Togliatti	24	C6
Togo ■	55	G5
Toinya	53	G4
Tojikiston = Tajikistan ■	29	F8
Tojo	39	E2
Tokala	39	E2
Tōkamachi	32	A6
Tokanui	65	G3
Tokar	53	E6
Tokarahi	65	F4
Tokat	46	B4
Tokelau Is.	65	K13
Tokmak	29	E8
Tokushima	32	B4
Tokuyama	32	B2
Tōkyō	32	B6
Tolaga Bay	64	C8
Tolbukhin = Dobrich	22	C6
Toledo, Spain	18	C3
Toledo, U.S.A.	72	D4
Toledo, Montes de	18	C3
Tolga	54	B6
Toliara	59	J8
Tolima	90	C3
Tolitoli	39	D2
Tolo	56	E3
Tolo, Teluk	39	E2
Toluca	84	D5
Tomakomai	32	F12
Tomar	18	C1
Tomaszów Mazowiecki	16	C4
Tombé	53	G5
Tombouctou	55	E4
Tombua	58	B2
Tomelloso	18	C4
Tomingley	63	B4
Tomini	39	D2
Tomini, Teluk	39	E2
Tomorit	23	D3
Tomsk	29	D9
Tonantins	90	D5
Tonawanda	73	C6
Tondano	39	D2
Tonekābon	44	B2
Tong Xian	35	C6
Tonga ■	65	L13
Tonga Trench	65	L13
Tongareva	65	K15
Tongchuan	35	C5
Tonghua	35	B7
Tongjiang	35	B8
Tongking, G. of = Tonkin, G. of	35	D5
Tongoy	94	C2
Tongren	35	D5
Tongsa Dzong	41	D8
Tongue →	76	B2
Tonk	42	F9
Tonkin, G. of	35	D5
Tonlé Sap	36	B2
Toompine	63	A3
Toora	63	C4
Toowoomba	63	A5
Topeka	77	F7
Topki	29	D9
Topol'čany	16	D4
Topolobampo	84	B3
Torata	91	G4
Torbalı	23	E6
Torbat-e Heydārīyeh	44	C4
Torbat-e Jām	45	C5
Torbay	11	F5
Tordesillas	18	B3
Torgau	15	C7
Torino	20	B1
Torit	53	H5
Tormes →	18	B2
Torne älv →	8	E12
Torneå = Tornio	8	E12
Torneträsk	8	E11
Tornio	8	E12
Tornquist	94	D4
Toro, Cerro del	94	B3
Toroníios Kólpos	23	D4
Toronto, Australia	63	B5
Toronto, Canada	69	D3
Toropets	24	B3
Tororo	57	D6
Toros Dağları	46	C3
Tôrre de Moncorvo	18	B2
Torre del Greco	21	D5
Torrejón de Ardoz	18	B4
Torrelavega	18	A3
Torremolinos	18	D3
Torrens, L.	62	B2
Torrente	19	C5
Torreón	84	B4
Torres	84	B2
Torres Vedras	18	C1
Torrevieja	19	D5
Tortosa	19	B6
Tortosa, C. de	19	B6
Ţorūd	44	C3
Toruń	16	B4
Tosa-Wan	32	C3
Toscana □	20	C3
Toshkent	29	E7
Tostado	94	B4
Tosya	46	B3
Toteng	58	C4
Totma	24	A5
Totten Glacier	96	A12
Tottenham	63	B4
Tottori	32	B4
Touba	55	G3
Toubkal, Djebel	54	B3
Tougan	55	F4
Touggourt	54	B6
Tougué	55	F2
Toul	13	B6
Toulepleu	55	G3
Toulon	13	E6
Toulouse	12	E4
Toummo	52	D1
Toungoo	41	H11
Touraine	12	C4
Tourane = Da Nang	36	A3
Tourcoing	13	A5
Touriñán, C.	18	A1
Tournai	14	C2
Tournon	13	D6
Tours	12	C4
Towamba	63	C4
Towang	41	D8
Townsville	61	D8
Toyama	32	A5
Toyohashi	32	B5
Toyonaka	32	B4
Toyooka	32	B4
Toyota	32	B5
Tozeur	54	B6
Trá Li = Tralee	11	E2
Trabzon	46	B4
Trafalgar, C.	18	D2
Trail	71	D8
Tralee	11	E2
Trancas	94	B3
Trang	36	C1
Trangan	39	F4
Trangie	63	B4
Trani	20	D6
Transantarctic Mts.	96	C3
Transilvania	17	F7
Transilvanian Alps = Carpații Meridionali	17	F7
Transylvania = Transilvania	17	F7
Trápani	21	E4
Traralgon	63	C4
Trasimeno, L.	20	C4
Traun	15	D8
Travemünde	15	B6
Travers, Mt.	65	E5
Travnik	20	B6
Trébbia →	20	B2
Třebíč	16	D2
Trebinje	20	C7
Treinta y Tres	94	C6
Trelew	95	E3
Tremp	19	A6
Trenčín	16	D4
Trenque Lauquen	94	D4
Trent →	11	E6
Trento	20	A3
Trenton	73	D8
Trepassey	69	D5
Tres Arroyos	94	D4
Três Corações	93	G4
Três Lagoas	93	G3
Tres Montes, C.	95	F1
Tres Puentes	94	B2
Tres Puntas, C.	95	F3
Três Rios	93	G5
Treviso	20	B4
Triabunna	62	D4
Trichinopoly = Tiruchchirappalli	43	P11
Trichur	43	P10
Trida	63	B4
Trier	14	D4
Trieste	20	B4

Triglav 20 A4
Tríkkala 23 E3
Trikora, Puncak 39 E5
Trinidad, Bolivia 91 F6
Trinidad,
  Colombia . . . 90 B4
Trinidad, Cuba 86 B3
Trinidad,
  Uruguay 94 C5
Trinidad, U.S.A. 78 A1
Trinidad, I. . . . 95 D4
Trinidad &
  Tobago ■ . . . 87 D7
Trinity ⇥ 79 E6
Trinity B. 69 D5
Trinity Range . . 80 E4
Trinkitat 53 E6
Tripoli =
  Tarābulus,
  Lebanon 46 D3
Tripoli =
  Tarābulus,
  Libya 52 B1
Trípolis 23 F4
Tripura □ 41 F8
Trivandrum . . . 43 Q10
Trnava 16 D3
Troglav 20 C6
Trois-Rivières . 69 D3
Troitsko
  Pechorsk 28 C6
Trollhättan 9 G10
Tronador 95 E2
Trondheim 8 F10
Trondheimsfjorden
  . . . . 8 F10
Trout L. 70 B7
Trouville-sur-
  Mer 12 B4
Troy, Turkey . . 23 E6
Troy, Ala.,
  U.S.A. 74 D5
Troy, N.Y.,
  U.S.A. 73 C9
Troyes 13 B6
Trucial States =
  United Arab
  Emirates ■ . . 44 F3
Trujillo,
  Honduras . . . 85 D7
Trujillo, Peru . 91 E3
Trujillo, Spain . 18 C3
Trujillo,
  Venezuela . . . 90 B4
Truk 64 J10
Trundle 63 B4
Truro, Canada . 69 D4
Truro, U.K. 11 F4
Truskavets . . . 17 D6
Trutnov 16 C2
Tsaratanana . . 59 H9
Tsarevo =
  Michurin 22 C6
Tsau 58 C4
Tselinograd =
  Astana 29 D8
Tsetserleg 34 B5
Tshabong 58 D4
Tshane 58 C4
Tshela 56 E2
Tshikapa 56 F4
Tshofa 57 F5
Tshwane 58 C4
Tsihombe 59 K9
Tsimlyansk Res.
  =
  Tsimlyanskoye
  Vdkhr. 25 D5
Tsimlyanskoye
  Vdkhr. 25 D5

Tsinan = Jinan 35 C6
Tsinghai =
  Qinghai □ . . 34 C4
Tsingtao =
  Qingdao 35 C7
Tskhinvali 25 E5
Tsna ⇥ 24 C5
Tsu 32 B5
Tsuchiura 32 A7
Tsugaru-Kaikyō 32 F12
Tsumeb 58 B3
Tsumis 58 C3
Tsuruga 32 B5
Tsurugi-San . . 32 C4
Tsuruoka 33 G11
Tsyelyakhany . 17 B7
Tual 39 F4
Tuamotu Arch.
  = Tuamotu Is. 65 L16
Tuamotu Is. . . . 65 L16
Tuamotu Ridge 65 M17
Tuao 38 A2
Tuapse 25 E4
Tuatapere 65 G2
Tubarão 94 B7
Tubau 37 D4
Tübingen 14 D5
Tubruq 52 B3
Tubuai Is. 65 M16
Tucacas 90 A5
Tucson 83 D7
Tucumcari 78 B2
Tucupita 90 B6
Tucuruí 92 C4
Tucuruí, Reprêsa
  de 92 C4
Tudela 19 A5
Tudmur 46 D4
Tuen 63 A4
Tuguegarao . . . 38 A2
Tukangbesi,
  Kepulauan . . 39 F2
Tükrah 52 B3
Tuktoyaktuk . . . 70 B6
Tukuyu 57 F6
Tula, Mexico . . 84 C5
Tula, Russia . . 24 C4
Tulak 45 C5
Tulancingo 84 C5
Tulare 82 B3
Tulcán 90 C3
Tulcea 17 F9
Tulchyn 17 D9
Tuli, Indonesia 39 E2
Tuli, Zimbabwe 59 C5
Tullamore,
  Australia . . . 63 B4
Tullamore,
  Ireland 11 E3
Tulle 12 D4
Tullibigeal 63 B4
Tulmaythah . . . 52 B3
Tulsa 79 A6
Tulua 90 C3
Tulungagung . . 37 F4
Tum 39 E4
Tumaco 90 C3
Tumatumari . . . 90 B7
Tumba, L. 56 E3
Tumbarumba . . 63 C4
Túmbes 90 D2
Tumby Bay . . . 62 B2
Tumeremo 90 B6
Tumkur 43 N10
Tump 42 F3
Tumpat 36 C2
Tumu 55 F4
Tumucumaque,
  Serra 92 B3

Tumut 63 C4
Tuncurry 63 B5
Tunduru 57 G7
Tundzha ⇥ . . . 22 D6
Tunga Pass . . . 41 C10
Tungabhadra ⇥
  . . . . 43 M11
Tungaru 53 F5
Tunguska,
  Nizhnyaya ⇥ 30 C6
Tunis 54 A7
Tunisia ■ 54 B6
Tunja 90 B4
Tunuyán ⇥ . . . 94 C3
Tunxi 35 D6
Tupelo 74 B3
Tupinambaranas 90 D7
Tupiza 94 A3
Tupungato,
  Cerro 94 C3
Túquerres 90 C3
Tura 30 C8
Turabah 47 E5
Tūrān 44 C4
Turayf 47 E5
Turda 17 E6
Turek 16 B4
Turfan = Turpan 34 B3
Turfan
  Depression =
  Turpan Hami 34 B3
Tŭrgovishte . . . 22 C6
Turgutlu 23 E6
Turhal 46 B4
Turia ⇥ 19 C5
Turiaçu 92 C4
Turiaçu ⇥ 92 C4
Turin = Torino 20 B1
Turkana, L. 57 D7
Turkestan =
  Türkistan . . . 29 E7
Turkey ■ 46 C3
Türkistan 29 E7
Turkmenistan ■ 29 F6
Turks & Caicos
  Is. ■ 87 B5
Turku 9 F12
Turnagain, C. . . 64 D7
Turneffe Is. . . . 85 D7
Turnhout 14 C3
Tŭrnovo =
  Veliko
  Tŭrnovo 22 C5
Turnu Măgurele 22 C5
Turnu Roşu, P. . 17 F7
Turpan 34 B3
Turpan Hami . . 34 B3
Turukhansk . . . 30 C6
Tuscaloosa . . . 74 C4
Tuscany =
  Toscana □ . . 20 C3
Tuticorin 43 Q11
Tutóia 92 C5
Tutong 36 D4
Tutrakan 22 B6
Tuttlingen 14 E5
Tutuala 39 F3
Tutuila 65 L13
Tuvalu ■ 64 K12
Tuxpan 84 C5
Tuxtla Gutiérrez 85 D6
Tuy 18 A1
Tuz Gölü 46 C3
Ţūz Khurmātū . 46 D6
Tuzla 20 B7
Tver 24 B4
Tweed Heads . 63 A5
Twillingate 69 D5
Twin Falls 81 D6

Twofold B. 63 C4
Tyachiv 17 D6
Tychy 16 C4
Tyler 79 C6
Tyre = Sūr 46 D3
Tyrol = Tirol □ 14 E6
Tyrrell ⇥ 62 C3
Tyrrell, L. 62 C3
Tyrrhenian Sea 21 E4
Tyumen 29 D7
Tzaneen 59 C6
Tzukong =
  Zigong 35 D5

U

U.S.A. = United
  States of
  America ■ . . 67 F10
Uarsciek 49 G4
Uato-Udo 39 F3
Uatumã ⇥ . . . 90 D7
Uaupés 90 D5
Uaupés ⇥ 90 C5
Ubá 93 G5
Ubaitaba 93 E6
Ubangi =
  Oubangi ⇥ . 56 E3
Ubauro 42 E6
Ube 32 C2
Ubeda 18 C4
Uberaba 93 F4
Uberlândia 93 F4
Ubon
  Ratchathani . 36 A2
Ubort ⇥ 17 B9
Ubundu 57 E5
Ucayali ⇥ 90 D4
Uchiura-Wan . . 32 F12
Udaipur 43 G8
Udaipur Garhi . 40 D6
Udgir 43 K10
Udhampur 42 C9
Udi 55 G6
Údine 20 A4
Udmurtia □ . . . 28 D6
Udon Thani . . . 36 A2
Udupi 43 N9
Ueda 32 A6
Uele ⇥ 57 D4
Uelzen 14 B6
Ufa 29 D6
Ugab ⇥ 58 C2
Ugalla ⇥ 57 F6
Uganda ■ 57 D6
Ugljane 20 B5
Ugolyak 30 C10
Uibhist a Deas
  = South Uist 10 C3
Uibhist a Tuath
  = North Uist 10 C3
Uíge 56 F2
Uinta Mts. 81 E8
Uitenhage 59 E5
Ujjain 43 H9
Ujung Pandang 39 F1
Ukerewe I. 57 E6
Ukhrul 41 E10
Ukhta 28 C6
Ukraine ■ 25 D3
Ulaanbaatar . . . 35 B5
Ulaangom 34 A4
Ulan Bator =
  Ulaanbaatar . 35 B5
Ulan Ude 30 D8
Ulcinj 22 D2

Ulhasnagar ... 43 K8
Ulladulla 63 C5
Ullapool 10 C4
Ulm 14 D5
Ulmarra 63 A5
Ulonguè 59 A6
Ulster □ 11 D3
Ulubat Gölü ... 23 D7
Uludağ 23 D7
Ulungur He ➝ 34 B3
Uluru = Ayers
  Rock 60 F5
Ulutau 29 E7
Ulverstone ... 62 D4
Ulyanovsk =
  Simbirsk 24 C6
Ulyasutay 34 B4
Umala 91 G5
Uman 17 D10
Umaria 40 F3
Umarkot 43 G6
Umba 28 C4
Umbrella Mts. . 65 F3
Ume älv ➝ ... 8 F12
Umeå 8 F12
Umera 39 E3
Umm al
  Qaywayn ... 44 E3
Umm Bel 53 F4
Umm Lajj 47 F4
Umm Ruwaba . 53 F5
Umnak I. 71 C3
Umniati ➝ ... 59 B5
Umtata 59 E5
Umuarama ... 93 G3
Una ➝ 20 B6
Unalaska 71 C3
Uncía 91 G5
Underbool 62 C3
Ungarie 63 B4
Ungarra 62 B2
Ungava B. 68 C4
Ungava Pen. .. 68 B3
Ungeny =
  Ungheni 17 E8
Ungheni 17 E8
União da Vitória 94 B6
Unimak I. 71 C3
United Arab
  Emirates ■ .. 44 F3
United
  Kingdom ■ . 11 E5
United States of
  America ■ .. 67 F10
Unnao 40 D3
Unst 10 A6
Ünye 46 B4
Upata 90 B6
Upemba, L. ... 57 F5
Upington 58 D4
Upper Hutt 65 D6
Upper Volta =
  Burkina
  Faso ■ 55 F4
Uppsala 9 G11
Ur 47 E6
Uracara 90 D7
Ural =
  Zhayyq ➝ .. 29 E6
Ural 63 B4
Ural Mts. =
  Uralskie Gory 28 D6
Uralla 63 B5
Uralsk = Oral . 24 C7
Uralskie Gory . 28 D6
Uranquinty ... 63 C4
Urawa 32 B6
Uray 29 C7
Urbana 72 D1

Urbino 20 C4
Urbión, Picos de 19 A4
Urcos 91 F4
Urda 25 D6
Urdzhar 29 E9
Ures 84 B2
Urfa = Sanliurfa 46 C4
Urganch 29 E7
Urgench =
  Urganch ... 29 E7
Uribia 90 A4
Urla 23 E6
Urmia =
  Orūmīyeh ... 46 C6
Urmia, L. =
  Orūmīyeh,
  Daryācheh-ye 46 C6
Uroševac 22 C3
Uruana 93 F4
Urubamba 91 F4
Urubamba ➝ . 91 F4
Uruçuí 92 D5
Uruguai ➝ ... 94 B6
Uruguaiana ... 94 B5
Uruguay ■ ... 94 C5
Uruguay ➝ .. 94 C5
Urumchi =
  Ürümqi 34 B3
Ürümqi 34 B3
Usakos 58 C3
Usedom 15 B8
Ush-Tobe 29 E8
Ushant =
  Ouessant, I. d' 12 B1
Ushuaia 95 G3
Üsküdar 25 E2
Usman 24 C4
Usoke 57 F6
Uspallata, P. de 94 C3
Uspenskiy 29 E8
Ussuriysk 31 E11
Ust-Aldan =
  Batamay 31 C10
Ust Ilimpeya =
  Yukti 30 C8
Ust Ishim 29 D8
Ust-
  Kamenogorsk
  = Öskemen . 29 E9
Ust-Karenga .. 31 D9
Ust Kuyga 31 B11
Ust Muya 30 D9
Ust Olenek 30 B10
Ust Port 28 C9
Ust Tsilma 28 C6
Ust Urt =
  Ustyurt,
  Plateau 29 E6
Ust Vorkuta .. 28 C7
Ústí nad Labem 16 C2
Ustica 21 E4
Ustinov =
  Izhevsk 28 D6
Ustye 30 D7
Ustyurt, Plateau 29 E6
Usu 34 B3
Usuki 32 C2
Usumacinta ➝ 85 D6
Usumbura =
  Bujumbura .. 57 E5
Uta 39 E5
Utah □ 81 F8
Utete 57 F7
Utiariti 91 F7
Utica 73 C8
Utrecht 14 B3
Utrera 18 D3
Utsunomiya ... 32 A6

Uttar Pradesh □ 42 F11
Uttaranchal □... 40 C2
Uttaradit 36 A2
Uummannarsuaq
  = Farvel, Kap 68 C6
Uusikaupunki . 8 F12
Uvat 29 D7
Uvinza 57 F6
Uvira 57 E5
Uvs Nuur 34 A4
Uwajima 32 C3
Uyuni 91 H5
Uzbekistan ■ .. 29 E7
Uzerche 12 D4
Uzh ➝ 17 C10
Uzhgorod =
  Uzhhorod ... 17 D6
Uzhhorod 17 D6
Uzunköprü 22 D6

V

Vaal ➝ 58 D4
Vaasa 8 F12
Vác 16 E4
Vach ➝ =
  Vakh ➝ ... 29 C8
Vadodara 43 H8
Vadsø 8 D13
Vaduz 13 C8
Váh ➝ 16 E4
Vahsel B. 96 B5
Vaigach 28 B6
Vakh ➝ 29 C8
Val d'Or 69 D3
Valahia 22 B5
Valandovo 22 D4
Valcheta 95 E3
Valdayskaya
  Vozvyshennost
  .... 24 B3
Valdepeñas ... 18 C4
Valdés, Pen. ... 95 E4
Valdez 71 B5
Valdivia 95 D2
Valdosta 75 D6
Valença 93 E6
Valença do Piauí 92 D5
Valence 13 D6
Valencia, Spain 19 C5
Valencia,
  Venezuela ... 90 A5
Valencia □ ... 19 C5
Valencia, G. de 19 C6
Valencia de
  Alcántara ... 18 C2
Valencia I. 11 F1
Valenciennes .. 13 A5
Valentim, Sa. do 92 D5
Valera 90 B4
Valjevo 22 B2
Vall de Uxó ... 19 C5
Valladolid,
  Mexico 85 C7
Valladolid, Spain 18 B3
Valle de la
  Pascua 90 B5
Valledupar 90 A4
Vallejo 80 F2
Vallenar 94 B2
Valletta 21 G5
Valls 19 B6
Valognes 12 B3
Valona = Vlóra 23 D2
Valozhyn 17 A8
Valparaíso ... 94 C2

Vals, Tanjung . 39 F5
Valsad 43 J8
Valverde del
  Camino 18 D2
Van 46 C5
Van, L. = Van
  Gölü 46 C5
Van Gölü 46 C5
Van Rees,
  Pegunungan 39 E5
Vanadzor 25 E5
Vancouver,
  Canada 71 D7
Vancouver,
  U.S.A. 80 C2
Vancouver I. .. 71 D7
Vänern 9 G10
Vanga 57 E7
Vangaindrano . 59 J9
Vännäs 8 F11
Vannes 12 C2
Vanrhynsdorp . 58 E3
Vanua Levu ... 64 L12
Vanuatu ■ 64 L11
Vapnyarka 17 D9
Varanasi 40 E4
Varangerfjorden 8 D13
Varaždin 20 A6
Varberg 9 G10
Vardak □ 45 C7
Vardar =
  Axiós ➝ ... 23 D4
Varese 20 B2
Varna 22 C6
Varzaneh 44 C3
Vasa Barris ➝ 93 E6
Vascongadas =
  País Vasco □ 19 A4
Vasht = Khāsh 42 E2
Vasilevichi 17 B9
Vasilkov =
  Vasylkiv 17 C10
Vaslui 17 E8
Västerås 9 G11
Västervik 9 G11
Vasto 20 C5
Vasylkiv 17 C10
Vatican City ■ . 20 D4
Vatomandry ... 59 H9
Vatra-Dornei . 17 E7
Vättern 9 G10
Vaupés =
  Uaupés ➝ .. 90 C5
Vawkavysk ... 17 B7
Vaygach, Ostrov 28 C6
Vedea ➝ 22 C5
Vega 8 E10
Vegreville 71 C7
Vejer de la
  Frontera 18 D3
Velebit Planina 20 B5
Vélez 90 B4
Vélez Málaga . 18 D3
Vélez Rubio .. 19 D4
Velhas ➝ 93 F5
Velika Kapela . 20 B5
Velikaya ➝ ... 24 B2
Veliki Ustyug . 24 A6
Velikiye Luki . 24 B3
Veliko Tŭrnovo 22 C5
Velikonda Range 43 M11
Velletri 20 D4
Vellore 43 N11
Venado Tuerto 94 C4
Vendée □ 12 C4
Vendôme 12 C4
Venézia 20 B4
Venézia, G. di . 20 B4

Venezuela ■ .. 90 B5
Venezuela, G. de 90 A4
Vengurla 43 M8
Venice =
  Venézia 20 B4
Venkatapuram . 40 H3
Ventotene ... 21 D4
Ventoux, Mt. .. 13 D6
Ventspils 24 B1
Ventuarí → .. 90 C5
Ventura 82 C3
Venus B. 63 C4
Vera, Argentina 94 B4
Vera, Spain ... 19 D5
Veracruz 84 D5
Veraval 43 J7
Verbánia 20 B2
Vercelli 20 B2
Vorde → ...., 95 E3
Verden 14 B5
Verdun 13 B6
Vereeniging ... 59 D5
Verga, C. 55 F2
Verín 18 B2
Verkhnevilyuysk 30 C10
Verkhniy
  Baskunchak . 25 D6
Verkhoyansk .. 31 C11
Verkhoyansk Ra.
  =
Verkhoyanskiy
  Khrebet 31 C10
Verkhoyanskiy
  Khrebet 31 C10
Vermilion 71 C8
Vermont □ 73 C9
Vernon, Canada 71 C4
Vernon, U.S.A. 78 B4
Véroia 23 D4
Verona 20 B3
Versailles 12 B5
Vert, C. 55 F1
Verviers 14 C3
Veselovskoye
  Vdkhr. 25 D5
Vesoul 13 C7
Vesterålen 8 E11
Vestfjorden ... 8 E10
Vesuvio 21 D5
Vesuvius, Mt. =
  Vesuvio 21 D5
Veszprém ... 16 E3
Vetlugu → ... 28 D5
Vettore, Mte.. . 20 C4
Veys 47 E7
Vezhen 22 C5
Viacha 91 G5
Viamão 94 C6
Viana 92 C5
Viana do
  Alentejo ... 18 C2
Viana do Castelo 18 B1
Vianópolis 93 F4
Viaréggio 20 C3
Vibo Valéntia .. 21 E6
Vicenza 20 B3
Vich 19 B7
Vichy 13 C5
Vicksburg 79 C8
Viçosa 93 D6
Victor 43 J7
Victor Harbor .. 62 C2
Victoria, Canada 71 D7
Victoria, Chile . 94 D2
Victoria, Guinea 55 F2
Victoria = Labuan,
  Malaysia 36 C5
Victoria □ 62 C3

Victoria, L.,
  Africa 57 E6
Victoria, L.,
  Australia 62 B3
Victoria Beach . 71 C10
Victoria de
  Durango =
  Durango 84 C4
Victoria Falls .. 59 B5
Victoria I. 70 A8
Victoria Ld. ... 96 B14
Victoria
  Taungdeik .. 41 G9
Victoria West .. 58 E4
Victorica 94 D3
Vicuña 94 C2
Vidin 22 C4
Vidisha 43 H10
Viedma 95 E4
Viedma, L. .. 95 F2
Vienna = Wien 15 D9
Vienne 13 D6
Vienne → 12 C4
Vientiane 36 A2
Vierzon 12 C5
Vietnam ■ 36 A3
Vigan 38 A2
Vigévano 20 B2
Vigia 92 C4
Vigo 18 A1
Vijayawada ... 40 J3
Vikeke 39 F3
Vikna 8 F10
Vila da Maganja 59 B7
Vila de João
  Belo = Xai-Xai 59 D6
Vila do Bispo .. 18 D1
Vila Franca de
  Xira 18 C1
Vila Machado . 59 B6
Vila Nova de
  Gaia 18 B1
Vila Real 18 B2
Vila Real de
  Santo António 18 D2
Vila Velha 93 G5
Vilaine → 12 C2
Vilanculos ... 59 C7
Vileyka 17 A8
Vilhelmina 8 F11
Vilhena 91 F6
Vilkitskogo,
  Proliv 30 B8
Vilkovo =
  Vylkove 17 F9
Villa Ahumada 84 A3
Villa Ángela ... 94 B4
Villa Bella ... 91 F5
Villa Bens =
  Tarfaya 54 C2
Villa Colón ... 94 C3
Villa de María . 94 B4
Villa Dolores .. 94 C3
Villa Hayes ... 94 B5
Villa María ... 94 C4
Villa Mazán .. 94 B3
Villa Montes .. 94 A4
Villa Ocampo . 94 B5
Villacarrillo ... 18 C4
Villach 15 E7
Villagarcía de
  Arosa 18 A1
Villaguay 94 C5
Villahermosa .. 85 D6
Villajoyosa ... 19 C5
Villalba 18 A2
Villanueva de la
  Serena 18 C3

Villanueva y
  Geltrú 19 B6
Villarreal 19 C5
Villarrica, Chile 95 D2
Villarrica,
  Paraguay ... 94 B5
Villarrobledo .. 19 C4
Villavicencio .. 90 C4
Villaviciosa ... 18 A3
Villazón 94 A3
Villena 19 C5
Villeneuve-
  d'Ascq 13 A5
Villeneuve-sur-
  Lot 12 D4
Villingen-
  Schwenningen 14 D5
Vilnius 24 C2
Vilyuy → 31 C10
Vilyuysk 31 C10
Viña del Mar .. 94 C2
Vinaroz 19 B6
Vindhya Ra. ... 43 H10
Vineland 73 E8
Vinkovci 20 B7
Vinnitsa =
  Vinnytsya ... 17 D9
Vinnytsya 17 D9
Virac 38 B2
Viramgam 43 H8
Viranşehir .. 46 C4
Virden 71 D9
Vire 12 B3
Vírgenes, C. ... 95 G3
Virgin Is. (U.K.
  -U.S.A.) ■ .. 87 C7
Virginia □ ... 73 F6
Virginia Beach . 73 F8
Vlrovitica 20 B6
Virudunagar .. 43 Q10
Vis 20 C6
Visalia 82 B3
Visayan Sea .. 38 B2
Visby 9 G11
Višegrad 20 C7
Viseu, Brazil ... 92 C4
Viseu, Portugal 18 B2
Vishakhapatnam 40 J4
Viso, Mte. ... 20 B1
Vistula =
  Wisła → ... 16 A4
Vitebsk =
  Vitsyebsk ... 24 B3
Viterbo 20 C4
Viti Levu 64 L12
Vitigudino 18 B2
Vitória, Brazil .. 93 G5
Vitoria, Spain . 19 A4
Vitória da
  Conquista ... 93 E5
Vitsyebsk 24 B3
Vittória 21 F5
Vittório Véneto 20 B4
Vivero 18 A2
Vize 22 D6
Vizianagaram . 40 H4
Vjosa → 23 D2
Vladikavkaz ... 25 E5
Vladimir 24 B5
Vladimir
  Volynskiy =
  Volodymyr-
  Volynskyy ... 17 C7
Vladivostok ... 31 E11
Vlissingen 14 C2
Vlóra 23 D2
Vltava → 16 C2
Vogelsberg ... 14 C5

Voghera 20 B2
Vohibinany ... 59 H9
Vohimarina ... 59 G10
Vohimena,
  Tanjon' ... 59 K9
Vohipeno 59 J9
Voi 57 E7
Voiron 13 D6
Vojvodina □ .. 22 B2
Volga → 25 D6
Volga Hts. =
  Privolzhskaya
  Vozvyshennost
  .... 24 C6
Volgodonsk ... 25 D5
Volgograd 25 D5
Volgogradskoye
  Vdkhr. 24 C6
Volkhov → ... 24 A3
Volkovysk =
  Vawkavysk .. 17 B7
Volochanka ... 30 B7
Volodymyr-
  Volynskyy ... 17 C7
Vologda 24 B4
Vólos 23 E4
Volovets 17 D6
Volozhin =
  Valozhyn ... 17 A8
Volsk 24 C6
Volta → 55 G5
Volta, L. 55 G5
Volta Redonda 93 G5
Volterra 20 C3
Volturno → ... 20 D4
Volzhskiy 25 D5
Voríai
  Sporádhes .. 23 E4
Vorkuta 28 C7
Voronezh 24 C4
Voroshilovgrad
  = Luhansk .. 25 D4
Voroshilovsk =
  Alchevsk ... 25 D4
Vosges 13 B7
Vostok I. 65 L15
Vouga → 18 B1
Voznesensk ... 25 D3
Voznesenye ... 28 C4
Vrangelya,
  Ostrov 31 B15
Vranje 22 C3
Vratsa 22 C4
Vrbas → 20 B6
Vrede 59 D5
Vredenburg ... 58 E3
Vršac 22 B3
Vryburg 58 D4
Vryheid 59 D6
Vukovar 20 B7
Vulcan 17 F6
Vulcaneşti ... 17 F9
Vulcano 21 E5
Vulkaneshty =
  Vulcaneşti .. 17 F9
Vung Tau 36 B3
Vyatka = Kirov 28 D5
Vyatskiye
  Polyany 24 B7
Vyazma 24 B3
Vyborg 28 C3
Vychegda → . 28 C5
Vychodné
  Beskydy 17 D5
Vylkove 17 F9
Vynohradiv ... 17 D6
Vyshniy
  Volochek ... 24 B3
Vyškov 16 D3

W

Wa 55 F4
Waal → 14 C3
Wabash → ... 72 F1
Waco 78 D5
Wad Banda .. 53 F4
Wad Hamid .. 53 E5
Wâd Medanî .. 53 F5
Waddington, Mt. 71 C7
Waddy Pt. 63
Wadi Halfa .. 52 D5
Wafrah 47 E6
Wager B. 68 B2
Wager Bay ... 68 B1
Wagga Wagga 63 C4
Waghete 39 E5
Wah 42 C8
Wahai 39 E3
Waiau → 65 E5
Waibeem 39 E4
Waigeo 39 E4
Waihi 64 B6
Waihou → ... 64 B6
Waikabubak ... 39 F1
Waikari 65 E5
Waikato → ... 64 B6
Waikerie 62 B2
Waikokopu 64 C7
Waikouaiti ... 65 F4
Waimakariri → 65 E5
Waimate 65 F4
Wainganga → 43 K11
Waingapu ... 39 F2
Wainwright,
 Canada 71 C8
Wainwright,
 U.S.A. 71 A3
Waiouru 64 C6
Waipara 65 E5
Waipawa 64 C7
Waipiro 64 C8
Waipu 64 A6
Waipukurau .. 64 D7
Wairakei 64 C7
Wairarapa, L. .. 65 D6
Wairoa 64 C7
Waitaki → 65 F4
Waitara 64 C6
Waiuku 64 B6
Wajima 32 A5
Wajir 57 D8
Wakasa-Wan .. 32 B4
Wakatipu, L. .. 65 F3
Wakayama 32 B4
Wakefield 65 D5
Wakema 41 J10
Wakkanai 32 E12
Wakool 63 C3
Wakool → 62 C3
Wakre 39 E4
Wałbrzych ... 16 C3
Walcha 63 B5
Wałcz 16 B3
Wales □ 11 E4
Walgett 63 A4
Walgreen Coast 96 B1
Walhalla 63 C4
Walla Walla .. 80 B4
Wallachia =
 Valahia 22 B5
Wallal 63 A4
Wallaroo 62 B2
Wallerawang .. 63 B5
Wallis & Futuna,
 Is. 64 L13
Wallowa Mts. . 80 C5
Wallsend 63 B5
Wallumbilla ... 63 A4

Walvisbaai 58 C2
Wamba 57 D5
Wamena 39 E5
Wamulan 39 E3
Wana 42 C6
Wanaaring ... 63 A3
Wanaka 65 F3
Wanaka L. 65 F3
Wanapiri 39 E5
Wanbi 62 B3
Wandoan 63 A4
Wangal 39 F4
Wanganella .. 63 C3
Wanganui ... 64 C6
Wangaratta .. 63 C4
Wangary 62 B2
Wangerooge .. 14 B4
Wangiwangi .. 39 F2
Wanxian 35 C5
Warangal 43 L11
Waratah 62 D4
Waratah B. ... 63 C4
Warburton ... 63 C4
Ward 65 D6
Ward → 63 A4
Wardha 43 J11
Wardha → ... 43 K11
Warialda 63 A5
Wariap 39 E4
Warkopi 39 E4
Warmbad,
 Namibia 58 D3
Warmbad,
 S. Africa 59 C5
Warner Mts. .. 80 E3
Warracknabeal 62 C3
Warragul 63 C4
Warrego → .. 63 B4
Warren 63 B4
Warrenton ... 58 D4
Warrenville ... 63 A4
Warri 55 G6
Warrina 62 A2
Warrington, U.K. 11 E5
Warrington,
 U.S.A. 74 D4
Warrnambool . 62 C3
Warsa 39 E5
Warsaw =
 Warszawa ... 16 B5
Warszawa ... 16 B5
Warta → 16 B2
Warthe =
 Warta → ... 16 B2
Waru 39 E4
Warwick 63 A5
Wasatch Ra. .. 81 E8
Wash, The 11 E7
Washim 43 J10
Washington .. 73 E7
Washington □ . 80 B3
Washington, Mt. 73 B10
Wasian 39 E4
Wasior 39 E4
Waskaganish .. 69 C3
Wasserkuppe .. 14 C5
Watangpone .. 39 E2
Waterbury ... 73 D9
Waterford ... 11 E3
Waterloo,
 S. Leone 55 G2
Waterloo, U.S.A. 77 D8
Waterton-Glacier
 International
 Peace Park .. 81 A6
Watertown ... 73 C8
Waterville ... 73 B11
Watford 11 F6
Watling I. = San
 Salvador 86 B5

Watrous 71 C9
Watsa 57 D5
Watson Lake .. 70 B7
Watsonville ... 82 B2
Wattiwarriganna
 Cr. → 62 A2
Watuata =
 Batuata 39 F2
Watubela,
 Kepulauan .. 39 E4
Watubela Is. =
 Watubela,
 Kepulauan .. 39 E4
Wauchope 63 B5
Waukegan 72 C2
Waukesha ... 72 C1
Wausau 77 C10
Wauwatosa ... 72 C2
Waverley 64 C6
Wâw 53 G4
Wâw al Kabir .. 52 C2
Waxahachie ... 79 C5
Wayabula Rau . 39 D3
Wayatinah 62 D4
Waycross 75 D6
Wazirabad ... 42 C9
We 36 C1
Weda 39 D3
Weda, Teluk .. 39 D3
Weddell I. 95 G4
Weddell Sea .. 96 A4
Wedderburn .. 62 C3
Wee Waa 63 B4
Weemelah 63 A4
Weiden 15 D7
Weifang 35 C6
Weimar 15 C6
Weipa 61 C7
Weir → 63 A4
Wejherowo ... 16 A4
Welbourn Hill . 62 A1
Welkom 59 D5
Wellesley Is. .. 60 D6
Wellington,
 Australia 63 B4
Wellington, N.Z. 65 D6
Wellington, I. .. 95 F1
Wellington, L. .. 63 C4
Wels 15 D8
Welshpool 11 E5
Wemindji 69 C3
Wenatchee ... 80 B3
Wenchi 55 G4
Wenchow =
 Wenzhou ... 35 D7
Wendesi 39 E4
Wensu 34 B3
Wentworth ... 62 B3
Wenut 39 E4
Wenzhou ... 35 D7
Werda 58 D4
Werder 49 F4
Weri 39 E4
Werra → 14 C5
Werribee 63 C3
Werrimull 62 B3
Werris Creek .. 63 B5
Wersar 39 E4
Weser → 14 B5
Wesiri 39 F3
West Bengal □ . 40 F7
West Beskids =
 Západné
 Beskydy ... 16 D4
West Falkland . 95 G4
West Fjord =
 Vestfjorden .. 8 E10
West Ice Shelf . 96 A11
West Nicholson 59 C5

West Palm
 Beach 75 F7
West Pt. 62 C2
West Virginia □ 72 E5
West Wyalong . 63 B4
Westall Pt. 62 B1
Westbury 62 D4
Westerland ... 14 A5
Western
 Australia □ .. 60 F3
Western Dvina
 =
 Daugava → .. 24 B1
Western Ghats 43 N9
Western
 Sahara ■ ... 54 D2
Western Samoa =
 Samoa ■ ... 65 L13
Westerwald ... 14 C4
Westland Bight 65 E4
Weston 36 C5
Weston-super-
 Mare 11 F5
Westport,
 Ireland 11 E2
Westport, N.Z. .. 65 D4
Westray 10 B5
Wetar 39 F3
Wetaskiwin .. 71 C8
Wetzlar 14 C5
Wewak 61
Wexford 11 E3
Weyburn 71 D9
Weymouth 11 F5
Whakatane ... 64 B7
Whale → 68 C4
Whale Cove .. 70 B10
Whales, B. of .. 96 B16
Whangamomona
 .... 64 C6
Whangarei 64 A6
Whangarei Harb. 64 A6
Wheeling 72 D5
White →, Ark.,
 U.S.A. 79 C8
White →, Ind.,
 U.S.A. 72 E2
White Cliffs ... 62 B3
White I. 64 B7
White Nile = Nîl
 el Abyad → .. 53 E5
White Russia =
 Belarus ■ .. 24 C2
White Sea =
 Beloye More . 28 C4
Whitecliffs 65 E4
Whitehaven ... 11 D5
Whitehorse ... 70 B6
Whitemark ... 62 D4
Whitfield 63 C4
Whitianga 64 B6
Whitney, Mt. .. 82 B3
Whittlesea ... 63 C4
Wholdaia L. ... 70 B9
Whyalla 62 B2
Whyjonta 62 A3
Wichita 78 A5
Wichita Falls .. 78 C4
Wick 10 B5
Wickham, C. .. 62 C3
Wicklow Mts. .. 11 E3
Wieluń 16 C4
Wien 15 D9
Wiener Neustadt 15 E9
Wiesbaden ... 14 C5
Wilcannia 62 B3
Wildspitze ... 14 E6
Wilhelm, Mt. .. 61 B8
Wilhelm II Coast 96 A11

Wilhelmshaven 14 B5
Wilkes-Barre .. 73 D8
Wilkie 71 C9
Willandra
  Billabong
  Creek ⇢ ... 63 B4
Willemstad ... 87 D6
William Creek . 62 A2
Williams Lake . 71 C7
Williamsburg .. 73 F7
Williamsport .. 73 D7
Williamstown . 63 C3
Williston 76 A3
Willowmore ... 58 E4
Willunga 62 C2
Wilmington,
  Australia 62 B2
Wilmington,
  Del., U.S.A. . 73 E8
Wilmington,
  N.C., U.S.A. . 75 B9
Wilpena Cr. ⇢ 62 B2
Wilson 75 B9
Wilson ⇢ 62 A3
Wilsons
  Promontory . 63 C4
Wimmera ⇢ . 62 C3
Winchester ... 11 F6
Wind River
  Range 81 D9
Windau =
  Ventspils ... 24 B1
Windhoek 58 C3
Windsor,
  Australia ... 63 B5
Windsor, N.S.,
  Canada 69 D4
Windsor, Ont.,
  Canada 69 D2
Windward Is. .. 87
Wingen 63 B5
Wingham 63 B5
Winisk ⇢ 69 C2
Winneba 55 G4
Winnipeg 71 D10
Winnipeg, L. .. 71 C10
Winnipegosis L. 71 C9
Winona 77 C9
Winston-Salem 75 A7
Winterthur 13 C8
Winton,
  Australia 61 E7
Winton, N.Z. .. 65 G3
Wirrulla 62 B1
Wisconsin □ .. 77 C10
Wisła ⇢ 16 A4
Wismar 15 B6
Witbank 59 D5
Wittenberg 15 C7
Wittenberge ... 15 B6
Wkra ⇢ 16 B5
Włocławek 16 B4
Włodawa 17 C6
Wodonga 63 C4
Wokam 39 F4
Wolfsberg 15 E8
Wolfsburg 15 B6
Wolin 16 B2
Wollaston, Is. . 95 H3
Wollaston Pen. 70 B8
Wollongong ... 63 B5
Wolseley 62 C3
Wolverhampton 11 E5
Wondai 63 A5
Wongalarroo L. 63 B3
Wŏnsan 35 C7
Wonthaggi 63 C4
Woocalla 62 B2
Woodburn 63 A5
Woodenbong . 63 A5

Woodend 63 C3
Woodland 80 F3
Woodroffe, Mt. 60 F5
Woods, L. of the 71 D10
Woodstock 69 D4
Woodville 64 D6
Woolamai, C. .. 63 C4
Woolgoolga ... 63 B5
Woombye 63 A5
Woomera 62 B2
Worcester,
  S. Africa 58 E3
Worcester, U.K. 11 E5
Worcester,
  U.S.A. 73 C10
Workington ... 11 D5
Worms 14 D5
Worthing 11 F6
Wosi 39 E3
Wou-han –
  Wuhan 35 C6
Wour 52 D2
Wousi = Wuxi . 35 C7
Wowoni 39 E2
Woy Woy 63 B5
Wrangel I. =
  Vrangelya,
  Ostrov 31 B15
Wrangell 71 C6
Wrangell Mts. . 71 B5
Wrath, C. 10 B4
Wrexham 11 E5
Wright 38 B3
Wrigley 70 B7
Wrocław 16 C3
Września 16 B3
Wu Jiang ⇢ .. 35 D5
Wuhan 35 C6
Wuhsi = Wuxi . 35 C7
Wuhu 35 C6
Wukari 55 G6
Wuliaru 39 F4
Wulumuchi =
  Ürümqi 34 B3
Wum 55 G7
Wuntho 41 F10
Wuppertal 14 C4
Würzburg 14 D5
Wutongqiao ... 34 D5
Wuwei 34 C5
Wuxi 35 C7
Wuyi Shan ... 35 D6
Wuzhi Shan ... 35 E5
Wuzhong 35 C5
Wuzhou 35 D6
Wyandotte 72 C4
Wyandra 63 A4
Wyangala Res. 63 B4
Wyara, L. 63 A3
Wycheproof ... 62 C3
Wynbring 62 B1
Wyndham,
  Australia 60 D4
Wyndham, N.Z. 65 G3
Wynnum 63 A5
Wynyard 62 D4
Wyoming □ ... 81 D10
Wyong 63 B5

X

Xai-Xai 59 D6
Xainza 34 C3
Xangongo 58 B3
Xankändi 25 F6
Xánthi 22 D5
Xapuri 91 F5

Xi Jiang ⇢ ... 35 D6
Xiaguan 34 D5
Xiamen 35 D6
Xi'an 35 C5
Xiang Jiang ⇢ 35 D6
Xiangfan 35 C6
Xiangtan 35 D6
Xiao Hinggan
  Ling 35 B7
Xiapu 35 D6
Xichang 34 D5
Xigazê 34 D3
Xinavane 59 D6
Xing'an 35 D6
Xingren 35 D5
Xingtai 35 C6
Xingu ⇢ 92 C3
Xining 34 C5
Xinjiang Uygur
  Zizhiqu □ ... 34 B3
Xinjin 35 C7
Xinxiang 35 C6
Xinyang 35 C6
Xinzhu 35 D7
Xique-Xique .. 93 E5
Xisha Qundao =
  Hsisha
  Chuntao 36 A4
Xixabangma
  Feng 40 C5
Xizang □ 34 C3
Xuanhua 35 B6
Xuchang 35 C6
Xuzhou 35 C6

Y

Ya'an 34 D5
Yaapeet 62 C3
Yabelo 53 H6
Yablonovy Ra. =
  Yablonovyy
  Khrebet 30 D9
Yablonovyy
  Khrebet 30 D9
Yacuiba 94 A4
Yadgir 43 L10
Yagoua 56 B3
Yahuma 56 D4
Yakima 80 B3
Yakutat 71 C6
Yakutsk 31 C10
Yala 36 C2
Yalinga 56 C4
Yalong Jiang ⇢ 34 D5
Yalova 22 D7
Yalta 25 E3
Yalutorovsk ... 29 D7
Yam Ha Melah
  = Dead Sea . 47 E3
Yam Kinneret . 46 D3
Yamagata 33 G12
Yamaguchi ... 32 B2
Yamal,
  Poluostrov .. 28 B8
Yamal Pen. =
  Yamal,
  Poluostrov .. 28 B8
Yamantau, Gora 29 D6
Yamba, N.S.W.,
  Australia 63 A5
Yamba,
  S. Austral.,
  Australia 62 B3
Yâmbiô 53 H4
Yambol 22 C6

Yamdena 39 F4
Yamethin 41 G11
Yamma-Yamma,
  L. 62 A3
Yamoussoukro 55 G3
Yampil 17 D9
Yampol =
  Yampil 17 D9
Yamuna ⇢ ... 40 E3
Yamzho Yumco 34 D4
Yana ⇢ 31 B11
Yanac 62 C3
Yanbu 'al Baḥr 47 F4
Yancannia 62 B3
Yanco Cr. ⇢ .. 63 C4
Yandoon 41 J10
Yangambi 56 D4
Yangch'ü =
  Taiyuan 35 C6
Yangchun 35 D6
Yangjiang 35 D6
Yangon –
  Rangoon 41 J11
Yangquan 35 C6
Yanji 35 B7
Yanna 63 A4
Yanqi 34 B3
Yantabulla ... 63 A4
Yantai 35 C7
Yanykurgan ... 29 E7
Yao 53 F2
Yaoundé 56 D2
Yapen 39 E5
Yapen, Selat .. 39 E5
Yaqui ⇢ 84 B2
Yar-Sale 28 C8
Yaraka 61 E7
Yaransk 24 B6
Yardea P.O. .. 62 B2
Yaremcha 17 D7
Yarensk 28 C5
Yarí ⇢ 90 D4
Yarkand =
  Shache 34 C2
Yarkhun ⇢ ... 42 A8
Yaroslavl 24 B4
Yarram 63 C4
Yarraman 63 A5
Yarranvale 63 A4
Yarras 63 B5
Yartsevo 30 C7
Yaselda 17 B8
Yasinya 17 D7
Yass 63 B4
Yatağan 23 F7
Yathkyed L. .. 70 B10
Yatsushiro ... 32 C2
Yauyos 91 F3
Yavari ⇢ 90 D4
Yavatmal 43 J11
Yavoriv 17 D6
Yavorov =
  Yavoriv 17 D6
Yawatahama .. 32 C3
Yazd 44 D3
Yazd □ 44 C3
Yazdän 45 C5
Yazoo ⇢ 79 C8
Ye Xian 35 C6
Yebyu 41 K12
Yecla 19 C5
Yedintsy =
  Edinița 17 D8
Yeelanna 62 B2
Yegros 94 B5
Yei 53 H5
Yekaterinburg . 29 D7
Yekaterinodar =
  Krasnodar .. 25 D4

Yelarbon 63 A5
Yelets 24 C4
Yelizavetgrad =
 Kirovohrad .. 25 D3
Yell 10 A6
Yellow Sea ... 35 C7
Yellowhead Pass 71 C8
Yellowknife ... 70 B8
Yellowknife → 70 B8
Yellowstone → 76 B3
Yellowstone
 National Park 81 C8
Yelsk 17 C9
Yemen ■ 49 E3
Yenangyaung . 41 G10
Yenbo = Yanbu
 'al Baḥr 47 F4
Yenda 63 B4
Yenice 23 E6
Yenisey → ... 28 B9
Yeniseysk 30 D7
Yeniseyskiy
 Zaliv 28 B9
Yenyuka 31 D10
Yeola 43 J9
Yeovil 11 F5
Yerbent 29 F6
Yerevan 25 E5
Yermak 29 D8
Yershov 24 C6
Yerushalayim =
 Jerusalem .. 47 E3
Yessey 30 C8
Yeu, I. d' 12 C2
Yevpatoriya ... 25 D3
Yeysk 25 D4
Yezd = Yazd .. 44 D3
Yiannitsa 23 D4
Yibin 35 D5
Yichang 35 C6
Yichun 35 B7
Yilan 35 D7
Yinchuan 35 C5
Yingkou · 35 B7
Yingtan 35 D6
Yining 34 B3
Yinmabin 41 F10
Yishan 35 D5
Yíthion 23 F4
Yiyang 35 D6
Yog Pt. 38 B2
Yogyakarta ... 37 F4
Yokadouma ... 56 D2
Yokkaichi 32 B5
Yoko 53 G1
Yokohama 32 B6
Yokosuka 32 B6
Yola 53 G1
Yonago 32 B3
Yongji 35 C6
Yonibana 55 G2
Yonkers 73 D9
Yonne → 13 B5
York, U.K. 11 E6
York, U.S.A. ... 73 E7
York, C. 61 C7
Yorke Pen. ... 62 B2
Yorkton 71 C9
Yos Sudarso,
 Pulau 39 F5
Yosemite
 National Park 82 B3
Yoshkar Ola ... 24 B6
Youghal 11 F3
Young 63 B4
Younghusband,
 L. 62 B2
Younghusband
 Pen. 62 C2

Youngstown .. 72 D5
Yozgat 46 C3
Ysyk-Köl, Ozero 29 E8
Yu Jiang → .. 35 D6
Yu Shan 35 D7
Yuan Jiang → 35 D6
Yuanling 35 D6
Yuanyang 34 D5
Yuba City 80 F3
Yūbari 32 F12
Yucatán □ 85 C7
Yucatán, Canal
 de 85 C7
Yucatán,
 Península de 85 D7
Yucatan Str. =
 Yucatán,
 Canal de 85 C7
Yuci 35 C6
Yugoslavia ■ .. 22 B3
Yukon → ... 71 B3
Yukon
 Territory □ .. 70 B6
Yukti 30 C8
Yuma 82 D5
Yumen 34 C4
Yun Xian 35 C6
Yungas 91 G5
Yunnan □ ... 34 D5
Yunta 62 B2
Yurgao 29 D9
Yuribei 28 B8
Yurimaguas .. 91 E3
Yuryung Kaya . 30 B9
Yushu 34 C4
Yuzhno-
 Sakhalinsk .. 31 E12
Yvetot 12 B4

Z

Zabid 49 E3
Zābol 45 D5
Zābol □ 45 D6
Zābolī 45 E5
Zabrze 16 C4
Zacapa 85 E7
Zacatecas 84 C4
Zacoalco 84 C4
Zadar 20 B5
Zadetkyi Kyun . 36 C1
Zafra 18 C2
Żagań 16 C2
Zagazig 52 B5
Zagorsk =
 Sergiyev
 Posad 24 B4
Zagreb 20 B6
Zāgros, Kūhhā-
 ye 44 C2
Zagros Mts. =
 Zāgros,
 Kūhhā-ye .. 44 C2
Zāhedān 45 D5
Zahlah 46 D3
Zaïre =
 Congo → .. 56 F2
Zaïre = Congo,
 Dem. Rep. of
 the ■ 56 E4
Zaječar 22 C4
Zakhodnaya
 Dzvina =
 Daugava → . 24 B1
Zākhū 46 C5
Zákinthos 23 F3

Zakopane 16 D4
Zalaegerszeg .. 16 E3
Zalău 17 E6
Zaleshchiki =
 Zalishchyky . 17 D7
Zalew Wiślany . 16 A4
Zalingei 53 F3
Zalishchyky ... 17 D7
Zambeze → .. 59 B7
Zambezi =
 Zambeze → 59 B7
Zambezi 58 A4
Zambia ■ 59 B5
Zamboanga ... 38 C2
Zamora, Mexico 84 D4
Zamora, Spain 18 B3
Zamość 17 C6
Zanaga 56 E2
Zanesville 72 E4
Zanjān 46 C7
Zanjān □ 46 C7
Zante =
 Zákinthos ... 23 F3
Zanzibar 57 F7
Zaouiet El-Kala
 = Bordj Omar
 Driss 54 C6
Zaouiet Reggane 54 C5
Zap Suyu =
 Kabīr, Zab
 al → 46 C5
Zapadnaya
 Dvina 28 D4
Zapadnaya
 Dvina → =
 Daugava → . 24 B1
Západné
 Beskydy 16 D4
Zaporizhzhya .. 25 D4
Zaporozhye =
 Zaporizhzhya 25 D4
Zara 46 C4
Zaragoza 19 B5
Zarand 44 D4
Zaranj 42 D2
Zaria 55 F6
Zaruma 90 D3
Żary 16 C2
Zarzis 52 B1
Zaskar Mts. ... 42 C10
Zavāreh 44 C3
Zawiercie 16 C4
Zāyandeh → . 44 C3
Zaysan 29 E9
Zaysan, Oz. ... 29 E9
Zbarazh 17 D7
Zdolbuniv 17 C8
Zduńska Wola . 16 C4
Zeebrugge 14 C2
Zeehan 62 D4
Zeerust 59 D5
Zeila 49 E3
Zeitz 15 C7
Zelenograd ... 24 B4
Zémio 57 C5
Zemun 22 B3
Zenica 20 B6
Žepce 20 B7
Žêzere → ... 18 C1
Zgorzelec 16 C2
Zhabinka 17 B7
Zhailma 29 D7
Zhambyl = Taraz 29 E8
Zhangaqazaly . 29 E7
Zhanghua 35 D7
Zhangjiakou ... 35 B6
Zhangye 34 C5
Zhangzhou ... 35 D6
Zhanjiang 35 D6

Zhanyi 34 D5
Zhaotong 34 D5
Zhashkiv 17 D10
Zhayyq → ... 29 E6
Zhdanov =
 Mariupol ... 25 D4
Zhejiang □ ... 35 D7
Zhengzhou ... 35 C6
Zhenjiang 35 C6
Zhenyuan 35 D5
Zhezqazghan . 29 E7
Zhigansk 30 C10
Zhijiang 35 D5
Zhilinda 30 B9
Zhitomir =
 Zhytomyr ... 17 C9
Zhlobin 17 B10
Zhmerinka =
 Zhmerynka .. 17 D9
Zhmerynka ... 17 D9
Zhodino =
 Zhodzina ... 17 A9
Zhodzina 17 A9
Zhongdian 34 D4
Zhumadian ... 35 C6
Zhuzhou 35 D6
Zhytomyr 17 C9
Zibo 35 C6
Zielona Góra .. 16 C2
Zigey 53 F2
Zigong 35 D5
Zigui 35 C6
Ziguinchor ... 55 F1
Zile 46 B3
Žilina 16 D4
Zillah 52 C2
Zimbabwe ■ .. 59 B5
Zimnicea 22 C5
Zinder 55 F6
Zion National
 Park 83 B6
Zipaquirá 90 C4
Ziway, L. 53 G6
Zlatograd 22 D5
Zlatoust 29 D6
Zlin 16 D3
Zlītan 52 B1
Zmeinogorsk .. 29 D9
Znojmo 16 D3
Zolochev =
 Zolochiv 17 D7
Zolochiv 17 D7
Zomba 59 B7
Zongo 56 D3
Zonguldak ... 46 B2
Zorritos 90 D2
Zouar 52 D2
Zouérate 54 D2
Zrenjanin 22 B3
Zuetina = Az
 Zuwaytīnah . 52 B3
Zufar 48 D5
Zug 13 C8
Zugspitze 14 E6
Zula 53 E6
Zumbo 59 B6
Zungeru 55 G6
Zunyi 35 D5
Zürich 13 C8
Zuwārah 52 B1
Zvishavane ... 59 C6
Zvolen 16 D4
Zwettl 15 D8
Zwickau 15 C7
Zwolle 14 B4
Żyrardów 16 B5
Zyryan 29 E9
Zyryanovsk =
 Zyryan 29 E9
Żywiec 16 D4